Islam from Within: Anthology of a Religion

The Religious Life of Man
Frederick J. Streng, Series Editor

Texts

Understanding Religious Man, 2nd edition
Frederick J. Streng

The House of Islam, 2nd edition
Kenneth Cragg

Japanese Religion: Unity and Diversity, 2nd edition
H. Byron Earhart

Chinese Religion: An Introduction, 3rd edition
Laurence G. Thompson

The Christian Religious Tradition
Stephen Reynolds

The Buddhist Religion, 2nd edition
Richard H. Robinson and William L. Johnson

The Way of Torah: An Introduction to Judaism, 3rd edition
Jacob Neusner

The Hindu Religious Tradition
Thomas J. Hopkins

Anthologies

The Chinese Way in Religion
Laurence G. Thompson

Religion in the Japanese Experience: Sources and Interpretations
H. Byron Earhart

The Buddhist Experience: Sources and Interpretations
Stephan Beyer

The Life of Torah: Readings in the Jewish Religious Experience
Jacob Neusner

Islam from Within: Anthology of a Religion
Kenneth Cragg and R. Marston Speight

Islam from Within

Anthology of a Religion

Kenneth Cragg
R. Marston Speight

Wadsworth Publishing Company Belmont, California

Islam from Within: Anthology of a Religion was edited and prepared for composition by Lucretia Lyons. Interior design was provided by Amato Prudente. The cover was designed by Oliver Kline.

Library of Congress Cataloging in Publication Data
Main entry under title:

Islam from within.
1. Islam. I. Cragg, Kenneth. II. Speight, R. Marston
BP161.2.I87 297 78-24004

ISBN 0-87872-212-2

Printed in the United States of America
1 2 3 4 5 6 7 8 9 – 83 82 81 80 79

Contents

Foreword

The Religious Life of Man series is intended as an introduction to a large, complex field of inquiry—human religious experience. It seeks to present the depth and richness of religious concepts, forms of worship, spiritual practices, and social institutions found in the major religious traditions throughout the world.

As a specialist in the languages and cultures in which a religion is found, each author is able to illuminate the meanings of a religious perspective and practice in a community. To communicate this meaning to readers who have had no special training in these cultures and religions, the authors have attempted to provide clear, nontechnical descriptions and interpretations of religious life.

Different interpretive approaches have been used, depending upon the nature of the religious data; some religious expressions, for example, lend themselves more to developmental, others more to topical studies. But this lack of a single interpretation may itself be instructive, for the experiences and practices regarded as religious in one culture may not be the most important in another.

The Religious Life of Man is concerned with, on the one hand, the variety of religious expressions found in different traditions and, on the other, the similarities in the structures of religious life. The various forms are interpreted in terms of their cultural context and historical continuity, demonstrating both the diverse expressions and commonalities of religious traditions. Besides the single volumes on different religions, the series offers a core book on the study of religious meaning, which describes different study approaches and examines several modes and structures of religious awareness. In addition, each book presents a list of materials for further reading, including translations of religious texts and detailed examinations of specific topics.

During a decade of use the series has experienced a wide readership. A continuing effort has been made to update the scholarship, simplify the organization of material, and clarify concepts through the publication of revised editions. The authors have been gratified with the response to their efforts to introduce people to various forms of religious life. We hope readers will also find these volumes "introductory" in the most significant sense: an introduction to a new perspective for understanding themselves and others.

Frederick J. Streng
Series Editor

Acknowledgments

Our warm thanks are extended to the four reviewers of the anthology in its formative stages, Frederick M. Denny, University of Virginia; Charles Wendell, University of California, Santa Barbara; Glenn Yocum, Williams College; and A.H. Mathias Zahniser, Central Michigan University. Even when we were not able to implement their suggestions, we shared many of their sentiments.

Special gratitude and indebtedness is acknowledged to Mohamed Nakhli and the late Al-Shādhilī Ibn al-Qādī, both of Tunis, for their help in interpreting some difficult passages in the translated material.

The authors are also indebted to the following:

Heinemann Educational Books Ltd. (London) and Éditions Denoël (Paris) for permission to reprint from pp. 43–44, from Driss Chraibi, *Le Passé Simple* [Heirs to the Past], trans. by Len Ortzen, 1971.

Faber and Faber Ltd. (London) and E.P. Dutton for permission to reprint from p. 265, from Lawrence Durrell, *Mountolive,* © 1958.

Luzac & Co. Ltd. (London) for permission to reprint excerpts from Henri Mercier, *The Koran,* trans. by L. Tremlett, 1956.

Maison Tunisienne de l'Edition (Tunis) for permission to reprint from pp. 27–28, from Muḥammad al-Nāsir al-Saddām, *Ibtihālāt,* 1968; and pp. 42–47, from Muḥammad Ṭalbī, *Islam et Dialogue,* 1972.

Sh. Muḥammad Ashraf (Lahore, Pakistan) for permission to reprint from pp. 107–28, 274–79, from Muḥammad 'Alī, *My Life, A Fragment,* 1942; and pp. 149, 152–54, 156–58, 171–72, 174–75, from F.K. Khan Durrani, *The Meaning of Pakistan,* 1944.

George Allen & Unwin (Publishers) Ltd. (London) for permission to reprint from pp. 56–60, from W. Montgomery Watt, *Faith and Practice of Al-Ghazālī,* 1953; and pp. 47–48, 50–51, from Sayyid Ḥossein Naṣr, *Ideals and Realities of Islam,* 1966.

George Allen & Unwin (Publishers) Ltd. (London) and Columbia University Press for permission to reprint from pp. 75–76, 194–96, 226, 268, 271–72, 276, from Niyazi Berkes, *Turkish Nationalism and Western Civilization,* 1959.

George Allen & Unwin (Publishers) Ltd. (London) and the University of California Press for permission to reprint from pp. 53–55, 58–59, 89–90, 102, 107, 117, 145, 160, 199–200, 202–03, 204, 207, from Martin Ling, *A Muslim Saint of the 20th Century,* 1961.

John Wiley & Sons, Inc. for permission to reprint from pp. 21, 23, 26–27, 34–36, from *Islam, The Straight Path: Islam Interpreted by Muslims,* edited by K.W. Morgan, © 1958 by The Ronald Press. Reprinted by permission of John Wiley & Sons, Inc.

Hashim Amir Ali and Shalimar Publishers (Hyderabad, India) for permission to reprint from pp. 121–22, from *The Student's Qur'ān,* 1959.

Institute of Islamic Culture (Lahore, Pakistan) for permission to reprint pp. ix–x, xi, xvi, 20, 21–26, 27, 29–31, 37, 63, 74, 83, 104, 149–50, 154, 159–64, 169, 180, from Khalifa Abdul-Hakim, *Islamic Ideology,* rev. ed., 1961.

John Murray (Publishers) Ltd. (London) for permission to reprint from pp. 173, 231, from A.J. Arberry, *Discourses of Rumi,* 1961; and pp. 40, 42, from Jogendra Singh, *The Invocations of Ansari of Herat,* 1939.

E.J. Brill (Leiden, Netherlands) for permission to reprint from pp. 18–19, from Daud Rahbar, *God of Justice: A Study of the Ethical Doctrine of the Qur'ān,* 1960; and act 2, scene 2, *The Tragedy of Al-Hallāj,* trans. by K.I. Semaan, 1972.

World Council of Churches (Geneva) for permission to reprint from pp. 68–72, 121–25, from S.J. Samartha and J.B. Taylor, eds., *Christian Muslim Dialogue: Papers from Broumana,* 1972.

Presses Universitaires de France (Paris) for permission to reprint from pp. 4–5, 7–8, 17, 21–24, 74–84, from Muḥammad Laḥbābī, *Le Personnalisme Musulman,* 1964.

Dār-āl-Ma'ārif (Cairo) for permission to use pp. 200–05, 343–46, 353–59, from Aḥmad Amīn, *Ḥayātī,* 1950.

Grove Press, Inc. and Hutchinson Pub. Group Ltd. (London) for permission to reprint from pp. 327–32, 341–43, 349, from *The Autobiography of Malcolm X,* copyright © 1964 by Alex Haley and Malcolm X. Copyright © 1965 by Alex Haley and Betty Shabazz.

The Society for Promoting Christian Knowledge (London) for permission to reprint from pp. 146–47, 214–19, from Constance E. Padwick, *Muslim Devotions,* 1961.

Oxford University Press for pp. 20–22, 39, 96–100, from Muḥammad Fāḍil Jamālī, *Letters on Islam,* © Oxford University Press 1965; pp. 170–71, 191, from J. Spencer Trimingham, *The Sufi Orders in Islam,* © Oxford University Press 1970; and extracts from *The Koran Interpreted,* trans. by Arthur J. Arberry, © Oxford University Press 1964. Reprinted by permission of Oxford University Press.

Muḥammad 'Amāra, ed., *Rasā'il al-'Adl wa-l-Tawḥīd* [Treatises on Justice and Unity] (Cairo: Dār al-Hilāl, 1971), for permission to reprint from vol. 1, pp. 105, 109, 168, 271.

Dover Publications, Inc. for permission to reprint from pp. 36–37, from T.W. Arnold, ed., *Painting in Islam,* 1928.

American University of Beirut for permission to reprint from pp. 115–21, from Charles Malik, ed., *God and Man in Contemporary Islamic Thought,* 1972.

Middle East Center, University of Utah, for permission to reprint from pp. 165, 167, 169, 171–72, 173–75, 179, from P.J. Chelkowski, ed., *Studies in the Art and Literature of the Near East,* 1974.

Cambridge University Press for permission to reprint from pp. 86–87, 88, 98–99, 113, 118–20, 125–27, 141–42, 152, 155–56, 165, 166–67, from A.J. Arberry, *The Doctrine of the Sufis,* 1935; vol. 1, pp. 425, 436, 439, 441–42, vol. 2, p. 537, from E.J. Brown, trans., *Literary History of Persia,* 1909; p. 397, from R.A. Nicholson, *Literary History of the Arabs,* 1914; and pp. xiii, xx, xxvi, xxxii, xl, xliv, from R.A. Nicholson, trans., *Dīwān Shams al-Din Tabrīzī,* 1898, reprinted 1952.

Routledge & Kegan Paul Ltd. (London) for permission to reprint from pp. 247, 264, 268–70, from H.A.R. Gibb, ed. and trans., *Travels of Ibn Baṭṭuṭa in Asia and Africa, 1325–1359,* 1953; and p. 87, from R.A. Nicholson, *Mystics of Islam,* 1975.

Macdonald Center for the Study of Islam and Christian–Muslim Relations, Hartford Seminary Foundation, for permission to reprint from pp. 8–9, from I.H. Qureshī, "The Foundations of Pakistani Culture," *The Muslim World,* 44 (January 1954).

Public Affairs Press for permission to reprint from pp. 33–36, 55–59, from Jamāl 'Abd al-Nāṣir, *Egypt's Liberation,* intro. by Dorothy Thompson, 1955.

Longman Group Ltd. (London) for permission to reprint from pp. 159–60, 168, 176, 178, from 'Ali Mazrui, *On Heroes and Uhuru Worship,* 1967.

Schenkman Pub. Co., Inc. for permission to reprint from pp. xv–xvi, 2, 4, 11–14, 79, 102–03, from Fāṭimah Mernissi, *Beyond the Veil: Male-Female Dynamics in a Modern Muslim Society,* 1975.

Princeton University Press and Routledge & Kegan Paul (London) for permission to reprint from vol. 2, pp. 438–39, 443–46, vol. 2, pp. 249–50, 388–89, from Ibn Khaldūn, *The Muqaddimah: An Introduction to History,* ed. and trans. by Franz Rosenthal, Bollingen series 43, © 1958.

Javid Iqbal for permission to reprint from pp. 10–11, 17–18, 56–57, 127–28, 138–40, 147, 167–68, 179, from Muḥammad Iqbal, *The Reconstruction of Religious Thoughts in Islam,* 1944.

Introduction

The circle of Arabic script presents a puzzling face. Its meaning is opaque, indeed impenetrable, without the needed clues. It suggests to the uninitiated a closed world, constituted to exclude access to itself. Clearly here is a thing of fascination for the scribe himself, joyously devising his script till it becomes a design where he can indulge, at one and the same time, a deep reverence for his document and its authority, and a lively ingenuity of skill in its celebration.

For the reader in the know, beginning at the lower right and moving to the upper left, the shapes yield their secret and spell themselves into Surah 3.139 of the Muslims' Scripture, the *Qur'ān.* The verse, repeated not quite verbatim in Surah 47.35, is a call to endurance, tenacity, and noncapitulation in the face of adversity. "Do not weaken and fall prey to grief, and (literally, present for future) you are the upper ones." It is a sort of: "We shall overcome," and so do not lose heart or give way to grief. It is a verse that gave the Prophet and his first followers the necessary staying power in face of hardship and danger; and it has long informed Islamic attitudes, clinging to rights and looking for vindication, not least in contemporary history. Behind the scribe's careful complexity and within the original's ample significance, much wealth, as well as much seeming mystery, is hidden.

This is taken here as a parable. Islam itself, out of which the scribe comes with his skilled calligraphy, requires an attentive perception. How can the outsider reach a genuine appreciation of what he sees and explores? The genesis of Islam, its long history, and its present quality of thought and movement can only be read if there is discernment for the clues involved. These, plainly, must be sought from those who belong.

In this anthology all sources are Islamic. The *Qur'ān* itself, its exegetes, the legists, traditionalists, apologists, and current exponents are left to speak for themselves. The only exceptions are Rudyard Kipling, Lawrence Durrell, and Alan Villiers with descriptions of Muslim worship.

Anthologies, of course, are numerous. This one is concerned with the religious life, insofar as this can be isolated, in spirituality, from history, chronicle, constitutions, institutions, and the rest. The reader will find here no details of Islamic empires, wars, battles, caliphates, and insurrections. Nor are we concerned primarily with literature, philosophy, biography, or society, for their own sake, but rather for the light they may shed on the feel and practice of religion. Islam is loathe to recognize such an isolation of "religion" from the totality of its existence, and this reluctance must be respected. But it is one that Muslim thinking is having to abandon in the evident necessity to explore—and when the need arises—to concentrate, for motive and for final criteria, on the essence of devotion and the "reasons of the heart" from which all else flows.

It is this Islamic quality of the contents that makes appropriate the title: *Islam from Within,* restricted by the subtitle: *Anthology of a Religion.* These are linked naturally with *The House of Islam* earlier published in the *Religious Life of Man* series. The analogy of house and household (*Dār al -Islām*), which is the Muslims' own, obviously invites across a threshold, into "living space" where those who dwell will be found "at home." Whereas *The House of Islam* had a single author, two contributors have collaborated here. R. Marston Speight contributes chapters 3 and 4 on Law and Tradition and chapter 5 on Theology and Kenneth Cragg chapters 1, 2, 6, 7, and 8 on the *Qur'ān,* Worship and Religion, Art and Architecture, Mystics and Saints, and Contemporary Issues. The overall title will be sufficient explanation for the inclusion of the themes of chapter 6. The mosque, after all, is the primary living space of Muslim religion, while calligraphy is the spring of its artistic skills and design the main preoccupation of its nonrepresentational art.

Several passages from Arabic sources have not previously been translated or published. The whole, of course, is intended as parallel to *The House of Islam* and that assumption allows us to dispense with explanatory detail and related contextual discussion that would otherwise have been required. In that way, explanations from the compilers have been kept to a minimum, except in chapter 6, where the elements of Muslim art seemed to call for more explicit, though still brief, elaboration. Art, anyway, is so much the insider's birthright and does not signify outside its culture as readily as it does to those within.

There is some continuity of interest between chapters, especially chapters 1, 2, and 8. Themes belonging with the *Qur'ān* are obviously central to Contemporary Issues. Chapter 1 has to do primarily with the content and role of the Scripture in Islamic life and devotion, including patterns of commentary and citation, while chapter 8 is concerned with matters of recent debate and tension. But the two areas are not sharply isolated. Clearly they belong together. Worship and Religion (chapter 2) is meant to embrace a wide range of Muslim self-expression, namely, the five pillars (except Zakāt, which figures under Tradition and Law), prayers other than those of ritual obligation, mosque sermons, and expositions of the Muslim's awareness of self, religious duty and communal history. All these are seen as providing an index, selective, it is true, but none the less adequate, to the understanding of Islam by its own criteria.

In our intention, the chapters on the *Qur'ān* and the Tradition comprise also the anthology's material on the Prophet Muḥammad himself. The *Qur'ān* is understood in Islam as the origin, in the eternal sense, of the experience of Muḥammad and that experience mediated the heavenly Scripture into the life of the world. Therefore the surest access to the mind of the Prophet is in the text and the texture of the Book it was his destiny to bring to mankind. The vast corpus of tradition communicates to us how that destiny was fulfilled and the biography in which it was achieved. The personality and imprint of Muḥammad are everywhere in the items we have chosen, whether celebrations of his *Maulid*, or birthday feast, or invocations of his example, or exhortations to the imitation of his character.

There exists through the centuries a sort of mutual possession of Muḥammad and his people—he shaping them in authority and ideal, they receiving and conceiving him in loyalty and commitment. That mutuality can hardly be an item in an anthology because it is the life stream of the whole.

Each contributor to this text is left to take his or her own stand and to present the case or opinion about each and all of the issues handled. The reader will not expect, or find, unanimity of mind. Divergence and debate, contrast and convergence are part of the living quality of faith and devotion. Beyond identifying and locating particular figures and interpretations in their context, no effort is made to take up the unresolved tensions or to reconcile opposing minds. Where opinions may be thought to be awry or claims extravagant, an alert reader may judge for oneself. But if one is to know the faith, one must penetrate its own assessments and try to overhear it in the wide range of its own assurance, its self-scrutiny, and its self-commendation. The task of anthologists is simply to arrange the encounter.

CHAPTER 1

The Qurʾān

SELECTED SURAHS

There is some wisdom in the newcomer to the *Qur'ān* beginning, Arabic style, at the back of the book and reading forward to the second Surah; the *Fātiḥah,* or first Surah, being in a class by itself. Certainly the two last pieces, by the actual order, immediately introduce one to the atmosphere of Muḥammad's world of listeners, while the third from the last states, in ringing terms, the core of his affirmation about God.

> In the Name of the merciful Lord of mercy. Say:
>
> "I take refuge with the Lord of the daybreak
> From the evil of what He has created,
> And from the evil of the enveloping darkness,
> And from the evil of those who bind their spells,
> From the evil of the envier and his envy."
>
> **—Surah 113**

> In the Name of the merciful Lord of mercy. Say:
>
> "I take refuge with the Lord of men,
> The King of men, the God of men,
> From the evil of the whispering insinuator
> Who whispers in the hearts of men,
> From jinn and men."
>
> **—Surah 114**

In the Name of the merciful Lord of mercy. Say:

> "He is God, One, God the ever self-sufficing,
> He begets not, nor is begotten.
> None is like unto Him."

—Surah 112

Close at hand is an inclusive directive for the time of Islamic success.

> In the Name of the merciful Lord of mercy. When God's help comes and victory with it and you see men thronging into God's religion, then occupy yourself in the praise of your Lord and seek His forgiveness. He is ever cognisant of repentance.

—Surah 110

The Surah entitled 'The Unbelievers' asserts in the sharpest terms the irreconcilable antagonism between the Prophet and the pagan Quraish.

> Say: "O you who believe not, I do not worship what you worship, nor are you worshipping what I worship. What you have served that serve not I: nor are you servants of what I serve. You have your religion, and I have mine."

—Surah 109

Those pagans are named in the intriguing verses of 'Surah Quraish', describing the commerce of Mecca that passed from Aden and Hadramaut in the south to Damascus and Aleppo in the north, with tribes en route in pact with the Quraish to give it safe-conduct under the fear of the Lord of the *Ka'bah.*

> The convoying of the Quraish, the caravans of winter and
> summer that go under covenant. Bounden are they to
> serve the Lord of this house—He whose provision has kept them from hunger and who made them safe from fear.

—Surah 106

How urgent, and how precarious, such protection could be is indicated by the graphic lines that describe and deplore the *ghazū*, or desert raid:

> By the snorting war horses that strike fire with their hoofs as they storm forward at dawn, a single host in the midst of their dust cloud. Man is indeed ungrateful to his Lord: witness what he does. Violent is he in his passion for wealth. Is he not aware that their Lord is cognisant of everything about them on that day when the tombs yield up their dead and all men's hidden thoughts are public knowledge?

—Surah 100

Muḥammad's experience of revelation is vividly intimated in two early and definitive Surahs.

Truly We revealed the Qur'ān on the night of authority.
Would that you knew what the night of authority means!
Better than a thousand months is the night of authority.
Thereon come the angels and the Spirit down,
By leave of their Lord, for every behest.
It is a night of peace until the breaking of the day.

—Surah 97

Recite: In the Name of Your Lord the Creator, Created man from an embryo.

Recite: By your Lord the most gracious, He who taught by the pen, taught man what he knew not. Nay! for sure man grows presumptuous, complacent in his self-sufficiency. Verily, to your Lord is all that accrues.

Have you seen him who forbids a servant at his prayers?

Was he, did you think? acting out of guidance and enjoining piety, or did you realise that he was giving the lie to truth and subverting it? Did he not know how God sees all?

No! No! If he does not desist, we will take him by the forelock, by his lying, sinning forelock. Let him call on whom he wills: We will call up the palace-guard of Hell!

No! No! pay him no heed! Worship and come near!

—Surah 96

That strident summons, with its deep irony, echoes in the "Surah of the Most High."

Praise the Name of your Lord most high, He who created and fashioned, He who measured and guided, who caused the pasture to spring forth and then turned its green to decay. We will cause you to recite: so forget not, except as God wills. For He knows what is uttered and what is concealed.

We are your solace and succour. So then, be the means to the reminding Word, that by the reminder there may come what profits. He who fears will take the reminder to heart, while the ne'er-do'-well will hold himself aloof from it, and he shall burn in the great fire, where there is neither dying nor living.

Whosoever has purified himself, he it is who flourishes—the man who mentions the Name of his Lord and prays the prayer. No, but it is the life of this present world that you people prefer, though the one to come is better and more abiding. Truly this is how it is in the pages of old, the pages of Abraham and Moses.

—Surah 87

And again, in the chapter called: "He (that is, Muḥammad) Frowned":

. . . Death to man! how thankless he is! From what did God create him? From a drop of sperm He made him and ordered his being, facilitating his course, and then of God comes his dying and his being laid in the grave. Then, when He wills, He brings him forth to life again,

Nay! man has not done what God decreed. Let man behold his provender, how We sent down the copious rain in torrents to cleave watercourses in the earth, where We made the grain to grow, and vines and reeds and olives and palms and dense orchards with their fruits, and pastures, delightsome to yourselves and to your flocks.

When the resurrection trump is heard, on a day when a man shall flee from his brother, his mother and his father, from his wife and children—on that day every human living will have more than enough on his hands. On that day there will be shining faces, blithe with joy, and there will be faces blackened with dust—the faces of the faithless and the graceless.

—Surah 80:17-42

The themes and the temper of Muḥammad's early preaching, his sense of nightly vigilance, and his continuity with God's other warners are evident in a Surah which addresses him as "The Enmantled One." This is perhaps to be understood as a symbol of office or it may belong with a tradition that, in anguish over the tense drama of the first revelations, Muḥammad ran to his wife, Khadījah, crying: "Envelope me! Envelope me!"

You who are enmantled, keep station well nigh the night long, or half the night within an hour or so either way. Chant the Qur'ān with due care. We will bring down upon you a weighty saying. Truly in the freshness of the night impressions are weightiest and words most telling. By day you have pressing business. Remember the Name of your Lord, devote yourself wholly to Him. He is the Lord of the east and of the west. There is no god but Him. Take Him for your trust. Be patient over what men are saying and dissociate yourself from them—but courteously. Leave to Me those who give the lie to you, who preen themselves on grace. Let them be awhile. Here before us there are fetters and a fire, a food to choke on and sore punishment, on a day when earth and mountains will be convulsed and the hills be shifting mounds of blown sand.

Truly We have sent to you an apostle to be a witness upon you, just as We sent to Pharaoh a messenger. Pharaoh rejected the messenger, so We gave him a condign handling. How then, disbelieving as you are, will you secure yourselves against a day fit to turn the very children grey-headed, when the heaven will be rent asunder and all that is promised is performed? This is truly a reminder. Let him who so wills betake his way to his Lord.

Your Lord knows how you, and those who take your part, hold station for the first two thirds of the night, or maybe a half or a third. It is God who measures night and day and He knows you would in no way stint your vigil. He has turned towards you [plural], so together recite the Qur'ān, so far as reciting may be feasible. He knows that some among you will be sick, others on their journeys in the land in quest of God's bounty, while others are fighting in the way of God. So recite as far as you are readily able, perform the prayer-rite and bring the alms, and lend to God a worthy loan. For whatever well-doing you remit to your soul's account you will find with God a greater reward and an ampler good. Seek God's forgiveness. For God is a merciful forgiver.

—Surah 73

The bounty and wisdom of God in the natural order, and man's responsive duty of gratitude and wonder, are constant themes of the *Qur'ān.* Here is a selection of passages.

The Lord of mercy, He has taught the Qur'ān. He created man. He taught him the how and where of understanding. The sun and the moon have their measured circuits, stars and trees alike bring their worship. As for the heaven, He raised it and He established the Scale—in the scales you should not transgress. In those scales weigh with justice and do not make the balance cheat—and the earth He established for all living creatures, wherein are fruits and palm trees with their sheaves, and grain in the blade and herbs of fragrance. Which, then, of the benefits of your Lord will you, O heaven and earth, deny?

He created man from clay as a potter might and He created jinn from smokeless fire. Which, then, of the benefits of your Lord will each of you deny?

Lord of the two easts and Lord of the two wests, which then of the benefits of the Lord of each of you will you deny?

The two waters [that is, salt and fresh] which flow together are His handiwork and the bound which they may not pass. Which then of the benefits of the Lord of each of you will you deny?

From these are drawn the pearl and the coral. Which then of the benefits of your Lord will you deny?

His also are the ships that stand out on the face of the waters like banners. Which then of the benefits of your Lord will you deny?

All that is in these is passing away. Only the face of your Lord abides, in majesty and glory all its own. Which then of your Lord's benefits will you deny?

Whatsoever is in the heavens and the earth seeks Him. Every day He is at work. Which then of your Lord's benefits will you deny?

—Surah 55:1–29

Have they not beheld the heaven above them? How We established and adorned it in its unbroken reach? And the earth also We stretched out and set thereon mighty hills, where We made every kind of joyous thing to grow, for insight and for token to every penitent servant. And from heaven We have sent down the blessed rain whereby We make the gardens grow and grain of harvest and tall palm trees laden with clustered dates, in provision for men, thereby bringing again to life a land that was dead—similitude of 'the coming forth'.

—Surah 50:6–11

We will show them our signs in the horizons and in themselves, that it may be evident to them that it is the truth. Does it not suffice you that your Lord is witness over all things? Does He not encompass everything, that they should be thus in doubt that it is with Him they have to do?

—Surah 41:53–54

It is God who made the earth for you as an abode and the heaven for a building. He fashioned you: comely did He fashion you and with good things did He provide you. Blessed, then, be God your Lord, this God, Lord of all being. He is the living God: there is none save Him. Call upon Him in sincerity of worship. Praise be to God, the Lord of all being.

—Surah 40:66–67

> We have set in the heaven constellations, making them glorious to behold, protecting them from every accursed Satan, save him who by stealth hears and is accompanied by a trail of fire that all can see. And the earth have We stretched out, whereon are borne great mountains where We have caused everything to grow accordingly, providing there a livelihood for you and for those for whom you take no liability. There is nothing whose treasure sources are not Ours and all are constituted from above in their appointed measure. We send the fertilizing winds and bring down the rain from heaven, giving you to drink of reservoirs that are not yours.
>
> **—Surah 15:16–22**

Often the invocation of nature in the *Qur'ān* is the setting for the assurance of the truth of the revelation to the Prophet. Here the most famous passage of all is that in the "Surah of the Star."

> By the star when it sets your kinsman here (that is, Muhammad) is not astray nor does he err. He is not speaking out of whims. His word is nothing but an inspired revelation. One of awesome might has taught him, one endued with strength. Erect he stood, away on the far horizon: then he drew near, hovering down, two bows' length away, nearer still, and what he revealed to his servant he revealed. The heart does not lie: he saw. Are you disputing with him about what he sees? In another coming down he saw him by the lotus tree on the far bound of Paradise, close by the garden of the refuge, where the lotus tree was wrapped in a covering. His eye was transfixed, never turning from the sight. Truly he beheld the great signs of his Lord.
>
> **—Surah 53:1–18**

> By the winnowing winds, by the raid-laden clouds,
> By the swift-running courses, by all that disposes,
> Faithful is all that you are pledged, the judgment will indeed befall.
>
> **—Surah 51:1–6**

The much loved "Surah of Light," with its symbolism of the sanctuary lamp (v. 35–37) and its celebration of monastic piety, contains this poetry in parable.

> As for those who are unbelieving, their works are like a mirage across a plain, which a man consumed with thirst takes to be water, until, when he comes up to it, he finds nothing there. What he finds is God, paying him his full account—God who is swift to the reckoning. Or they may be likened to shadows on the vast waters of the sea swept by rolling billows, with dense clouds drifting over them, where a man can scarcely see his own hand stretched out in front of him. He to whom God appoints no light, no light has he.
>
> Do you not see that God it is whom all things praise, in the heavens and in the earth and the birds also on wings of flight? Each truly knows its prayer and its praising and God knows their every deed. For to God belongs the kingdom of the heavens and of the earth and unto Him is their becoming.
>
> Have you not seen how God drives the clouds, banks them into a rearing mass and then, behold! rain pouring down from within them? It is He who

from heaven ordains the mountains and sends hail storms over them, striking where He wills and exempting where He wills, the flash of whose lightning blinds men's eyes. God's is the revolution of the day and the night. Surely it is a lesson for those who have eyes to see. God has created of water every crawling thing, some go on their bellies and some on two feet and some on four. God creates what He wills. God is over all things sovereign.

—Surah 24:39–45

Abraham learns—and teaches—how to look through and beyond nature, to the Lordship of "the Lord of all being."

Accordingly, We showed Abraham the kingdom of the heavens and of the earth, that he might be one of sure faith. As night darkened round him he beheld a star and said: "This is my Lord." But when it set he said: "I cannot love what sets." And when he saw the moon rising he said: "This is my Lord." But when it set he said: "If my Lord does not guide me aright I shall surely be among the erring." And when he saw the sun rising he said: "This is my Lord, this is greater." But when it also set he said: "O my people, I have finished with all your idolatrous things. As for me my face is toward the One who created the heavens and the earth, as a man of pure faith. I am not a worshipper of false deities."

—Surah 6:75–79

In the "Surah of the Expropriation," it is possible to savor the mingled force of resolve and sharp irony with which the *Qur'ān* sustains the cause of Islam in the campaigns against its foes, and the interplay of relationships after the *Hijrah* between the emigrants and the Medinans who received them and also the allocation of the spoils of war.

God's is the praise of all that is in the heavens and the earth. He is the mighty and the wise. He it is who expelled those who were unbelieving of the people of the book, from their dwellings at the first rounding up. You had not imagined that they would depart and they took it for granted that their bastions would protect them against God. However, God got at them from an unexpected quarter, striking terror into their hearts so that they wrecked their houses with their own hands, apart from what believers did. So let those who have eyes use them perceptively!

It was by God's leave that you cut down palm trees as you did or left some standing with their roots. It was that He might confound the miscreants. As for what God has allotted to His messenger from these spoils—for they were not won by horse or camel that you spurred into battle—well, God empowers His messengers over whom He wills, since God is over all things sovereign. Whatever God has assigned to His messenger from the property of the people of the villages belongs anyway to God and to His messenger, and to those near of kin, to the orphans and the poverty-stricken and to the son of the road, so that it may not just circulate among you that are rich. Take what the messenger brings you and what he withholds from you, well, let it alone. Fear God. For He is truly a strong retributor.

Let it be for the emigrant poor who were expelled from their dwellings and their property [at the *Hijrah*], as they sought the good pleasure of God and His favor, in the good cause of God and His messenger—for those are the men of good faith. As for those in the faith who had their abode before, they love every one who has emigrated to them, disclaiming in their hearts any need for what has been brought to them, giving others precedence over themselves even in straitened circumstances. It is such—those preserved from inward greed for themselves—who are the ones who flourish. Those who arrived later after them say: "Our Lord, forgive us and our brothers who preceded us in the faith. Let there not be in our hearts any ill-will towards those who have believed. Our Lord, You are gentle in mercy."

Have you not noted [Muḥammad] those who acted hypocritically, saying to the unbelieving among the people of the book: "In the event of your being expelled, we too, definitely, will go out with you and we'll be bounden to no one in what relates to you. If you are involved in battle, we, for sure, will come to your aid." God is witness what deceivers they are! They do not go forth with the expelled people, nor do they take part with them when battle is joined. Even if they did they would surely turn tail and that would be no aid at all.

Truly you yourselves arouse more fear in their bosoms than God Himself, for the simple reason that they are people who are quite witless.

They will not join battle with you as a whole except in fortified places and from the cover of ramparts. They have a formidable valor when you take them together but at heart they are at sixes and sevens. They are a people who lack understanding. Like those who just a while back tasted the dire results of their doings, so these, too, are due for condign punishment. Satan once said to the man: "Say No! to God." And when he did so, Satan said: "It's nothing to do with me. I fear God, the Lord of the worlds." That is how it is with these people too. The end of both is the fire, where they are eternally. For that is the due retribution of the wrongdoers.

O you who believe, hold God in awe. Let a soul look to what he has forwarded for a morrow. Hold God in awe. God is cognisant of all you do. Do not be like those who forgot God and God caused them to forget themselves. These are the wanton with life. The denizens of the fire are not as the denizens of the garden. The denizens of the garden theirs is the triumph.

Had We caused this Qur'ān to come down upon a mountain you would have seen it disintegrating in humility and awe before God. Those similitudes We employ for the sake of men: it may be they will ponder them.

He is God: there is none but Him: He knows what is hidden and what is evident. He is the merciful Lord of mercy. He is God: there is no god but Him. He is the king, the holy, the peace, the faithkeeper, the preserver, the strong, the all-disposing, whose greatness is ever self-affirming. Praise be to God above all that idolaters conceive. He is God, the Creator, the Maker, the Fashioner; His are the beautiful names. All that is in the heavens and in the earth magnifies Him. He is ever mighty and wise.

—Surah 59

A typical late Surah with the perennial themes of judgment, the future state, the vicissitudes of *Jihād* for Islam and how to cope with them, and the duties of fidelity is the "Surah of the House of 'Imrān."

To God belongs whatsoever is in the heavens and the earth. He forgives whom He wills and punishes whom He wills, and God is the merciful forgiver. O you who have believed do not give yourselves up to usury, doubling and doubling again. Fear God: perhaps that will be your prosperity. Have fear of the fire made ready for the gainsayers. Obey God and His messenger, perhaps you will find mercy. Outdoing each other, hasten toward that forgiveness which is from your Lord and to that garden whose breadth is wide as the heavens and the earth, made ready for the God-fearers, those who give in alms both in good times and in hard, who curb their anger and pardon their fellows. For God loves the well-doers, who when they themselves do something evil or commit a wrong, remember God and seek forgiveness for the evil they have done—who shall forgive sins but God only?—and who do not still go on knowingly in the same deeds. For such, their reward is forgiveness from their Lord and gardens with rivers flowing through them where the righteous live forever. How excellent is the reward of those who labour.

Before you there have been traditions of life that have ceased to be. Traverse the earth and see to what an end they came who gave the lie to truth.

This is a disclosure for mankind and a guidance and an admonition for the God-fearers. So do not lose heart or be sad of soul, for you will have the mastery if you keep the faith.

If *you* have suffered wounds, wounds have also befallen the folk against you. That is how it goes with the days of battle that We make to fluctuate among men, so that God may know who are believers and that He may take martyrs from among you. God does not love those who work evil. It is that He may purify those who believe and put away the evildoers. Or did you count on entering the garden without God knowing whom they were who struggled in *Jihād* and endured with patience?

In advance of meeting it, you were eager to face death. Truly now you have seen it before your own eyes.

Muḥammad is only a messenger: messengers before him have passed away. If he were to die or be killed, would you then turn tail and take to your heels? Anyone who does so—well, he'll be doing God no harm. God's reward is for the thankful. It is only by the permission of God anyway that any soul dies: it is all down in a book, a register. The reward of this world will be given to him who wants it; and on him who seeks the reward of the other world We bestow it, recompensing the thankful.

Many a prophet has there been of old with whom bands of godly men have gone forth in battle, without faltering in the face of adversities in the way of God, without weakening or accepting humiliation. God loves those who steadily endure. What they said was simply: "Lord, forgive us our trespasses: forgive where we have exceeded our brief: make us to stand firm and grant us victory over the unbelieving people."

So God rewarded them in this world and gave them the more excellent reward of the world to come. For God loves the well-doers.

O you who have believed, if you obey those who are unbelievers, it will be a right-about-turn for you and spell total loss. But God is your Lord-guardian and He is the best of helpers. Into the hearts of those who believe not We will strike terror. For they have done what no revealed mandate allows—they have violated the divine unity. The fire is their abode, the wretched haunt of the wrong-doers.

God faithfully kept His word to you when, by His leave, you put them to the sword. The trouble was you faltered and fell into quarreling among yourselves over it and so broke discipline just when God set before your very eyes the thing you longed to see. There are some among you who crave after this world: and there are some who yearn for the world to come. So it was that He tested you in letting them drive you back. He has pardoned you. For God is a gracious Lord to those who believe.

—Surah 3:129–152

From commentary on the fortunes of war and their meaning for the faithful, we turn finally to a sample passage of Quranic legislation for the guidance of the *Ummah* in Medina and beyond.

> O you who have believed, eat of the good things with which We have provided you and give thanks to God—if indeed it is Him you serve. He has, however, ruled out for you carrion flesh, blood, and the flesh of swine and any meat ritually consecrated in any other name than God's. But anyone who is compelled against his desire and who is not deliberately doing wrong, no guilt will be his. For God is forgiving and merciful. Those who suppress what God has sent down and barter the Book for a little price, they will have only the fire for their fodder. God will have no word to say to them on the day of resurrection, nor will He purify them. Theirs is a painful punishment. These are they who purchase delusion with the price of guidance and doom instead of forgiveness. In the fire what endurance they will need!
>
> So be it. For God has caused the Book to come down with the truth. Those who differ as to the Book surely are in total schism.
>
> Righteousness does not consist in turning your faces in the direction of the east or of the west. Rather, righteousness is theirs, whoever they be, who believe in God, in the last day, in the angels, the Book, and the prophets; who make what they possess and cherish available to kinsfolk and orphans, to the needy and the wayfarer and those who beg and for the ransom of slaves; who perform the prayer rite and bring the alms; who fulfill the covenant they have undertaken and who endure patiently when trouble, adversity and tribulation come their way. Those are the ones who keep faith: it is such who are the true God-fearers.
>
> O you who have believed, retaliation is prescribed for you in cases of murder—the freeman for the freeman, the slave for the slave, the woman for the woman. But in the case of a homicide being pardoned by the brother, payment must be made appropriately, and let the due compensation be transacted kindly. This is an alleviation from your Lord and a merciful thing. However, anyone who then does not let it rest there, his will be a painful requital.
>
> In [such] retaliation there is life for you—you who are endowed with intelligence. Perhaps you will let the fear of God prevail.
>
> It is prescribed for you, when death draws near for any of you with property to leave, that testamentary bequest be made to the two parents, and to the next of kin according to honourable custom, as is properly due from those who fear God. Anyone who changes it after he has heard it, the guilt will be on those who connive with the change. God is He who hears and knows. But, in the case of a fear that there has been partiality or evil-doing on the part of the testator, putting it right between those concerned will not be transgressing. God is forgiving and merciful.
>
> O you who have believed, fasting is prescribed for you, as it was prescribed for those before you. Perhaps you will fear God. The fast days are fixed. Any among you who is sick or on a journey, let him fast the same number of other days. For those who are undertaking the fast, there is an expiation for breaking it, namely feeding a destitute person. But it is better that such good be done spontaneously and the fast, duly done, is better for you too, did you but realise. The [fast] month is Ramaḍān, in which the Qur'ān was sent down as a guidance for mankind, guidance in clear terms, and as the criterion. So when the month is visibly upon you, let each of you fast during it. As for the sick and any who are journeying, let them fast a number of other days. God

wills to ease you in this. For He does not will for you hardship, but that you should achieve the number of days and so magnify God who has guided you. Perhaps you will be grateful.

And when My servants ask you [Muḥammad] about Me—I am near to answer the call of the suppliant when he calls upon Me. Let them, too, respond to Me and believe in Me, so that they may be led in the right way."

—Surah 2:172–186

But the very essence of all the *Qur'ān* is in the Opening Surah, *Surat al-Fātiḥah*

In the Name of God, the merciful Lord of mercy.
Praise be to God, the Lord of all being,
The merciful Lord of mercy, Master of the day of judgment.
You alone we serve and to you alone we come for aid.
Guide us in the straight path,
The path of those whom You have blessed,
Not of those against whom there is displeasure,
Nor of those who go astray.[1]

—Surah 1

THE 'FEEL' OF THE BOOK

"You will never understand this power and warmth of religion among us until you can feel in your own heart the poetry and music of the *Qur'ān al-Sharīf* ("the noble Scripture"). There was never music in the world before like that." (Zaka Ullah, an Indian Muslim leader, to his Christian friend, the famous Charles Freer Andrews.)

This "feel" of the *Qur'ān* in the Muslim soul is vividly described by Driss Chraïbi, in an autobiographical novel, *Heirs to the Past.* The occasion is the funeral of the old father of the family, for which the emigré son, Driss Ferdi, has returned from the chill secular rationalism of Paris, where he has spent the last sixteen years in a steady erosion of his Muslim convictions and identity. So he is no merely traditional witness. The emotion he registers is all the more significant for his very reluctance to yield to it.

Then a man stood up . . . and began to chant. What he chanted was of no importance. It was not the words, nor the meaning, nor even the symbolism, which moved our hearts, the men, women and children who were there. We forgot why we were there the moment he began to chant. It was the incantation, and the end of our woes and miserable little problems, the aching and yet serene longing for that other life which is ours and to which we are all destined to return, the victors and the defeated, the fully developed and those who are still at the larva stage, the faithful and the atheists, through God's great compassion. There was all of that in the voice of the man who stood chanting in the sun, and we were in his voice, I was in his voice despite the

> vast legacy of incredulity that I had received from the West. When he reached the end of a verse, he paused, and so it came about—an outburst of fervour. And while he chanted it was like a man in the wilderness chanting his faith. And the voice rose and swelled, changed in tone, became tragic, soared and then floated down on our heads like a seagull gliding gently and softly, little more than a whisper. And so—never again will I go in search of intellectuals, of written truths, synthetic truths, of collections of hybrid ideas which are nothing but ideas. Never again will I travel the world in search of a shadow of justice, fairness, progress, or schemes calculated to change mankind. I was weary and I was returning to my clan. The man who was not even aware of his voice or of his faith was alive and held the secret of life—a man who could not even have been a dustman in this world of founts of knowledge and of civilization. Peace and everlasting truth were in him and in his voice, while all was crumbling around him and on the continents.[2]

A narrative of Muslim seamen, sailing in a dhow on the route between Muscat and Zanzibar, entitled: *Sons of Sinbad,* describes the place of the *Qur'ān* in a seafaring religion.

> The only book on board was a copy of the Qur'ān, in which Ḥamad, 'Abdallāh, the nakhoda's brother, and the passengers, often read. When he came to a good part Ḥamad would sometimes call a small group together and read aloud in a very pleasant and well-modulated voice, and they would discuss whatever they read for hours. They seemed to find perfect content in this book and never tired of reading it. Sometimes one or another of them would chant chapters from memory.[3]

Lawrence Durrell's well-known works of imagination, based on life in Alexandria, Egypt, contain the same witness, as, for example, the following:

> They waited now with emotion for that old voice, melodious and worn with age, to utter the opening strophes of the Holy Book, and there was nothing feigned in the adoring attention of the circle of faces. Some licked their lips and leaned forward eagerly, as if to take the phrases upon their lips: others lowered their heads and closed their eyes as if against a new experience in music. The old preacher sat with his waxen hands folded in his lap and uttered the first Surah, full of the soft, warm coloring of a familiar understanding, his voice a little shaky at first, but gathering power and assurance from the silence as he proceeded. His eyes now were as wide and lustreless as a dead hare's. His listeners followed the notation of the verses as they fell from his lips with care and rapture, gradually seeking their way together and into the main stream of the poetry like a school of fish following a leader by instinct out into the deep sea.[4]

There are several forms of Quranic recitation, but each is determined in measure by the demands of the Arabic vowel forms. There is a single tonality in any recitative pattern. In his French translation of the *Qur'ān,* Henri Mercier offers the following punctuation in a Muslim psalmody (as it were) applied to the opening verse of Surah 14, which reads: "A Book which We have brought down to thee, to lead men out of darkness into light by leave of their Lord into the path of the Mighty, the Praiseworthy."

The quaver represents a short syllable, the crotchet a long, and the minim a very long. Where, unlike this verse, the last syllable of a rhythmic phrase is short, its value is a dotted quaver.[5]

A recent volume of poems by a Tunisian Muslim, Muḥammad al-Nāṣir al-Ṣaddām, includes a poem on the *Qur'ān* that conveys a representative sense of what the Scripture means in terms of simple, contemporary piety. The title of the volume is *Ibtihālāt* [Supplications], Tunis, 1968.

> Good shall never be lacking to the community that speaks the Arabic tongue as long as they cleave to the guidance of the Qur'ān. It is the Book whose bright beams shone forth, disclosing the truth and dispelling the dark.
>
> There God called to everyone on earth together, summoning them to a right mind. Arabs and non-Arabs alike responded. Its verses are explicit and by them we do not go astray, for by them is wisdom, guidance and sound truth. Those who are led by them are true in what they proclaim and their deeds are not their pretensions and their prognostications. For the Qur'ān is our authority in religion and mind and deed, and what it contains has graced both moral principles and practice.
>
> By means of the Qur'ān the very gist of earth's sciences came into being, harmonizing in every age with the movement of events. Its verses reveal wonders to us as new things, while it is itself the enduring thing which old

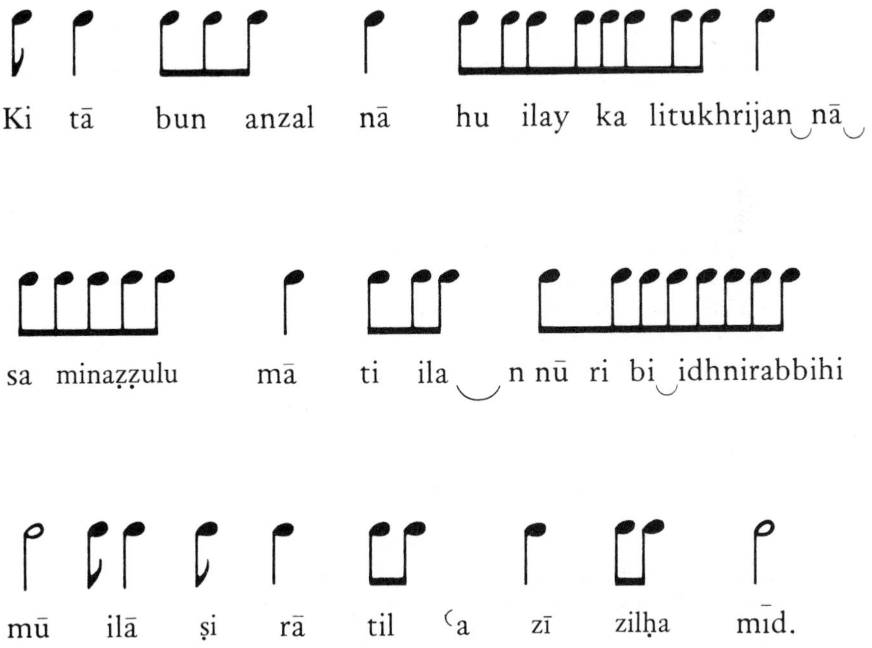

FIGURE 1. Quranic Notation. (Henri Mercier, The Koran, *trans. by L. Tremlett. London Luzac & Co., 1956. Reproduced by permission.*

times have not made obsolete. It is salvation to whosoever seeks it and only by it are the things that intimidate defied. By God, peoples who did according to it have not gone wrong, nor have adversities disintegrated or destroyed them.

Let us then ask God that we may conform to its directive and in our goings forth our steps will not stumble.[6]

One interesting and suggestive witness to the role of the *Qur'ān* in Muslim personal and political life is Muḥammad 'Alī (1878–1931). In his autobiography, *My Life, A Fragment,* he describes his role in the leadership of the Khilafatist Movement within Indian Islam in the 1930s. This movement sought to maintain the Khalifat (which Turkey abolished in 1924) as the main buttress of communal security for Muslims in the subcontinent. During his imprisonment for political leadership Muḥammad 'Alī 'discovered' the *Qur'ān* in a new and compelling way. That he was a great thinker—even though, by his own confession, no theologian—was indicated by the rare distinction accorded to him at his death of being buried within the precincts of the *Ḥaram al-Sharīf* in Jerusalem.

At Chindwara [internment place], where we passed three and a half years, we had enough leisure and undisturbed peace and quiet to read the Qur'ān and thoroughly soak ourselves in that perennial foundation of Truth that the gathering dust of thirteen centuries has not been able to choke or dry.

For the first time in my life I read it through in an intelligent and comprehending manner. Neither my brother nor I had been able to acquire any real proficiency in Arabic. But the late Maulvie Nazir Ahmad . . . had utilized his leisure on retirement to translate the Qur'ān into Urdu. . . . He made an entirely new departure in not being so literal as to offend against the Urdu idiom and, for the first time, Indian Muslims had a translation which was not only readable, but a pleasure to read. . . . With the help of this both my brother and I commenced our first regular study of the Qur'ān and the amount of Arabic we knew was enough to make our daily study of absorbing interest.

This wonderful book is full of repetitions, in spite of being but a small volume, abrupt in its transitions from topic to topic. I can well understand that Europeans who read it in translation, more or less out of curiosity and are able to go through it in a few days, so often pronounce it to be incoherent and disjointed. But they do not realise that it was not revealed as a complete volume all at once, but piecemeal and in the course of no less than twenty-three years of the Prophet's mission. Moreover, they do not realise that even God's Word, when it appears in human language, has to take on the characteristics of the particular language in which it makes its appearance. Those who are familiar with the Arabic language and Arab literature know that jerkiness is characteristic of both. In fact it is characteristic of the very mentality of the people whose thought flits from topic to topic with breathless rapidity. Ideas do not continue to glow with a steady light but seem to flash dazzlingly, as it were, through the gloom from time to time. Even in long poems the same idea hardly runs through more than a few couplets and this peculiarity has made the *ghazal* the favorite metric form in which the metre and the rhyme in the first and second verses and then only in the even numbered verses are the only marks of continuity, while the topic of each couplet is distinct and unconnected with the rest. Apart from this jerky abruptness characteristic of all Arabic literature, each fragment of the Qur'ān was revealed from time to time, so that the circumstance in which it was revealed, and which in fact necessitated the revelation, supplied a relevance and a context, which are not to be found in the text itself. . . .

There are several passages in the Qur'ān which explain why the revelation was so gradual [here citing 17:41, 17:105, 106, and 25:32]. For the unbelievers the warnings and the arguments were repeated day after day, and through logic, parable and history, every facet of the great eternal Truth was presented before their eyes. For the Muslims the fragments that were revealed from time to time were so many messages from their Maker who was watching their daily and hourly growth with more loving care and vigilance than the most anxious parent, and helped them every now and then with a word of caution or of courage. His commandments were not promulgated in the humdrum manner of the laws enacted by human legislators, indifferently received by those who are required to obey them. They descended as occasion required on a people waiting and watching anxiously to conform to them.

And on His side the ever vigilant God, too, who knew how weak after all was the human creature He had made, did not demand impossibilities from these first believers who had just been weaned from heathenism with its lax morals. "God lays not on a soul a heavier burden than it can bear," and "the religion of God is easy." In their probation, the Companions were by degrees habituated to the austere life that Islam, with all its abhorrence of anchoritism, expects a Muslim to live. . . .

When the commandments were being revealed they were engraved, as it were, on the tablets of the Muslims' memories because of the incidents connected with their revelation. A blind man pleads his disability when all Muslims are called upon to bear arms in defense of their faith; a group of men through sheer procrastination tarried behind so long, when the Prophet marched out with the Muslims on an expedition, that they could not catch him up and became defaulters in their duty as Muslims; a woman states before the Prophet the pitiable case of her daughters whom Arab custom had totally disinherited while distant relatives were succeeding to the estate of their deceased father . . . Hostile critics have characterized this as hand-to-mouth legislation. But they have totally missed the object which would have been defeated if an artificial code of laws, like the Priestly Code . . . had descended all at once upon the Arabs, many of them uncouth warriors or worse still barbarian nomads of the desert. A Pallas Athene, rising ready armed from the head of Zeus, would have altogether bewildered such worshippers. Finally, for the Prophet himself, these revelations coming, as they did, from time to time provided a Prophet's sustenance that strengthened his heart and supplied the necessary stimulus throughout a long and arduous mission. This piecemeal revelation fully served its three-fold purpose. At the most trying moments in his prophetic career it comforted and consoled him, and at no time did it take on a surer note in predicting ultimate triumph than when to all outward appearances the Prophet's condition was hopeless. As for the infidels, unrelaxing repetition and reiteration wore down their prejudice and hostility and truth at last triumphed and falsehood finally vanished from Arabia. . . .

If Islam has endured through so many and such strange vicissitudes, it was because truth had trickled down on the early Muslims drop by drop and soaked them through and through.

Throughout the day the Companions used to be in attendance on Muḥammad, some to jot down on paper and skins, on tablets and bones and palm branches shorn of leaves, the Word of God as the official scribes of 'the illiterate Prophet' the moment he recovered from the trance-like condition in which he used to receive the revelation, and others to memorize it for their own use both as lessons for their lives and for liturgical purposes. Those whose business did not permit them to be in attendance every day . . . paired with others and thus arranged with them to be in attendance by turns. Thus not a syllable of the Holy Writ was lost or confounded with human utterance and the chief topic of conversation among the thousands at Medina used to be the day's revelations which, along with the customary, explanatory comments of the Prophet, were treasured in the most retentive of memories.

After narrating in these devout terms the traditional reconstruction of the *Qur'ān's* descent upon Muḥammad and his audiences' receptivity, Muḥammad 'Alī goes on to describe his own encounter with the text.

When we commenced our study of the Qur'ān, we wisely decided to read only a little every day, so that it took us no less than eight or nine months to finish our first reading of it, and although I am now able to obtain equal pleasure in reading four or five times as much in the same space of time, I still prefer to keep up the old rate of progress. In reading so little every day, . . . the repetitions do not produce the same effect as they are apt to do if one reads the whole book, say, in seven days which many Muslims do to this day, and in still less time as is customary with them, when they fast in the Month of Ramaḍān, and no part of the freshness is thus lost. . . . How often have we not felt as if the passages we happened to be reading on a particular day were revealed only that instant in response to our own prayer, or to settle some point about which we happened to be unsure or uneasy. My brother would call out to me from his room and recite to me a verse, or I would do the same to him, pointing out how apposite it was to the question we happened to be debating only a little before. These coincidences were of such frequent occurrence that by degrees a habit of expectancy was formed, and we began to expect all unconsciously a response from the day's reading of the Qur'ān to unexpressed references to Heaven! . . .

To us, therefore, who read such small portions every day, even when for the first time we had abundant leisure, it never seemed to lack freshness, and its repetitions and the variety of ways in which its main theme was presented to us day after day, as it had been presented to the Arabs thirteen centuries ago, only served to enable us to learn a much-needed lesson that we were apt to forget and even ignore in the distractions of the world. Ever since, this Book, which so many European critics pronounce to be incoherent, disjointed and dull, had had the invariable effect of intoxicating us by its simple grandeur, its intense directness and its incessant flow of motive power for the manifold activities of life.

And long before I had read it through, *Eureka!* I had found a new meaning in life and in this world and an entirely new significance in Islam. I had been familiar enough with the main tenets of Islam; but they had been little more than a bundle of doctrines and commandments, each for a particular department of life or situation, though, of course, I had looked upon them as superior to the dogmas and ethical codes of other faiths. Now, however, they acquired a new coherence and, as it were, fell suddenly into place, creating an effect of unity such as I had never realised before.

They were no longer a bundle of doctrines but a single divine purpose running through all creation from the remote genesis of the world to the very minute of our present existence. . . . Nothing stood apart: nothing was alien: nothing could exist for itself unrelated to others. The entire universe was one. The unity of the Creator postulated the unity of His creation and all was one vast Theocracy with Allah for its King and Man for His earthly Viceregent. Man, made in the image of his Creator, was not the sport of chance and slave of destiny, but master of his fate. Of all His creatures in the world, we know Man alone has been endowed by the Creator with a will of his own, and was to that extent responsible for his actions and fit to be God's deputy or agent on earth. But, nevertheless, man made a voluntary and complete surrender of himself and became the rightless slave of his Creator, or, rejecting the purpose for which he was created, he chose to surrender himself to another master than God. . . . The key word of the Qur'ān was 'Serve,' and while man was free to serve whom he would, his inherent, inborn faith, the nature with which his Creator had endowed him at his creation, told him that he was to serve none other but the One God, Creator, Sustainer and Developer of all creation and this 'testimony' of his own soul was supported by the testimony of all nature and was finally confirmed by the teaching of those whom God had given a more acute intuition, the Prophets on whom had descended a yet more impressive revelation than his own. . . .

This was my unique discovery in that small volume revealed more than thirteen hundred years ago to an Arab of the desert whose name I bore—unique to me even though thousands, tens of thousands and hundreds of thousands of other Columbuses had discovered the same new world, after the first revelation to the solitary worshipper in the cave of Hirā' one night towards the end of the month of Ramaḍān. Nay, the first revelation was in fact far earlier. It was in that infinitely earlier epoch that people call the Genesis when God revealed Himself to the first Man. . . . I had discovered God and in discovering Him and His message to mankind I had discovered myself. I had found a new meaning and a hitherto unrealized fullness in life, contrasted with which my previous existence, which I had thought to be crowded enough for a somewhat somnolent continent of the east like India, appeared to be empty and barren. . . . The moment this eternal truth had dawned upon me in all its refulgence I was too full of it to keep it to myself, even if I could have desired it. I was literally bursting with my new discovery and felt impelled to shout it to all and sundry.[7]

THE 'MIRACLE' OF THE *QUR'ĀN*

A characteristic, classical statement of the literary miracle (*I'jāz*) of the *Qur'ān* is that of the famous Quranicist, Al-Suyūṭī (1445–1505) in his *Al-Itqān,* a much prized manual of Quranic sciences.

Among those who have occupied themselves in composition on this subject are Al-Khaṭābī, Al-Ramānī, Al-Zamalkānī, the Imām al-Rāzī, and Al-Bāqīllānī. Ibn 'Arabī, whose work is unsurpassed, said that [the] miracle is something transcending the ordinary and, though open to be emulated, is beyond the reach of imitation. It is either a thing of the senses or a thing of the mind. The majority of the miracles of the children of Israel were in the realm of the senses, because of their simplemindedness and the poverty of their understanding: while the larger part of the miracles of this [Islamic] people are intellectual, because of their ample intelligence and the perfection of their understanding and because this religious law, enduring as it does upon the pages of time until the day of resurrection, has been characterized by enduring intellectual miracles for the intellectually competent to perceive.

As Muḥammad said: "There is no prophet among the prophets who was not given the like of that in which humanity believed. Nevertheless, that which was brought to me was a revelation God inspired in me and I hope to have more followers than them all."

Al-Bukhārī elucidates this: "It was reported that his meaning was that the miracles of the prophets were confined to their own times and only their contemporaries witnessed them. The miracle of the Qur'ān, however, abides until the day of resurrection. The miracle is its transcending the natural in style and eloquence and in its revelation of the hidden mysteries. There will never come an age in which something of its message will not be manifest. It will continue to give evidence of the authenticity of its claims."

The point here is that the evident miracles of the past were sensible, that is, they were seen by the sight of the eye, like Ṣāliḥ's camel, and Moses' rod, whereas the miracle of the Qur'ān is recognized by the intelligence. Thus those who are disciples to it will be more numerous. For that which is seen by the actual eye is limited to the immediate witnesses, while that which is observed by the eye of the intelligence abides and all who come after its original time perceive it as an abiding thing. . . .

There is no disagreement among intellectuals that the Book of God most exalted is a miracle which no one can imitate when challenged to do so. God [exalted] said: "If any one of the polytheists seeks your protection, guard him until he hears the words of God." [Surah 9:6] Were hearing not in fact a proof for him, the matter would not be made to turn upon hearing and it would not constitute a proof unless the Book were a miracle. And God [exalted] also said: "They said: Why have there not been sent down upon him [Muḥammad] signs from his Lord? Say: The signs are only with God and I am a plain warner. Does it not suffice them that We have sent down upon thee the Book recited to them?" [Surah 29:50, 51] Know then that the Book is among His signs sufficient as guidance and taking the place of miracles other than itself and the signs of those among the prophets other than itself.

When the Prophet brought it to them—and they the most eloquent and the most quick witted of speakers—and challenged them to bring forth the like of it and, through the years gave them plenty of opportunity, they were unable to do so. As God said: "Let them produce a discourse like it, if they are sincere." [Surah 52:34] Then he challenged them to ten surahs like it, saying: "Do they say: 'He has forged it?' Say: Then bring ten surahs like it, forgeries too and call upon whomever you can other than God, if you are honest men. Then, if they do not respond to you, know that it has been brought down by the knowledge of God." [Surah 11:13] Then he challenged them to one surah when he said: "Do they say: 'He forged it?' Say thou: Then produce a surah like it." (Surah 10:38). Then He reiterated the point, saying: "If you are in doubt concerning what We have sent down upon Our servant, then bring a surah like it." [Surah 2:23] When they were incapable of emulating it or of producing a comparable surah, despite the surfeit of orators among them and of eloquent speakers, he called upon them to recognize their incapacity and the surpassing quality of the Qur'ān. And He said: "Say: If men and jinns came together to produce the like of this Qur'ān, they would never avail to do so, not even were they to back each other." [Surah 17:88] And that is so though they are eloquent ones.

The thing they were most anxious to do was to extinguish the light of the Qur'ān and explain away what it required. If it had been within their power to counter it, they would certainly have returned to the point in order to make an end of the argument. But it is not related of any of them that they did anything of the kind, even though they eagerly desired to do so. So they had recourse sometimes to hostility and sometimes to contempt. Sometimes they said: Witchcraft! and at other times: Poetry! Or again they said: "It is legends of the primitive times!" All that derived from their perplexity, their being at the end of themselves. Then they were pleased to appeal to the arbitrament of the sword, in their stiff-neckedness—a thing which resulted in the captivity of their women folk and the destruction of their property, when, as a matter of first priority, they were at all costs most anxious to protect them.

Had they known that just bringing the like of a surah was within their power, they would surely have hastened to do so as much the easiest thing for them.[8]

"Whoever reads the *Qur'ān* rightly," wrote Shaikh Muḥammad 'Abduh in his pioneer work of modern Islamic apologetic (see pp. 217–219) "will find new impulse and initiative and unfailing treasure." 'Rightly', of course, is the crucial word. How the Shaikh himself meant it can be sensed from his own exposition of what may be called the excellence of the *Qur'ān* as Muslims find it.

A recurrent tradition which is undoubtedly reliable relates that the Prophet was . . . brought up illiterate. It is equally maintained down the years among the nations that he brought a Scripture of which he said that it had been sent down upon him. That Book was the Qur'ān, written on pages and preserved in the hearts of those Muslims who in their care committed it to memory, down to today.

It is a Book which contains such chronicles of the nations of the past as hold a moral for present and future generations, proving the true and jettisoning the false and imaginary, and thus alerting us to the lessons they afford.

It relates of the Prophets what God wills us to know of their story and course of life, the issues between them and their peoples and believers in their message.

It blamed the learned leaders of the various sects for the degree to which they had corrupted their beliefs and 'alloyed' their precepts, and for the exegetical alterations they made in their Scriptures. The Qur'ān laid down for men the principles by which their interests might be rightly served. Nothing could be clearer than the benefit which comes from being guided by them and preserving them jealously. Justice rests on them and the whole special order remains secure within their authority. Contrariwise, their neglect and abandonment, or any departure even from their spirit, entails great loss. In these ways the laws of the Qur'ān are superior to all the legislation of the nations, as will be evident to any one who studies their history.

The Qur'ān, moreover, contains rules, exhortations and moral precepts that bow men's hearts and win a kindly way into men's minds. In their wake resolutions take their forward way, in the cause of human society. . . .

The mighty Book was vindicated as being speech *par excellence,* and its judgments superior to all others. Is not the appearance of such a Book, from the lips of an illiterate man, the greatest miracle and clearest evidence that it is not of human origin? Is it not rather the light that emanates from the sun of divine knowledge, the heavenly wisdom coming forth from the Lord upon the illiterate Prophet?

Furthermore, the Book brought tidings of the unseen world, which terrestrial events have confirmed. . . .

Muḥammad's awareness of the hidden world of things is implicit also in his challenge to the Arabs about producing a comparable chapter and his readiness to stake his mission on it—if one keeps in mind the extent of Arab lands, the wealth of population within their wide borders, the diffusion of his message on the part of the delegations come to Mecca from every corner, and the further fact that Muḥammad himself had not circulated in those parts or made the acquaintance of their leading men. One man's knowledge is ordinarily inadequate to cover the potential of so great a nation as the Arab people. We must take it then that his unhesitating assertion that they would not ever be able to produce anything like it was not a merely human judgment. It would be not only very difficult but impracticable for an intelligent person to involve himself in such an undertaking and put himself under such a pledge. Any thinking person would naturally assume that the world would not lack a match for him. Thus it is God Who addresses men in these words of challenge. On Muḥammad's lips, the All-knowing, the All-aware is speaking. God's knowledge comprehends the universal incapacity to rise to what is required and meet the challenge. . . .

The matchlessness of the Qur'ān is an actuality beyond the powers of humanity. Its eloquence remained unparalleled. We say deliberately 'the powers of humanity.' For the Qur'ān came to an Arabic speaking prophet. Writing was well known everywhere among the Arabs at that time. . . . Yet for all that the Arabs quite failed to produce from their whole mental effort anything to oppose it. It is then irrational to think that some Persian, or Indian, or Greek, could have commanded such Arabic skill to achieve what had defeated the Arabs themselves. The powers of the Arabs quite failed them, despite their having comparable origins and education to Muḥammad, and many of them special advantages of science and study. All of this is proof positive that the words of the Qur'ān are in no way the sort of thing to originate from man. No! it was a unique, divine gift to him on whose lips it came. And so its statements about their inability to equal it and its readiness to meet head on all that their skill could contrive are plain proofs of its assurance as to its identity. The speaker is undoubtedly the Lord, Who knows the unseen and the visible, and no man preaching and counselling in the ordinary way. This is the conclusion of all the evidences now accumulated, of contents quite impossible to merely human intelligence to sustain for so long.

And thus, the great wonder of the Qur'ān is proved. This eternal Book, untouched by change, susceptible of no alteration, demonstrates that our Prophet Muḥammad is God's messenger to His creation. His message is to be believed, and the whole contents of the heaven-sent Book. It is ours to follow all that it lays down as guidance and law. It is written in the Qur'ān that Muḥammad is the seal of the prophets and this is for us *de fide*. . . .

When one has sound training does one need a mentor: or a guardian when one's mind is fully ripe? Hardly! For the true had been distinguished from the false and all that remains is to follow the guidance and from the hands of mercy take the way that brings one to happiness here and hereafter.

For this reason, Muḥammad's prophecy brought prophecy to an end. His message terminated the work of messengers, as the Book affirms and the

> authentic tradition corroborates. The fact is evidenced by the collapse of all pretensions to prophethood since Muḥammad, as well as by the world's contentment with what has come to it from him. The world knows that there is no acceptability now in claims made by pretenders after mission with laws and revelation from God. It acknowledges the heavenly word which says: "Muḥammad is not the father of any man among you. He is the messenger of God and the seal of the prophets. God truly knows all things." [Surah 33:40] [9]

The orthodox view of the *Qur'ān*, as perfect, final revelation, has been set out in characteristic form by Muḥammad 'Abd Allāh Draz, one time Professor of *Tafsīr* (Exegesis) at the Al-Azhar University, Cairo. In K.W. Morgan: *Islam, the Straight Path,* he writes:

> The greatest miracle was the revelation of the Qur'ān which was transmitted by the Prophet in passages of unequal length at different times over a period of twenty-three years. . . . The explicit and implicit testimony of the Qur'ān is that the author is God Himself. It is never the Prophet who speaks in the Qur'ān. The Scripture either refers to him in the third person or addresses him directly—O Prophet, O Messenger, We reveal to thee, We send thee, do this, recite this: such is the language of the Qur'ān.
>
> The direct proof of the divine origin of the Qur'ān is manifest all through the Scripture itself. It is shown by the peculiar phenomena which accompanied every revelation of the Qur'ān, according to the testimony of the true tradition. The Prophet's contemporaries were objective witnesses of the visible, tangible, and audible signs of the mysterious accompanying phenomena which made evident the real source of the Qur'ān and opened the eyes of the truth-seekers. In the presence of the Revealer Spirit the Prophet's inspired face was illumined, like a mirror: there was silence: conversation stopped as if in moments of absence of mind: his body relaxed as if in sleep and a mysterious buzz was heard around him—as in a telephone conversation where the one listening is the only one who can hear distinctly enough to understand. There was nothing voluntary about these phenomena, for the Prophet could neither avoid them when they came nor bring them into being when he earnestly desired to receive a message. . . .
>
> The literary style and contents of the text are conclusive evidence of the divine origin of the Qur'ān. [After ruling out all suggestions about historical, human contacts and sources, Muḥammad Draz continues:] It is clear that the teachings of the Qur'ān cannot be attributed to the influence of the environment on Muḥammad. There remains the question as to whether or not he could have created the Qur'ān by himself through the use of meditation or reason. To a limited extent reason could have revealed the falseness of idolatry and the senselessness of superstition, but how could it know how to replace them? It is not by mere thinking that facts can be known, that previous events can be described, yet the Qur'ān was always in perfect accord with the essential data of the Bible, even those hidden from Muḥammad by scholars. The Qur'ān confirms that before the revelation Muḥammad did not know any book nor even the meaning of faith [42:52]. He was ignorant of all the legislative, moral, social and ritual details which are included in the revelation of the Qur'ān. . . .
>
> The literary form of the Qur'ān is distinguished clearly from all other forms, whether they be poetry, rhythmic or non-rhythmic; prose, the style of the

common people, or that of the Prophet himself. The exceptional eloquence of Muḥammad was always acknowledged and is known to us in countless instructions which he gave after careful thought, or dictated as non-Quranic insights. In all such passages there is not the slightest resemblance between them and the revealed messages.

We feel such ascendant power in the revealed texts that they penetrate the soul. The infidels in the time of the Prophet considered the form of the text such an extraordinary phenomenon that they used to call it magic. Even in modern times those who can understand the Arabic text recognise its sublime character without being able to explain it. . . .

At the same time there is such a profundity, flexibility, suggestivity and radiance in the Qur'ān that it serves as the basis of the principles and rules for the Islamic sciences and arts, for theology and for the juridical schools. Thus it is almost impossible in each case to express the ideas of a text by one interpretation only, either in Arabic or in a foreign language, even with the greatest care.

Quranic speech appears to be superhuman in its transcendence of the psychological law that intellect and feeling are always found in inverse proportions to each other. In the Qur'ān we find constant co-operation between the two antagonistic powers of reason and emotion. For we find that in the narrations, arguments, doctrines, laws, and moral principles, the words have both a persuasive teaching and an emotive force. Throughout the whole Qur'ān the speech maintains a surprising solemnity and powerful majesty which nothing can disturb.

Finally, when we pass from the structure of a sentence, or a group of sentences dealing with the same subject, to the structure of the Surah and of the Qur'ān as a whole, we find an over-all plan which could not have been created by man.

[After discussing the sequences of the Qur'ān and its architectural order, and reviewing its teaching, the writer proceeds:]

In addition to the Qur'ān's primary aim of revealing religious and moral truths, there are secondary objectives designed to strengthen faith in the Creator or to support the faithful in their hope. It is striking to discover the extent to which explanations of the natural world, God's creation, correspond precisely with the latest discoveries of cosmology, anatomy, physiology, and the rest of the positive sciences. For instance, consider these remarkable examples of scientific knowledge: the sphericity of the earth [39:5], the formation of rain [30:48], fertilization by the wind [15:22], the aquatic origin of all living creatures [21:30], the duality of the sex of plants and other creatures, then unknown [36:35], the collective life of animals [6:38], the mode of life of the bees [16:69], the successive phases of the child in his mother's womb. [22:5; 23:14]

A constant support to the faithful in their hope is the fulfillment of prophecies. . . . Who could ever give guarantees against space and time other than the Master of Space and Time Himself?

The divine origin of the Qur'ān is evident for all the reasons which have been considered in this discussion. The possibility of human origin has been eliminated. Nowhere in the Qur'ān is the personal character of the Prophet reflected, nowhere is there an echo of his daily joys and sorrows or of his earthly surroundings. There are no indications of geographical, atmospherical, racial, tribal, or individual peculiarities in the subjects treated. Only that which is necessary for the education of humanity is found in the Qur'ān. The revelations were accompanied by visible signs of their divine origin. The linguistic and stylistic form of the Qur'ān gives positive signs of its divine origin, free from the possibility of borrowing from other books.

It is for this reason that the Qur'ān holds the highest place in Islam. For Muslims, the Qur'ān is not only the text of prayers, the instrument of prophecy, the food for the spirit, the favorite canticle of the soul. It is at the same time the fundamental law, the treasure of the sciences, the mirror of the ages. It is the consolation for the present and the hope for the future.

In what it affirms the Qur'ān is the criterion of truth. In what it orders or prohibits, it is the best model for behavior. In what it judges, its judgment is always correct. In what it discusses it gives the decisive argument. In what it says, it is the purest and most beautiful expression possible in speech. It calms and incites most effectively.

Since the Qur'ān is the direct expression of the divine will, it holds supreme authority for all men.[10]

QURANIC COMMENTARY

Muslim commentary on the *Qur'ān,* known as *Tafsīr,* or exegesis, has a long and honored history but, for the most part, follows very traditional lines. It is concerned with grammatical comments and elucidations, and breathes a deep, devotional reverence for the text. One of the most esteemed and authoritative commentators was 'Abdallāh ibn 'Umar al-Baiḍāwī (1226–1260), who lived and wrote mainly in Tabriz, Iran. His celebrated commentary had the title *Anwār al-Tanzīl wa Asrār al-Ta'wīl,* "The Lights of Revelation and the Secrets of its Elucidation." Here is a section on Surah 3:4–10, as translated by D.S. Margoliouth. Certain abstruse technicalities are omitted and a few expressions adapted for the sake of clarity. The passage contains in verse 5 one of the main observations of the *Qur'ān* about its own verses, as a guide to its interpretation.

Verily nothing is concealed from God in earth or heaven. That is, nothing which comes to pass in this world, be it universal or particular, faith or unbelief. He expresses this by the terms "earth and heaven" because the senses cannot go beyond them. He mentions the earth first in order to ascend from lower to higher, and because what is intended to be mentioned is what is committed on earth. The verse is, as it were, a proof that He is alive, whereas the following

He it is who forms you in the wombs as He will. That is, out of different forms, is, as it were, a proof of His quality of sustainer, and is like an argument that He is wise, based upon the perfection of His work in creating and forming the embryo. Others read: "formed you for Himself and for His worship."

There is no god but He, the Mighty, the Wise. Since none except Him knows what He knows or can do what He does. Indicated is the perfection of His power and the absoluteness of His wisdom. It has been said that this passage is an argument against those who say: "Jesus is Lord:" for when the envoys from Najrān argued with the Prophet on this matter, the Surah was revealed as far as the eightieth verse to confirm the arguments which he used against them and his answers to their quibbles.

He it is who has sent down unto thee the Book wherein are categorical verses: they are the mother of the Book, and others ambiguous. Categorically expressed in that they are preserved from ambiguity and obscurity. "The mother . . ." means the foundation to which other texts are referred. Analogy would suggest the plural 'mothers,' but the singular implies that the plural pronoun which relates to it is to be interpreted as 'each of them,' or that all these verses count as one verse. The ambiguous are those whose drift is not clear—owing to their generality, or to their contradicting some clear text—except by examination and study, in order that the excellence of the learned be displayed over them, and that their zeal may be increased for their study and for the acquisition of the sciences on which the development of their meaning is based, and that they may rise to the highest ranks by employing their talents in educing their meaning and harmonizing them with the categorical texts. As for the expression [Surah 11:2] "a Book whose verses are made decisive" the meaning is that they are preserved from false notions and improper phrases. The expression in 39:24, "a Book whose parts are mutually consistent," means that it is uniform throughout in correctness of idea and beauty of language. . . .

As for those in whose hearts is a turning back, they follow the ambiguous verses, seeking to mislead and explaining it tendentiously. These reject the truth like the schismatics and adhere to their letter or to a false interpretation of them, seeking to explain the text to mean what they want. Now it is possible that the cause of their following the ambiguous texts may be both these desires together, or each of them alternately. Now the first corresponds with the case of the hardened opponent, while the second suits the fool.

And none knows its explanation except God and those who are firm in knowledge who say: We believe therein; all is from our Lord. That is, the explanation according to which it is to be taken. "Those who are firm . . ." means those that are steadfast and have possession of it. If we stop at "Except God . . ." [and connect the next clause with the relative that follows] then the ambiguous part refers to what God has reserved for His own knowledge, that is, the duration of the world, the time of the arrival of the Hour, and the properties of the numbers, such as the number of the warders of Hell, or as referring to those texts of which the letter is shown by decisive argument not to be the meaning, while there is no other indication of what their meaning is. "They say we believe . . ." a fresh sentence explaining the conduct of those who are firm. . . . Both the categorical and the ambiguous are from God.

Yet there reflect not save those that are possessed of minds. Tribute of praise to the fine intelligence and careful study of those who are steadfast, and an indication of the apparatus with which they provide themselves in order to be guided to its interpretation, namely the abstraction of the intellect from the clouds of sense. . . .

Our Lord, do not cause our hearts to stray after Thou hast guided us and give us mercy from Thee. Verily Thou art the Giver. Part of the speech of the 'steadfast,' or according to others a fresh sentence. The meaning is: Do not divert our hearts from the path of truth to follow the ambiguous texts according to interpretations that do not please Thee. The Prophet said: "The heart of man is between two of the fingers of the Merciful: if He will, He establishes him in the truth and if He will He diverts him from it." Others make the meaning: Do not try us with afflictions in which our hearts may go astray, after Thou has guided us to the truth, or to belief in both portions. . . . Give us mercy which shall bring us near Thee, and which we shall possess with Thee: or else help towards abiding in the truth; or, forgiveness of sins. Here is evidence that guidance and misdirection come from God, and that He does a favor when He does good to His servants and that nothing is obligatory upon Him.

Our Lord, verily Thou shalt gather mankind for a day wherein is no doubt. Verily God will not break the appointment. For the reckoning of a day or for the recompense of a day, of whose occurrence there is no doubt, or of the gathering and recompense taking place thereon. They call attention by their words to the fact that their chief aim in their two prayers is what concerns the future world, for that future world is the aim and the result. God's divinity contradicts the notion that He might break an appointment. In order to call attention to this, and to magnify that which is promised, there is a change of person. The Wa'īdites used this verse as evidence of their doctrines: the answer given them is that the menace to the evildoers is conditional on their not being forgiven, as is shown by special proofs, just as it is conditional on non-repentance, as we are all agreed. [The Wa'īdites held that God could not pardon evildoers and that the punishment spoken of in the Qur'ān was irrevocable.] [11]

The *Al-Muqaddimah,* [Introduction to the Study of History], by Ibn Khaldūn (1332–1406) is one of the most admired and influential works in the study of human society. It is in these terms that this great writer analyses what he calls "the sciences of *Qur'ān* interpretation."

The Qur'ān is the word of God that was revealed to His Prophet and that is written down between the two covers of copies of the Qur'ān [*Al-Mashaf al-Sharīf*]. . . . It should be known that the Qur'ān was revealed in the language of the Arabs and according to their rhetorical methods. All Arabs understood it and knew the meaning of the individual words and composite statements. It was revealed in chapters and verses, in order to explain the oneness of God and the religious duties according to the [various] occasions. . . . The Prophet used to explain these things, as it is said: "So that you may explain to the people that which was revealed to them." [Qur'ān 16:44]

These [explanations] were transmitted on the authority of the men around Muḥammad and were circulated by the men of the second generation after them on their authority. They continued to be transmitted among the early Muslims, until knowledge became organized in scholarly disciplines and systematic scholarly works were written. At the time most of these [explanations] were committed to writing. . . .

The linguistic sciences then became technical discussions of the lexicographical meaning of words, the rules governing vowel endings [*i'rāb*] and style [*balāghah*] in [the use of] word combinations. Systematic works were written on these subjects. Formerly, these subjects had been habits with the Arabs. No recourse to oral and written transmission had been necessary with respect to them. Now, that (state of affairs) was forgotten, and these subjects were learned from the books of philologists. They were needed for the interpretation of the Qur'ān because the Qur'ān is in Arabic and follows the stylistic technique of the Arabs. Qur'ān interpretation thus came to be handled in two ways.

> One is traditional, based upon information received from the early Muslims. It consists of knowledge of the abrogating verses and of the verses abrogated by them, of the reasons why a (given) verse was revealed, and of the purposes of individual verses. All this can be known only through traditions based on the authority of the men around Muḥammad and the men of the second generation. . . .
>
> The other kind of Qur'ān interpretation has recourse to linguistic knowledge and the stylistic form used for conveying meaning, through the appropriate means and methods. This kind of Qur'ān interpretation rarely appears separately from the first kind. The first kind is the one that is wanted essentially. The second kind made its appearance only after language and the philological sciences had become crafts. However, it has become preponderant as far as certain Qur'ān commentaries are concerned. . . .
>
> These traditional sciences are all restricted to Islam and the Muslims, even though every religious group has to have something of the sort. The Islamic traditional sciences are remotely comparable in that they are the sciences of a religious law revealed by God to the lawgiver who transmits it. But as to the particulars [Islam] is different from all other religious groups, because it abrogates them. All the pre-Islamic sciences concerned with religious groups are to be discarded and their discussion is forbidden.
>
> The religious law has forbidden the discussion of all revealed scriptures except the Qur'ān . . . When the Prophet saw a leaf of the Torah in 'Umar's hand, he became so angry that his anger showed in his face. Then he said: 'Did I not bring it to you white and clean? By God, if Moses were alive, he would have no choice but to follow me.'[12]

Al-Ikhwān-al-Muslimūn, [The Muslim Brethren], (see: *The House of Islam,* p. 117) have been an important influence in the life of Arabian Islam, especially Egyptian, since the foundation of the society in the 1920s. After the charismatic founder, Ḥasan al-Bannā (1906–1949), one of their most memorable figures was Sayyid Quṭb (1906–1966), who was executed for alleged political offences. He published an eight-volume commentary on the *Qur'ān, Fī-Ẓull al-Qur'ān* [In the Shade of the *Qur'ān*]. Here is part of the commentary on Surah 92, the "Surah of Night." It is representative of how a strongly conservative reader expounds the text. The verses, as the English version has them, are in italics.

> Within a framework of scenes from the universe and the nature of man, this Surah emphasizes the essence of Action and Reward. This essence has many different aspects: *Truly your striving is diverse. As for him who gives and is dutiful towards God, and God-fearing, and believes in the best, We will facilitate for him the way to perfect ease. As for him who hoards and deems himself to be self-sufficient* (that is, a person who has a lot of wealth which he hoards and thinks that because of his wealth he does not need the help of anyone) *and disbelieves in the best, We will indeed facilitate for him the way to affliction. His riches will not be of any help to him when he falls headlong. Lo! Ours it is to provide the guidance. Therefore do I* (God) *warn you against a fire blazing fiercely, which only the most wretched shall suffer . . . he who denies the truth and turns away* (from the truth). *But far removed from it will be the righteous who spends his wealth in charity seeking self-purification.* [v. 5–18]

Since this essence has two aspects and two directions, so the framework selected for it at the beginning of the Surah has also two aspects—the universe and man himself. *By the night enshrouding and the day resplendent.* Thus it is that when the night enshrouds it covers and conceals the land, and the day when it brightens and is resplendent, makes every object apparent and visible. The two times are contrasting in the earthly cycle and in their respective scenes, qualities and effects. God also swears by His creation of all species in two opposite sexes: *And Him Who has created male and female.* This completes the aspects of contrast in the general atmosphere of the Surah as well as in the facts it states and underlines. The night and day are two comprehensive phenomena [that is, well-known events and objects] with a certain message with which they inspire the human heart. They have also another message which they deliver when man contemplates and meditates [thinks seriously] on them and what lies beyond them.

The human soul is automatically affected by the cycle of night and day, the former when it spreads and covers over and the latter when it shines and brightens. This unfailing movement of the cycle has its message and its inspiration. It talks about this universe with its mysterious secrets and the phenomena, natural events, over which man has no control. It inspires one to think that beyond this movement there is a power which moves time in the universe like a simple wheel.

When he thinks about these things, man gets the message that there is a hand beyond, which runs the universe and makes the night and the day follow each other so perfectly. The message goes on to say that He Who runs the universe also controls the lives of men. He does not leave them without reason or purpose, nor does He create them for nothing.

However, the disbelievers and those who have gone astray try to drown this reality and turn attention away from it. The human heart will remain linked to this universe, seeing and thinking about the changes and variations in it. It will automatically understand what it also realises, namely that there is a controller who must be felt and recognized in spite of all nonsense, diversions and denials.

The same is the case with the creation of male and female. In both man and mammals [animals whose young drink their mothers' milk] creation starts with a drop in a womb, a sperm united with a cell. What is the reason, then, for this difference in the outcome? What power is it that says to one drop: "Be a male," what power says to another: "Be a female"? The discovery of the factors which make one seed result in a male creature and another in a female does not make the matter any different. What provides the male factors in the one and the female in the other? And how come that the result of a male and a female is so fitting with the course of life as a whole and is a guarantee that it will go on breeding and procreating?

Is it all a coincidence? Did it just happen that way? There is a rule which shows that it is impossible for all things to come together by themselves and fit in with each other so exactly, just by chance or accident.

The only explanation then is that there is a controller in charge, who creates the male and the female, with a designed purpose and a definite objective. There is no room for chance in the precise order of the universe.

Moreover, the system of males and females is not limited to mankind and the animals whose young drink milk from their mothers. It is the system, the method, by which *all* living things, including plants, breed and procreate. The *system* is the same, unfailingly, for all creation. Singularity and individuality belong *only* to the Creator, Praised and blessed be He, Who has no parallel whatever.

These are some of the inspirations of these scenes of the universe, and that human fact by which God swears, due to its great message and its strong influence. The Qur'ān uses them to provide a framework for the statement of action and reward in this life and in the life Hereafter.

God swears by these contrasting aspects and facts of the universe and of mankind that the striving and methods of human beings are not alike, hence their reward also is not alike. Good is not the same as evil, right guidance is not the same as waywardness and righteousness is different from wrongdoing. So, the one who is charitable and Godfearing is unlike the one who hoards wealth and claims that he is self-sufficient.

Again, those who believe and accept the Faith are *not* the same as those who disbelieve and turn away from the faith. Each group has its own way, its own destiny and its appropriate reward.

Truly your striving is diverse, as for him who gives and is dutiful towards God and God-fearing, and believes in the best, We will indeed facilitate (make easy) for him the way to perfect ease. And as for him who hoards and deems himself self-sufficient, and disbelieves in the best, We will indeed facilitate for him the way to affliction (suffering and misery). *His riches will not be any help to him when he falls headlong.*

Your striving is diverse. It is different in essence, motives, directions and results. Men are of diverse and different temperaments, environments, concepts and concerns, so much so that every man seems to be a distinct world by himself, living in his own special planet.

This is a fact, but along with it there is another general fact which consists of all scattered human beings and their different little worlds together. It groups them in two different [distinct] classes and in two contrasting positions and under two general headings:

a. *He who gives and is God-fearing and believes in the best.*
b. *He who hoards and deems himself to be self-sufficient and disbelieves in the best.*

These are the two positions where all different souls line up and where all the different efforts, the differing desires and objectives *end*. . . .

The second part of the Surah states the fate of each group. First of all this part of the Surah states that the end and the reward are *fair,* just and inevitable. God has beforehand provided guidance for man and warned men against the fire blazing fiercely. No one will have any excuse for not following the Guidance:

Lo! Ours it is to provide the Guidance and Lo! unto Us belong the end and the beginning. Therefore, do I warn you against a fire blazing fiercely, which only the most wretched shall suffer, he who denies the truth and turns away. But far removed from it will be the righteous, who spends his wealth in charity seeking self-purification. And none has with him any favor for which a reward is expected in return, except as seeking the pleasure of his Lord, the most High. He will indeed have satisfaction. [v. 13–21]

As an aspect of His grace and mercy which He bestows on His servants, God has taken upon Himself to provide guidance and has put it clear before man's nature and mind, explaining it through His messengers, the messages they deliver and the signs He provides. Thus *no one* will have a valid argument for his deviation [for not following the guidance] and no one will suffer injustice. *Ours it is to provide the guidance.*

The next verse is a straightforward and clear statement of the essence of the power controlling man and the things around him, so that he can have no shelter against it: *Unto Us belong the end and the beginning.*

To make clear and drive home the two facts mentioned about God's promise to provide guidance and that to Him belong this life and the Hereafter—places of action and reward—there is a reminder that He has cautioned, warned and forewarned them: *Therefore do I warn you against a fire blazing fiercely.* But this fire burning furiously is one *which only the most wretched shall suffer,* that is, the most wretched of mankind. But, is there any wretchedness worse than suffering that Hell?

Then comes an explanation of who the most wretched is: it is he *who denies the truth and turns away.* He denies [in words and deeds] this Message and turns away from it and from guidance. He does not answer his Lord's call to him to guide him as He has promised any one who comes towards Him with an open mind.

But far removed from it will be the righteous, who will be the happiest in contrast to the most wretched. Then follows a statement explaining who the righteous is. It is he *who spends his wealth in charity seeking self-purification.* He spends his money in order to purify himself, not for any vanity or snobbery. He spends it voluntarily [not when somebody begs him for it], not out of indebtedness for anybody's favor, and not seeking gratitude from any one. His only objective is the pleasure of his Lord the Exalted.

And none has with Him any favor for which a reward is expected in return, except as seeking the pleasure of his Lord the most High.

Then, what? What does this righteous person expect in return for spending his wealth in self-purification and for the pleasure of his Exalted Lord? The reward which the Qur'ān states before the believing souls is unfamiliar, surprising and astonishing: *he will indeed have satisfaction.* It is the satisfaction in the heart of this righteous person which fills his soul, flows over his whole being and radiates through him. It is a satisfaction which fills his life with ease and happiness. What a reward! What a great act of grace! He will *indeed have satisfaction.*

He will be satisfied with his religion, with his Lord, with his destiny and his lot. He will be contented with whatever he comes across of comfort or discomfort, wealth or poverty, ease or hardship. He will be inwardly content and happy, free of anxiety, free of hard feeling or hate. He does not think his burden to be too heavy or his objective to be too far. This satisfaction is indeed a reward, a reward much greater than any other. It is a reward deserved by the one who sacrifices himself and his wealth for it, who seeks self-purification and the pleasure of his most Exalted Lord.

It is a reward which can only be granted by God Who pours it into the hearts which are submitted to Him with all sincerity so that they recognize none but Him. *He will indeed have satisfaction.* He will be satisfied after having paid the price and given what he had to give. It is a surprise at this point. But it is the surprise awaited by the one who attains the standard of righteousness. *Who spends for self-purification,* not in return for any favor from anyone, but for the pleasure of his Lord the Exalted, *he will indeed have satisfaction.*[13]

It is useful to compare Sayyid Quṭb's *In the Shade of the Qur'ān* with the brief notices on the same Surah in *The Student's Qur'ān* by Dr.

Hashim Amir Ali, an agricultural scientist from Hyderabad, India. He concentrates on what he considers to be the first twenty-five Surahs, chronologically, and pleads for patience with new ideas and for a lively awareness of how much the Arabic of the *Qur'ān* requires of the reader, not simply linguistic exactness but a psychological sympathy for the very feel of it. Here follow his notes on Surah 92.

> A particular feature to note is the common rhyme in all the twenty-one lines of this Surah. Every one of these rhyme words ends in sounds expressed in Arabic by long 'a' sound carried on the silent 'y' letter.
>
> The meaning of the Surah, too, is plain and sustained throughout. It is merely a re-statement of the principle the Qur'ān emphasizes over and over again and particularly in this early period, namely: man cannot escape from the working of the moral law: those inclined to the good *shall* prosper; those inclined to the evil *shall* suffer. But every time this basic message is presented in a fresh form adorned with words of rhythm and beauty.
>
> Explaining Indian arts and crafts, an Indian writer says: "The more abstract the truth you wish to teach, the more you must allure the senses to it." Essentially that observation expresses a real need of human nature. But the Qur'ān has none of the usual means to tickle the senses, no vehicles of art to effect such allurement. It cannot make use of form, or color, line or melody. It has nothing but the use of the words of a then primitive desert language. But this it uses with unbelievable skill to allure the soul itself.
>
> In that sense, this is not rugged Nature: it is nearer to chiselled art. Nor is the chiselling that of a master craftsman. As the product of a process in the mind of a man who claims to be neither a poet nor a scholar, it is nothing less than Inspiration from the divine. That is why it is incomparable.
>
> But how is it possible to convey the magic effect of this inspired construction by merely translating the words and by trying to express only the meanings of the lines? It is precisely such characteristics of the Qur'ān which make it impossible to render its scintillating message adequately in any other language.
>
> The pivotal words of this Surah are those of the fourth verse which comes as a climax to the opening trio of asseverations and explains what is meant: "Verily, your [respective] tendencies are leading you to widely different destinations."
>
> The strongly worded asseverations in the first three lines [wrongly called 'oaths'] draw attention to natural phenomena which have conspicuously opposite characteristics. The gloom of night as contrasted with the brightness of the day, the male and female principles so noticeably permeating all that we call 'life'. To put it in prosaic language, the opening passage would, in short, mean something like this: "As much as night differs from day, as conspicuously as male differs from female, even so clearly differ the paths of some of you from those of others." The word *a'ṭa* in verse 5 is generally translated as one who gives alms. But the stage of teaching in this early period does not justify that meaning. The almost opposite meaning of the same word fits in more appropriately. 'One who is amenable to learning', 'receptive to new ideas', 'capable of being trained', that is what is meant here according to Abū-l-Fazl in his *Gharīb al-Qur'ān* [1947]. The other qualification mentioned immediately afterwards bears out this contention.

Hashim Amir Ali ends his notes here on Surah 92. At the conclusion of his discussion of his twenty-five "first" Surahs, he summarizes what he believes to be the significant elements of the message with which original Islam began—the message that drew the first disciples and set the stage of all that subsequently ensued. After vindicating his interest in chronology and noting that these twenty-five chosen chapters have less than one hundred and fifty verses out of the more than six thousand of the whole *Qur'ān* (that is, less than three percent of all), he goes on:

> Let us stop . . . and look back at the path we have travelled. What are the landmarks that we saw? . . .
>
> 1. God: *Rabb* We started with the idea of the Deity as *Rabb,* the Master of all earthly masters and of all earthly slaves: He Who is alone deserving of servitude, He Who is the source of all creation, Who made men through love and for love, He Who developed man's emotional life through affection and attachment and provided for him his mental repertoire through knowledge inherited and enlarged by means of the Pen, the written word. [96:1]
> 2. God: *Allāh.* Later we came to the same Deity emphasized as *Allāh the* Deity: that supreme Being Who is One, the eternal Refuge of all. He is neither begotten nor begets. That is, He has no beginning, no end. He, like unto whom *there can be no other.* [112]
> 3. Inspiration, Illumination. We heard first the majestic call to call upon man—in the name of the supreme Master: the order to announce the advent of the inspired Message. Then we heard the experience of illumination related, vaguely, but as clearly as words can convey, a mystic experience to the non-illumined consciousness. We realized that such beatific lucidity of mind and blossoming of vision comes only after a lifetime of seeking and surrender of the self. It is an experience of Peace after turmoil until the meaning of existence—the rhythm of the Universe—the Music of the Spheres—the Order pervading the cosmos—all this is manifested, like the breaking of the dawn. [97:2]
> 4. Guidance. This relation between the illumined individual human mind and the Omnipotent, Omnipresent THAT, then assumes a different form. It becomes the inner voice, offers consolation in the midst of discouragement: encourages the sagging spirit of the chosen man facing the heavy odds confronting him, guides him in his loneliness.
>
>   This inner voice also prompts him as to how he should avoid or extricate himself from the negative attitudes of doubt, fear and misgiving by seeking refuge in Him Who is the Master of men, the King of men, the God of men, for with Him alone are courage and safety and peace. [113; 114]
> 5. Reckoning. There is the oft-repeated lesson of the inevitable reckoning. No human action, however insignificant, goes unrecorded on the tablet of existence. It brings its reward or punishment, that is, its consequences, in the form of well-being or misery. The accumulation of evil necessarily ends in an eruption: the special fabric bursts asunder often to the utter consternation of man. And then he realizes, often too late, what has involved him in the collective disaster. [101:5; 99:17; 102:6]
> 6. Examples are given of those that transgressed and brought down upon themselves the retribution that became due to them. [105:9; 95:19; 89:25]

7. The Wrong Path. What are the actual transgressions which are deprecated in this early period? First: persecution is wrong. Second: Individual hoarding and perpetual competition are futile and detrimental to the social good. Third: hypocrisy is despicable. Merely formal prayers, unaccompanied by sympathy towards fellow men, are worse than useless. [107:11]
8. And what is the right path? The answer is that time itself is evidence. Men flounder on the way, except those who have faith in the law of God, who engage in good works and leave behind examples of truth and perseverance. The right path is essentially one of sympathy and love for those human beings who are most in need of them—the orphan, the deprived, those who are poor, or those who are lonely. [90:24]
9. Whom shall we take as our Guide? The only true guide is within ourselves: the tiny lens through which our hearts see. He who keeps it bright and clear, burnished and sensitive, he it is who will be on the right road to prosperity. And he who allows it to accumulate rust or deliberately refuses to see through it, he it is who will suffer and be damned.

   And this little inner voice constantly prompts man to take the upward and difficult path. But often, O so often, he takes the path of least resistance and tends to slide down lower and lower. [90:24]
10. Denunciations, Ambiguities. We also came across several denunciations of incorrigible individuals whose identity is thickly or thinly veiled. Also we met instances of passages which are not clear, at least to this student, and needed the intuition of the poet rather than the erudition of the scholar to explain them. [104:8; 90:24]
11. Withdrawal. And, finally, we were shown the technique of dignified but courteous withdrawal when faced, not with those who cannot see, but with those who *will* not see. Even in this early stage of teaching we were told that at such times we should "Say . . . To you is your reckoning, and . . . to me, mine." [109:13]

In these few paragraphs, an attempt has been made to summarize the message of these twenty-five Surahs of the earliest period of Islamic teaching. Even to hope that this portion has been adequately summarized is to display one's utter ignorance of the depth and width of meaning which most words of the Qur'ān possess.

No, I have *not* succeeded. But success in explaining the Qur'ān or even a portion of it is not my aim. If I can succeed in convincing even one individual that here lies a still little-explored mine of universally applicable moral teaching and persuade him to carry this study further, I will have achieved all the success I have ever aspired to.

May He forgive me where I have transgressed. "But is there one who will pay heed?" [Surah 54:17] [14]

The attitude of Sufism (see chapter 7), generally speaking, to the *Qur'ān* can be well gauged in the response made by Shaikh al-'Alawī, of Algeria, to an orthodox critic of the claims of mystical knowledge.

Who told you that the Sufis say Islam is based on any other principles than those of the Book of God and the Wont of His Messenger? They say, however, that in the Book of God there is a doctrine which is beyond most men's attainment. The poet Ibn al-Fāriḍ wrote: "There lieth a lore beneath the words of the text too subtle to be grasped by the farthest reach of sound intelligence."

It may well be that one who cleaves to externals can see nothing in the Book of God but what his own intelligence, such as it is, can apprehend and that he may belie what goes beyond this without realizing that in knowing the outside of the Book only he is as one who knows a fruit by nothing but its peel. And beyond that lies "what no eye hath seen and what no ear hath heard and what the heart of man cannot conceive." Let him examine himself: if what his heart hides is more precious than what his tongue tells of, then he is "one whom his Lord has made certain" [Surah 11:17], but, if not, then he has missed far more than he has gained. . . . The Prophet said: "Knowledge of the inward is one of the Secrets of God. It is wisdom from the treasury of His Wisdom which He casteth into the heart of whomsoever He will of His slaves." And: "Knowledge is of two kinds, knowledge in the heart which is knowledge that availeth, and knowledge upon the tongue which is God's evidence against His slave." This shows that secret knowledge is different from the knowledge that is bandied about. . . .

In saying: "Islam is nothing other than the Book of God and the Wont of the Apostle," it is as if you said: "Islam is what *I* understand of the Book and of the Wont and no more," which means that you set your own innermost perceptions on a level with the innermost perceptions of the Companions and even of the Prophets."

The Prophet said: "The earth shall never be found lacking in forty men whose hearts are as the Heart of the Friend of the All-Merciful." One has only to study the traditions to find that they tell us explicitly that there is within the community an elect to whom God has revealed the secrets of the Book and the Wont, and where else is this body of men to be found save among the Rememberers who are marked out for having devoted their lives to God? It was of such of them that Dhū al-Nūn al-Miṣrī said: "In my travels I met a slave girl and asked her whence she came. She said: 'From one whose sides shrink away from beds'. Then I asked her whither she was going and she said [in the words of Surah 24:36]: 'To men whom neither bartering nor selling divert from the remembrance of God.'"[15]

FURTHER ISSUES IN INTERPRETATION

A notable index to the potential role of the *Qur'ān* in undergirding, through judicious quotation and interpretation, a current philosophy of man and nature, may be had in the Lectures of Muḥammad Iqbāl, the pioneer and cherished symbol of the Pakistan identity, whose thoughts will figure widely in subsequent areas of this anthology. If the juxtaposition of Iqbāl's ideas and the claimed import of the verses he cites is left sharp and crisp in these extracts, it only serves to emphasize the point at issue, namely the recruiting of the *Qur'ān* for the user's case. (*Qur'ān* quotation in Iqbāl's English.)

The main purpose of the Qur'ān is to awaken in man the higher consciousness of his manifold relations with God and the universe. . . . What, then, according to the Qur'ān, is the character of the universe which we inhabit? In the first place it is not the result of a mere creative sport: "We have not created the heavens and the earth and whatever is between them in sport. We have not created them but for a serious end: but the greater part of them understand it not." [Surah 44:38–39]

It is a reality to be reckoned with: "Verily in the creation of the heavens and the earth and in the succession of the night and the day, are signs for men of understanding: who, standing and sitting and reclining, bear God in mind and reflect on the creation of the heavens and the earth and say: 'O our Lord, Thou has not created this in vain.'" [Surah 3:188]

Again, the universe is so constituted that it is capable of extension: "He [God] adds to His creation what He wills." [Surah 35:1] [The immediate reference of the verb 'to add' is in reference to angels' wings—two, three or four.] It is not a block universe, a finished product, immobile and incapable of change. Deep in its inner being lies, perhaps, the dream of a new birth: Say: "Go through the earth and see how God has brought forth all creation: hereafter He will give it another birth." [Surah 29:20] In fact, this mysterious swing and impulse of the universe, this noiseless swim of time which appears to us, human beings, as the movement of day and night, is regarded by the Qur'ān as one of the greatest signs of God. [Surah 24:44] This is why the Prophet said "Do not vilify time; for time is God." And this immensity of time and space carries in it the promise of a complete subjugation by man whose duty is to reflect on the signs of God, and thus discover the means of realizing his conquest of nature as an actual fact. [Surah 31:19; 16:12] . . . No doubt the immediate purpose of the Qur'ān in this reflective observation of nature is to awaken in man the consciousness of that of which nature is regarded as a symbol. But the point to note is the general empirical attitude of the Qur'ān which engendered in its followers a feeling of reverence for the actual and ultimately made them the founders of modern science . . . The Prophet of Islam was the first critical observer of psychic phenomena. . . . A better appreciation of the spirit of the Qur'ān . . . initiated the cultural movement terminating in the birth of the modern empirical attitude. . . .

To my mind nothing is more alien to the Quranic outlook than the idea that the universe is the temporal working out of a pre-conceived plan. As I have already pointed out, the universe, according to the Qur'ān, is liable to increase. It is a growing universe and not an already completed product . . . . Nature, as we have seen, is not a mass of pure materiality occupying a void. It is a structure of events, a systematic mode of behavior, and as such organic to the ultimate Self. Nature is to the divine Self as character is to the human self. In the picturesque phrase of the Qur'ān it is the habit of God. . . . It is in that sense that the Qur'ān says: "And of Him is the change of night and day."

It is in tapping these sources of knowledge (that is, nature and history) that the spirit of Islam is seen at its best. The Qur'ān sees signs of the ultimate reality in the sun, the moon, the lengthening out of the shadows, the alternation of day and night, the variety of human colors and tongues, the alternation of the days of success and reverse among the peoples—in fact the whole of nature as revealed to the sense perception of man. . . .

Thus all lines of Muslim thought converge on a dynamic conception of the universe. . . . History, or in the language of the Qur'ān, "the days of God," is the third source of human knowledge according to the Qur'ān [with nature and prophecy]. It is one of the most essential teachings of the Qur'ān that nations are collectively judged and suffer for their misdeeds here and now. In order to establish this proposition the Qur'ān constantly cites historical instances and urges upon the reader to reflect on the past and present experience of mankind. [Surahs 14:5; 7:181; 3:131; 3:134; 7:32)

However, the interest of the Qur'ān in history, regarded as a source of human knowledge, extends further than mere indications of historical generalizations. It has given us one of the most fundamental principles of historical criticism. Since accuracy in recording facts which constitute the material of history is an indispenable condition of history as a science, and an accurate knowledge of facts ultimately depends on those who report them, the very first principle of historical criticism is that the reporter's personal character is an important factor in judging his testimony. The Qur'ān says: "O believers, If any bad man comes to you with a report, clear it up at once." [Surah 49:6] [The passage goes on to say: "Lest you afflict a people ignorantly. . . ." and may well refer to an act of punishment or retaliation based on false innuendo or treachery. The whole Surah is watchful against suspicion and hypocrisy. It would seem excessive to build a whole philosophy of historical criticism on a directive to a community finding its way amid competing loyalties and tensions. But Iqbal pursues his conviction.] It is the application of the principle . . . out of which were gradually evolved the cannons of historical criticism.

Finally, explaining his belief about the nature of prophecy in the *Qur'ān* and of its finality, Iqbāl concludes:

The world-life intuitively sees its own needs and at critical moments defines its own direction. This is what, in the language of religion, we call prophetic revelation. It is only natural that Islam should have flashed across the consciousness of a simple people untouched by any of the ancient cultures and occupying a geographical position where three continents meet together. The new culture finds the foundation of world-unity in the principles of *Tauhīd.* Islam as a polity is only a practical means of making this principle a living factor in the intellectual and emotional life of mankind. It demands loyalty to God, not to thrones. And since loyalty to God is the ultimate spiritual basis of all life, loyalty to God virtually amounts to man's loyalty to his own ideal nature. . . . A society based on such a conception of Reality must reconcile in its life the categories of permanence and change. . . . "To those who exert We show our path." [Surah 29:69]

Far from leaving no scope for human thought and legislative activity the intensive breadth of the legal principles in the Qur'ān virtually acts as an awakener of human thought. . . . The teaching of the Qur'ān that life is a process of progressive creation necessitates that each generation, guided but unhampered by the work of its predecessors, should be permitted to solve its own problems. . . .

The Muslim . . . is in possession of these ultimate ideas on the basis of a revelation, which, speaking from the inmost depths of life, internalizes its own apparent externality. With him, the spiritual basis of life is a matter of conviction for which even the least enlightened man among us can easily lay down his life. In view of the basic idea of Islam that there can be no further revelation binding on man, we ought to be spiritually one of the most emancipated peoples on earth. Early Muslims, emerging out of the spiritual slavery of pre-Islamic Asia, were not in a position to realize the true significance of this basic idea. Let the Muslim of today appreciate his position, reconstruct his social thought in the light of ultimate principles and evolve, out of the hitherto partially revealed purpose of Islam, that spiritual democracy which is the ultimate aim of Islam.[16]

In his autobiography *My Life, A Fragment,* Muḥammad 'Alī has some confident, if not always cautious, thoughts about the average Muslim and his sense of the *Qur'ān*'s meaning. He writes:

> Where the Qur'ān excels in style apart from its contents is in the universality of its appeal and its intelligibility to fools as well as to philosophers, to dull, prosaic men not less than poets. . . . To all it conveys clearly enough the concluded message God sent to mankind. There are no such things as literal meaning and interpretation. If speech is not the art of concealing thought but of expressing it, the Qur'ān, like every other literary product, must have some thought to convey, some meaning to express, and it is immaterial *how* we arrive at a comprehension of these thoughts and an understanding of that meaning, so long as we do arrive there.
>
> If literal meaning would take us to our destination, by all means let us take that road, philosophers as well as fools. If, on the contrary, interpretation alone can lead to it, let us all follow that path, fools as well as philosophers. But if either literal meaning or interpretation fails to lead us to our destined goal, of what earthly use is it? No road in the world runs absolutely straight and always on the same level. . . . The Qur'ān's great miracle is that all without exception find some beauty or other in the road, and to none is the way dull and wearisome.
>
> The Qur'ān is God's Word, truly enough: but it is, and must be, in man's ill-coin.
>
> The Qur'ān repeatedly . . . tells the Arabs that God's message is worded in their own Arabic tongue. And it repeatedly asserts its clarity. The Qur'ān must, therefore, be simple enough, if it was meant by God, Whose message it contains, to be intelligible to the dwellers of the desert. For an *Ummī*, [that is, an unlettered] nation even the Apostle chosen was an *Ummī*. How then could the Qur'ān be a mystery to all mankind, except the philosopher who could solve it by the 'open sesame' of his interpretation? The only way to make it a riddle is to look in it for riddles. And if we understand anything of the psychology of simple folk such as the dwellers of the desert, who were to preach the new evangel, God must have talked in the Qur'ān in pictures and parables. Not philosophical concepts and abstractions but images sufficiently concrete for the untutored mind must have been employed. And that is precisely what we find. But if we must look for riddles in the Qur'ān and thereby make it a philosopher's riddle, we must not be so wooden-minded as to have no use for a metaphor.
>
> If there is one thing worse than turning rhetoric into a syllogism, it is petrifying a parable. Metaphysics and anthropomorphism are alike foreign to the whole spirit of the Qur'ān and if we just let it soak into our consciousness, as it must have soaked into the consciousness of the Arabs more than thirteen hundred years ago, we shall get all the philosophy we need to last us through life and to carry us into the great beyond.
>
> This is the only possible cannon of interpretation to be applied to a book like the Qur'ān. . . . Remember the message was first addressed to the untutored Arabs and even if we are as bad as the bedouin and no worse, by following the same road we can, with God's help, find our destined goal. . . . There is still ample room in the Church of Islam for all philosophers. Only they must not make Muslim theology their battleground and divert the energies of Muslims from righteous action into vain disputations.
>
> There is ample room for the mystic also. But let him develop his *kashf,* or

gnosis, to the fullest extent that his deep religious emotions are capable of, without letting Sufism degenerate into a wild, fantastic ritual, or worse still leading him to consider his kind above and beyond the claims of Islamic Sharī'ah, which prescribes the simplest of duties for all alike.[17]

What the Khilafatist Muḥammad 'Alī lacks in alertness to genuine issues of long standing and deep controversy, he makes amends for in the vigor and assurance of his views. Other passages from other minds will indicate how much his attitude omits.

A useful measure of the utilization of the *Qur'ān* in current Islamic thinking can be had by tracing the form and accents of Quranic citation in the work of any single thinker concerned to relate his faith to his overall philosophy. Such a writer would be Dr. Khalifa Abdul-Hakim, formerly Dean of Osmania University, Hyderabad, whose study, *Islamic Ideology,* first appeared in 1951. His range of themes is wide, and his approach is alert to philosophical and social issues in general. Here, taken serially from a major coverage of human problems, are his methods of employing the *Qur'ān* either to argue or to support his case. The translations are his own.

"And there is not a people but a warner has gone among them." [Surah 35:24] Islam, being the religion of harmony, promulgated the doctrine of the unity of religions. Islam, however, considers theistic religion only as true religion, so its doctrine of the unity of religions covers only those creeds in which the Oneness of God was realised: all else is barbarity and ignorance which degrades man to such an extent that he becomes sub-human. The Qur'ān says: "They are as cattle: nay they are in worse error." [Surah 7:179] In the sense in which the term is used in the Qur'ān, Islam is a universal religion. Wherever there is true religion, there is no monopoly of salvation.

Like every other creed or discipline, Islam has its ritual, but gives it a very subordinate and secondary place. . . . Fearing lest turning to the *Qiblah* should be considered as part of the essence of prayers, the Qur'ān says there is no special virtue in this, that you turn your face to the east or to the west. It says: "And God's is the east and the west: therefore, whither you turn, thither is God's purpose," and: "It is not righteousness that you turn your faces toward the east or the west." [Surahs 2:115, 117]

An antithesis springs out of the inevitable inner contradictions of a thesis, but the thesis or the previous state is not completely annihilated: it acts along with its antithesis to create a new synthesis. This is a general law of life and a progressive realization of its values. This law is recognized by the Qur'ān when it says: "Whatever communication We abrogate or cause to be forgotten, We bring one better than it or like it." [Surah 2:106]

In Islam, physical nature is pointed out as a great divine manifestation and Islam firmly believes that the working of physical nature also shows enough signs of rationality, method and adaptation for goodness, to give a knowledge of God to those who ponder with pure reason, without any narrow prejudices or cramping hypotheses. Then it appeals to us to study the adaptations in the organic realm. The study of the anatomy of the camel is sufficient to convince one of the rationality of nature. The Qur'ān calls all nature the nature of God. As it is said about man: "The nature of God in which He made man."

[Surah 30:30] Then it says: "In your own souls too there are signs: why do you not see?" [Surah 51:21] The stars moving in their orbits with measure and exactitude are also pointed out as signs of God. The Qur'ān calls itself a book of wisdom: It never asks us to believe without giving a rationale of that belief. We are asked to study the seen very carefully, because this study would lead us to a belief in the nature of the unseen. The unseen is in direct line with the seen.

The Qur'ān says that God is the cause of all causes, and the ultimate cause of all existence. He is the Being as the foundation of all becoming, the stable Reality which creates and supports all change. "He is the beginning and He is the end: He is the outer appearance and He is the inner Reality." [Surah 57:3] He is the phenomena and He is the noumena. He is immanent as well as transcendent.

According to the Qur'ān, the entire creation is a realm of reason and order, but reason and order work at different levels of existence. "And there is not a thing but with Us are the treasures of it, and We did not send it down but in a known measure." [Surah 15:21] Chaos and chance have no part in His creation. If man were endowed with real insight, he would find no flaw in the universe. Where he observes disorder he should know that he has not yet seen aright. Creation is at every step an ordered realm . . . Causation in phenomenal existence is God-established sequence.

There is no scripture of any great religion in which observation of nature and its rational working are so emphasized and profusely recommended as proofs of the existence of God. Entire nature is presented as a great miracle. "And in the earth there are signs for those who are sure and in your own souls too: will you not then see?" [Surah 51:21]

In the Qur'ān we find no appeal to the supernatural as the basis of belief. Man must outlive his demand for miracles and proceed from nature and reason to God. . . . One can proceed from God to nature, or from nature to God: whether we ascend or descend it is the same road. This is the meaning of the words of the Qur'ān that God is the beginning and God is the end. It . . . was this ideology of Islam which made the Muslims the great investigators of nature and appreciators of all philosophies which attempted to discover the meanings of life.

Self-surrender is found in all nature. According to Islam the earth and the heavens and all that they contain are Muslims. The earth that is spread, the trees that grow, the rivers that flow, the birds that sing, the meanest worm that crawls, all glorify their Creator in a tongue that man does not understand. Their living according to the natures with which they are endowed is their worshipful self-surrender and their silent, wordless prayer.

Revelation which according to the Qur'ān is a supreme source of guidance may be natural, instinctive, or supra-rational. Animal instinct, too, is called in the Qur'ān guidance by revelation, as it said: "And your Lord revealed to the bee, saying: 'Make hives in the mountains and in the trees.'" [Surah 16:68]

The Qur'ān asserts that there is no natural or cosmic evil. "Who created the seven heavens alike: you see no incongruity in the creation of the beneficent God: then look again, can you see any disorder?" [Surah 67:2] . . . Islam denies the existence of cosmic evil: the problem arises out of ignorance or narrowness of vision. . . . So the question that if God is omnipotent why does He allow evil to exist in nature, is answered in the Qur'ān by the denial of evil in nature. Nature works according to universal laws which are rational and work for good. If sometimes their working does not suit our personal convenience we call it evil. The problem of evil in nature is not raised by nature itself but by importing our narrow anthropomorphism and anthropopathism into nature. Our narrow human passions and human relativity create a problem which is not raised by any contradiction in the nature of things themselves.

When the Qur'ān says that God created man so that he may worship Him—worship in its essential significance means not verbal praise and begging for benefits, but living in accordance with the will of God. Every right action is an act of worship. . . . If God is truth the pursuit of all truth is an act of submission to God and hence an act of worship.

Prayer is a great instrument for self-realization. Without prayer one might attain to partial well-being or gain some material and transitory benefit, but if the human spirit is not attuned to the contemplation of the Highest, the ultimate human destiny is not realised. In another place the Qur'ān says: "Successful indeed are the believers who are humble in their prayers." [Surah 23:2]

The Muslims are called in the Qur'ān "the nation of the middle." [Surah 2: 143] It is a very significant designation. Before Islam there had been great nations that had hit on great truths but they had gone to extremes in their one-sided development. . . . The truths of these concepts were taken up by Islam and incorporated in a complete harmony with other aspects of life. We find Islam following a middle path and synthesizing all these truths. It is one of the oft-repeated theses of the Qur'ān that all great religions of civilized humanity were essentially true but were later on perverted. We see, historically, how this perversion takes place.

Islam is a religion of complete integration. For the first time in history we see the doctrine of the development of the whole man in complete integration with himself, with society and with nature, and the whole integration based on belief in a single Creator who is the unity of all creation. Being is graded but all being is teleologically and organically related. The doctrine of the unity of humanity is repeatedly presented in the Qur'ān. "Be careful of your duty to God your Lord, who created you from a single being." [Surah 4:1]

"Let not men cut asunder what God has joined." [Surah 2:27] We now follow this text further into other spheres of social life. . . . God has joined the life of the two sexes to co-operate in the birth and bringing up of every child, male or female . . . Islam means peace and a Muslim home must be a peaceful home. Any element which disrupts this peace must be eliminated. . . . Islam attempted integration everywhere—God and nature, body and soul, reason and instinct, law and love, were all integrated in Islam.

About merely speculative knowledge the Qur'ān says: "Conjecture will not avail aught against the truth." [Surah 10:36]

God is the unity of all unities and the harmony of all harmonies. "His are the most excellent Names," says Surah 59:24, that is to say, He is the transcendental locus of all intrinsic and abiding values.

Wherever Islam prohibits killing it always qualifies it as killing without justice. "Thou shalt not kill" is not an absolute injunction. There are situations in life where killing becomes a paramount duty. The word *Fitnah* is often used in the Qur'ān wherever the permission to kill an evildoer is given. This word is difficult to translate with a single English word. . . . It means persecution, social tyranny or disorder and compelling a man to unlawful submission, or forcibly keeping a man from pursuing the right path, or misleading a man into false pursuits or into deviation from truth. . . .

FIGURE 2. Names of God.

Khalifa Abdul-Hakim quotes, as a comprehensive verse, the familiar Surah 13:11: "God does not change the condition of a people until they change their own condition." He quotes further from a French writer: "Dogma is the living faith of the dead that has become the dead faith of the living." What has been culled here from a major work of Muslim self-projection and interpretation does not, of course, do justice to the author's whole philosophy. But by isolating his many Quranic citations, with the immediate context around them of his own writing, it presents a picture of the way in which the *Qur'ān* both shapes and in exegesis, is shaped by, the believing Muslim. This is the more clear when it is noted that many of the passages cited are quoted repeatedly and the same sentiments recur in a variety of themes.[18]

The student of the *Qur'ān* has to cope with the frequent and often bewildering distinction made by Muslims between the inner and the outer, the esoteric and the exoteric, senses of the text. Jalāl al-Dīn Rūmī, in his famous *Mathnawī*, expressed it this way:

> Know the words of the Qur'ān are simple,
> But within the outward sense is an inner secret one.
> Beneath the secret meaning is third
> Whereat the highest wisdom is dumbfounded.
> The fourth meaning has been seen by none
> Save God, the Incomparable, the All Sufficient.
> Thus they go on, even to seven meanings, one by one,
> According to the saying of the Prophet without doubt:

Do thou, O son, confine not thy view to the outward meaning,
Even as the demons saw in Adam only clay.
The outward meaning is like Adam's body:
For its semblance is visible but its soul is hidden.[19]

The allusion is to Surah 17:61, where the angels are enjoined to worship Adam. Iblis, or the devil, refuses, seeing only a creature of clay and not the precious dignity of the human spirit.

This approach to the *Qur'ān,* which distinguishes an inner meaning for sophisticates from an outer sense perceptible to the ordinary reader, plays a large part in the Sufi or mystical reception of the Book—a theme that will be more luminous in the light of disciplines and figures to be pondered in chapter 7. The general theory of the inner and the outer has been strongly advocated in recent years, for example, by Sayyid Ḥossein Naṣr in Iran. To understand the concept in its full implications, it is necessary to set it in the whole context of his exposition of the status of the *Qur'ān.*

Many people, especially non-Muslims, who read the Qur'ān for the first time are struck by what appears to be a kind of incoherence from the human point of view. It is neither like a high mystical text nor a manual of Aristotelian logic, though it contains both mysticism and logic. It is not just poetry though it contains the most powerful poetry. The text of the Qur'ān reveals human language crushed by the power of the divine Word. It is as if human language were shattered into a thousand fragments like a wave shatters into drops against the rocks at sea. One feels through the shattering effect left upon the language of the Qur'ān, the power of the divine whence it originated. . . .

The Qur'ān contains a quality which is difficult to express in modern language. One might call it a divine magic, if one understands this phrase metaphysically and not literally. The formulae of the Qur'ān, because they come from God, have a power which is not identical with what we learn from them rationally by simply reading them and reciting them. They are rather like a talisman which protects and guides man. That is why even the physical presence of the Qur'ān carries a great grace and *barakah* (blessing) with it. When a Muslim is in difficulty he reads certain verses of the Qur'ān which pacify and comfort him. And when he wants something or is in dire need again he turns to appropriate verses from the Qur'ān. . . . All these words, phrases and sentences possess a divine magic which is connected with the presence of the divine in the sacred language where He has chosen to reveal His Word. . . . The Qur'ān possesses a *barakah* for believers which it is impossible to explain or analyze logically. But because of this divine presence and *barakah* it endures from generation to generation. People read and memorize it by heart: they chant and recite it from day to day and there have been saints who have spent their whole life only in chanting the Qur'ān. That is because the divine presence in the text provides food for the souls of men. It is in fact a sacred act to recite the Qur'ān. Its reading is a ritual act which God wishes man to perform over and over again throughout his earthly journey. . . .

The Qur'ān is like the universe with many planes of existence and levels of meaning. . . . It is essential to realize that we cannot reach the inner meaning of the Qur'ān until we ourselves have penetrated into the deeper dimensions of our being and also by the grace of heaven. If we approach the Qur'ān superficially and are ourselves superficial beings floating on the surface of our existence and unaware of our profound roots, then the Qur'ān appears to us also having only a surface meaning. It hides its mysteries from us and we are not able to penetrate it. It is by spiritual travail that man is able to penetrate into the hidden meaning of the sacred text.[20]

In his *Discourses,* Jalāl al-Dīn Rūmī, poet of Persian mysticism, has a variety of intriguing images by which to convey the believer's relation to the *Qur'ān.* He likens it to a husband's enjoyment of his wife or a suckling child's delight in its mother's milk but suggests how these may be transposed.

> Some men are infants of the way and take pleasure in the literal meaning of the Qur'ān and drink that milk. But those who have reached years of full discretion have another enjoyment and a different understanding of the inner meanings of the Qur'ān.
>
> (For) the Qur'ān is a bride who does not disclose her face to you, for all that you draw aside the veil. That you should examine it and not attain happiness and unveiling, is due to the fact that the act of drawing aside the veil has itself repulsed and tricked you, so that the bride has shown herself to you as ugly, as if to say: "I am not that beauty!" But if you do not draw aside the veil and seek only its good pleasure, watering its sown field and attending on it from afar, toiling upon that which pleases it best, it will show its face to you without your drawing aside the veil.
>
> The Qur'ān is a double-sided brocade. Some enjoy one side and some the other. Both are true inasmuch as God most High desires that both peoples should derive benefit from it.[21]

One of the most illuminating initiatives in study of the *Qur'ān* is that taken by Muḥammad Daud Rahbar in his *God of Justice: A Study in the Ethical Doctrine of the Qur'ān.* He insists on the necessity of relating all exegesis firmly to the context of the passage, not simply in the familiar sense that takes the reader back to tradition to learn the setting of events (if he can) in which particular Surahs (or parts of them) were placed but to the linguistic context of recurrent terms and vocabulary. Much light, he holds, is shed on the sense of the *Qur'ān*, and any long-standing misinterpretations corrected or excluded, if careful note is made of the norms of usage that become clear when attention is paid to the themes in which they recur. Dr. Rahbar works out his contextual method by surveying all the major terms of the Quranic vocabulary. For him the Quranic concordance, intelligently used, is a vital key.

> We must now define what we mean by the context of a word or a phrase in the Qur'ān. Let it be understood at the outset that a single verse, whose reference we find in the concordance against a word, is very seldom the full context of that word. Very few verses of the Qur'ān are complete in themselves in point of subject matter. The verses, although they, for the most part, mark a pause either in the rhyme or in the sense, are sometimes arbitrary divisions in respect of either. If we print a copy of the Qur'ān with no numbers on

verses, and ask an educated Arab to number its verses, he will find no consistently applicable principle to separate a passage as one verse. In some cases a verse contains only half a sentence, the other half continued in the next. . . . Often a whole verse is left meaningless if isolated and hung in the air. . . .

The following passage is part of a narrative speaking of Abraham's denunciation of idol worship. [Surah 37:90–95]

90. And he [Abraham] went aside unto their gods and said: "Will you not eat?"
91. "What ails you that you will not speak?"
92. And he went aside to them smiting with the right hand.
93. And they [the people of the city] rushed towards him.
94. Said he: "Do you serve what you have hewed out?
95. When God has created you and what you make?"

The original of verse 95, if read in isolation, will admit of two alternative translations: (a) "God has created you and what you do." (b) "God has created you and what you manufacture."

The context of the verse reveals that the words are addressed by Abraham to idol-worshippers, telling them that the idols manufactured by them are helpless creatures of God. But by isolating this verse from its context, a great Imām like Al-Ghazālī, in all good faith, makes it mean "God has created you and what you do," thus contriving to provide scriptural support for the theological idea that God himself is the creator of each and every deed that men do [this leading to a totally determinist view]. . . .

Dr. Rahbar proceeds to apply his method to a variety of terms, of names having to do with the divine attributes and crucial verbs in which divine action is denoted. In central perspective throughout, the theme is of divine justice and, with it, a repudiation of the notion of arbitrary determinism that Islamic theologians have variously deduced from—as Dr. Rahbar sees it—a mistaken, because noncontextual, reading of the *Qur'ān.* He notes how repetitious the *Qur'ān* is, as "a collection of revelatory speeches connected with a movement of reform." Each exhaustive examination he makes leads him to conclude that nowhere does the text of the *Qur'ān* sustain the subsequent theology of arbitrary determinism on the part of God. By this principle of exegesis he proposes to liberate the original message from the accretions or mistaken emphases of later theology.

Islam is basically an anti-idolatrous campaign. The theology of Islam, therefore, seems a development upon this anti-idolatrous movement, which, when intellectualized, took the form of anti-anthropomorphism as regards the conception of God. So all the energy of theologians was spent on developing the conception of God as an Essence with a minimum number of non-anthropomorphic attributes. . . . This phase of Muslim theology has obscured Quranic thought. The Qur'ān on the contrary is engaged primarily on the subject of God's ethical nature. When the question is put What is the Qur'ān's conception of God? . . . a balanced answer has to be obtained by actually going through the Book, by ascertaining the original meanings of the phrases, by being better acquainted with its rhetorical style, and through reconstructing by these means the broad unity of thought which the Prophet in his inspired moments of revelation sought. . . . The idea of God's justice is the central theme of the Qur'ān and consistently dominates in the Book.

We shall now give a very brief summary of the aspects of the Qur'ān's simple doctrine of God discussed in the present work. According to the Qur'ān, God is the true deity [*ḥaqq*]. The idols and any partners associated with God are false gods. God is the first and the last. He created the heavens and the earth in order that He may reward and punish men with justice on the judgment day. His promise is true. None can escape the weight of an atom on judgment day. All will receive a portion of what they have earned. He has the power to reward and punish. He has the power to quicken the dead. He knows what men conceal and display. He will let them know on judgment day what they have done. All will be there in writing. He knows how to quicken the dead. His will is supreme. His mercy, forgiveness and love are only for those who believe in Him, and act aright, and who, when they have done something wrong, repent, and thence act aright. Men must guard themselves fearfully against His wrath by obeying Him and by believing in Him and His apostles. He sends prophets with messages of guidance to all nations. Those who accept His guidance He guides them more. Those who refuse His guidance persistently, He condemns them as hopeless and increases them in error. All earlier nations received apostles. Those who belied the apostles were destroyed. All those who belie the Prophet Muḥammad will be destroyed. . . .

The central idea throughout is God's justice on the judgment day. All themes are subservient to this central theme. When the Qur'ān speaks of God's knowledge, it reminds that God knows men's conduct and is recording all their deeds vigilantly. When it speaks of God's power, it reminds us that God has power to requite and to raise the dead. When it speaks of God's Creatorhood, it often alludes to it as a proof of His power to recreate and raise the dead on the resurrection day. In short, whatever discourse we select from the Qur'ān it almost invariably turns out to have reference to that central idea of resurrection and God's justice. . . .

We must admit the priority of the Quranic doctrine of God over the political campaign into which the Prophet was pushed because of circumstances. The Prophet had a doctrine of God and a divine mission before he thought of political campaigns. He did not think out a doctrine of God to suit any premeditated political plans. He was forced into political campaigns because the doctrine he brought was opposed. . . . "It was under the pressure of circumstance, and by the necessities of thoughts which carried him further than he could possibly have divined, that he became a prince and a conqueror. . . ."

What we have tried to achieve in this study is the realization of a sharp distinction between scriptural and non-scriptural thought. When making an objective study of the Qur'ān we must never forget that the commentaries we consult are from the pens of writers belonging to Muslim sects and therefore whatever they say has to be accepted or rejected with the utmost caution. Likewise when we look up Quranic words in lexicons, we must never forget that their authors are Muslims. . . . We must use our own judgment in deciding the *original* signification of Quranic words and phrases, instead of depending carelessly or blindly on commentaries that are full of fictitious traditions. For a scientific re-interpretation of the entire Qur'ān therefore great caution and scepticism are required.[22]

In the last resort, every faith is in trust with itself, rather than merely in possession of its tradition. Its obedience has to be seen as responsible, rather than simply dogged or automatic. Dr. Ali Merad, an Algerian writer and philosopher, has explored what such renewed and perceptive loyalty to the *Qur'ān* and the Prophet requires, in his view, of Muslims today. Posing the question: How to obey? he answers:

> The idea which immediately comes to mind is that the Revelation represents an indivisible whole, which, in its totality, invites the obedience of the believer. From the purely orthodox point of view, it is not possible to conceive of an obedience which would limit itself to certain aspects of the Revelation. The Qur'ān guards against such a restrictive attitude: "Would you then believe certain parts of the Scripture, while you would reject others?" [Surah 2:85]
>
> The attitude of strict fidelity to the entirety of the Scripture is characteristic of classical Islam. Nowadays, this attitude is likewise represented by the different orthodox currents, and doubtless with more brilliance and fervor by the Muslim Brothers, who preach the necessity for Muslims to assume the totality of the Quranic message, so that the total control of Man's destiny by the Word of God may be realized. In the perspective of this integrating movement, to live through and for the Qur'ān would be the ideal conduct for Muslims.
>
> If such a conception is perfectly legitimate, it nevertheless raises some problems when it is a question of defining the terms of this apparently unconditional obedience. Does obedience to the Revelation involve a language whose verbal images and moral content refer to the social and cultural situation of the Arab *milieu* of the seventh century? In many cases, Quranic verses, taken literally, offer a meaning that is difficult to reconcile with moral ideas and social values that prevail in our age. Note these several examples which call for an oral commentary:
>
> "Those of whom you fear indocility (that is, womenfolk) exhort them! Leave them alone in their rooms, even beat them!" [Surah 4:34]
>
> "Cut off the hands of thieves." [Surah 5:38]
>
> "Prepare against them [enemies] everything you can in forces and cavalry." [Surah 8:60]
>
> "The bedouin are the strongest in ungodliness and hypocrisy." [Surah 9:97]
>
> One often encounters in the Qur'ān such concrete and precise instruction which interpretation does not help to reconcile with the modern intellect. It is certainly possible to interpret the third example in the sense of the necessity of the community to reinforce in time of war its defensive and offensive means. But the second example resists all interpretation. To cut off or not to cut off the hands of thieves: that is the question. Would obedience to the Revelation consist exclusively in cutting off the hand of a thief? . . . Would it not also be obeying the plan of God, as well as preventing theft, to rehabilitate the thief and, in a general manner, to build the type of society in which the human being would not experience material need or the temptation to steal? In the same way, would it be obeying revelation to accept impiety and hypocrisy as the specific mark of the bedouin? Should this judgment in the Scripture, motivated by historical circumstances and specific human beings [the hostility of bedouin tribes near Medina to Muḥammad and their continual violations of the given word] be considered as a curse falling forever on bedouin society? Is it necessary to draw on the argument of Revelation to justify a Manichean conception of the world?
>
> Should obedience to the Revelation be likened to the obedience which is due to a law? Under the circumstances, is it a question of a code whose pro-

visions are set forever, and remain applicable in all ages and in a form rigorously identical to that expressed in their primitive conception? . . .

How ambiguous can be the notion of obedience, often even of Truth? To respond appropriately to Revelation, it is essential to grasp correctly the truths that issue from it. The origin of the ambiguities is in the reading of the revealed datum.

1. The general inclination in the Muslim *milieu* consists in regarding the Qur'ān as the perfect expression of the supreme and total truth. This is not merely a vague sentiment in the collective consciousness, but a conviction based on principles resulting from the Qur'ān itself. See the numerous verses proclaiming the unquestionable truth of the Quranic account: "This is the truth on the part of your Lord," "Such is the truth coming from your Lord." [Surah 2:147, 149; 3:60; 6:114; 10:94; 11:20; 13:1, 19; 16:103; 18:29; 22:53; 32:2; 41:38] See also 6:38: "We have omitted nothing in the Book," the traditional interpretation of which is such as to contribute to convincing Muslims that the Qur'ān suggests the totality of everything known, at the same time as it announces the totality of that which can be known.

   From this textual and cultural data arises a conception of revealed truth which promotes a type of idolatry for the sacred Book considered in itself as absolute, outside which there is nothing but vanities, and not only on the level of secular productions of the mind. Hence the attitudes of self-complacency, if not plain and simple rejection with regard to the former Scriptures. . . . It is nevertheless necessary to point out—and to welcome—a new attitude, full of tolerance and understanding, which is appearing in contemporary Quranic exegesis.
2. Another consequence of the identification of the Qur'ān with the exhaustive and definitive expression of divine truth is the risk of unjustifiably encasing the work of God in the plan offered for our meditation through the Quranic ideas. Is there some presumption in thinking that the Truth of God is collected, condensed in one Book, however perfect, however miraculous it may be, and believing that this Book gives the ultimate state of the wills of God, of Him Who "each day calls one new work" [Surah 5:29] Is it as if, in spite of our attentive fervor, our reading of the revealed text could allow us as rigorously to trace the outlines of divine intentions? Is it as though the approximations of our efforts in exegesis could adequately render the Truth of God, when our formulations of this Truth that we think we have grasped are themselves conditioned by the moral and cultural universe in which our thought and entire being are steeped?
3. Our manner of understanding revelation is often only a product of our desires or dreams. From a certain reading of the revealed message, one is tempted to construct a system of values and references in terms of which it will be possible to justify such and such type of human action. . . .

We are at the end of a long period of historical and cultural evolution, during which obedience to the Revelation was conceived, in the Muslim *milieu,* as the unconditional adherence to the norms and values elaborated within the community and more or less unanimously accepted by it. One can also witness ceaseless invocations of the values of community, cohesion and confessional solidarity. These call us to condemn, if not repress, nonconformism, attempts at breaking away and even innovations, except of course those which the community feels itself in a position to accept.

This shows how difficult can be the position of those who feel that obedience does not mean passive adherence to the common wisdom and more or less resigned submission to collective taboos. There are those who see in obedience an active participation in the Work of God, and not simply a mechanical response to exterior injunctions. Obedience can have a finality differently charged with spiritual meaning, namely the patient quest for the plans of God, through the signs that He lavishes on men in the Revelation of the Scripture, but also in the Revelation He unfolds in His creation, in the course of human evolution.[23]

CHAPTER 2

Worship and Religion

> "Allāhu akbar"—then a pause while another muezzin somewhere in the direction of the Golden Temple takes up the call: "Allāhu akbar." Again and again, four times in all, and from the bedsteads a dozen men have risen up already. "I bear witness that there is no god but God." What a splendid cry it is, the proclamation of the creed that brings men out of their beds by scores at midnight! Once again he thunders through the same phrase, shaking with the vehemence of his voice: and then, far and near, the night rings with "Muḥammad is the apostle of God." It is as though he were flinging his defiance to the far off horizon, where the summer lightning plays and leaps like a bared sword. . . . Christian churches may compromise with images and chapels where the unworthy or abashed can traffic with accessible saints. Islam has but one pulpit and one stark affirmation—living or dying, one only—and where men have repeated that in red-hot belief through centuries, the air still shakes to it.[1]

THE CONFESSION OF FAITH

The significance of *Shahādah,* or witness, the first of the pillars of Islam, has been developed in lively form in Muḥammad Laḥbābī's *Le Personnalisme Musulman,* Paris, 1964 (see following pp. 237–239). In the formula of witness, the first person singular verb is used: . . . "*I bear* witness." (*ashhadu*). Basing himself on this important point, and noting the instinctive tribalism of the pre-Islamic society, Dr. Laḥbābī considers that:

> Islam brings together several variant forms of being a person. To live as Muslim is essentially to take up one's being as consciousness, set in flesh and engaged in the world, with a view to finding personal authenticity. Embodied,

conscious and committed, each of us is charged to transform himself in transforming the world and improving it in every area, in accordance with the laws willed and revealed by God, the *Sunan Allāh.*

All human beings are alike persons, because they have been created by the same God. The difference between them is not specific . . . it is only qualitative. That is to say, there are believers and there are unbelievers. The divine message, in addressing each and all, recognises by that very fact their specific equality or personal value, individually. There are no 'me's' upper and 'me's' lower, but simply equal 'me's'—equal before God and society. The believer and the unbeliever alike have the same power to change their category or qualification: the one may apostacize, the other convert. An individual exists as a person in proportion as he aspires, or decides, for example, to convert, to be apostate, to take up any deliberate position.

It is in the fire of action that beliefs are tested and proved. To appreciate the personalism of Islam we must clarify its basic ideas (the *Credo*), the way in which its metaphysics expound these and, above all the firm bonds it establishes between belief and action.

(In this sense of personal autonomy) one is far from the pre-Islamic, bedouin mentality which only thought of the human creature in a gregarious context, where all the members, in one way or another, were just copies more or less conformed to all the rest. The fact of the tribe meant in some senses a dilution of personality. Its *esprit de corps* knew no solidarity, no ties of heart, outside agnate and cognate kinships. The clan itself was founded on the cult of the same ancestors. Even at a more advanced stage of the pagan period of the *Jāhiliyyah* discrimination continued to hold. The limits of the tribe were in some measure transcended but there was no affirmation of the human person as an inclusive denominator. . . . By contrast, in Islam, it is the human person which obtains, whatever his ethnic, linguistic or 'color' identity. The *'ajamī* (that is, "Persian," or, simply non-Arab) is the same as the Arab.

After analysing in this context the several terms used in Arabic to denote the person (*shakhṣ*), the individual (*fard*), face (*wajh*), and even nose (*anf*), as well as *dhāt* (essence), Laḥbābī continues:

This brief research into vocabulary makes us realise how alert and weighty is this sense of the person in primitive Islam. If during the first century of the *Hijrah* an adequate term has not yet been found to express this concept, it is not the less present, coming into focus and being elaborated. We witness a total change in the mentality of the Arab, a transition from the diffused to the individualized, from the confused to the clear—a transition to consciousness. It is no longer the tribe alone which determines reality and value: each member of the tribe, irrespective of age, station or sex, senses his or her real self and proceeds upon it as something inviolate in itself. He/she is a person created by God and so a sacred being. . . .

All human beings are called upon to bear witness to the existence of their Creator, to His unity and His Almightiness. In pronouncing the *Shahādah,* or profession of faith, one is considered a Muslim.

However, this witness must not be merely verbal. The believer must make it concrete in his ritual acts (the obligatory pillars of Islam: ritual prayer, *Zakāt* or alms, fasting and pilgrimage to Mecca) and by participation in the social order [ethics and law]. Oral witness [the profession of the monotheistic faith] together with the performance of duties towards God and attitudes towards our neighbor take our will and our reason to fulfilment.

Nevertheless, none of our actions have their due religious validity apart from purity of intention [*niyyah*], Muḥammad insisted that acts have worth only from their intention. That rule is basic in Islam. The *niyyah* distinguishes heartfeltness and reflective fulfilment from habit and sheep-like rote. . . . All the acts upon which the Islamic faith is built make their appeal to that in each of us which is most universal [that is to say, specifically human] and at one and the same time the most intimate and individual, so that the whole religious behavior recruits the totality of our being, of our being as personal.

To bear witness that God is One, is to affirm oneself also as a unity. For to acknowledge divine omnipotence is at the same time to recognize one's own power to judge and to decide, in the very act of bearing witness. In prayer the Muslim presents himself alone before God, apart and yet in communion. In these privileged moments of prayer, of invocation and of prostration, it is always the one before the One: two infinites. One is not over against God, but standing in relation to Him, just as our distinction from other beings stands in our locating ourselves in the setting of the likenesses and unlikenesses we share with them. . . .

The *Shahādah,* then, is bipolar. In witnessing one avows the existence of God and the Witness is at the same time the affirmation of the personal reality of him who witnesses. It is a perpetual crossroads between transcendence and immanence, between the Absolute and finitude, between the spiritual and the institutional, the metaphysical and the psychic. At the beginning and the end of the *Shahādah* the person apprehends himself and herein lies his ontological value. The believer witnesses in face of the world and humanity. "We have made you an *Ummah* in the midst, in order that you may witness to man and that the Prophet-messenger may be a witness to you." [Surah 2:143]

It follows, psychologically that the *Shahādah* constitutes a relationship with others since the 'I' and the others participate in the same witness, and it means sociologically a partnership in making it concrete in adapting *our* existence and *our* shape of things in regard to others. The believer participates in a 'we' where the faith of some is set in opposition to the non-faith, the atheism, of all the others. An essentially contradictory attitude to it requires of the faith constantly to put itself to the question, to develop in great measure a militancy of thought [involving meditation and return, mystical sense and reason, engagement and disengagement] and a necessary *Kalām,* or speculative theology, all the time developing and continuing. Metaphysically, the person, whether believing or unbelieving, finds himself set within a dialectic where the alternatives, the options deriving from the 'I', converge upon God, the Creator-Ordainer, even when His existence is denied. Do we not find at the core of ourselves the most important of the 'signs' [*āyāt*] of the divine omnipresence?[2]

Risālat al-Tauḥīd (The Theology of Unity) by Shaikh Muḥammad 'Abduh of Egypt (see pp. 217–219) was the most formative, popular work of Islamic thought in Arabic through the first decades of the 1900s. The writer rounds off a long exposé of doctrine and a confident picture of history with this brief summary of the pillars of religion.

Such is Islam, and the forms of divine obedience according to its Book and its authentic tradition, as befits the majesty of God and His transcendent glory beyond all likeness, and in accord with the mind and sound thinking.

Prayer includes kneeling and prostration, movement and stillness, petition and entreaty, praise and ascription of greatness—all of which arise from that awareness of the divine authority which overwhelms men and claims every energy. To Him the heart is bowed in awe and the soul brings homage. In all there is nothing beyond reason's range, except an abstruse question like why the prescribed number of ritual movements or the stone-throwing on pilgrimage—about which one can readily defer to the wisdom of the All-knowing, the Ever-aware, in the knowledge that there is nothing evidently futile, or meaningless, or inconsistent with the principles of thought with which God has furnished the mind.

Fasting is an abstinence which serves to impress on the spirit the greatness of God's command and a means to appreciate His gifts through foregoing them and, by exercise in His lovingkindness, to know its quality in truth. "Fasting is prescribed for you, as it was for those before you, perhaps you may truly fear Him." [Surah 2:183]

As for the pilgrimage ceremonies, they recall to man his most elemental needs and—if only once in a life-time—serve notice on him forcibly of the equality among all men, in that there the distinction between rich and poor, pauper and prince, is annulled. All are present in a common garb, bare-headed, without adornment, and with the single aim of worship before God, the Lord of all the worlds. By the circumambulation of the *Ka'bah* and the running and the standing and by the touching of the Stone they perpetuate the memory of Abraham, father of faith. Yet they are all aware that none of these material things, for all their sanctity, have the power to harm or to profit superstitiously. Each of the various parts of Islamic worship, when men truly submit themselves to them, proclaim the divine transcendence and His holy separation from all that man vainly associates with Him.

When will anything comparable be found in the rites of other nations, where reason goes awry and there is no clear way to the pure secrets of the unity and transcendence of God? . . .

For reason is the pioneer of authentic belief. Nor is it in any way onerous for human nature, which is the true criterion of what best serves and befits human needs. . . . Islam lifts the souls of men by an awareness of the divine to a point where men almost transcend the lower world and become a part of the heavenly kingdom. Islam invites men to the daily renewal of that awareness of God through the five times of prayer, yet for all that it does not impede the delight of pleasurable things. It does not impose disciplines and acts of asceticism that would be a burden upon natural human proclivities. It considers that the body should have its rights, consistently with pure conscience and proper intention and it takes such an attitude to be pleasing to God and meritorious. If any man is carried away by passion and succumbs, there is divine forgiveness for him when he duly repents and turns back.

Readers of the Qur'ān were much impressed with the simplicity of this religion and the way of life of its true and pure followers had great appeal. They realized the difference between the incomprehensible creeds and one whose essentials could be taken in at a glance. They almost stampeded into it to be free of the heavy, oppressive thing they had endured.

Now the nations had what they were looking for—a religion with a mind to think. Now they had a faith which gave justice its due place.[3]

Prayer in Arabian waters on a sailing dhow.

> They began the day with prayer. First ablutions, then prayer. The dawn prayer was not communal: each man prayed as best pleased him, having first washed hands and face and feet in water hauled up from the sea. They always stood facing the direction of Mecca . . . stood silent a moment or two in meditation, putting from their minds all worldly thoughts, and then fell easily and rhythmically into the exercise and words of the set prayers. It was interesting to watch the changes which came over some of their faces. The lines would soften, the flash fade from imperious eyes and whatever there might have been of arrogance, pride, vanity, quite disappear.
>
> There was no hypocrisy in those strong faces which looked towards Mecca. It was obvious that their religion was a real and living thing. Their prayers were not simply a formula to be mouthed, but a form of real communion with a very real god. None of them prayed hurriedly: they always spent a few moments first in silent meditation, in this discard of their worldly thoughts.[4]

Sirdar Iqbal Ali Shah, in his *Lights of Asia,* presents a description of canonical Muslim prayer.

> The saying of prayer [*Ṣalāt*] is obligatory upon every Muslim, male or female, five times a day, *viz.* early in the morning, a little after midday, in the afternoon, immediately after sunset and in the first part of the night before going to bed. The service consists of two parts—one part to be said alone, preferably in private, and the other in congregation, preferably in a mosque, but in case there is no congregation of Muslims both parts may be performed alone. Each part consists of a number of *Raka'āt,* as we will explain below.
>
> The morning or *Fajr* prayer consists of two *Rak'ahs* said alone, followed by two said in congregation. The midday or *Ẓuhr* prayer consists of four *Raka'āt* said alone, followed by four said in congregation, and these again followed by two said alone. The afternoon or *'Aṣr* prayer consists of four *Raka'āt* said in congregation. The sunset or *Maghrib* prayer consists of three *Raka'āt* said in congregation, followed by two said alone. The night or *'Ishā'* prayer consists of four *Raka'āt,* said in congregation followed by two, and again by three, said alone. Besides these, there is the *Tahajjud,* or after midnight prayer, which is not obligatory, consisting of eight *Raka'āt* said in twos.
>
> Description of a *Rak'ah*:
>
> One *Rak'ah* is completed as follows.
>
> **1.** Both hands are raised up to the ears in a standing position, with the face towards the *Qiblah* in Mecca, while the words *Allāhu Akbar* [God is the greatest of all] are uttered. This is called the *Takbīr.*
>
> **2.** Then comes *Qiyām.* The right hand is placed straight upon the fore-arm of the left, over the navel, while the standing position is maintained and the following prayer is recited (though there are other prayers too): "Glory to Thee, O God, Thine is the praise and blessed is Thy Name and exalted is Thy majesty, and there is none to be served beside Thee. . . . I betake me for refuge to God against the accursed satan."
>
> After this the *Fātiḥah,* or opening Surah of the Qur'ān, is recited in the same position. At the close is said *Amen,* be it so, and then any portion of the Qur'ān which the devotee wishes is recited by heart. Generally one of the shorter chapters at the close of the Holy Book is repeated and the Chapter termed *Ikhlāṣ* [Surah 112] is the one recommended.

3. Then, saying *Allāhu Akbar* the worshipper lowers his head down, so that the palms of the hands reach the knees. In this position, which is called *Rukū'*, phrases expressive of the divine glory and majesty are repeated at least three times. They are the following: "Glory to my Lord the great."

4. After this, the standing position is resumed, with the words: "God accepts him who gives praise to Him. O our Lord, Thine is the praise."

5. Then the worshipper prostrates himself, the toes of both feet, both knees, both hands, and the forehead touching the ground, and the following words expressing the divine greatness are uttered at least three times. This is the first *Sijdah.* "Glory to my Lord the most High."

6. Then the worshipper sits down in a reverential position [on his haunches]. This is the *Jalsah.*

7. This is followed by a second prostration, or *Sijdah,* (as described under 5) with the repetition of the same words.

8. This finishes one *Rak'ah.* The worshipper rises and assumes a standing position for the second one, which is finished in the same manner as the first. But at the end of the second one, instead of assuming the standing position he sits down in a reverential position called the *qaḍā',* and with the glorification of God he combines prayers for the holy prophets, for the faithful and for himself, called the *Taḥīyah,* which runs as follows: "All prayers and worship rendered through words, actions and wealth, are due to God. Peace be upon you, O Prophet and the mercy of God and His blessings. Peace be on us and the righteous servants of God. I bear witness that none is worthy to be worshipped save God and I bear witness that Muḥammad is His servant and His Apostle."

9. If the worshipper intends more than two *Raka'āt* he repeats also the following prayer of blessings upon the Prophet: "O God, magnify Muḥammad and the followers of Muḥammad, as Thou didst magnify Abraham and the followers of Abraham. For surely Thou art praised and magnified. O God, bless Muḥammad and the followers of Muḥammad, as Thou didst bless etc."

The following prayer may also be added to this: "My Lord, make me, and my offspring also, to continue prayer. Our Lord, accept the prayer: grant Thy protection to me and to my parents and to the faithful on the day when the reckoning shall be made."

10. This closes the prayer, which ends at the *Salām,* or the greeting, being also the greeting of the Muslims to each other. The worshipper turns his head first to the right and then to the left, saying with each turn of the head: "Peace be upon you and the mercy of God."

11. Thus the prayer finishes . . . the last act being always *Taḥiyah* and the concluding prayer, followed by the *Salām.*

12. The prayer known as the *Qunūt* is recited after rising from the *Rukū'* [see above], or immediately before assuming that position, when standing and generally only in the last of the three last *Raka'āt* of the *'Ishā'* prayer. The most wellknown *Qunūt*, or rest, is the following: "O God, we ask help of Thee and we ask Thy protection and believe in Thee, and trust in Thee in the best manner and we thank Thee. We are not ungrateful unto Thee and we cast off and forsake him who disobeys Thee. O God, Thee do we serve and to Thee do we fly, and we are quick in hope of Thy mercy and we fear Thy punishment. For surely Thy punishment overtakes the unbeliever."[5]

Dr. Ḥasan al-Askari, sociologist and theologian, from Osmania University, Hyderabad, India, writes on Worship and Prayer and, after first noting the collective form of religion, cites Surah 2:238: "Watch over prayers," and continues:

> When one keeps watch over prayers, one is aware of the difference between [communal] self-gathering and [personal] self-surrender, the former referring to the emphasis gained through prayer, on personal and group identity, and the latter demanding the surrender of this very identity. Each principle reflected in the *Fātiḥah,* the opening chapter in the Qur'ān, calls forth this surrender. The act of surrender presupposes a judgment on the self and the world: prayer, like love, is not merely tenderness and humility, but also judgment. The principle of "All praise to God," one of the fundamental principles of Islamic prayer, is also a principle of constant vigilance over, and criticism of, one's position within one's tradition and in history. . . .
>
> From the Islamic point of view, *Ṣalāt* is an act of obedience to God's command: "Establish prayer." [*uqīmu-l-Ṣalāt*] It is rewarding to note that the divine command is not just to pray, or to *say* the prayers. The imperative is "to establish." To establish a form is to make it a part of the rhythm of nature and of society, and also to transcend this rhythm. The form is both a subjective medium and an objective symbol. . . .
>
> "And when you have performed the acts of worship prescribed for you, celebrate the praises of God as you celebrate the praises of your fathers, or even more than that." [Surah 2:200] . . . The believer is called upon to remember God after the specific act of worship is over . . . "as you celebrate the praises of your fathers. . . ." One does not praise one's father [identity, heritage, tribe, nation, culture] only in subjective terms. The entire edifice of society is erected for that purpose. Hence the celebration of the praises of God should be read into this edifice. By remembering God in place of one's fathers, one brings about a universal and transcendent basis of human relationships, of justice and understanding between men. A specific act of worship, however universal its idiom, may not uplift man from his narrow identities if it is not followed by the praises of God expressed in each social and cultural situation. . . . Spiritual attitudes are never really privative limitations and prejudices: they are always realized on the plane of what seems to be their opposite, which implies that fundamentally every village and town is normally the extension of a sanctuary and ought to remain as such, and that every human collectivity is a spiritual association. . . . The metaphysical invisible [the Hidden God of worship] should be supported by a sociological visible [God as Manifest].[6]

Characteristic phrases in Muslim person *Du'ā*, or private prayer, used of God, or to Him, are these.

> My adequacy is in God, the best of the trustworthy.
>
> He who has hallowed and made holy His nature beyond all likening, sanctified from all resemblance.
>
> Whose attributes are exalted beyond all comparison, known only limitlessly and described never finally, unto Whom no progeny is ascribed, Whom the years do not change nor the lapse of time cause to pass away.
>
> The sincere are well-versed in remembrance of Him.
>
> Those who believe in the Unity rejoice in His One-ness: those who obey Him are led into a straight path and the people of His love learn the blissful gardens.

The movements of the ants' feet He sees in the dark night.
At the remembrance of Him the fears of apprehensive hearts are laid to rest.
Thou Succorer of those who seek for aid, Thy face is glory manifest and Thy strength is Thy majesty.
God's it is to make us followers of His holy law and lovers of His perfect nature.
Be merciful toward me with a mercy Thou wilt never afterward reverse into affliction.
Ease for us that of which we are afraid for its exactingness: how simple is that unto Thee!
Open to us the portals of Thy mercy, O Thou our refuge and our hiding-place.
O God, as those who have repented before Thee we ask Thy forgiveness though we have returned into that of which we repented. We ask forgiveness for every good we sought to gain before Thy face and what was not right before Thee we confused with it.
In Thee we shelter and in Thee alone.
Set us free for Thy worship and for seeking unto Thee, and for the reading of Thy Book and make Thy blessing great upon us. Forgive us our misusing of ourselves, for all our desire is toward Thee that Thou wouldest grant us a faith unalloyed by doubt.[7]

KEEPING THE FAST

In the collected essays and papers of Kemal A. Faruki, of Karachi, is a noted lawyer's rationale of the meaning and significance of Ramaḍān.

The Muslim fasts because, as a believer in God, he wishes to carry out God's commands and he understands that God wishes him to fast from sunrise to sunset for thirty days during the month of Ramaḍān. But why should God want him to undertake this every year or at all? God, Who does nothing without purpose, is surely not interested in imposing upon His creatures a meaningless ritual. He asks human beings to do things for their own benefit.

The benefit of fasting is primarily in terms of character. The abstention from food and drink and other material pleasures for the long hours between dawn and dusk during the month of Ramaḍān is an act of self-discipline by which an individual asserts his or her ability to gain control over material pleasures and habits. There is a triumph of mind over matter. The desire to quench thirst, to soften the pangs of hunger, or to light a cigarette, are placed in their proper perspective as things which can be postponed, and in some cases given up altogether, if necessary. This, in itself, constitutes a victory for the human being over his or her material environment. His or her values, or assessment of a situation, or the truth of a matter, are all too often clouded and obscured unknowingly by material considerations over which it is thought that the individual has no power or control. Nor can he or she even hope to begin to move in a direction that is recognized to be best, or intelligent, as long as the dead weight of habit pushes him or her elsewhere. The act of fasting breaks such habits and makes it possible for the individual to conceive of adopting the most suitable course of action, undeflected by the fear that the force of habit . . . will prevent its implementation.

Self-discipline is the phrase which perhaps best describes the movement which fasting can inaugurate, and with this self-discipline comes a definite slowing down of activity during the month of Ramaḍān. This slowing down of impulses and actions is sometimes held to be one of the defects of fasting for this century, where speed and restless activity are often thought to be virtues in themselves. But restless activity . . . often conceals a neurotic sense of aimless dissatisfaction with things as they are. . . . Fasting, by slowing down this action places thought once more where it rightly belongs.

Coupled with these sterner experiences which the fast-er knows is, paradoxically, a richer appreciation of material pleasures themselves. . . .

These obviously are intensely personal experiences and yet, as in most other religious disciplines, there is a social dimension of equal importance. The community sense of those who fast and break their fast together is greatly heightened and a necessary element for concerted social action is added. The traditional virtues . . . can only develop effectively when an individual possesses an awareness of how the other person feels and thinks . . . One who can afford food and yet abstains from it, is better able to understand the person who does not have the food because he or she cannot afford it. . . .

It may be asked, notwithstanding these benefits of fasting, why is it necessary seemingly to clothe it with religious sanction? Partly, the religious nature of fasting . . . gives the intending fast-er the necessary impulse to carry him or her over the hill of doubt, indecision and lassitude, and that firmness of *niyyah* or intention, to abstain from material needs and pleasures during the long, daylight hours. . . . There remains that golden thread of guidance that comes from religion, continuous through the centuries, which gives assurance that there will be at least an active minority possessing these qualities, however much the world might change.

However, it would be a misunderstanding of the nature of the development which fasting inculcates to think that the change is dramatic. Often enough, to begin fasting merely arrests the drift into increasing lack of discipline of the self. The rigors of abstention may initially provoke a reaction of indulgence in the evening. An understanding of the less fortunate may appear, at best, a faint glimmer in the early phases of the change to fasting. Only through a period of years does the change and development of character assume a more decisive shape. . . . "Islam," as Iqbal put it, "is aspiration not achievement."

This leads to one other, and last consideration. Is it necessary to fast the entire month from dawn to dusk for any religious merit or practical benefit to be obtained? By no means. It is certainly better to have fasted for one solitary day than not to have fasted at all . . . In a purely religious sense, the value and merit attaching to an act can only be assessed against the background of the effort involved for the individual concerned. God, in the Qur'ān tells us that while we may be able to measure the quantitative amount of an individual's acts, only God can measure its qualitative value [Surah 73:20]. So it is with fasting. God lays not upon any soul a burden "except to the extent of its ability." [Surah 23:62] [8]

A typical pocket manual of devotions for the month of Ramaḍān, published in Sidon, Lebanon, in 1930 but echoing petitions familiar for centuries, opens with a long prayer with reiterated themes and refrains and then turns to the last ten nights of the month with a liturgy for each prefaced by this inclusive plea.

I seek refuge in the majesty of Thy gracious countenance. May this month of Ramaḍān not pass, nor the dawn of this night of mine break, while Thou hast before Thee any deed or guilt of mine for which Thou dost requite me.

Prayers for the last Ten Nights of Ramaḍān

O God, send down blessings upon Muḥammad and his people. Grant or apportion unto me a vision which will close up for me forever the door of ignorance. Bestow upon me guidance from every error; wealth that will bar the door to all poverty; strength whereby Thou wilt remove from me all weakness; power whereby Thou wilt ennoble me above all unworthiness. Grant me also the exaltation by which I may be lifted above humiliation; the security to repel from me every fear; mercy whereby to be defended from all calamity; knowledge to open unto me all certainty; and certainty to banish all doubt. Grant me that prayer by which Thou mayest extend unto me, on this night of Ramaḍān and at this hour, a gracious answer, O Thou Who art kindly. Give me that awe whereby Thou wilt bring me all mercy, and a protecting virtue between me and my transgressions so that I may prosper thereby and be among those who enjoy security with Thee, by Thy mercy, O Thou most merciful.

O Thou aid of those who seek refuge, send down blessing upon Muḥammad and the people of Muḥammad. Be unto me a fortress and a sure haven, O Thou shelter of those who have recourse unto thee, and down blessing upon Muḥammad and the people of Muḥammad. Be unto me a shelter and a succour and a helper, O Thou who comest to the aid of those who cry unto thee in need. Send down. . . . Be unto me a hiding place and a champion, O Thou Lord of the believers. Send down. . . . Be thou unto me a sovereign, O Thou who savest the believers from overwhelming sorrows. Send down. . . . Aid my sorrow and cheer my grief, make me glad in this great month with a happiness that will have no sequel of wretchedness for me, O Thou most Merciful.

O God, extend my years, enlarge my livelihood, make healthy my frame, bring to pass my hope. If I have been written down among the wretched, blot out my place with the wretched and write me down among the blessed. For Thou annihilatest what Thou wilt and what Thou wilt Thou establishest. With Thee is the Mother of the Book [the dossier of decrees?]. O God, upon Thee do I rely in my need this night. From Thee I have accepted my poverty and lowliness that the night may enlarge me, through Thy mercy and Thy pardon. I have more hope in Thy mercy than I have in what I do. For Thy forgiveness and Thy compassion are more ample than my transgressions. Do Thou supply my every need as is good for me and acceptable unto Thee, by virtue of Thine ability so to do, seeing it is so easy for Thee. For verily I shall find no good whatsoever save from Thee. None other than Thou will ever rid me of evil. My hope for my religious duty-done, for my place in this world and the next, for the day of my destitution and abasement and the day I lie in the grave, and people are sundered from me, is not in what I have done. My hope is none other save Thou, O Lord of the worlds.

O God, O my Lord, I beseech Thee, as one who is poor and needy, who fears and supplicates Thee; I beseech Thee my Lord, to send down blessing upon Muḥammad and his people and to protect me from disgrace in this world and from retribution in the next, to double unto me that which I do this night and during this month. Have mercy upon my dwelling place and protect me from the punishment of those things which Thou hast reckoned against me, the things which are concealed from Thy servant and which Thou, of Thy mercy towards me, hast veiled from me, delivering me from their shame and disgrace and reproach in this transitory world. Unto Thee be praise for this mercy. In every circumstance, I beseech Thee, O Lord, to send down blessing upon Muḥammad and his people and to fulfil upon me Thy grace, under the protecting shield thereof, in the world to come. Save me from shame and disgrace by Thy favour unto me, O Thou of all most merciful.

O God, I pray Thee to make complete according to my finest hopes the reward of Thy mercy. Rid me of all that is evil. Verily I cannot ward off the things I must beware of, save by Thee. Indeed I have come to be like a mortgaged man by the things which I have done and the disposition rests in Thy hands. There is no suppliant more beggarly than I. So send down blessing upon Muḥammad and the people of Muḥammad and pardon me my wrongdoing, my ignorance, my deserts, my follies, and every transgression that I have committed. Cause me to attain my inheritance without toilsome obstacles. Do not let me perish in body or soul in seeking anything that is not decreed for me, O Thou of all most merciful.[9]

FULFILLING THE PILGRIMAGE

The mood of devout anticipation of the Pilgrimage is well communicated in a popular novel by one of Egypt's foremost writers. A character, Riḍwān Ḥusseini, revered by his neighbors as a man of deep, personal piety, is about to depart for Mecca, as narrated in *Zaqāq al-Midāq* (*Midāq Alley*) by Najīb Maḥfūẓ.

It was a joyful day of leave-taking. Riḍwān . . . had hoped that God would choose him to make the holy Pilgrimage to Mecca and Medina and this year so He had. Every one knew this was the day when he would leave for the Holy Land. His house was filled with well-wishers, lifelong friends and devout Muslims. They clustered in his modest room which had so often echoed with their pious and friendly discussions. They chatted about the Pilgrimage and their reminiscences of it, their voices rising from every corner of the room and mixing with a trail of smoke billowing up from the brazier. They told tales of the modern Pilgrimage and those of bye-gone days and rehearsed holy traditions and beautiful verses concerning it. One man with a melodious voice chanted verses from the Holy Qur'ān and then they are listened to a long and eloquent speech by Riḍwān that expressed his heart's goodness. A pious friend wished him a happy and safe return, to which Ḥusseini beamed and replied in his most gentle manner:

"Please, my friend, don't remind me of my return. Anyone who visits God's house with a longing for home deserves to have God deny him his reward, ignore his prayers and destroy his happiness. I will think of returning only when I have left the scene of the revelation on my way back to Egypt. And, by 'returning' I mean going back on the Pilgrimage again, with the help and permission of the All-Merciful. If only I could spend the rest of my life in the Holy Land, seeing the ground which was once trodden by the Prophet, the sky once filled with the angels singing and listening to the divine revelation coming to earth and rising to the skies again from the souls on earth. There

> one's mind is filled only with the revelations from eternity. One throbs with love for God. There are the remedy and the cure. O my brother, I long for Mecca and its bright heavens. I long for the whisper of time at every corner and to walk down its streets and lose myself in its holy places. How I long to drink from the well of Zamzam and take the road of the Messenger on his flight, followed by the multitudes of thirteen hundred years ago and those of today, too. I long to feel my heart grow chill when I visit the grave of the Prophet and pray in the holy garden. I can see myself now, my brothers, walking through the lanes of Mecca, reciting verses from the Qur'ān just as they were first revealed, as if I were listening to a lesson given by the Almighty Being. What joy! I can see myself kneeling in the garden imagining the beloved face of the Prophet before me, just as it appears to me in my sleep. What joy! I can see myself prostrating low before the edifice and pleading for forgiveness. What peace I'll have, going to the well of Zamzam, saturating with water those wounds of passion and crying out for their cure. What peace! My brother, speak not to me of my return, but pray with me to God to fulfill my hopes."

It is notable in this passage of deep emotion that the novelist has his pilgrim Riḍwān dwell on his private piety rather than on the several sequences within the pilgrim ritual. Muḥammad's *Hijrah* to Medina from Mecca is followed in deep veneration by most pilgrims, in order also to greet the Prophet's tomb. But it is not part of the canonical pilgrimage. The allusion to the angels' singing is an echo of Surah 97 and "The Night of Power."[10]

Pilgrimage is described in simple direct terms by Sayyid Abū-l-'Alā al-Maudūdī, leader of the *Jamā' at-i-Islāmī* in Pakistan, in his *Towards Understanding Islam.*

> On the present site of Mecca, thousands of years before now, Abraham, the Prophet (God's blessing be upon him), had built a small house for worshipping God. In appreciation of his sincerity and pure love for Himself, God blessed and consecrated that House as His own, and ordained that whoever worshipped Him should do so facing that House. He also commanded that he who wished to please Him more should go to it in the same simple dress which Abraham used to wear, and circumambulate the House with the same love which Abraham had cherished for Him. He further ordered: "When you come to my House, purify your hearts, suppress your physical desires, avoid bloodshed, bad acts and bad tongue, present yourselves here with the same reverence and humility which you ought to observe in the presence of your Master. Consider that you are going in the presence of a King who governs the earth and the heavens, and before Whom all men are but indigent and helpless. When you come to Me with humility I will enrich you with My favors.
>
> In one respect pilgrimage is the most important of all duties. If one does not cherish true love for God, how would he be ready to part with his friends and relatives, stop his own occupation, and take upon himself the trouble and inconvenience of a long journey. To intend to perform pilgrimage, therefore, of itself shows the love and sincerity of the pilgrim for God. This journey is not like the ordinary journeys taken in worldly interest: in it the man always has the attitude of attention and devotion towards God. The further he advances the keener becomes his love and zeal: the nearer he approaches

the *Ka'bah,* the fire of sacred love becomes stronger. His heart of itself despises sin and disobedience, and feels remorse for his past commissions. He prays God to grant him strength for obedience to Him in the future. He feels gratification in his remembrance of God and his devotion to Him. He tarries longer in his prostrations and does not like to lift his head from that position. In reciting the Qur'ān he feels a new joy, and experiences a new pleasure in keeping fast. When he enters the Hijaz he at once mentally surveys the whole history of the early Islam. Everywhere he sees the relics of those who loved God, and sacrificed their lives for His sake. Every grain of its sand witnesses the glory and grandeur of Islam, and every piece of stone declares: "This is the land where Islam took birth, and whence God's word rose high." Thus the Muslim's heart becomes full of love for God, and he returns to his house with deep impressions so that they remain stamped on his mind till death.

Along with the spiritual improvement effected by the *Ḥajj,* it is so ordained by God as to promote our worldly interests in numerous ways. Through *Ḥajj* Mecca has been the center for the Muslims of the whole world, from every corner of which the votaries of Islam gather there at one fixed time of the year. They mix with each other and a bond of love is established among them, together with the impression that Muslims of whatever race or country they be are of one nation, and are brothers to each other. In this respect, if *Ḥajj* is a religious duty in one aspect, it is at the same time a conference of all the Muslims of the world, and the best means of producing unity among them.[11]

Abū-l-'Alā al-Maudūdī does not mean by 'conference' any formal political gathering of heads of state or delegates with agenda for debate. Nevertheless the indirect potential of the *Ḥajj* as a symbol and experience of Islamic togetherness has been developed, in more sophisticated terms than those of Maudūdī, by Kemal A. Faruki (see p. 55). Writing in 1972, in *Islam, Today and Tomorrow,* he observes:

The pilgrimage to Mecca, like most other duties laid upon the Muslim, will be found to possess both personal and universal significance: personal, because it is the individual who hopes to become, by performing this pious act, a better person in this world and increases his prospects of reward in the Hereafter: universal, because the pilgrimage represents the largest of the concentric circles around which the Muslim institution of prayer is built. At the center is daily personal prayer in solitude, followed by prayer in Friday congregation in an individual's particular locality, and then there are the annual *'Id* prayers comprising all the people in a town, culminating once in a lifetime in the pilgrimage, in which an individual prays with Muslims from all over the world. The pilgrimage thus constitutes a most dramatic visual illustration of how belief in the One God leads to a union of people of different parts of the world and of different ethnic origins in a brotherhood of man.

There is a carefully prescribed ritual to be observed during the pilgrimage [as indeed there is for the other *arkān,* or pillars, of the faith], and this ritual and external form have their essential functions in ensuring order and discipline amongst the vast concourse at the pilgrimage, as well as emphasizing, through uniformity in practice, the unity which the pilgrimage symbolizes.

Important, and indeed essential, as are the ritual aspects and the outer form of the pilgrimage, they become little more than empty, meaningless shells, if they do not contain a living, heartfelt understanding of the purpose of pilgrimage. For instance the pilgrimage should inculcate a living conviction of true brotherhood, and, by the dress prescribed for the pilgrim, eradicate from the heart and mind of the pilgrim any false notions of a superiority or unjust privilege between men, which is based on differences of social class, economic wealth, race or genealogy. In the last analysis, unjust privilege can only be effectively and permanently removed from a society when people really believe that such privilege is unjust and wrong.

Hence, it is far from sufficient for an intending pilgrim to repeat like a parrot the rituals and outward forms of piety, devoid of any understanding or attempt to understand the spirit underlying this institution and the type of transformation in human character which it is sought to bring about through the pilgrimage. . . .

It should be remembered that when any group of people becomes Muslim . . . the change is far from being complete or total. The recitation of the *Kalimah,* the act of circumcision, the construction of the first mosque, and the observance of Muslim festivals, are usually mixed up with a multitude of pre-Islamic customs and practices. It is true that many of these are not necessarily in contradiction with an Islamic society: but at the same time, many of them are not in harmony with their new Islamic faith. For a variety of reasons, the pre-Islamic customs and outlook of a particular society persist for many years and even for centuries, side by side with the external acceptance of Islam.

One of the important ways in which the Islamic outlook and way of life slowly and peacefully win acceptance over those pre-Islamic habits and customs which are in conflict with Islamic ideas, consists in the fact that every year, a small group from every town and village in the newly converted society goes to Mecca to perform the pilgrimage. There, at the House of God, they see the Islamic norms in their original starting-place and absorb the common denominator amongst the many-colored, many-tongued pilgrims. They then return to their towns and villages with the added prestige of having made the sacred journey: and they point out to their fellow-villagers or townsmen the practice of Islam which they observed at Mecca during the *Ḥajj* and they contrast this with the customs of the newly converted society that were being continued under the mistaken notion that they were either part of the Islamic way of life or, at any rate, not in contradiction with it. . . .

Islamic brotherhood will become more and more a living reality, and in this task, the annual pilgrimage has its essential role, provided that the outer forms and ritual are not thought to be substitutes for the inner spirit of this essential Muslim duty and when, on the contrary, ritual and inner spirit truly complement and strengthen each other.[12]

The Autobiography of Malcolm X contains a vivid narrative of his experiences as an American Muslim pilgrim. These, among other factors, weaned him away from the Black Muslims' distortion of historical Islam into an instrument or an advocacy of black racialism and contributed to his decisive break with Elijah Muḥammad, head of Black Islam. The extracts here concentrate on Malcolm X's impressions of the pilgrimage itself, omitting the details of his permit and diary.

In Cairo airport scores of pilgrims were becoming *Muḥrim,* that is, entering upon the state of *Iḥrām,* the assumption of a spiritual and physical state of consecration. . . . We took off our clothes and put on two white towels. One, the *izār,* was folded round the loins. The other, the *ridā',* was thrown over the neck and shoulders, leaving the right shoulder and arm bare. Over the *izār*, a waist-wrapper, a money belt was worn and a bag . . . with a long strap. . . . Every one of the thousands at the airport was dressed in this way. You could be a king or a peasant and no one would know. . . .

Planeloads of pilgrims were taking off every few minutes, but the airport was jammed with more, and their friends and relatives waiting to see them off. Those who are not going ask others to pray for them at Mecca. . . . The Jeddah airport seemed even more crowded than Cairo's had been. Our party became another shuffling unit in the shifting mass with every race on earth represented. . . . Each party was assigned to a *muṭawwif* who would be responsible for transferring that party from Jeddah to Mecca. . . .

I had to go before . . . the Muslim High Court which examined all possibly non-authentic converts to the Islamic religion seeking to enter Mecca. It was absolute that no non-Muslim could enter Mecca. . . . My guide gestured me into a compartment that contained about fifteen people. Most lay curled up on their rugs asleep. An old Russian Muslim and his wife were not asleep. They stared frankly at me. Two Egyptian Muslims and a Persian roused and also stared. With gestures my guide indicated that he would demonstrate to me the proper ritual prayer postures. Imagine, being a Muslim minister, a leader in Elijah Muḥammad's *Nation of Islam,* and not knowing the prayer ritual!

I tried to do what he did. I knew I was not doing it right: I could feel the other Muslims' eyes on me. . . . Watched by the Muslims, I kept practicing the prayer posture. I refused to let myself think how ridiculous I must have looked.

After much suspense, occupied with practicing the ritual and reflecting on the panorama of Jeddah airport and, later, streets and crowds, Malcolm X was satisfactorily admitted to pilgrim status.

Two young Arabs accompanied me to Mecca. A well-lighted modern turnpike highway made the trip easy. . . . I was at once thrilled, important, humble and thankful. Mecca, when we entered, seemed as ancient as time itself. Our car slowed through the winding streets, lined by shops on both sides and with buses, cars and trucks, and tens of thousands of pilgrims from all over the earth were everywhere. . . . We parked near the Great Mosque. We performed our ablution and entered. Pilgrims seemed to be on top of each other, there were so many, lying, sitting, sleeping, praying, walking . . . carrying my sandals I followed the *muṭawwif.* Then I saw the *Ka'bah,* a huge black stone house in the middle of the Great Mosque. It was being circumambulated by thousands upon thousands of praying pilgrims, both sexes, and every size, shape, color, and race in the world. I knew the prayer to be uttered when the pilgrim's eyes first perceive the *Ka'bah*: "O God, You are peace and peace derives from You. So greet us, O Lord, with peace." Upon entering the Mosque, the pilgrim should try to kiss the *Ka'bah* if possible, but if the crowds prevent him getting that close he touches it and if the crowds prevent that he raises his hand and cries out: *Takbīr* [that is, *Allāhu akbar*]. I could not get within yards.

My feeling there in the House of God was a numbness. My *muṭawwif* led me in the crowd of praying, chanting pilgrims moving seven times round the *Ka'bah.* Some were bent and wizened with age. It was a sight that stamped itself on the brain. I saw incapacitated pilgrims being carried by others. Faces were enraptured in their faith. The seventh time round, I prayed two *Rak'ahs,* prostrating myself. . . . As I did so the *muṭawwif* fended pilgrims off to keep me from being trampled.

He and I next drank water from the well of Zamzam. Then we ran between the two hills, Safā and Marwa, where Hagar wandered over the same earth, searching for water for her child Ismā'īl. Three separate times after that I visited the Great Mosque and circumambulated the *Ka'bah.* The next day we set out after sunrise toward Mount 'Arafāt, thousands of us crying in unison: *Labbaika, Labbaika,* and *Allāhu akbar.* Mecca is surrounded by the crudest mountains I have ever seen: they seem to be made of the slag of a blast furnace. No vegetation is on them at all. Arriving about noon, we prayed and chanted from noon until sunset and the *'aṣr* and *maghrib* prayers were performed.

Finally we lifted our hands in prayer and thanksgiving, repeating God's words: "There is no god but God. He has no partner: His are authority and praise. Good emanates from Him and He has power over all things."

Standing on Mount 'Arafāt had concluded the essential rites of being a pilgrim to Mecca. . . . The *Iḥrām* had ended. We cast the traditional seven stones at the devil. Some had their hair and their beards cut. I decided that I was going to let my beard remain. I wondered what my wife Betty and our little daughters were going to say when they saw me with a beard when I got back to New York. New York seemed a million miles away. . . .

I remember one night at Muzdalīfah with nothing but the sky overhead, I lay awake amid sleeping Muslim brothers and I learned that pilgrims from every land—every color and class and rank, high officials and beggars alike—all snored in the same language.[13]

There are numerous manuals of prayers for the *Ḥajii.* Malcolm X, in the preceding narrative, quotes the prayer of entering at *Bāb al-Salām,* the gate of Mecca. Here are devotions translated from *Manāsik al-Ḥajj wa Ad'iyat al-Ṭawāf* (Liturgy of the *Ḥajj* and Petitions during Circumambulation), Cairo, 1357 AH

Upon beholding the noble sanctuary, let him bless God thrice and recite the Takbīr (the ascription: God is most great) *thrice, and say:*

There is no god save God alone. He has no like and unto Him is the power and unto Him the praise. He is mighty over all things. I take refuge with the Lord of the house from unbelief and poverty, from the torment of the grave and from a narrow heart and an anguished bosom. May the blessing of God be upon our Lord Muḥammad, upon his people and his companions. Peace upon them all.

O God, let this house increase in honour, reverence, grandeur, awe, exaltedness, and righteousness. Increase, O Lord, those who do it honour, who magnify and esteem it among those who have made pilgrimage thither and who resort hither in veneration, honour, worship, in awe, dignity, and righteousness.

This is the confession of intention to circumambulate the Ka'bah:

O God, I desire the circumambulation of Thy holy house: enable me thereto and accept of me seven circuits, the circuits of the pilgrimage, of the holy visit, seeing it is performed unto God, the Exalted, to Him be power and majesty.

Then he kisses the Black Stone and raises his hands saying:

In the Name of God; God is most great; unto God be praise.

Prayer of the First Circuit

Praise be to God, glory to God. There is no god save God. God is most great. There is no might and no strength save in God most High, the great. Blessing and peace be upon the Apostle of God, may God send blessing and peace upon him. O God, I come unto Thee out of faith in Thee and belief in Thy words, in reliance upon Thy covenant and in obedience to Thy law, the *Sunnah* of thy Prophet and Thy beloved, Muḥammad, may peace and blessing be upon him, O God, I ask Thee for pardon and favour and constant clemency in the things of religion, in this world and in the next, safety in paradise and escape from the fire.

Prayer of the Second Circuit

O God, truly this house is Thy house, the sanctuary is Thy sanctuary, the security is Thine. The servant is Thy servant. I am Thy servant and the son of Thy servant. This is the doing of one seeking refuge with Thee from the fire. Then make our flesh and our frame inviolate from the fire. O God, cause us to love faith and adorn it in our hearts. Cause us to detest unbelief, transgression, and disobedience. Make us to be among the rightful. O God, defend us from Thy punishment on the day when Thou raisest Thy servants. O God, cause me to inherit paradise without a reckoning.

Prayer of the Third Circuit

O God, I take refuge with Thee from doubt, from *shirk* [polytheism], separatism and hypocrisy, from evil character and evil outlook, from calamity of substance or kindred or child. O God, I ask Thee Thy favour and paradise. And I seek refuge with Thee from Thy wrath and the fire. O God, I take refuge with Thee from the terror of the grave and I take refuge with Thee from danger in living and danger in dying.

Prayer of the Fourth Circuit

O God, cause it to be a righteous pilgrimage and a grateful striving. Let guilt be forgiven. Let this be a righteous and accepted deed, a transaction which is never voided, O Thou who knowest what is in the heart. Lead me forth, O God, from the shadows into the light. O God, I ask of Thee the things that properly belong to Thy mercy and the sureness of Thy forgiveness, security from all iniquity and a full share [booty] of righteousness, safety in the garden and escape from the fire. Lord, make me assured with that wherewith Thou hast endowed me and bless me in Thy gifts. Cause everything of which I am repentant to be retrieved by good from Thee.

Prayer of the Fifth Circuit

O God, shelter me under the shadow of Thy throne on that day when there is no shelter save the shadow of Thy throne, and nought abides save Thy countenance. Give me water from the reservoir of Thy Prophet, our Lord Muḥammad asked of Thee—may the blessing and peace of God be upon him—a joyous, health-giving draught, which we shall never thirst again. O God, I ask of Thee the good which Thy Prophet, our Lord Muḥammad—may the blessing and peace of God be upon him—asked of Thee. I take refuge with Thee from the evil from which he sought refuge with Thee, he, They Prophet our Lord Muḥammad. O God, I ask of Thee paradise and its favour and whatever will bring me nigh unto it—of word or deed or work. I take refuge with Thee from the fire and from whatever, in word or deed or work, would bring me nigh to it.

Prayer of the Sixth Circuit

O God, Thou has much against me in respect of my relations with Thee and with Thy creation. O God, forgive me what is due unto Thee and unto Thy creation and take it off from me. By Thy gracious glory make me well-satisfied without what Thou hast disallowed. By obedience unto Thee keep me from rebelliousness against Thee and by Thy goodness keep me from any save Thee, O Thou who art of wide forgiveness. O God, verily Thy house is great and Thy countenance is gracious. Thou, O God, art forbearing, gracious, and great. Thou lovest to pardon: therefore, pardon me.[14]

DEVOTIONS OF THE SHĪ'AH

The Passion Play of Shī'ah Islam (see: *House of Islam,* pp. 79–80) during the month of Ramaḍān commemorates the tragedy of Karbalā' in lower Iraq, where Ḥusain, grandson of the Prophet, was put to death by the forces of Yazīd, the second Umayyad Caliph. A nineteenth century English publication in two volumes, *The Miracle Play of Hasan and Ḥusain,* presents a fascinating text of the commemorative drama, as gathered from oral tradition by Lewis Pelly. His documentation was a notable contribution to study of a deep religious expression within the minority segment of the house of Islam. There is no single authoritative text, as the content varies in detail in the Shī'ah dispersion. But the theology of the theme of innocent suffering and the mystery of vicarious merit runs through the whole story and its expressive liturgical dramatization. The central martyrdom of Ḥusain is prefaced by a series of shorter enactments of other sacred sufferers, whose tribulations are seen as prophetic of those in which they culminate at Karbalā'. Thus in the Play of Joseph, Gabriel says to Jacob:

> Peace be to thee, thou wise prophet: the incomparable God, sending thee salutation says: "What thinkest thou, O afflicted one? Is thy son Joseph more precious than Muḥammad's dear grandson?"
>
> Jacob replies: "O may a thousand ones like me and my Joseph be a ransom for Ḥusain. May a thousand Josephs be the dust of his feet."
>
> Gabriel: "Come and peep through my finger: behold thence the land of Karbalā'. . . . One shall hear no cry from that holy family but for bread and water. Their sad voices shall reach the very throne of the Majesty on high. They shall subsist only on the tears of their own eyes."

In the play about the death of his infant son, Ibrāhīm, Muḥammad himself yields up to Ḥusain the propitiatory merit for his people's sins and declares: "We are one another's soul and body," and is assured: "Since thou (Muḥammad) makest Ḥusain a man of sorrow and acquainted with grief on behalf of thy people, no doubt God will forgive all of them in that day for that Imām's meritorious blood's sake." In a play called *The Disobedient Son,* Ḥusain's intercession suffices to bring back a son from perdition, when all other intercessors have failed. Ḥusain achieves this by pleading, in prospect, the virtue of his death at Karbalā' and in conclusion Muḥammad prays: "O God, be gracious towards my sinful followers for the merit of the blood of Ḥusain."

A later scene depicts Muḥammad on his deathbed telling Ḥusain of the Karbalā' that is to be. Ḥusain declares his readiness for any sacrifice and adds: "My heart within me is sounding like a flute. Where-ever I set my face, first or last, there is a Karbalā'." Later again, Muḥammad speaks to him from the sepulchre and calls him "the pilgrim of God . . . a little more and thou shalt pitch thy tents in the plain of tribulation." Ḥusain answers that he is going to offer himself voluntarily for the sake of his people. "Now I am free, I have washed my hands of life: I have girded myself to do the will of God."

The climax of the historical tragedy is steadily built up—Ḥusain's departure from Medina, premonitions of impending sorrow, the killing of three servants of Ḥusain, each of whom protests a willingness to die in the cause. Then follows the final onslaught.

'Alī Akbar, son to Ḥusain, dies first, citing the example of the ram sacrificed instead of Ismā'īl in the Quranic account of the testing of Abraham. Cannot he, 'Alī Akbar, be as a ram in the stead of Ḥusain? "I, being a sacrifice," he cries, "must proceed toward the altar and, being a traveller on the way of faith, must repair to my destiny." His shroud is his nuptial robe.

Scene xviii deals with the death of Qāsim, son of Ḥasan, who was bridegroom to Fāṭimah, daughter of Ḥusain. It opens with Ḥusain saying: "The host of grief (that is, Ḥusain) is inviting souls to the banquet of lamentation, Moses on Mount Sinai is shedding tears at my pitiable condition. Jesus, Son of Mary, is groaning aloud over my miserable state." 'Alī Akbar rides out against the hostile forces and dies, then follow 'Abbās, Hāshim, and others, who die defending Ḥusain. Scene xxiii brings his final martyrdom. He puts on an old dirty garment, representing the foulness of his murderers, the chief of whom, Shimar, cries: "I care not about the conflict of the Day of Judgement. I am a worshipper of Yazīd and have no fear of God. . . . I can make the great throne of the Lord to shake. . . . I am one who has no share in Islam."

Muḥammad appears and comforts Ḥusain and says: "At present thou art thirsty but tomorrow thou shalt be a distributor of the water of Al-Kauthar (stream of Paradise)." Ḥusain's mother, Fāṭimah, daughter of the Prophet, also appears. The women mourn and bewail. "The wolf of death tore my Joseph's coat in pieces." Ḥusain cries: "All the sorrows and troubles of this world have overwhelmed me."

A series of imaginary scenes follow, all enlarging the theme of Karbalā' as the very fulcrum of earth's tragic stories. An envoy from Europe, oppressed at the sight of Ḥusain's head impaled at Damascus, denounces the Caliph Yazīd and is slaughtered for his temerity. He dies as a Muslim wondering why Jesus did not descend from heaven when Ḥusain's head was struck off his body: Miraculously the severed head recites Surah 24:35: "God is the light . . ." and a lady who, years later, passes by the field of Karbalā' is struck by its beauty, halts and pitches camp, only to find that blood oozes out where the tent pegs are struck in. Sleeping, she learns the story of Husain and by a vision of him is constrained to Islamize.

Accompanied as the *Miracle Plays* are by the deep emotions of Shī'ah rituals and chanting, they represent a powerful discord (to borrow a musical metaphor) in the harmony of power and success, of victory and strength, by which Sunnī history and instinct are expressed.[15]

CELEBRATING MUḤAMMAD

The devotional life of Islam and the role Muḥammad plays in simple piety may be understood from the numerous manuals written for celebration of the Prophet's *Maulid,* or birthday, when poems and tributes appear in all the newspapers. The following extracts are taken from one such manual (4th edition), published at Damascus in 1941, and written by Shaikh Yūsuf ibn Ismā'īl al-Nabahānī, who died in 1932. It has the title: *Al-Naṭm al-Badī 'fī-Maulid al-Nabī al-Shafī',* "The Sweet Order (of verses) for the Birthfeast of the Prophet Intercessor." After quoting Surah 9:128: "Verily there has come to you a messenger from among yourselves, one who sets great store by what you undergo, watchful over you, gentle and merciful to believers. If they turn their backs, say: 'God is my sufficiency. There is no god but He: in Him is my trust. He is the Lord of the mighty throne,'" it continues:

> Praise be to God for His benefits, the praise of one who is sincere in his indebtedness. I praise Him. Praise be for His goodnesses in that He has favored us with His prophets, with Muḥammad who is lord of every servant. I bear witness that God is alone the worshipped, and that Muḥammad is the best of His creation, His culminating apostle, the renewer. Every one who believes in Him is without doubt eternalized in the gardens of eternity. May his Lord bless him and send him peace, his people likewise and those whose desire is towards them, his companions, the leaders, the stars of the heaven and their followers and all the *'ulamā'* and from every guide among mankind. . . .
>
> Every single invocation made upon him God makes tenfold. This is dependably clear in the tradition according to Muslim, the traditionalist, which has a wide fame. It is true beyond all criticism. If God Himself, my Lord, were to call down blessing upon him once, then a thousand thousands more would be appropriate. So see how great the benefit avails from your invocation and what reward of enlightenment. Be alert to it, if you be of rightful mind.
>
> The light of Muḥammad was the first creation of God and the genesis of mankind. He is lord of every lord who prophesied of old before the body's clay, he being the origin alike of both parent and child, being before, and after, the creation of Adam.
>
> His light was the first creation of God, whence came mankind, their hidden things and their open things. Around the throne [of God] was his expansive

fullness. His fame is a record after him inexhaustibly wherever existence goes.

From the light of the Prophet all things came to be: the height was his creation and the depths also. The universe is derivative, the Prophet primary. In the worlds there is nothing comparable to him. But for him, mankind would never have been freed to be.

Then the Creator created Adam from a clay, following the creation of the world and singularly favored him with the light, the light of Hāshim (name of Muḥammad's family)—Muḥammad, the guide, the father of the worlds. So let man be a wonder to you down all the generations.

God made for him Eve and he inclined towards her with longing and in his presence she showed reluctance and it was said: "Give her her bridal right justly and invoke blessing on Muḥammad the praiseworthy."

And they dwelt together in the garden of the All-Merciful, well pleased with their happy lot, until *Iblīs,* the devil, came with his lying accusation and they ate and were confounded, both of them and came to a settled abode in the earth—in India. And sons were born to Adam and Shith was the best of them assuredly and there was bestowed upon him the light of virtue and he was commanded to be a faithful preserver, giving commands to those who came after him in their sequence.

At length there came the best of mankind, purest in lineage and esteem, from the finest of all the diversity of peoples, noblest in breeding, his grandfather, his mother, his father alike the worthiest. His glory spreads its splendor everywhere. The light of the most perfect of prophets passed unfailing from master to master, like a torch before the brow, a light which the thoughtful and the thoughtless alike can see, like a star riding in its blessed sky.

At length the light rested on the brow of our master 'Abdallāh, to the chosen one the best of fathers. There is nothing opprobrious attaching to 'Abdallāh's glorious name and his mother, too, is exempt from all things mean. Was not their faith in what had to be? From them came the guide of the world: how, then, could he who is the mercy to the worlds be other than mercy to his own two parents? Cut off the tongue of one who says this Nay! . . .

Alas! alas! decreed it was in his orphanhood that his father died before his mother bore him. The very angels of heaven grieved with his grief and cried unto their Lord in His decree. And He said: "Leave to me my pure one and my servant."

Neither of them passed the age of twenty years and they had no others sons but him. Had they survived he would have been the very apple of their eyes. How delighted they would have been with him in things both mundane and religious. Theirs would have been happiness in every realm.

But his Lord wanted to separate him into His love alone, other children apart. He did not grant him others of his parents' begetting, guidance being given into his sole custody, that he might to none be beholden. . . .

Listen to the attributes whose bringing to birth is light, the light of the chosen prophet, the bringer of good tidings, the adornment of the pure, the . . . splendour of the ages, the guide of humanity into his righteous religion. His law has not ceased to be . . . the guide within them.

God of His favor manifested wonders to his mother while she bore him to show her the greatness of his rank. . . .

Concluding these paeans of celebration of Āminah and of Muḥammad's natal glory, the singer turns to petition.

We beseech Thee, O Lord, by his standing before Thee, as those who rely upon Thee, . . . our Lord and seek of Thee the good we desire, inspire all into the path of true guidance. By his merit, O Lord, hear us, and grant us and those we love our petition. O my God, accept our word and our deed and in truth make good ourselves and our people, defending them from every thing of ill.

Forgive, O Lord, our misdeeds and cover our faults: facilitate what we hope and bear down hard on what we dread. Set hateful things far away. Forgive . . . our parents and our patriarchs, our brethren and our sons; do well to them in this world and the next and bring all to the secure abode and we with them to the gardens of immortality.

Our Lord, do Thou preserve the Sultan, make his well being and ours to increase; give him, victory, O Lord, over his enemies and, O my God, protect our religion and our world. . . . of things through him, our laborers, too, and our army.

Prosper his subjects and his workers, beautify their state and bring him to the satisfaction of his hopes. Let his words and his deeds be such as may evoke our praise. . . .

O Lord have mercy upon . . . the *Ummah* of the chosen one, in every age and in every . . . haunt: guard them from the power of the fates, in every land and clime on plateau and in valley.

By the Prophet, O Lord, hear our petitions: by him, O Lord, set at rest our fears, enhance our state and exchange our ills for good, delivering us from envy and from hatred. . . .[16]

Dalā'il al-Khairāt (Guides to Goodnesses), a very widely favored book of personal prayers, contains this eulogy of the Prophet, to be used at *Maulid* season and at any time. It celebrates Muḥammad as

The man of the stalwart staff,
The man who wore sandals, the man of argument,
The man of sound reason, the man of power,
The wearer of the turban,
The hero of the night of ascent, the hero of the sword,
The rider of Burāq, the noble rider,
He who traversed the seven spheres,
The intercessor for all creatures,
The man who gave thanks when he abstained from taking food,
The man for whom the palm trees wept
And sighed at his departure.
He from whom the birds of the air sought influence,
To whom the very stones did homage at his self restraint.
He of whom the gazelles sought intercession in clear speech,
The devoted evangelist, the brilliant lamp,
The man to whom the camel made its complaint,
For whom the sparkling water burst forth in the midst of his comrades.
He who was pure and yet purified,
The light of lights.
He for whom the moon opened out.
He who was good and did good,
The Apostle to whom was given the privilege of access.
The spreading dawn, the brilliant star,
The trusty hand-hold,

Monitor of the people of the earth . . .
The man at whose light the flowers opened,
The man at whose blessing the fruits matured.
The man at whose promise the trees moved themselves from every direction.
The man at whose lights all other lights shone forth,
The man to the skirts of whose robes
Wild creatures clung when he was travelling in desert lands.[17]

THE MOSQUE PREACHER

The mosque sermon has been a vital instrument in the interpretation and application of Islam within its household and is, therefore, an important index to the Muslim dimensions of religion. Here is a sermon translated from *Dīwān al-Khuṭab al-Ḥadīthah fī-l-Wa'ẓi wa-l-Irshād,* "A collection of Modern Sermons in the Art of Preaching and Guidance," by a former Grand Shaikh of Al-Azhar, Muṣṭafā al-Marāghī. The theme is "Faith in God."

Praise be to God, Who guides the hearts of His chosen by faith and makes tranquil the hearts of His elect in confidence. I bear witness that there is no god but God. In His dominion nothing occurs save by His willing it. I bear witness that our Lord Muḥammad is the apostle of God, whose resolution was not weakened by adversities.

O God, bless, preserve and be gracious to our Lord Muḥammad, his people, his companions and those who follow him.

God most High has said in His glorious Book: "He who believes in God, his heart is guided, and God is in all things most knowing." [Surah 64:11]

You who worship God: faith is man's devoting of his heart to God and his acceptance of what God has revealed to His prophets. It is his belief in His determination and His will. It is a breath from the spirit of God whereby He confirms those who sincerely believe among His worshippers in trials. It is a torch lighted from the light of God, irradiating the hearts of the chosen ones among those who love Him. Faith has signs which point the way to it, and conviction has indications which guide men towards it. God most High said: "Those believers whose hearts glow at the mention of God, and whose faith is increased when His signs are read to them, those who rely upon their Lord and perform the prayer and give generously of what We have bestowed upon them—these are the true believers indeed, they have honor with their Lord, and forgiveness and gracious benefits." [Surah 2:2–4]

These are the marks of true faith: the fear of God which impels a man to magnify Him and extol Him; meditation on His signs which stimulates him to trust in His promise; reliance upon God . . . leading him to conformity to divine decree, so that he reverences God in his prayers and is obedient in his almsgiving. God will increase him in honor and forgive him his evil deeds, bestowing upon him gracious blessings and guiding him in the path of the upright.

Ye worshippers of God, how wondrous it is that the things of the believer are altogether for good: it is only so for him who believes. If some good fortune befalls him, he gives thanks and it becomes to him a blessing: if some misfortune befalls, he is patient and it becomes a blessing. A gift does not make him negligent, nor does catastrophe anger him. That is how Muḥammad was. God tried him with blessings and he received them with great gratitude: He tested him with calamity and he met it with splendid patience. He went one day to the people of Al-Ṭā'if to preach to them the message of his Lord. They stoned him until the blood flowed. He took refuge under a vine and sought shade there. Then he turned unto God and said: "O God, I plead with Thee in the feebleness of my strength which has borne with men. O Thou most merciful, Thou art the Lord of those who acknowledge their weakness. Thou art my Lord. If it is not Your anger which is upon me I will not care anything of it."

Such also was the life of his companions, the believers. They did not weary under the animosity of the unbelievers and did not despair at their seeming victory. They drew out of failure the means of success and out of disaster the road to victory, taking refuge with their Lord in loyal resolve and in entire confidence. They it was who hearkened to God and to the apostle after wounds befell them. They it was to whom the people said: "Verily men have gathered together against you, so fear them." But such words only increased their faith and they replied: "We have considered God and the grace of the One we trust." So they overcame by grace and favor from God and no evil touched them. They followed a course well pleasing to God, who is the Lord of great goodness.

O ye worshippers of God, faith guides believers, both individuals and communities, to bear hardships, however great they be, and to cleave open the way to a happy life, however difficult its attainment, and to the performing of religious obligations, however arduous. Hardships reward the believer with rest, with quiet and confidence. Difficulties repay him with strength and courage. Acts of worship make him grow in faith. Fasting is half of patience: patience is half of faith. How great is our need in this life of a disposition that will implant fasting in men's souls. For it nourishes the feeling of mercy and trains the power of the will and the purpose, and lifts man to the loftiest character. Prayer is a link between the servant and his Lord, and between the believer and his fellow believers. Pilgrimage means mutual awareness and mutual goodwill, sacrifice, patience and fortitude. *Zakāt* is goodness, liberality, righteousness, and the payment of debt.

Then fear God, O ye worshipper of God, and lay hold of the bond of faith. For that is the rope of God, strong to bind the word of believers. Take delight in God's blessings and in His glories beautify yourselves. May God cause quietness to descend upon you and bring your hearts into unity.

Tradition records that the apostle of God said to his companions: "Ask me anything you wish." A man cried: "O Apostle of God, what is faith?" He said: "Sincerity." "And what is conviction?" And he said: "Honest dealing."[18]

REFLECTIVE EXPERIENCE AS A MUSLIM

Muḥammad Fāḍil Jamālī, Prime Minister of Iraq in the 1950s, and a well-known Shī'ah thinker and statesman, was imprisoned after the Revolution in Baghdad in July, 1958, and for a year and a half lay under sentence of death. During his incarceration he wrote letters to his son, 'Abbās, at the University of Beirut. One, dated 25 March 1961, gives a brief summary of the meaning of Islam. The translation from Arabic is by Dr. Jamālī.

Dear 'Abbās,

After presenting you my good greetings, I pray for your safety, success and guidance. . . . I have read again your letter, dated February 11. In it you say: "What is religion? Let us take Islam as an example of a religion. I do not believe that it is an easy matter to define the Islamic religion, as you can hardly find two groups of people who agree in their opinion about it."

I answer you with the following:

1. I have already referred in a previous letter to what I think is the meaning of religious experience, as well as to the evolution of religions and their development, and I told you that the highest stage which the spiritual evolution of man has reached is faith in God, the One and Only, the God of Abraham, Moses, Jesus and Muḥammad, peace on them all.

Islam is ". . . the faith of your father Abraham: he named you Muslims before. . . ." [Surah 22:78]

2. Islam, as I understand it, is not blind fanaticism and sectarianism. It is not doctrinal squabbles and philosophical and theological argumentation. It is not laziness and negligence in development and construction, moral and material. It is not intellectual stagnation and superstition. It is not charlatanism and quackery. It is not hypocrisy and sycophancy, asceticism and self-deprivation, or poverty and disease, or dirt and ugliness. It is not indulgence in sensual pleasures and hareems. None of these belong to Islam.

If you dismiss all these from the field of Islam you will find that Islam is clear and simple, easy to understand, and no two who are guided by God and whose hearts have been enlightened by the light of faith could disagree about it.

3. Literally Islam means man's surrender of himself to God and his complete submission and resignation to the guidance of God. If man submits and surrenders to the will of God, the Almighty, spiritually, intellectually, physically, and in action, then he is a Muslim in the literal sense.

4. In legal terms a Muslim is one who says: "I bear witness that there is no god but God and Muḥammad is the messenger of God." On this all Muslims are agreed.

5. Realistically Islam is a divine order which directs the life of the Muslim in all its phases, spiritual, social, political and economic. For it consists of: (a) a creed, (b) rituals, (c) a social order, (d) morality.

I may describe the religion of Islam as a totalist religion which is liberal and liberating. It differs from those religions which care for the spiritual aspects subject to external influences.

It also differs from all political totalitarian systems like Fascism, Nazism, or Communism, which are despotic towards the individual and which make the individual subject to the leader or the Party. All these totalitarian systems try to control the individual by external pressure. They limit his freedom, unlike Islam, which liberates the individual from any external authority of material greed. Unless man trespasses against his brother man, he fears nobody but God, and, as long as man obeys the commands of his Creator and accepts His prohibitions, he enjoys complete freedom.

Islam is a democratic system with no excess. It controls individuals without subjugation. Islam liberates man from fear and need, guarantees freedom of conscience and calls to social inter-dependence. Besides all this, it is the religion of peace—peace that is founded on right and justice between individuals and nations. . . .

I do not believe that a person with an enlightened outlook faces any obstacle which could not be surmounted. Muslim youth today could be directed towards Islam and imbued with its upright principles. I hereby transcribe for you verse 177 of the Surah [2], The Cow.

"It is not righteousness that you turn your face towards the east and the west, but righteousness is this—that one should believe in God and the Last Day and the angels and the Book and the prophets, and give away wealth out of love for Him to the near of kin, and orphans and the needy and the wayfarer and the beggars, and for (the emancipation of) the captives, and keep up prayer and pay the poor-rates: and the fulfillers of their obligation, when they undertake one, and the patient in distress and affliction and in time of conflict—it is these who are sincere and God-fearing."

This verse contains the bases of the creed, rituals, and some of the important aspects of social and moral life of the Islamic religion.

In conclusion I ask God to grant us all the blessings of faith and to save us from the slippery path of the philosophers and theologians and from the argumentations of the atheist-materialists.

Fāḍil

In a later letter he confides:

I am reading the Qur'ān for the thirty-fifth time since entering the prison and every time I read it I discover wisdom and hidden things to which I had not been attentive in previous readings. The enjoyment of the blessings of the Qur'ān requires persistence in reading it and also requires a good knowledge of the Arabic language. For Quranic expression possesses beauty and grandeur which has not been approached by the highest of what the Arabs produced in terms of entrancing expression.[19]

A representative picture of traditional Muslim piety can be drawn from Aḥmad Amīn's sensitive portrayal of the life of his father, a Quranic scholar in Cairo, in the second half of the nineteenth century. Aḥmad Amīn himself (1888–1954) was a historian, a man of letters, a judge, and an educationalist. His story in *Ḥayātī,* 'My Life,' published in Cairo in 1950, gives many revealing glimpses into patterns of society, of schooling, of family life, as well as the ebb and flow of political events. Not least of the valuable features of his autobiography is its acute awareness of the shift of culture attitudes, between his own modest political and intellectual interests on the one hand, and the dogged, static, dutiful religious submissiveness of his father on the other—not to mention the contrasted ebullience and acquisitive brusqueness of the next generation, his own offspring in the third generation. He writes of his father:

He was about eighty years old. . . . I was by his side when he died, commending to my care my mother and sisters, and calling upon God to be my help.

So ended an assiduous, difficult life, filled with toil and effort in the pursuit of knowledge and of a livelihood. Seldom was he without some book he was reading or writing, and his income was dependent on the knowledge he imparted by teaching, or a book he was editing and the like. His illness did not hinder him from pursuing his work, nor did any trouble that befell him. He was utterly religious, frequent in the prayers and much given to the reading of the Qur'ān and of tradition. He observed *Zakāt* and gave his alms to the poor among his neighbors. He kept the fast and went on pilgrimage. He used even to pray during the night and make intercession before God. If he fell into any wrong, or something he felt to be wrong, he was profuse in his penitence and his desire for forgiveness. He took an ascetic attitude to this world and renounced the seeking of wealth beyond what was necessary for the needs of his family. Anything he had in excess he saved as far as he could for an emergency.

His recollection of death was frequent and he had by heart many traditions about the emptiness of the world and the worthlessness of its affairs before God. He prepared a burial place for himself where he recited the Qur'ān whenever he visited it, hoping that thereby it would become a blessed abode for him after his decease. He despised the world and its pomp and pleasure.

I saw him on one occasion dressed in ceremonial clothes to attend the *Mahmal* Festival (the ceremony of preparing to send the sacred carpet from Egypt to Mecca to cover the *Ka'bah*—an annual feast day). He stood awhile hesitantly in the room and then took them off and threw them into a corner with the words: "This world's life is play and show." Seating himself he recited the Qur'ān.

Every one in the quarter where he lived respected him, for he was the outstanding religious personage. People were deferential to him when he passed. Both rich and poor resorted to him over religious questions and *fatwas* on matters like marriage, divorce and inheritance. The notables of the district asked him to give them religious studies in the home of one or another of them and at feasts and festivals they lavished gifts on him.

In food, drink, dress and sleep he was temperate and simple. He ate what was laid before him without complaining and slept on a coarse mattress without a bedstead. His dress was neat, but plain and unpretentious.

He was a strict family disciplinarian and only gave his children necessities, in order that they should not be spoiled. He supervised their studies rigorously, testing them constantly in their memorizing of the Qur'ān and texts and in their grasp of their lessons. If they made mistakes he would recite the formulae: "God is our sufficiency," and: "In God only is there power and strength." He might be angry and beat them. Our only intercourse with him was either a new lesson or a test on an old. I do not recollect that he was ever playful with us and he seldom laughed with us. Our few occasions of relaxation and fun were when he was absent. When he was about it was all fear and awe and keeping our spirits in check.

The world he really knew was his beloved Azhar, the mosque, his books, and the neighbors in the garden with whom he had contact. Politics, the British Occupation, economic affairs, social and cultural life—of these, and anything else beyond the quarter he inhabited, he knew nothing. He only read the newspapers when they chanced to come to hand and only rarely did he meet with people who talked about general matters. . . .

He was intelligent and excelled in his knowledge of Azharite books. He was fond of reading literary and historical works, but without going deeply into them or reading systematically. He wrote poetry on occasions, but only after choosing some piece out of a collection of verses, whose accent and rhythm he could imitate, and whose sentiments he could borrow. Thus his versification was ponderous and flat. . . . Despite his parental severity, he was tender towards his children—a tenderness which made itself evident in his distress when his son fell sick, and his anguish of heart when he died, as well as in his yearning over his children's absence.

He was more solicitous for my education than he was for my brothers'. . . . When I ceased to be under his care and discipline after I entered the School of Jurisprudence, I began to appreciate his goodness. My fear of him was replaced by a fondness and a deep respect. . . . This change of relationship was mutual: he repaid love with love. He left the disposal of his property and his affairs to me and, relieved of that distraction, he lived with his grief, his illness and his religion.

When he died I felt a burning sorrow. An irreplaceable pillar had fallen, leaving a gap which would never be filled. God have mercy on him.

For his own part, Aḥmad Amīn ends the story of his career in scholarship, his long engagement with Arabic letters and Islamic history, by musing on the vicissitudes through which he had personally passed and the significance of his inner biography. In his prose at the close of *Ḥayātī*, the reader has access to a modest, reflective, questing, yet staunch form of Islam, all the more communicative for being less explicit.

The foregoing are the major events that befell during my life from youth to old age, events which in their succession have shaped my character as it is today. They might have been otherwise, and then I would be other than I am. But by divine will what happened happened and the flow of things fashioned me accordingly.

I once wrote an article describing a friend and using my characterisation of him as a means to self-description. This was how it ran:

"I have a friend whose contrasts and contradictions of character and scholarship I find readily familiar. He is very sensitive and shy and comes to the Senate with a faltering step and an uneasy air about his movements. He sits down nervously on the first bench he can find, consumed with bashfulness. His hand shakes when coffee is offered to him and he is all of a tremble. Perhaps he manages to disguise his shyness and make it seem that coffee does not interest him or that he does not require it. . . . He leaves as he came in and wearily utters a sigh of relief when the session is over. . . . He loves solitude, not out of any misanthropic feeling but simply to avoid meeting people.

Yet for all his shyness he is bold to the point of peremptoriness . . . giving his mind without diffidence or compunction. He may even be outspoken to the point of wounded feelings. . . .

The enigma goes further: for he is at once ambitious and content, alert and languid, seeking after the heights with unstinted endeavor and with set mind enduring the most tedious and strenuous labors to that end. Yet for all his decisive resolution, he has something of the Sufi about him and despises this world and its ways, its pleasures and miseries, retreating with a sort of scorn into a posture of indifference. He is satisfied with his lot as time unfolds. With all that he cherishes hope of great fame. . . . He finds himself going back constantly to his Sufi saying: 'Bury your existence in obscurity and whatever befalls you that you cannot so bury will produce no effect.' . . .

It was indeed a strange quality—this high measure of himself and his capacities, combined with a humility prone to self-depreciation and a clipping of the wings of pride. His self-esteem has to do with what is insignificant to big men, and where small men have airs he deems himself unimportant. He is haughty in his relations with the great and takes company with the poor, commiserating with them and supplying their needs. . . . His ways are enigmatic, attraction and repulsion mingled.

His head might be likened to a disordered store, a shop all topsy-turvy, with threadbare clothes side by side with precious stones, where the traditional *Sunnah* and the theory of evolution and progress jostle with each other, the school of the determinists with the voluntarists. In his library ancient manuscript books on old subjects, which white ants have eaten and where time has left its traces, sit cheek by jowl with the most modern European works, up to date in printing, binding, and in outlook. Yet both sorts persist in his receptive mind.

There is a certain impulse towards atheism in his thinking, though it goes very much against his nature. If his intellect has sometimes known doubt, his heart has always held with faith. He has both ascetics and heavy drinkers, profligates and worshippers, in his circle of friends."

After concluding his third-person portrait of himself, Aḥmad Amīn elaborates certain other features of his pilgrimage through life and of his attitude to writing. After assessing his habitual ways, he adds:

There is within me, perhaps enigmatically, a real Sufi strain. At times I feel a religious urge which fills my soul and thrills my heart. It manifests itself most of all when I am impressed by the scenes of nature, such as broad acres under cultivation, ripening trees, the brilliance of the stars, sunrise and sunset, the surge of the sea, and the music of the birds. All these I feel I want to make my own, to take into my embrace and to drink, as it were, the cup of them. I find a certain rapture at the sight of them and of God in them. Yet I know too within myself a real regret that I have not nourished this inner sense as I ought. I have not kept faith with it, nor cherished it, as it deserved. . . .

Were I to pass in review my whole life from first to last it would be a sequence with many twists and turns and some strange episodes. What a far cry it is from the closed book back to the beginning! How many new departures and changes of course and conflicting possibilities! . . . My intellectual outlook has changed, too, with the movement of my life. I no longer belong with the Azharite mentality, nor yet with that of my associates in the School of Law. A little while ago I met one who had been among my closest friends there and a man then most congenial to my thinking. We had a long conversation, only to realize that we were worlds apart. It is a difference like that of which Al-Jāḥiẓ spoke and Imrū-l-Qais knew:

"While you speak, the stream has carried us along together:
My camel is worn out. O Imrū-l-Qais, dismount."

And the lines of 'Alī ibn al-Jahm:

"We have turned in together for the night:
But were a glass of wine to be poured out,
It could not blend what is betwixt us."

In my youth, I let my imagination play around my future. I had the highest ideals for myself—in character, conduct and self-improvement—ideals which by and by came into collision with things as they are and with the context around me and the trials I encountered. I was disappointed, too, at how many people let me down. All of this meant a slow attrition of my idealism. I tried hard to maintain my standards in face of these currents, but was incapable of holding them intact. In lesser or greater degree, I was myself overborne and for this reason regard myself as having been a better person in my youth than I am in my old age. I had more and better hope then than I have now. When I was young I held loyally to principle even when it was disadvantageous to me. I repudiated gainful actions when I considered them to involve my honor. I had high hopes of being able to achieve great things and put the world to rights. But I have seen many of these hopes evaporate: many intentions have gone awry. Here I am as an old man, tolerating what I used to repudiate, and declining from principles I used to hold obligatory. Environment, popular convention, large family burdens, weakness of will, successive tribulations—all these, with the lapse of time, may oblige a man to abandon some at least of his ideals. I am very fond of the lines:

"I curbed my inclinations while I was young,
And when time had left me gray and old
I yielded to those baser things, and contradicted progress.
Would I had been born adult
And in reverse grown younger. . . ."

It is difficult indeed rationally to analyse how it all was as it was. It is something which defies explanation by reference to social or personal factors. I have known many people with greater intelligence than I, people with stronger character and steadier resolve, folk whom every indication suggested would succeed in all they put their hands to, but who in fact failed and came to grief. There is, indeed, no fathoming it, except to say: "The goodness of God, it is bestowed on whom He wills. For in God great grace has its perfect source."

Aḥmad Amīn's retrospect is certainly a very human one. In its time and place, as well as in its temper and content, it could also be claimed that it is a very Muslim one. For the index of a religion has to be looked for in places of honest life-reflection, as well as in the more deliberate propositions, and positions, of tradition and theology.[20]

CHAPTER 3

Tradition

ḤADĪTH LITERATURE

The *ḥadīth* literature has probably had as much influence as the *Qur'ān* in shaping the Muslim religious consciousness. The massive authoritative collections of this material preserve accounts of the Prophet's example to the Muslim community. These take the form of short unconnected texts, each of which is preceded by its chain of authorities. Recorded are events in the Prophet Muḥammad's life and facts about him, events in the lives of others, about which the Prophet was asked questions or made comments, speeches by the Prophet, and statements by his companions in which they refer to him as their authority. The *ḥadīth* texts were originally transmitted orally, and after they were written down they did not undergo literary recomposition. So they retain the distinctive characteristics of oral compositions.

For this presentation, only *ḥadīth* texts have been chosen which are generally accepted by Muslims as reliable. Also this choice is limited to texts that are either of importance to the Muslim community today, or help to understand the Muslims' way of thinking. Those texts that are merely curiosities or have to do with institutions that no longer exist are not used.

The collections, all dating from the ninth and early tenth centuries, from which the following texts have been taken are as follows: the *Musnad* (*Authenticated*) of Ibn Ḥanbal, the *Ṣaḥīḥ* (*Genuine*) of Muslim Ibn al-Ḥajjāj, the *Jāmi'* (*Collection*) of Al-Tirmidhī, the *Sunan* (*Principles of Right Action*) of Abū Dāwud and the *Sunan* of Al-Dārimī.

References will be made to these collections by use of the compiler's name, the title of the section, and the number of the chapter, except in the case of Ibn Ḥanbal, where the number of the original text will be indicated, as found in Aḥmad Shākir's unfinished edition of the *Musnad* (1949–1956), or the volume and page number of the older, standard edition (1895).

The Content of Faith

Theology in the *ḥadīth* is at a rudimentary stage of development. Questions are asked which in later centuries will be the center of massive intellectual endeavors. The terms of early controversy in the community are reflected. *Ḥadīth* texts also contain, in simple declarative style, the first systematic formulations of Islamic doctrine, and these are sometimes interspersed with lively remarks by the narrators and by the Prophet, which give a vivid and picturesque impression to the reader.

The full chain of authorities is included in this first text, as an example of how every *ḥadīth* has been authenticated. In subsequent texts this will be omitted, although occasionally the first transmitter's name will be indicated. The material shown in parentheses here and elsewhere in the translations of *ḥadīth* was added by one or more of the transmitters, usually indicating a variant reading of the text. The brackets are used to note the editorial comments.

> 1. Abū Mu'āwiyyah and Al-'Amash reported to us, upon the authority of 'Umarah, that 'Abd Al-Raḥmān Ibn Yazīd had heard 'Abd Allāh Ibn Mas'ūd say, "I was hidden behind the veil of the Ka'bah. [The focal point of the Muslim pilgrimage to Mecca, but also a holy place in pre-islamic Arabian religion.] Three men approached, one Qurayshī and two Thaqafī relatives [tribesmen from the region of Mecca who opposed the Prophet at the beginning of his ministry] (or one Thaqafī and two Qurayshī relatives). They had very fat stomachs but very little knowledge in their hearts. They spoke so that I could not quite understand.
>
> "One of them said, 'What do you think, will God hear these words of ours?'
>
> Another said, 'If we raise our voices He will surely hear, but if we do not raise them, He will not hear.'
>
> Another said, 'If He hears some of what we say He will hear all.'
>
> "I reported this to the Prophet and God, may He be exalted and glorified, revealed the following verses, 'Not so did you cover yourselves, that your hearing, your eyes and your skins should not bear witness against you,' up to the words, '. . . the thought you thought about your Lord, has destroyed you, and therefore you find yourselves this morning among the losers.'" (Surah 41:21, 22)*
>
> **—Ibn Ḥanbal, No. 3614**

The god whom the Arabian tribesmen address is Allāh, the principal deity of the preislamic pantheon. This is the name that was revealed to Muḥammad as that of the one true and living God. In this story the Qurayshī and the Thaqafī men are exposed to derision because of their

*All quotations from the *Qur'ān* in this chapter are from *The Koran Interpreted,* translated by Arthur J. Arberry, © Oxford University Press 1964. Reprinted by permission of Oxford University Press.

inadequate conception of God. As is the case in many *ḥadīth,* the incident reported here provided the occasion for the revelation of verses which later were incorporated into the *Qur'ān.*

2. God, may He be exalted and glorified, said, "My mercy has prevailed over my wrath."

—Ibn Ḥanbal, No. 7297

This is one of the many sayings which the Prophet reports as coming from God Himself. Such texts are called *ḥadīth qudsī* (holy traditions), and they belong in a category apart from the *Qur'ān.* The background for this statement is the Quranic verse in Surah 6:12, where it is said of God, "He has prescribed for Himself mercy." *Raḥmah,* or mercy, is considered to be one of the basic attributes of God. So, many interpret this *ḥadīth* as meaning that, whereas mercy is extended to all men at all times, regardless of whether they deserve it or not, His wrath only manifests itself when men commit reprehensible deeds.

3. A man asked the Prophet, "What is faith?"

He replied, "Faith consists of belief in God, His angels, the meeting with Him, His Apostles, and the resurrection."

The man said, "What is *islām?*" [not Islām, the name of the religion of the Muslims, but *islām,* the Arabic noun meaning 'surrender to God'] .

He replied, "*Islām* consists of the service of God, the refusal to associate anything with Him [in His deity and in His exclusive claim to allegiance] , prayer, alms-giving, and fasting during the month of Ramaḍān."

The man said, "What does it mean to do good?"

He replied, "To serve God [or, to worship God. . . . One Arabic word may be used to convey the ideas of service and worship. This fact is an indication of the integrated view of human life as related to God according to Islam.] as though you could see Him. Even though you cannot see Him, He can see you."

The man said, "When is the last hour?"

He replied, "The one who is asked does not know any more than he who asks, but I can tell you about the signs that point to it. When the slavewoman gives birth to her master, that is one of the signs. When the naked and the barefoot become the chiefs of the people, that is one of the signs. When the shepherds take insolent pride in constructing buildings, that is one of the signs [reference to enigmatic occurrences which seem to indicate momentous social upheavals] . Then there are five things that only God knows."

After that he recited, "Surely God—He has knowledge of the Hour; He sends down the rain; He knows what is in the wombs. No soul knows what it shall earn tomorrow, and no soul knows in what land it shall die. Surely God is All-knowing, All-aware." (Surah 31:34)

Then the man slipped away. The Apostle of God said, "Send that man back to me." They tried to do so, but they could not find him.

The Apostle of God said, "It was Gabriel who came to teach the people their religion."

—Muslim, imān, 1

In this narrative is found a primitive catechism, including the distinction, to be developed in later theology, between faith as the inward act of believing, and *islām* as the outward religious expression of belief. The *Qur'ān* itself mentions this distinction. (Surah 49:14)

4. The father of 'Abd Al-Raḥmān Ibn Abī Bakrah said, "The Apostle of God said, 'Shall I not tell you about the most serious of the great sins?'

"His listeners replied, 'Yes, indeed, O Apostle of God.'

"He said, 'Making someone an associate with God in His sovereignty, then disobedience to parents'—here he sat up from his reclining position—'then false testimony (or untrue words).' And the Apostle of God kept on talking about the great sins until we wished he would stop."

—Al-Tirmidhī, birr, 4

Taking their terminology and basic information from the *Qur'ān* (Surah 53:32; 6:151), the Muslims developed a doctrine of greater sins (*kabā'ir*) and lesser sins (*ṣaghā'ir*). However, even in later theology, this doctrine stops short of a fully elaborated casuistic system.

5. Ibn Mas'ūd said, "The Apostle of God spoke to us, and he is the truthful one, the one proven to be veracious, 'Verily the elements out of which each of you is created are gathered in his mother's womb for forty days. Then they become a clot of blood for forty days, then an embryo for forty more days. After that an angel is sent to breathe into them the breath of life and to announce four decrees; the livelihood of the new creation, its span of life and the nature of its works, whether they will issue in misery or in happiness. And, by the One beside whom there is no deity, one of you may do the deeds of the people of paradise, so that between him and it there lies but the space of a cubit, and yet the written decree will prevail, and he will end up by doing the deeds of the people of hell, and will enter into it. Likewise one of you may do the deeds of the people of hell, so that between him and it there lies but the space of a cubit, and yet the written decree will prevail. He will end up by doing the deeds of the people of paradise and will enter into it.

—Al-Tirmidhī, qadar, 4

The Quranic basis for this *ḥadīth* is Surah 22:5, which describes the steps in the development of a human embryo as one of the proofs of God's power to raise the dead in the last day. Here the Quranic verse is developed to declare the transcendental divine ordering of human life in all of its aspects. The reinforcement of the idea of predestination seen at the end of the text, is evidence of the importance of this doctrine in Islamic thought.

6. The Apostle of God said, "Comparing myself with the Prophets who were before me, it is like a man who built a building of great beauty and perfection except for one brick which was missing from one of the corners of the construction. People came to walk around it and to admire it."

"They said, 'We have never seen such a beautiful building as this, except for that space where the brick is missing.'

"And I am that brick."

—Ibn Ḥanbal, No. 7479

Muḥammad is called the Seal of the Prophets (Surah 33:40), that is, the one who completes the series of messengers sent by God to various peoples throughout the history of the world.

7. The Apostle of God said, "Not one of you will enter paradise by virtue of his works."

They asked, "Not even you, O Apostle of God?"

He replied, "Not I either, unless God covers me with His mercy and grace." He then placed his hand on his head [a gesture of respect for the deity].

—Ibn Ḥanbal, No. 7473

Although there arose a marked difference of opinion among theologians as to whether or not a person may be certain that he has faith, there has always been the strong conviction in the community that ultimately one's salvation depends entirely upon the goodness of God.

8. The Apostle of God said: "There are seven kinds of people whom God will shelter on the day when there is no shelter but His: the just ruler, the young person nurtured in the worship of God, the man whose heart is filled with thoughts of the place of prayer from the time he leaves it until he returns to it, two people who love one another in God, whether together or absent from each other; the man who, when free of preoccupation, remembers God until tears flow from his eyes; the man who, when praised for his good family and his excellent character, says, 'I fear God, may He be exalted and glorified,' and the man who gives alms, and then hides the deed so that his left hand does not know what his right hand has given."

—Al-Tirmidhī, zuhd, 41

The form of this utterance is a stereotyped coordination of items into an easily remembered list. First there is a statement of what all of the items have in common and then follows the listing. The content provides an impressive example of the way in which intense social and individual piety were balanced in early Islam.

9. 'Umar said, "O Apostle of God, what do you think, are the works we do creative (or inceptive) [that is, not anticipated by the divine decree], or are they settled in advance" [by the divine decree]?

The Apostle of God said, "They are indeed settled in advance, O Ibn Al-Khaṭṭāb, and everything has been facilitated [an allusion to Surah 80:20]. Whoever is of the people of happiness will do that which leads to happiness, and whoever is of the people of misery will do that which leads to misery."

—Al-Tirmidhī, qadar, 3

'Umar's question reflects an early confrontation in the Muslim community between the advocates of absolute predestination and the Qadariyyah (see *The House of Islam*, p. 12), who held to the principle of man's free will.

10. The father of Muṣ'ab Ibn Sa'd said, "I asked the Apostle of God, 'Who are the people who have the most severe tribulation?'

He said, "The Prophets, and then after them the exemplary people, always the exemplary ones. A man suffers affliction according to the quality of his religion. If he is firm in his religion then he suffers severe afflictions. But if he is weak in his religion, well, his suffering is measured according to the worth of his religion. A man will not be without tribulation until he leaves it behind, going forth upon the earth free of sin'" [an allusion to man's final deliverance from sin].

—Al-Tirmidhī, zuhd, 45

The New Testament expresses this same thought in the words, "For the Lord disciplines him whom he loves, and chastises every son whom he receives." (Epistle to the Hebrews 12:6).

11. A man came to the Apostle of God and said, "O Apostle of God, I recite the Qur'ān, but I find that my head does not understand it."

The Apostle of God replied, "Your heart lacks faith, for truly, faith is given to a believer first, and then the Qur'ān."

—Ibn Ḥanbal, No. 6604

RITUAL

Ritual Prayer

12. Ibn 'Umar said, "While the people were praying at the early morning hour in Buqā' [a locality in Medina], a messenger came to them and said, 'During the night the Apostle of God received a revelation in which he was commanded to face in the direction of the Ka'bah when praying. So, face in that direction.' We had been facing Syria, so we turned around to the direction of the Ka'bah."

—Muslim, masājid, 13

This text gives further details on the changing of the direction for prayer which is noted in Surah 2:136–140. See *The House of Islam*, pp. 59, 64.

13. Whenever the Apostle of God went on a journey of at least three miles (or three parasangs [an ancient unit of distance, one parasang being about the equivalent of four miles] —Shu'bah was not sure of the wording), he shortened his prayer (another version: he prayed two sets of postures).

—Muslim, ṣalāt al-musāfirīn, 12

Although the rules for observing the five times of daily prayer are very precise, the Prophet's example in unusual circumstances as seen in this selection offers the possibility of delaying and combining certain prayers.

14. The Apostle of God used to say at the end of each prescribed prayer, after he had given the salutation:

"There is no deity but God alone; He has no partner. To Him belongs sovereignty and praise. He gives life and He takes it away. He is the All-powerful One. O God, no one can prevent your giving, and no one can give what you withhold. The man who enjoys good fortune from you will not benefit from his good fortune." [This enigmatic utterance is taken to mean that, unless a man's life has been filled with good deeds, any good fortune which he may have enjoyed will be of no ultimate benefit to him.]

—Al-Tirmidhī, ṣalāt, 222

The recitations prescribed or recommended for ritual prayer are all derived from the example of the Prophet, even as are the required postures (see the next two selections).

15. Abū Al-Zubayr heard Ṭawus saying, "We asked Ibn 'Abbās about sitting on the feet during prayer. [One of the postures of the ritual prayer, the position of half sitting on the heels and half kneeling, which follows the touching of the forehead to the ground. While in this position the worshipper recites certain elements of the rite.]

"He said, 'It is the practice.'

"We said, 'It seems to us that it is hard on the feet.'

"Ibn 'Abbās replied, 'It was the practice of your Prophet.'"

—Ibn Ḥanbal, No. 2855

16. Ibn 'Abbās said, "I came up behind the Apostle of God while he was prostrated in prayer. I could see the white of his armpits. He was holding his arms out from his sides, with his hands far apart."

—Ibn Ḥanbal, No. 2405

A detail is given of the way in which the Prophet performed the prostration of ritual prayer, where the forehead touches the ground.

Almsgiving

17. Ibn 'Abbās addressed the people of Al-Baṣrah [a city in Iraq, founded by the Muslims in 638 A.D.] at the end of Ramaḍān [the month of fasting], saying, "O people of Al-Baṣrah, do your duty and give alms after fasting." The people looked at each other.

He said, "Who is here from Medina [the city in which the Muslim community was founded, and where it first flourished] ? Come forth and teach your brothers. Should they not know that the Apostle of God prescribed as alms to be given at the end of Ramaḍān, a half *ṣā'* [a cubic measure of varying quantity] of wheat, or a *ṣā'* of barley, or a *ṣā'* of dates, to be given by every person, slave and free, man and woman?"

—Ibn Ḥanbal, No. 3291

Even today the religious authorities in each Muslim country or community prescribe a fixed amount, either of money or of foodstuff, which should be given as alms by every person. Whether it is done or not is left up to the individual conscience.

Fasting

18. The Prophet mentioned Ramaḍān and said, "Do not fast until you see the new moon [in the evening preceding the first day of the lunar month] and do not break the fast until you see it [at the beginning of the following month]. If it is hidden from sight then calculate the time of its appearance."

—Muslim, ṣiyām, 2

19. Salmah Ibn Al-Akwa' said, "When this verse was revealed, 'O believers, prescribed . . . for those who are able to fast, a redemption by feeding a poor man', (Surah 2:180), whoever did not want to observe the fast did as the verse directed [that is, instead of fasting they gave food to the poor], until the following verse was revealed, abrogating the former one."

—Muslim, ṣiyām, 25

The following verse states that the fast of Ramaḍān is obligatory, with a few precise exceptions. The science of *Qur'ān* interpretation admits the fact that certain verses are abrogated by others, due to changing circumstances and other factors. Abrogation is the prerogative of the divine author of the Book (see Surah 2:106).

20. The Prophet said, "God will pay no heed to the fasting of one who does not abandon false words and deeds, as well as food and drink."

—Al-Tirmidhī, ṣawm, 16

21. The Apostle of God said: "Fasting provides protection [from committing sin and from hell]. Whenever one fasts, he should not behave obscenely or foolishly. If someone attacks or abuses him, let him say, 'I am fasting, I am fasting'" [that is, abstaining not only from food and drink, but also from contention and controversy].

—Ibn Ḥanbal, No. 7484

Pilgrimage

22. Ibn 'Abbās said, "Abraham brought Ishmael and Hagar and put them in Mecca, at the place where the well of Zamzam now is."

Then, remembering the tradition, he continued, "Hagar came from Al-Marwah [a mountain near Mecca where, according to the story, Hagar went several times in search of water for herself and Ishmael] back to Ishmael and she found that a spring had gushed forth where he was. She began to scratch up the ground where the spring had appeared so that water gathered in the crevice that she had dug. She scooped it up in her drinking cup and put it into the waterskin. The Apostle of God said, 'May God be merciful to her. If she had left it alone, it would have remained a flowing spring until the day of resurrection.'"

—Ibn Ḥanbal, No. 2285

This is an account of the significance of the Well of Zamzam which plays an important part in the ceremonies of the pilgrimage to Mecca.

The story of Ishmael and Hagar is important to Muslims because, according to tradition, the Arabs are descendants of Ishmael (see also the Biblical story in Genesis 16, 17, and 21).

23. Ibn 'Abbās said, "The Apostle of God addressed us saying, 'O people, the pilgrimage [to Mecca] is ordained for you.'

"Al-Aqra' Ibn Ḥābis arose and said, 'Every year, O Apostle of God?'

"He replied, 'If I had said so, it would have been necessary. But even if it had been necessary you would not have done it, because you would not have been able to do it. The pilgrimage is for one time only. If anyone does it more than that, it is a voluntary act.'"

—Ibn Ḥanbal, No. 2642

24. Sa'd Ibn Abī Waqqās and Al-Ḍaḥḥāk Ibn Qays were discussing the practice of combining the minor pilgrimage (*'umrah*) with the major one (*ḥajj*).

Al-Ḍaḥḥāk said, "No one would do that unless he were ignorant of the command of God Most High."

But Sa'd rejoined, "You are wrong in what you say, O nephew."

Al-Ḍaḥḥāk said, "But 'Umar Ibn Al-Khaṭṭāb forbade it."

Then Sa'd said. "The Apostle of God did it, and we did it in company with him."

—Al-Tirmidhī, ḥajj, 12

The *'umrah* and the *ḥajj* were two separate pilgrimages to Mecca which were taken over by the Muslims from preislamic religious practice. This conversational exchange reflects early discussion regarding the optional combination of the two ceremonies, a practice which later was codified with precise conditions. Both *ḥajj* and *'umrah* are mentioned in Surah 2:196.

Death and Burial

25. Marwān asked Abū Hurayrah, "What did you hear the Apostle of God say when he prayed for burials?"

He replied, "I heard him say, 'You created him, and you sustained him. You guided him to Islam, and you have taken his life. You know his secret thoughts and his manifest deeds. We act as intercessors, so grant him forgiveness.'"

—Ibn Ḥanbal, No. 7471

26. Umm 'Aṭiyyah said: "One of the Prophet's daughters died, and he said, 'Wash her three or four times consecutively, or more if you think it is needed. Wash her with water and lotus leaves, then afterwards put camphor on her body. When you finish, call me.'

"When we finished we called him. He brought us one of his garments and said, 'Wrap her in this,'"

—Al-Tirmidhī, janā'iz, 14

From this example there developed in Islamic law a detailed series of instructions for preparing the dead for burial.

27. The Apostle of God said, "When you see a funeral procession, stand up for it, until it has passed, or until the body is placed in its grave."

—Muslim, janā'iz, 24

28. A funeral procession passed by the Apostle of God and he said, "He is delivered; we are delivered."

He was asked, "O Apostle of God, what do you mean by 'He is delivered; we are delivered?'"

He answered, "In the case of a believing man he is delivered from evils of this world, but in the case of a wicked man, his fellows, the country and all of nature are delivered from him."

—Muslim, janā'iz, 21

29. The Prophet prayed, saying, "O God, grant that my grave will not become an idol. May God curse those people who use the graves of their prophets as places of prayer." [A text occasioned by the practices of excessive grief at funerals and the veneration of the dead.]

—Ibn Ḥanbal, No. 7352

SOCIAL AND ECONOMIC LIFE

Marriage

30. The Apostle of God said, "A widow should be consulted and asked for her opinion about possible remarriage, and a virgin should be asked permission before her marriage."

They asked him, "O Apostle of God, how should her permission be indicated" [that is, that of a virgin] ?

He replied, "By her silence."

—Ibn Ḥanbal, No. 7398

31. The Prophet said, "There is no celibacy in Islam."

—Ibn Ḥanbal, No. 2845

Although some ascetic practices have been admitted throughout the history of Islam, voluntary celibacy has always been reproved.

32. The Prophet said, "There shall be no marriage without a legal guardian. The ruler shall be the guardian for anyone who has none."

—Ibn Ḥanbal, No. 2260

Inheritance

33. Sa'd Ibn Abī Waqqāṣ said, "I became ill in the year of the conquest, and I almost died. The Apostle of God came to visit me, and I said, 'O Apostle of God, I have much wealth and only one daughter as heir. Shall I bequeath [that is, to others than members of his family] all of my wealth?'

"The Prophet said, 'No.'
"I said, 'Two thirds?'
"The Prophet said, 'No.'
"I said, 'A half, then?'
"The Prophet said, 'No.'
"I said, 'A third, then?'

"The Prophet said, 'A third, and a third is a lot. It is better to leave your heirs rich than to leave them destitute, having to beg from others.

"'Any expenditure for others will be rewarded, even to the morsel of food that you put in your wife's mouth.'

"I said, 'O Apostle of God, shall I be left behind, unable to complete my emigration?' [Sa'd had emigrated from Mecca to Medina. Now he finds himself ill in the place from which he had emigrated. There was concern in the Muslim community that those who had emigrated to Medina should stay there. See also Surah 4:101.]

"The Prophet said, 'You will not be left behind, and any work that you will do, by which you seek the face of God, will result in your advancing a step and a rank. Perhaps if you are left behind other peoples might be benefited because of you, and still others afflicted.'

'O God, complete the emigration of my Companions and do not send them back to where they came from.'

"But Sa'd Ibn Khawlah was the unfortunate one. The Apostle of God regretted that he had died in Mecca."

—Al-Tirmidhī, waṣāyā, 1

This is a complex *ḥadīth* composed of several separate traditions whose relationship to each other is not immediately apparent. The Prophet's restriction of the amount of property that can be bequeathed to others than the testator's own family is one of the basic principles of Muslim laws of succession.

34. Ibn 'Umar reported that the Apostle of God said, "Let no one stay away from home as long as three nights without having made his will in writing."

Ibn 'Umar then said, "After that I never went away from home for even one night without having my will by my side."

—Ibn Ḥanbal, No. 4469

Law and Judges

35. The Apostle of God said, "You come to me with your disputes, but I am only human. Perhaps some of you are more skillful and eloquent in presenting your cases than others. If I thus judge ignorantly and unjustly in your favor against your brother, what I am actually doing is assigning to you a portion of hell. You will not be able to take advantage of your brother." [Divine justice will finally correct fallible human efforts to administer justice.]

—Al-Tirmidhī, aḥkām, 11

36. 'Ā' ishah reported that the Quraish were concerned about the case of the Makhẓūmiyyah woman who had stolen.

They said, "Who will speak to the Apostle of God on her behalf?"

Others said, "Who would be bold enough to do it but Usāmah Ibn Zayd, the dear friend of the Apostle of God." So Usāmah spoke to him.

The Apostle of God said, "Are you interceding regarding the legal punishment for infraction of a divine statute?"

He got up and addressed the people, saying, "Surely what caused those people who lived before to perish, was that when one of their nobles stole, they let him go. But when one of their lowly ones stole they carried out the sentence against him. I swear by God that even if the thief is Faṭimah the daughter of Muḥammad, I shall cut off her hand."

—Al-Tirmidhī, ḥudūd, 5

Commerce and Finance

37. The Apostle of God passed by a pile of grain. He put his hand into the midst of it, and his fingers encountered moisture.

He exclaimed, "O merchant, what is this?"

The owner of the grain said, "It has been damaged by the rain, O Apostle of God."

Then he replied, "If that is the case, why not put the damaged grain on top of the pile so that people can see it?"

Then he concluded, "Whoever practices fraud is not one of us."

—Al-Tirmidhī, buyū', 72

38. Ibn Mas'ūd said, "The Apostle of God cursed the one who collected usury, the one who paid it, the two witnesses to the transaction and the one who recorded it."

—Al-Tirmidhī, buyū', 2

Usury, or the collecting of interest on a debt, is considered by the *Qur'ān* to be an illicit form of profit making (Surah 2:275, 276; 4:161; 30:39).

39. Ḥakīm Ibn Ḥizām said, "I asked the Apostle of God, if a man should come to me and ask me to sell him something which I do not have, may I purchase it later and then deliver it to him?"

He replied, "Do not sell that which you do not have."

—Al-Tirmidhī, buyū', 19

This is one circumstance leading to a general principle in Islamic law which forbids a delay in carrying out the terms of a commercial transaction.

Piety, Morals, and Good Manners

40. 'Abd Al-Raḥmān 'Abd Rabb Al-Ka'bah said: "I came up to 'Abd Allāh Ibn 'Amr Ibn Al-'Āṣ [the famous Muslim conqueror of Egypt, 640 AD]. He was sitting in the shade of the Ka'bah. I heard him saying, 'While we were with the Apostle of God on a journey, he stopped at a camp site; some of us

put up our tents, others tended to their livestock, and still others practiced their archery.

"'Then his crier called out, "Unite for prayer!"

"'We assembled, and the Apostle of God got up to address us. He said, "There was never a Prophet before me who did not guide his nation to that which he knew was good for them and warn them against that which he knew was bad for them. Truly, your nation has been granted its felicity at the beginning. At the end it will suffer severe tribulation, and practice things with which you refuse to have anything to do now. There will come temptations which will increase in severity. A temptation will come which will cause the believer to say, 'This is a deadly peril to me.' Then it will be removed. Then another temptation will come, and the believer will say the same thing, and it will be removed. Let a man be sure that death finds him believing in God and in the last day, that is, if he desires to escape hell and to gain paradise.

"' "Let a man do to others that which he would like for them to do to him.

"' "One who gives allegiance to a ruler concludes the act with a handclasp, thus assuring him of affection. He will do for him whatever he can. If someone arises to contest the ruler's authority then you must cast the rebel out by force."'

"I pushed myself forward from among the people and said, 'I adjure you by God, did you hear this from the Apostle of God?'

"He replied, putting his hands to his ears, 'I heard with my ears and I have retained it in my heart.'

"I said, 'I am thinking of that cousin of yours, Mu'āwiyyah [the first Umayyad Caliph, 661–680 AD]. He orders us to consume our goods between us in vanity and to kill one another. God Most High said, "O believers, consume not your goods between you in vanity."' (Surah 2:184)

"Ibn Al-'Aṣ put his hands together and placed them upon his brow. He bowed a little and then raised his head, saying, 'Obey him insofar as you can obey God in doing so, and disobey him if such disobedience is willed by God (may He be exalted and glorified).'"

—Ibn Ḥanbal, No. 6503

This *ḥadīth* is politically oriented, reflecting anti-Umayyad feelings. It is also a good example of the discourse form of expression in which several sayings of the Prophet are combined to form a kind of sermon.

41. Mujāhid said, "I went in to see Ibn 'Abbās and said to him, 'O Ibn 'Abbās, when I was with Ibn 'Umar he recited a certain verse and wept.'

"Ibn 'Abbās said, 'Which verse was it?'

"I replied, 'Whether you publish what is in your hearts or hide it, God shall make reckoning with you for it.' (Surah 2:284)

"Ibn 'Abbās said, 'When that verse was revealed the companions of the Apostle of God were filled with great distress; that is to say, they felt thoroughly exasperated.

"'They said, "O Apostle of God, we are doomed if what we have said and done is to be held against us. Besides, we have no control over our hearts."

"'The Apostle of God said to them, "Say, we have heard and we have obeyed." Then this verse takes the place of the other one, "The Messenger believes in what was sent down to him from the Lord, and the believers," up to "God charges no soul save to its capacity; standing to its account is what it has earned, and against its account what it has merited" [Surah 2:285–86]. So they were delivered from their worries and they accepted responsibility for their works.'"

—Ibn Ḥanbal, No. 3071

42. The Prophet said, "Islam is built on five pillars: the profession of the unity of God, the performance of prayer, the giving of alms, the fasting of Ramaḍān and the pilgrimage."

—Muslim, imān, 5

43. The Apostle of God said, "No one will go into hell who has even a tiny grain of faith in his heart. And no one will go into paradise who has even a tiny grain of pride in his heart."

A man asked him, "O Apostle of God, I like to keep my clothing freshly washed, my head anointed, my sandal thongs in good condition,"—and he mentioned other things, ending with the strap of his whip—"Is this a sign of pride, O Apostle of God?"

He said, "No, that shows comeliness. Truly, God is beautiful, and He loves comeliness [a good example of Semitic realism, to be compared with Psalm 27:4]. By contrast, pride is seen in one who acts in stupid ignorance and who despises other people."

—Ibn Ḥanbal, No. 3789

44. The Apostle of God said, "Food for two people is enough for three, and food for three people is enough for four." [The meaning is that a person should be content with sufficient food, without eating to satiety.]

—Al-Tirmidhī, aṭ 'ima, 21

45. Ibn Mas'ūd said, "When this verse was revealed, 'Those who believe, and have not confounded their belief with evildoing . . .' [Surah 6:82], it troubled the people.

"They said, 'O Apostle of God, who among us has not done evil?'

"He replied, 'You are not interpreting the verse correctly. Did you not hear what the righteous servant said, "O my son, do not associate others with God; to associate others with God is a mighty wrong" [Surah 31:12]. Indeed, by "evildoing" is meant associating others with God.'" [Evildoing is thus narrowly defined in this case as the sin of *shirk*, or polytheism.]

—Ibn Ḥanbal, No. 3589

46. Someone said to the Prophet about a certain woman, "O Apostle of God, So-and-So prays and fasts often. She gives alms generously, but she wrongs her neighbors with her tongue."

The Apostle of God said, "She is one of the people of hell."

Then someone said to him about another woman, "So-and-So reportedly fasts and prays little. She only gives pots of cheese as alms, but does not wrong her neighbors with her tongue."

The Apostle of God said, "She is one of the people of paradise." [In spite of the immense importance attached to ritual in Islam, it is always secondary to human goodness.]

—Ibn Ḥanbal, II, 440

47. The Apostle of God said, "The believers who show perfect faith, the best character, in short, the most excellent of believers, are those who treat their wives best."

—Ibn Ḥanbal, No. 7396

48. Abū Kharr asked, "O Apostle of God, what words does God most like to hear?"

He answered, "The words which God chose for His angels to say, 'May the Lord be glorified and praised, may the Lord be glorified and praised.'" [Praise and gratitude to God are fundamental aspects of Muslim piety.]

—Al-Tirmidhī, da'wāt, 11

49. The Apostle of God said, "Muslims are brothers. One should neither mistreat nor betray another. If one cares for the need of his brother, then God will care for his need. If one removes the worry of a fellow Muslim, then God will remove one of his worries on the day of resurrection. If one protects a fellow Muslim, then God will protect him on the day of resurrection."

—Al-Tirmidhī, ḥudūd, 3

50. Ibn 'Umar heard a man swear, saying, "No, I swear by the Ka'bah!" Ibn 'Umar said, "Swear by none other than God. I heard the Apostle of God say, 'Whoever swears by other than God commits blasphemy and makes someone or something an associate with God.'"

—Al-Tirmidhī, nudhūr, 8

51. The Apostle of God said, "Disputation about the Qur'ān constitutes unbelief." [This stricture reflects an early bias in Islam against commentaries on the Qur'ān.]

—Ibn Ḥanbal, No. 7499

52. The Apostle of God said, "You will not enter paradise unless you have faith. And your faith will be of no avail unless you love one another. Let me tell you something to do that will cause you to love one another; spread peace among yourselves." [Faith is inseparable from its expression in deeds of brotherly love.]

—Muslim, imān, 93

53. The Prophet said, "When you pray do not say, 'O God forgive me, if you will,' but rather be determined in the matter. God will not be displeased."

—Ibn Ḥanbal, No. 7312

This text illustrates a well-known point of discussion in classical Islamic theology. Sufyān al-Thawrī, the guarantor of the *ḥadīth,* represented a moderate position, which did not require a radical attitude of uncertainty regarding the believer's relationship with God. In the creedal statement by Ibn Ḥanbal, p. 119, is found another position on this question.

54. When a man enters his house he should say, "O God, I pray your blessing on our entering and on our going out. In God's name we enter and in God's name we go out. In God our Lord we put our trust." Then he should greet his family.

—Abū Dāwud, adab, 112

55. When the Prophet awoke he would say, "O God, it is you who enables us to wake up in the morning and it is you who brings us into the evening. You enable us to live. You cause us to die, and at the Resurrection we go to you." When evening came he would say, "O God, it is you who brings us into the evening, and it is you who enables us to wake up in the morning. You enable us to live. You cause us to die, and with you is the issue of our life."

—Ibn Ḥanbal, II, 354

56. The Bedouins asked the Apostle of God, "Shall we not use medicines?"

He said, "Yes, O people of God, use medicines. God provides either healing or a remedy for each disease, that is, except one."

They said, "O Apostle of God, what is that one?"

He said, "Old age."

—Al-Tirmidhī, ṭibb, 2

57. The Apostle of God passed by a camel so thin that its back met its abdomen. He said, "For God's sake, show regard for these dumb animals. Ride them properly and feed them properly."

—Abū Dāwud, jihād, 47

58. The Prophet said, "Every one of you is a shepherd; every one of you is responsible. A prince is shepherd over his people; he is responsible for his subjects. A man is shepherd over his family; he is responsible for them. A woman is shepherdess over her husband's household; she is responsible for it. The slave is shepherd over the property of his master; he is responsible. Are you not all shepherds, all responsible?"

—Ibn Ḥanbal, No. 4495

In Arabic the word "shepherd" (*rā'in*) also means "ruler" or "governor," and the word for "flock" (*ra'iyyah*) also means "subjects" or "citizens."

59. Suwayd Ibn Ghafalah said, "I went out with Zayd Ibn Ṣūḥān and Salmān Ibn Rabī'ah, and I found a whip.

"My two companions said, 'Leave it alone.'

"I said, 'No, if I leave it the wild animals will destroy it. I prefer to take it and get some good use out of it.' Then I went to see Ubayy Ibn Ka'b and I asked him about the matter.

"He said, 'You have done well. In the time of the Apostle of God I once found a purse containing one hundred dinars. I took it to him.

"'He said, "Let it be known for a year that you have found it." I did so but no one knew anything about it.

"'I returned to him with it and he said, "Let it be known another year." I did so and came back to him.

"'He said, "Let it be known still another year. Count the pieces of money, its compartments and its thongs. Then if someone looking for it comes to you, and he can tell you about the number of pieces, its compartments and its thongs, then you must return it to him. If not, you may use it." ' "

—Al-Tirmidhī, aḥkām, 35

60. The Apostle of God said, "Let a person take a rope, go into the mountains and gather fire wood; then let him carry it on his back and sell it so that he can eat. This is better than that he should beg.

"It is better for a person to put dirt into his mouth than that he should put something into his mouth that God has forbidden."

—Ibn Ḥanbal, No. 7482

Muslim scholars of *ḥadīth* recognize two completely different subjects in this text: the prohibition of begging and a warning against eating ritually unclean food. No attempt is made to connect the two subjects.

61. Al-'Aqra' Ibn Ḥābis saw the Prophet kissing Al-Ḥasan (Ibn Abī 'Umar said it was either Al-Ḥasan or Al-Ḥusayn). Then Al-'Aqra' said, "I have ten children, and I have never kissed one of them."

The Apostle of God replied, "Verily, he who shows no compassion will have no compassion shown him."

—Al-Tirmidhī, birr, 12

62. Abū Ma'mar said, "A man got up and started praising a certain prince. Al-Miqdād Ibn Al-Aswad threw dirt in his face and said, 'The Apostle of God directed us to throw dirt in the face of flatterers.' "

—Al-Tirmidhī, zuhd, 43

63. The Prophet said, "Close the door, secure the waterskin, turn the cooking pot over (or, cover the cooking pot), extinguish the lamp. Satan will not enter a closed door, nor open what is secured, nor uncover a covered pot. A little mouse can burn a dwelling down." [The last statement rightfully goes with the admonition to extinguish the lamp.]

—Al-Tirmidhī, aṭ 'imah, 15

64. Someone said, "O Apostle of God, what is disparagement?"

He said, "It is saying something offensive about your brother."

The other asked, "But what if that which I say about him is true?"

He replied, "If that which you say about him is true, then you have disparaged him. But if it is not true, then you have slandered him."

—Al-Tirmidhī, birr, 23

65. The Apostle of God said, "There are only two kinds of envy which are permissible: to envy a man whom God has given wealth, and who spends it night and day for others; and to envy a man whom God has given the Qur'ān, and who spends his time night and day, learning it, reciting it and putting it into practice."

—Al-Tirmidhī, birr, 24

66. The Apostle of God said, "Use olive oil for eating and for rubbing on the body. It comes from a blessed tree" [a reference to Surah 24:35].

—Al-Dārimī, aṭ 'imah, 20

HISTORY AND THE FUTURE

Life and Person of Muḥammad

67. The Apostle of God said, "Verily God chose Ishmael from the sons of Abraham. Then He chose the Banū Kinānah [a large tribal grouping in the central Hejaz] from the sons of Ishmael. Then He chose the Quraish [the Meccan tribe to which Muḥammad belonged] from the Banū Kinānah. Then He chose the Banū Hāshim from the Quraish. Then he chose from among the Banū Hāshim [the immediate family of Muḥammad]."

—Al-Tirmidhī, manāqib, 1

68. Ibn 'Abbās said: "The Prophet received his first revelation at the age of forty. He remained in Mecca for thirteen years after that, and then was for ten years in Medina. So he died at the age of sixty-three."

—Ibn Ḥanbal, No. 2242

69. The prophet said to Khadījah [his wife]. "I see a light, and I hear a voice, I fear that I am possessed by demons [explaining the circumstances of Muḥammad's initial revelatory experience]."

She said, "God would not do that to you, O Ibn 'Abd Allāh" [another part of Muḥammad's name]. Then she went to Waraqah Ibn Nawfal [Khadījah's cousin] and told him what had happened.

He said, "This is true; this is a divine law, like that sent to Moses. If it is sent while I am still alive I shall support it; I shall help it to prevail, and I shall believe in it." [In fact, Waraqah died just when Muḥammad began his public ministry.]

—Ibn Ḥanbal, No. 2846

70. Ibn Mas'ūd said, "I recited the Surah, 'The Women,' to the Apostle of God, and when I reached the verse, 'How then shall it be, when We bring forward from every nation a witness, and bring thee to witness against those?' [Surah 4:45] his eyes overflowed with tears, may the blessing and peace of God be upon him."

—Ibn Ḥanbal, No. 3551

71. Abū Hurayrah said, "After the early morning prayer, when the Apostle of God had finished reciting and pronouncing the formula, 'God is great,' he would raise his head and say, 'God hears the one who gives Him praise. O our Lord, to you be praise.' Then he would say, while maintaining a standing position, 'O God, deliver Al-Walīd Ibn Al-Walīd and Salmah Ibn Hishām and 'Ayyash Ibn Abī Rabī'ah, and all of the believers who are oppressed. O God, afflict Muḍar [an Arab tribe which opposed the Prophet] with severity. Cause them to suffer the "years of Joseph" [that is, drought and economic diffi-

culty, an allusion to the events recorded in Genesis 41]. O God, curse Liḥyān. Ri'l, Dhakwān and 'Uṣayyah [other Arab tribes which opposed the Prophet]. They disobeyed God and His Apostle.' Then later we learned that he gave up that kind of praying, after the verse had been revealed, 'No part of the matter is thine, whether He turns toward them again, or chastises them, for they are evil doers'" [Surah 3:123. Thus the Prophet learned that, instead of praying for vengeance against his enemies, he should leave the matter to God.]

—Muslim, masājid, 294

72. Jābir Ibn 'Abd Allāh said, "We went on an expedition with the Apostle of God in the direction of Najd. He brought us to a river valley where many thorn trees grew. There he dismounted and hung his sword on one of the branches of a tree. The others dispersed and sought shade under the trees.

"Afterwards the Apostle of God told them, 'A man came to me while I was sleeping. He took my sword, and I awoke to find him standing over me. Suddenly I realized that he held the drawn sword in his hand.

"'He said to me, "Who can prevent me from killing you?"

"'I said, "God!"

"'He said a second time, "Who can prevent me from killing you?"

"'I said, "God!" At that he put the sword back into its sheath. The man is sitting over there among you.' But the Apostle of God did not single him out."

—Muslim, faḍā'il, 4

73. Al-Barā' said, "There was no one better looking than the Apostle of God, with his long lock of hair and dressed in his red cloak. He had hair that came down to his shoulders. His back was broad, but in height he was neither excessively tall nor excessively short."

—Al-Tirmidhī, libās, 4

74. 'Ā'ishah said, "The mattress on which the Apostle of God slept was made of leather with palm fibers." [Naturally even the smallest detail regarding the Prophet's personal life was of the highest importance to the Muslim community.]

—Al-Tirmidhī, libās, 27

75. The Apostle of God said, "My eyes sleep, but not my heart." [This statement explains the Prophet's capacity to stay awake for prayers during the night.]

—Ibn Ḥanbal, No. 7411

The Early Community

76. When the Apostle of God went forth to Ḥunayn he passed by a tree belonging to the polytheists, and called Dhāt Anwāt [an object of pagan worship]. They used to hang their weapons upon it.

The Apostle's followers said to him, "O Apostle of God, make us a Dhāt Anwāt such as they have."

The Prophet replied, "God is great! You have spoken like the people of

Moses, who said to him, 'Make us a god like their gods.' By him who holds my life in his hands, you follow the customs of those who were before you."

—Al-Tirmidhī, fitan, 16

77. Ibn 'Abbās said, "When Abū Ṭālib [Muḥammad's uncle, who, although he took his nephew's part against those who opposed him, never became a Muslim] became ill a group from the Quraish came to see him. Among them was Abū Jahl [one of the Prophet's chief opponents in Mecca].

"They said, 'O Abū Ṭālib, your nephew reviles our gods. He says thus and so, and he does such and such. Send a warning to him.' So Abū Ṭālib sent for him. Just next to the sick man was a spot where a person could sit. Abū Jahl feared that if the Prophet came to see his uncle and sat in that place, he would arouse the pity of his uncle. So Abū Jahl jumped over to that seat and occupied it. When the Prophet came in he could only find a place beside the door.

"He sat down, and his uncle, Abū Ṭālib, said, 'O nephew, your people are complaining about you. They claim that you are reviling their gods, that you say thus and so, and that you do such and such.'

"The Prophet replied, 'O uncle, I really have only one word for them, a word by which the Arabs will submit to them, and because of which the non-Arabs will pay a head tax in return for protection [an allusion to the practice during the expansion of Islam and later of granting to non-Muslim minorities a special legal status which entitled them to protection by the Muslim rulers].

"They said, 'And what is it?'

"He said, 'There is no deity but God.'

"His listeners got up, shaking out their clothes and saying, 'What, has he made the gods One God? This is indeed a marvellous thing' [Surah 38:4].

Then he [Ibn 'Abbās] recited up to the verse, "They have not yet tasted My chastisement" [Surah 38:7].

—Ibn Ḥanbal, No. 3419

78. The Apostle of God sent Mu'ādh to Yemen and said, "You will come to a people who possess Scriptures [that is, Christians and Jews]. Invite them to testify that there is no deity but God, and that I am the Apostle of God. If they consent to do that, then inform them that God has prescribed for them five prayers a day. If they consent to that, then inform them that God has prescribed that they should give alms of their possessions to be taken from their rich people and to be returned to their poor people. And if they consent to that, then be careful not to take their most valuable possessions. Give your attention to the appeal of the oppressed, for between that appeal and God, there is no barrier."

—Al-Tirmidhī, zakāt, 6

Divine Secrets

79. The Apostle of God said, "There rose before me in the seventh heaven the *sidrat al-muntahā* [the lotus tree of the utmost limit; an allusion to the mysterious tree mentioned in Surah 53:14]. Its fruit was like earthenware jars made in Hajar, and its leaves were like the ears of an elephant. From its trunk flowed two rivers which could be seen, and two rivers which were hidden.

"I said, 'O Gabriel, what are these two?'

"He said, 'The two hidden ones have their origin in paradise, but the two that can be seen are the Nile and the Euphrates,'" [The Traditions report many details regarding the mystical journey of the Prophet to Jerusalem and to the seventh heaven. Surah 17:1 is the Quranic basis for the accounts.]

—Ibn Ḥanbal, III, 164

80. Iblīs [Satan] said to his Lord, "I swear by your honor and glory that I shall never cease leading men astray, as long as their souls remain within their bodies."

Then God said, "I swear by my honor and my glory that I shall never cease forgiving them that for which they ask me forgiveness."

—Ibn Ḥanbal, III, 29

81. The Apostle of God said, "Compared with the hereafter, the world is as though one of you should put his finger in the sea, and then look to see what he could hook with it."

—Al-Tirmidhī, zuhd, 10

82. The Apostle of God said, "If you knew what I know you would laugh little and weep much [in view of the realities of the day of judgment].

—Al-Tirmidhī, zuhd 7

83. The Prophet said, "By the One who holds my life in his hand, the Son of Mary is about to come down among you to judge with equity, and he will break up the crosses [which Christians have made objects of veneration], kill the swine [unclean animals] and dispense with the head tax on non-Muslims [symbol of the fact that all of the world is not yet united in the House of Islam]. Wealth will abound to such a degree that no one will want it." [This text predicts the imminent return of Jesus as judge of mankind and vindicator of Islam.]

—Al-Tirmidhī, fitan 45

84. The Apostle of God said, "The world will not come to an end until the Arabs are ruled by a man from my family, whose name will correspond to my name." [A prophecy of the coming of the Mahdī, or future deliverer, a Messiah-like figure. This prophecy has been highly developed in Shī'ah Islam.]

—Al-Tirmidhī, fitan, 44

CHAPTER 4

Law

THEORY OF JURISPRUDENCE

Islamic law may be most simply understood as the institution that sets forth the details of what man's practice should be when he submits to the authority of God. The divine will as understood by Muslims embraces all of human life. Every act of man should be a service rendered to the benevolent Creator. Some duties prescribed by law have to do with ritual practices, such as prayer and fasting. These are called *'ibādāt.* Other duties pertain to social relations, and they are called *mu'āmalāt*. The distinction between *'ibādāt* and *mu'āmalāt* is made for rational classification, but it does not constitute a division of human life into sacred and profane areas. To Muslims, buying and selling, as well as the correct granting of an inheritance, are religious acts, in the sense that they are carried out in accordance with the will of God as prescribed by Islamic law. As Kenneth Cragg remarks (in *The House of Islam,* p. 45), "the strictly ritual and devotional provisions are the sacramental *foci* of what is throughout religious." Another way of expressing this thought is that the *'ibādāt* are deliberate, symbolic acts which accentuate the attitudes and orientation of life which characterize the total existence of a Muslim. For example, ritual ablutions enable the believer to prepare thoughtfully for the intense practice of the presence of God which constitutes ritual prayer. However, as acts, neither the humble washing in preparation for prayer nor the dramatic prostration of the body in the exalted climax of worship, differs in kind from the everyday acts of one who lives constantly under the all-seeing eye of God.

Although this comprehensive, global vision of man's relationship to God profoundly marks the Muslims' outlook toward life, it is not quite accurate to say that the positive regulations of the *sharī'ah* (revealed law) apply to every institution of human society. Many fiscal matters and other questions of public law are not covered by the *sharīʻah.* So, the way is left open for modern Muslims to adopt social and economic legislation based upon European models and destined to regulate a life whose activities have been changed by technology. Much of the ferment in modern Islamic thought is motivated by the desire to define the scope of the *sharīʻah* in this age. There is a tendency to restrict its explicit application to the conduct of worship and to the defining of personal status in society. It may be expected, however, that in spite of all of the influx of foreign ideas into Islamic countries, the mature legal formulations of these societies will come to bear a particularly Islamic stamp.

The Sources of Islamic Law—Kitāb al-Muqaddimāt al-Mumahhadāt (The Book of Introductory Explanations) by Ibn Rushd

Ibn Rushd, the author of the following selection, was a Spanish Muslim who died in 1126 AD. He was an illustrious *qāḍī* (judge) of Cordova and a scholar of Islamic law according to the school of Mālik Ibn Anas of Medina (d. 795 AD). Ibn Rushd's grandson, who had the same name, was the famous philosopher, legist, and physician, known to the Latin world as Averroes. The book from which this passage has been taken is called *The Book of Introductory Explanations for the purpose of elucidating the duties recorded in al-Mudawwanah.* This last, *Al-Mudawwanah* (The Body of Laws), is the basic text book for Islamic law according to the Mālikī school. It was compiled by a Tunisian, Saḥnūn, who died in 854 AD. In its printed form, *Al-Mudawwanah* consists of six large volumes. Ibn Rushd's *Book of Introductory Explanations* contains 675 pages (published in Beirut by Dār Ṣādir without a date).

The Way to a Knowledge of the Ordinances of the Law

The ordinances of the Law derive from four sources.

1. The Book of God (may He be glorified), wholly untouched by anything false, which has been revealed by the All-wise, All-praiseworthy One [a reference to the Qur'ān].

2. The example (*sunnah*) of his Prophet (may God bless him and grant him salvation). God Most High has identified obedience to himself with obedience to his Prophet and has commanded us to follow his example. He said (may He be exalted), "Obey God and the Messenger" (Surah 3:29).* The Most High also said, "Whoever obeys the Messenger, thereby obeys God" (Surah 4:82), and, "Whatever the Messenger gives you, take; whatever he forbids you, give over" (Surah 59:7). He also said, "And remember that which is recited in your houses of the signs of God and the Wisdom" (Surah 33:34). "The Wisdom" is the example of the Prophet (*sunnah*). And He said, "You have had a good example in God's Messenger" (Surah 33:21).

The second source of law is related to the Islamic doctrine of prophethood. According to this belief, a prophet is one to whom God has

---

*All quotations from the *Qur'ān* in this chapter are from *The Koran Interpreted,* translated by Arthur J. Arberry, © Oxford University Press 1964. Reprinted by permission of Oxford University Press.

revealed a Divine Law (see the chapter on Theology). Since Muḥammad was granted such a revelation his whole life and personality are considered to have been of such exceptional quality that his words, acts, and attitudes, preserved in the memory of his followers, serve to repeat and to emphasize Quranic precepts, to elucidate principles enunciated in the *Qur'ān,* to give specific examples of general provisions, to illustrate the purpose of sacred texts, and to convey certain rules of behavior about which the *Qur'ān* is silent.

> 3. Consensus (*ijmā'*), of which the Most High has indicated the soundness by saying, "But whoso makes a breach with the Messenger after the guidance has become clear to him, and follows a way other than the believers', him We shall turn over to what he has turned to and We shall roast him in Gehenna—an evil homecoming" (Surah 4:115)! So God (may He be exalted) warned against following any other way than that of the believers. This constituted an obligatory command to follow their way. The Apostle of God (may God bless him and grant him salvation) said, "My people will not agree upon an error."

Ijmā' means the unanimous opinion of the community, or of reputed scholars representing the community, regarding legal questions which are not adequately covered by the first two sources. This principle is a mark of the democratic nature of the Muslim community. It is significant that in spite of debate through the centuries as to the validity, methods, and conditions of *ijmā'*, the practice never evolved into a uniform structure to implement the achieving of consensus. *Ijmā'* puts emphasis on mutual consultation, in whatever form it might take place, and the seeking of a unanimous opinion.

> 4. Deductive reasoning, which consists of drawing analogous conclusions (*qiyās*) from the other three sources, the Book, the example of the Prophet and consensus. God Most High has made the results of deductive reasoning into a science and the judgments which are based on it into precepts. He said (may He be exalted), "If they had referred it to the Messenger and to those in authority among them, those of them whose task it is to investigate [The word translated 'to investigate' here may also be translated 'to reason deductively.'] would have known the matter" (Surah 4:85). He also said (may He be exalted), "surely We have sent down to thee the Book with the truth, so that thou mayest judge between the people by that God has shown thee" (Surah 4:106); that is, what God has shown you in the Book with respect to deductive reasoning and analogy, for that which was shown the Prophet in the Book with respect to deductive reasoning and analogy was part of that which God revealed to him and that according to which he was commanded to judge, when God said, "So judge between them according to what God has sent down" (Surah 5:54). . . . [Here follows a brief discussion of the Qur'ān, the first source of law, its contents being classified according to those texts which are to be interpreted literally (*ḥaqīqah*) and those which are to be interpreted figuratively (*majāz*). Then the Prophetic example (*sunnah*) is summarily classified into four main types, not according to its subject matter, but according to the nature of the obligation imposed upon the community to observe it.]

Although deductive reasoning was used from the earliest days of Islam, its place as a proper source of law was often controverted. To many the process of human reasoning could not rightfully be joined with divinely revealed law. *Qiyās* was finally dependent upon *ijmā'* for its acceptance.

To picture the scope and the nature of the four sources, they may be said to resemble a pyramid. At the summit stands the *Qur'ān,* the inimitable, pure Word of God, but necessarily limited in its scope. Scarcely less authoritative, but nonetheless second in the descending scale, is the *sunnah* of the Prophet. Inevitably, Muḥammad was able, by his example, to broaden the range of man's duty. In the first two sources Muslims find the basic materials out of which they construct the edifice of jurisprudence. The other two sources, farther down on the scale, are tools rather than materials. *Ijmā'* is a method of authenticating, and *qiyās* is a method of reasoning. Both are also common processes in everyday human life, and their use broadens the applications of law almost indefinitely. Theoretically these four sources make possible a flexible and realistic approach to legal practice. During the historical development of Islam, however, the free interplay of the four sources with their complex interrelationships was interrupted, and law became a congealed and hidebound science. Much of the effort of modern Muslim leaders is directed toward the recovery of the early dynamic of Islamic jurisprudence.

Consensus

Consensus is not sought unless there is evidence for the need of it, whether in interpreting a tradition emanating from the Prophet (may God bless him and grant him salvation), or in making judgments based on the Qur'ān and the *sunnah,* or in formulating an independent judgment, such as, for example, the case of those who agreed by consensus to punish a wine drinker by flogging, and other similar cases.

Consensus is of two kinds. First there is the agreement of scholars and common people together, regarding things like ritual ablutions, ritual prayer, the alms tax and fasting. Secondly there is the agreement reached by the scholars, without the common people, although the common people agree subsequently on that concerning which the scholars reached accord, and in that way it becomes duty. This second kind of consensus involves the systematic elaboration of ritual duties (*'ibādāt*), the ordinances regulating divorce, the code of legal punishments and other similar matters. . . . [The author continues with a presentation of the fourth source, analogy. First he affirms Quranic and prophetic support of the principle as well as evidence that in the practice of seeking consensus, the community recognized the value of analogy. Then he mentions those who do not accept the source for legal science.]

Analogy

Analogy means bringing a particular case into relationship with a basic principle in order to determine whether, by virtue of a causal factor, a judgment of that case is valid or not. The evidence thus adduced indicates whether reference to the basic principle justifies the ruling or not, depending on the nature of the causal factor. This factor, or motive, is found in a particular case, and requires that a given case be linked up with a basic principle in order to verify the validity or the invalidity of a judgment based on the principle.

Once a judgment is made in a particular case, then this case becomes a basic principle for other judgments, and it is permitted to reason analogically from it by taking into account other effective causes which may be deduced from it. The legal action is called a case as long as it is being studied in relation to basic principles, and as long as a judgment has not yet been decided regarding it. Thus, when a case has been made a basic principle itself by the authenticating of its judgment, analogy can be drawn from it by another case, involving another effective cause, which is deduced from the basic principle. Then, finally, when this new case has its judgment confirmed, it too becomes in turn a source for analogical reasoning. There is no limit to the possibilities of this procedure. It is not as some ignorant people say, that legal questions are all secondary cases, and that there can be no analogies drawn from them. Such reasoning, they say, can rightfully only be exercised with reference to the Book, to the *sunnah* and to consensus. This is clearly an error, because, although the Book, the *sunnah* and consensus are the bases of legal evidence, and analogy is drawn from them first of all, when it is proven to be impossible to draw analogy directly from them, then such reasoning can rightfully be based on deductions from these basic sources. So, if legal action is undertaken, and if no text can be found to apply, either in the Book or in the *sunnah* or in the consensus of the people, and if no motivating cause can be found in any of those sources which could establish a link between them and the proposed legal action, and if such a link can be established by deductive inference, either from the sources or from judgments which have been deductively inferred from those sources, then analogical reasoning is required. . . . [Next Ibn Rushd compares analogical reasoning in jurisprudence with the same method in philosophical or theological speculation.]

A legal cause in itself does not necessitate a judgment based on a basic principle. It only renders a judgment necessary when the legal scholar makes it a cause. An example of this lies in the fact that the capacity to induce intoxication was present in wine, but this did not provide evidence for prohibiting winedrinking until the legal scholar made it a cause for such prohibition. Thus it is not a cause in essence, but it is rather an indication and an evidence for the judgment. . . . [In this way Ibn Rushd distinguishes legal causes from philosophical ones. The section on analogy is concluded by a description of two kinds of legal causes, those which are determined, and those which are conjectured.]

INSTITUTIONS

Ritual Ablution—Al-Risālah (The Treatise) by Ibn Abī Zayd Al-Qayrawānī

The most accessible edition of this much-published work is in two languages, Arabic and French, translated by Leon Bercher and published in a fifth Algiers edition in 1968.

To perform the ritual prayer in Islam a Muslim must be in a state of ritual purity. This is achieved by ablution [see pp. 57, 58 of *The House of Islam*]. Depending upon the degree of impurity which must be removed, the ablution can be partial (*wuḍū'*) or complete (*ghusl*). The following text gives detailed instructions as to how the partial ablution must be carried out. It is taken from a famous treatise on Mālikī law, written in the tenth century AD by a Tunisian legist, Ibn Abī Zayd Al-Qayrawānī. He composed this work, not for professional jurists, but for the edification and instruction of ordinary believers.

Impurity requiring an ablution may be caused by contact with any unclean substance, by excretions from the body, by loss of consciousness, and other circumstances. [For further information on the notion of impurity, see under '*ḥadath*' in the *Encyclopedia of Islam.*]

There is no doubt a complex range of symbolic meaning in the concepts of impurity and of purification in Islam if the preislamic background and origins of the ritual practices are taken into consideration, but little of such complexity is revealed in the texts of jurisprudence. Most of the causes of impurity are acts or bodily functions which are seen to render the body physically unclean. Ritual ablutions serve primarily to prepare the body, in the most prosaic fashion, for a specially planned meeting with God at the time of prayer. To wash oneself is to observe the propriety that is fitting for such an occasion. It should be observed, in addition, that the notion of moral purity is not absent. It is implied in a *ḥadīth* which says, "God will not accept prayer which is offered by an unclean person, nor will He accept the giving of alms by a deceitful person." In the last paragraph of the following selection it is explicitly stated that the ritually purified worshipper hopes to be purified as well from his sins.

Meticulously formalized acts such as ritual ablution are seriously criticized by some modern Muslims. There is a growing tendency, especially among youth, to minimize the importance of all rites in Islam, but as yet the antiritualist movement is little more than a vague and uneasy calling into question. A study of the following text reveals that ablutions, when performed in the spirit of Muslim piety, are not divorced from deep religious feeling.

On the Purity of Water, et cetera

The person who performs the ritual prayer speaks intimately with his Lord [an allusion to a *ḥadīth* which says, "The Prophet found his companions praying, and they were reciting with loud voices. He said, 'The one who prays is engaged in intimate conversation with his Lord. He must comtemplate that which he says. So, do not disturb one another with your reciting.'"], so he must prepare himself for this act either by ritual ablution (*wuḍū'*) or by washing the whole body, if the latter is necessary. [Ablution is one of the means of proving one's seriousness of intent in prayer.] Both ritual ablution and complete washing shall be carried out with pure water, that is to say, water unmixed with any uncleanness. No water shall be used whose color has been altered by anything, whether pure or impure, except when the change of color is due to the earth from which it is taken, as, for example, water taken from saline land, from muddy ground, or such like. Rain water, spring water, well water and sea water are good, pure, and capable of purifying. Water whose color has been altered by the presence of a ritually pure substance is pure, but cannot be used for the ritual ablution nor for the complete washing of the body. It is not capable of removing ritual impurity. Water which has been changed by the presence of an impure substance is itself impure. A small quantity of water is rendered impure by the presence of a small quantity of an impure substance, even if no alteration is apparent.

On Generalities Concerning Obligatory Actions, Recommended Actions and Desirable Actions

Ablution (*wuḍū'*) in preparation for ritual prayer is an obligatory action. The word *wuḍū'* is derived from *waḍā'a* [meaning "radiant cleanness"].

On the Nature of Ablution, et cetera

The person who desires to perform his ablution for having contracted an impurity, or having slept, or for any other cause which makes it necessary, must wash his hands before putting them into the vessel used for the ablution.

Recommended practices (*sunnah*) [The word, *sunnah*, here has a different meaning from that seen previously, "the example of the Prophet." Here it indicates one of the five classifications of human acts in Islamic law. They are: 1) *farḍ* or *farīḍah*, obligatory (see the following); 2) *sunnah*, recommended; 3) *mubāḥ*, indifferent; 4) *makrūh*, reprehensible; 5) *ḥarām*, forbidden.] connected with the ablution are the washing of the hands before putting them into the vessel, the rinsing of the mouth, the aspiration of water into the nostrils followed by its being expelled by expiration, and the wiping of the ears. The other details of the ablution are obligatory (*farīḍah*).

Some scholars say that the person desiring to perform his ablution after sleep or after contracting impurity for any other reason should pronounce the name of God. But others have not considered this to be an accepted practice. If the vessel is placed to the right of the person using it, he can reach it more easily. He begins by washing his hands three times before putting them into the vessel. . . . Then he puts his hand into it, takes out some water with which he rinses his mouth three times, either with the same water, or with three handfuls. If he cleans his teeth with his finger, this is a good practice. Then he draws water into his nostrils three times and expels it. To do this he puts his hand over his nose as he does when he blows his nose. Fewer than three rinsings of the mouth and three inhalations of water are considered sufficient. Both rinsing and inhalation can be carried out with one handful of water, but it is better to use the maximum number of handfuls.

Next he takes water as he wishes, either in both hands or in his right hand only, taking care in the latter case, however, to moisten both hands, and this water is brought to his face. He washes his face with his two hands, beginning at the top of the forehead, at the hairline, and going as far as the bottom of the chin [or beard]. This washing includes the whole face, from the edge of the two jawbones to the temples. He rubs his hands over the sunken-in parts of the eyelids, the wrinkles of the forehead and the lower external part of the nasal cartilage.

In this way he brings water to his face and washes it three times. In doing this with his two hands, he shakes his beard so that the water can penetrate it. This is necessary because the hair of the beard tends to repel water which touches it. But he is not required to comb the beard with his fingers during a ritual washing, according to the opinion of Mālik. He must only rub his two hands over it as far as the end.

Next he washes his right hand three times, or twice, pouring water over it. He rubs it with his left hand, interlacing the fingers of his two hands. Then he washes his left hand similarly. The two elbows are to be washed with the hands. Some say that they are not to be included, and so it is not obligatory that they be so. On the other hand, to include them is a good way to avoid having to go to the trouble of determining the precise area to be excluded from washing.

Next he takes some water in his right hand, pours it into the palm of his left hand, and then he passes his two hands over his head, beginning at the front where the hairline begins. To do this he puts the fingers of his two hands together and his thumbs rest on his temples. Then his hands go over the head back to the hairline on the neck, and afterwards he brings them back over the head to where the wiping began. His two thumbs move around the back of the ears and return to the temples.

Any way that this wiping is done is valid, provided that the whole head is included. However, the way described here is preferable. It is also permitted to dip the two hands into the vessel, to take them out dripping and to proceed with the wiping of the head.

Next he pours water on his two index fingers and on his two thumbs, and wipes his ears with them, both outside and inside.

The woman runs her hands over her head and ears in the manner described, and also over the hair which hangs over her temples and forehead. She does not wipe the protective covering of her hair, and in bringing her hands back to the front of her head she runs them under her tresses.

After that the feet are washed by pouring water from the right hand onto the right foot and rubbing it with the left hand, a little at a time until the whole foot is washed three times. If desired the fingers can be run between the toes, but this can be omitted without any objection. On the other hand, for the sake of scrupulosity, it is better to do it. The heels and the achilles tendons are rubbed. In the case of callouses or cracks in the skin where water does not penetrate easily, water must be poured upon them from the hand, and they must be rubbed vigorously. There is a tradition from the Prophet that says, "Woe to the heels in hell!" [if they are not thoroughly washed]. It should be noted that the "heel" of a thing is the end of it, or its extremity. [The author here clarifies which part of the body is meant, the "extremity" of the leg, by noting the more general meaning of the word translated by "heel."]

Thereupon the left foot is washed in the same way as the right.

The specifying of three washings of the members does not mean that fewer than three are not sufficient. Three times is only the maximum number. If each is washed completely less than three times, this is perfectly acceptable, provided it is done properly, which is not the practice of everyone. The Apostle of God (may God bless him and grant him salvation) said: "Whoever does his ablution and does it well, then raises his eyes toward heaven and says, 'I witness that there is no god but God alone, and that he has no partner; I witness that Muḥammad is his Servant and his Apostle,' that one will have the eight doors of paradise opened for him and he will go in by the one which he wishes." Some scholars considered it recommended to recite the following words immediately after having performed the ablutions: "O God, grant that I might be among the repentant and the purified."

Ablution is an act which must be offered to God Most High, since He has prescribed it. The worshipper hopes thereby to find acceptance with God and to obtain merit, being purified by this act from sins which he has committed. He should feel that thereby he is prepared and cleansed in order to converse with his Lord, to stand before him, to carry out his ordinances and to bow and prostrate himself in humble worship. Ablution should be performed with conviction and with care. Truly, the perfect accomplishment of each act depends upon the good intention which motivates it.

Almsgiving—Al-Hidāyah (Guidance) by Al-Marghīnānī

This selection deals with one of the basic institutions of Islamic society, *zakāt,* or almsgiving [see *The House of Islam,* pp. 46–48]. It is taken from an authoritative work of Ḥanafī law used widely in India.[1] This book, written by ʻAlī Ibn Abī Bakr Al-Marghīnānī (d. 1197 AD), is a commentary on two earlier treatises, one by Al-Shaybānī, and the other by Al-Qudūrī. However, the text upon which he comments is of his own formulation, a summary of the work done by the two earlier authorities. In order to give the reader a brief glimpse at the structure of a typical commentary prepared as a reference book for legists, the explanations of the first three paragraphs of the text are given in full. Thereafter, until the end of the selection, only the text is presented.

Zakāt is the institution that gives expression to a major concern of the *Qur'ān,* that is, the responsibility under God of those who have material wealth to share their possessions with the poor and weak members of society. Although it is prescribed as a duty in the *Qur'ān, zakāt,* in the form of a system of taxation, owes its origin to the *ḥadīth.* As Islamic civilization grew in complexity other forms of taxation, imposed by the state, vied with *zakāt* in making demands upon Muslim citizens. In modern times there are charitable associations, maintained by political parties and others, as well as government welfare systems that duplicate the services to the poor formerly assured by *zakāt* funds. Nowadays the carrying out of the duty of paying *zakāt* is almost everywhere left to the conscience of the believer. To his mind paying this tax is an act of worship. In modern thought, with its tendency to separate religion from secular life, it is stressed that *zakāt* is both a religious and a social duty. However, it is truer to the all-embracing spirit of Islamic faith to say that the social solidarity made possible by *zakāt* is simply an example of the living practice of Islam, which inextricably unites the devotional and social aspects of life. The beneficiaries of almsgiving are strengthened in their life of submission to God's will, and the givers gain fuller access to temporal and eternal blessings. In this last connection Muslim writers often refer to the basic meanings of the Arabic root from which the word *zakāt* is derived. These are "to grow, increase," and "to be pure." So by fulfilling the duty of *zakāt* a Muslim develops goodness in himself, and assures the healthy growth of his portion of this world's goods. His wealth is also "purified," or he himself is "purified," in the sense that he is granted a particular recompense for his faithfulness by God and that his possessions become an asset, helping him to attain both earthly and eternal happiness.

Book of Almsgiving

Almsgiving is obligatory for every free adult Muslim who is of a sound mind, and who for at least a year has been in full possession of at least the minimum property liable to payment of the alms.

The child and the mentally ill do not have to give alms, nor does the person who has purchased his own freedom from slavery.

One whose property is immobilized by a debt is not required to pay the alms, but if the value of his property exceeds the amount of the debt, then he is liable to pay provided the amount in excess is sufficient to constitute the minimum of assessable property.

Commentary Its obligation stems from the word of God Most High, ". . . and pay the alms" (Surah 2:40), and from the word of the Prophet (may God bless him and grant him salvation), "Set aside a portion of your goods as alms." The community has unanimously agreed upon this practice. [So, *zakāt* is founded upon three of the four sources of Islamic law, as explained above in the selection by Ibn Rushd, pp. 100–103.] The intent of the obligation is that is should be a precise duty, for there is nothing vague about it. The stipulation that a person who gives *zakāt* should be free is made because only a free man can fully own property. [Ḥanafī law provided for a limited form of property ownership by slaves.] A sound mind and legal age are specified for the same reason. The person must be a Muslim because almsgiving is an act of devotion, and an unbeliever cannot carry out an act of devotion. The amount of property owned must be at least the minimum which is liable to the assessment because the Prophet (may God bless him and grant him salvation) determined that it should be that amount [an allusion to a *ḥadīth* in which Muḥammad said that alms should not be assessed upon less than five ounces of silver money, et cetera]. The minimum period of one year's ownership is required because a certain length of time is necessary for any growth of the property to be realized. The law has determined this time as one year, according to the word of the Prophet (may God bless him and grant him salvation): "No alms shall be assessed until a year has passed." An owner expects his property to develop as the various seasons of the year go by. Usually the price that it is worth will change before a year has passed. So the application of the law of *zakāt* takes this into account.

Some say that the amount of *zakāt* should be collected when due, without delay, because it is an absolute rule without any qualification. But others say that there can be a delay because the obligation to fulfill the duty continues during the whole of life. It follows, however, that if, after payment is delayed, the assessable property is destroyed, this fact in no way removes the obligation to pay *zakāt* on it.

(*The child and the mentally ill do not have to give alms*), contrary to the opinion of Al-Shāfi'ī (may God have mercy on him) [founder of one of the four main schools of Islamic law (d. 820 AD)]. He said that *zakāt* is a financial responsibility like any other obligation to provide support, as for example, the money due for the maintenance of wives.

So to him it amounts to the same thing as the *'ushr* and the *kharāj* [two types of taxes on the land and its produce, *'ushr* required of Muslims and *kharāj* of non-Muslims].

In our view, however, it is an act of devotion and can only be carried out by free choice. It is one way of experiencing the meaning of the divine testing (*ibtilā'*). [The *Qur'ān* says that men will be tried or tested in their possessions and in their persons (Surah 3:183). By successfully enduring this testing, Muslims are purified in the sense to which reference is made above, p. 107.] So, for these two kinds of people, who lack intelligence, there can be no free choice. The *zakāt*, understood as an act of devotion, thus differs from the *kharāj*, which is a tax on the land. The *'ushr* is generally considered like the *kharāj*, although it may have the secondary meaning of an act of devotion.

If, for part of a year, the mentally ill person regains his reason, then his status is the same as that of one who regains his reason during a portion of the month of fasting. [That is, his property would be taxable only for that part of the year during which he enjoys mental health. A Muslim is required to fast during the month of Ramaḍān only when he is in good health.] Abū Yūsuf (may God have mercy on him) [one of the founders of the Ḥanafī school of law, who died in 798 AD] took into account only the greater part of the year [That is, if the person is mentally ill for most of the year and then regains health, his imposition, or rather the year's delay before his imposition, does not begin until the following year.], and made no difference between a permanent affliction and a temporary attack. Abū Ḥanīfah (may God be merciful to him) [the scholar from Al-Kūfah, for whom the Ḥanafī school is named (d. 767 AD)] considered the year's delay before paying alms as beginning from the moment of recovery, in the case of a mentally ill person, and in the case of a child, from the time that he attains adulthood, (*nor does the person who has purchased his own freedom from slavery*) because he is not an owner of property in the full sense of the word. The fact of his having been a slave takes this right away from him. Neither has he the right to free a slave.

(*One whose property is immobilized by a debt is not required to pay the alms*).

Al-Shāfi'ī said (may God be merciful to him) that such a one must pay the *zakāt*, for he is in full possession of his property.

In our view the assets of such a person are tied up in such a way that his property may be considered as nonexistent. *Zakāt* should not be required, even as water which is required to quench the thirst is not to be used to perform ritual ablution [In cases where there is not enough water to satisfy the thirst and to perform ablutions, the worshipper is authorized to rub his body with sand in preparation for prayer.], and even as material used for making clothing is not assessable for the alms tax.

(. . . *but if the value of his property exceeds the amount of the debt, then he is liable to pay provided the amount in excess is sufficient to constitute the minimum of assessable property*) since the amount in excess is no longer tied up.

No *zakāt* is required to be paid on dwellings, clothing, furniture, riding animals or hunting arms.

If a creditor cannot collect a debt because the debtor refuses to acknowledge his indebtedness for a period of years, and then if testimony is borne against the debtor, requiring him to pay, the creditor does not have to pay *zakāt* on the amount of the debt for the time elapsed of non-payment.

If a slave girl is bought for trade and then it is decided to keep her for service, then no *zakāt* is due. And if later it is decided to use her for trade, this decision does not become effective until the time when she is actually sold. Then *zakāt* must be paid on the price of her sale. If something is bought for purposes of trade, it should be so used, in order that the act might conform to the intention. A different situation arises if property is inherited, and subsequently it is decided that it be used in trade.

It is only possible to carry out the obligation of almsgiving if one does it with sincere intention, or if one sets aside the amount due with the same sincere intention.

If a person gives all of his property away as alms, without regard to *zakāt*, then, by common consent the obligation to pay the latter is removed. Even if he gives away only part of his minimum of assessable property (*niṣāb*) the obligation of *zakāt* is cancelled, at least according to Muḥammad [Muḥammad Al-Shaybānī (d. 804 AD), a celebrated Ḥanafī jurist]. Abū Yūsuf said, however, that in this case the obligation is not cancelled.

Those who are permitted to receive Alms, and those who are not

The basis for these rulings is found in the words of the Most High: "The free will offerings are for the poor and needy, those who work to collect them, those whose hearts are brought together, the ransoming of slaves, debtors, in God's way, and the traveller" (Surah 9:60).

There are eight different categories listed here. One no longer applies, that is, "those whose hearts are brought together," since God Most High honored Islam [by bringing them into full allegiance to the Muslim community. These were new converts whom the Prophet helped at first with gifts.] and became their sufficiency.

The poor are those who have the smallest quantity of possessions.

The needy are those who have nothing.

The one who works to collect the offerings is paid by the head of the community, provided he has worked well. He should be given enough both for himself and for those who helped him, and the amount should not be set in advance [since he should be paid in proportion to the alms which he has collected].

Then, alms should be given to slaves to help them purchase their freedom.

A debtor should receive alms when his debt prevents him from owning, in excess of the amount he owes, the minimum of assessable property.

"In God's way:" Abū Yūsuf (may God be merciful to him) interpreted this as referring to those who engage in military expeditions [in defence of Islam], whereas to Muḥammad Al-Shaybānī it meant those who go on pilgrimage.

The traveler is one who, although he may have property in his own country, finds himself in another place without resources.

These are the ways in which *zakāt* is distributed. The property owner can give to each category, or he can limit himself to one type of beneficiary.

The "protected citizen" (*dhimmī*) [meaning the member of the Christian or Jewish community] should not receive *zakāt*, but he may receive its equivalent as superogatory alms.

Zakāt shall not be used to build a mosque, nor to bury the dead, nor to settle the debt of a dead person, nor to buy a slave for the purpose of freeing him. *Zakāt* shall not be paid to a rich person.

The almsgiver shall not give *zakāt* to his father, nor to his grandfather, nor to any further ascendants. Neither shall he give to his children, nor to his grandchildren, nor to any further descendants. A man shall not give to his wife nor shall a woman give to her husband. *Zakāt* shall not be paid to a slave who has been freed after the death of his master or to one who has bought his own freedom, or to the mother of one's children [referring to concubines], or to a partially freed slave. Others who are excluded from receiving *zakāt* are the rich slave [It was possible for a slave in Islam to amass wealth and to enjoy it, although his actual ownership of it was limited to his legal status as a slave.], the young son of a wealthy man and the members of the Banū Hāshim tribe, who include the families of 'Alī, Al-'Abbās, Ja'far, 'Aqīl, Al-Ḥārith Ibn 'Abd Al-Muṭallib and their freed slaves. [The interdiction is derived from a tradition according to which the Prophet refused to accept alms for himself and his family. The Banū Hāshim is the tribe into which Muḥammad was born. 'Alī, 'Aqīl and Ja'far were the Prophet's cousins, Al-'Abbās and Al-Ḥārith were his uncles. It is also known that the Banū Hāshim received regular financial support from the state during the time of the Abbassid caliphs.]

Abū Ḥanīfah and Muḥammad Al-Shaybānī (may God have mercy on them) said that if *zakāt* is paid to a person who one thinks is poor, and then it turns out that he is rich, or that he is a Hāshimī, or that he is an unbeliever, the *zakāt* cannot be returned. The same is true if in the darkness *zakāt* is given to one who turns out to be father or son. Abū Yūsuf said, however, that in such cases the *zakāt* can be returned. If payment should be made to an individual who is found later to be either the slave or the self-freed slave of the giver, then there can be no substitution of beneficiary.

No *zakāt* shall be paid to a person who owns the minimum of assessable property of any kind. But it can be paid to one who owns less than the minimum, even if he is strong in body and able to make a living. It is not advisable to pay one person two hundred dirhams or more, but it is nevertheless permitted. It is permitted for a person to send *zakāt* to his relatives in another country or to people who might be more worthy than those in his own country.

Marriage—Sharā'i' Al-Islām (The Laws of Islam) by Al-Muḥaqqiq Al-Ḥillī

Both law and theology in Shī'ī Islam are dominated by the doctrine that gurantees the leadership of the community will be assumed by a series of divinely appointed Imams. This feature will be clearly seen in the text on Shī'ī theology chosen for the chapter on theology. (See also *The House of Islam,* pp. 78–81.) Shī'ī Muslims accept, like the Sunnī group, the *Qur'ān* and the *sunnah* as basic sources of law; but they reject consensus (*ijmā'*) and analogy (*qiyās*). This rejection is based upon their belief that the divinely appointed Imam is alone capable of interpreting the revealed law to mankind. In many respects, however, the content of Shīʿī law differs only slightly from that of Sunnī law. The norms concerning marriage in the following selection do not diverge in general from the Sunnī ideal (see *The House of Islam*, pp. 51, 53).

As his name indicates, the author of this selection came from the town of Al-Ḥillah on the Euphrates River. He died in 1277 AD and is celebrated as the author of one of the most authoritative textbooks on Shīʿī law, *Sharāʾiʿ Al-Islām*.[2] He belonged to the branch of the Shīʿah who believe in twelve Imams. They are called the Twelvers (Al-Ithnā ʿAsharīyah).

The Book of Marriage

The first part is a general view of permanent marriage [as contrasted with temporary marriage (*mutʿah*), a preislamic custom which persisted in some parts of the Muslim world, and which is admitted by the Ithnā ʿAshariyyah branch of Shīʿī Islam], comprising several sections.

The norms of conduct regarding the marriage contract, sexual relations and other related matters: As for the contract, its principles prescribe that marriage is recommended for any man or woman who desires it, and who, after legally declaring his intention, fulfills his responsibility, according to the following sayings of the Prophet (may God bless him and grant him salvation):

Marry and have children!

The most unfortunate of mortals are the bachelors.

Except for Islam, there is no greater benefit that a man can have than a Muslim wife who gives him joy when he cares for her, who is obedient to his command, who protects her reputation in his absence, both by her behavior and by taking care of his possessions.

Perhaps one who abstains from marriage can justify his action by evoking the example of John the Baptist (may peace be upon him), who lived a celibate life [see Surah 3:34]. Thus abstinence can be accepted, exceptionally, in spite of the natural repugnance for celibacy. It should be noted that the approbation of such a practice belongs to another law than ours. It does not merit a place in our law.

Seven things are recommended for the man who desires to marry. An eighth thing is reprehensible. It is recommended that he choose a woman who combines four traits: 1) honorable ancestry, 2) virginity, 3) fertility, and 4) uprightness. 5) He should not limit himself to the criteria of beauty and wealth. It is possible that both of these will be excluded. 6) Then a ritual prayer of two sets of postures is recommended, followed by the recitation of one of the prayers which have been handed down from the Prophet, such as:

O God, I desire to marry. Choose a wife for me, one of the most virtuous, one of the most respectful in her behavior, one who will be most careful in taking care of my possessions, one having the most wealth possible, and one of the most blessed.

Or, another similar prayer may be used. 7) It is also recommended that witnesses be called for the contract, that it be made known and that a betrothal ceremony be performed.

8) It is reprehensible to let a marriage occur under the sign of the Scorpion [one of the signs of the zodiac. This prescription reflects an ancient and widespread belief that new undertakings, such as building a house, buying and selling, choosing a wife or conceiving a child should not be initiated during the period when the moon is seen against the background of the constellation Scorpio.]

The norms of conduct regarding sexual relations, in two sections.

It is recommended that before consummating marriage a man should perform a ritual prayer consisting of two sets of postures and then that he make a supplication to God. When he brings the woman to take up residence with him she should also perform the ritual prayer and make supplication with him. To do this they should be in a state of ritual purity. Then as the man proceeds to consummate the marriage he should place his hand on the woman's side and say, "O God, in accordance with your Book I have married her. In your keeping I have taken her. According to your word, I have deemed it permissible to take pleasure in her. If you have decreed something for me in her womb, then make him a good Muslim; do not make him a snare of Satan."

The consummation should take place at night. At the moment of union the man should pronounce the formula, "In the name of God, the Merciful, the Compassionate," and he should ask God Most High to bless him with a male child, sound in body.

It is recommended that the wedding feast last one or two days. The fellow believers should be invited, but they are not obliged to attend; it is only recommended that they do so. If a person attends a wedding feast, he should partake of all that is set before the guests, even if it involves breaking a voluntary fast. On the other hand, food should not be taken away by the guests unless those in charge of the feast give their permission, or unless the circumstances permit.

There are eight times when it is reprehensible for sexual union to take place: 1) during an eclipse of the moon and during an eclipse of the sun; 2) at noon and at sunset, until twilight passes; 3) when there is no moonlight [especially during the last few nights of the lunar month] ; 4) between dawn and sunrise; 5) the first night of every month, except the month of Ramaḍān; and the night midway through the month; 6) on a journey when there is no water available to perform ablutions; 7) when the "black" wind and the "yellow" [epithets for particularly violent and malevolent winds] wind blow; 8) and during an earthquake. [These recommendations are motivated both by practical considerations and by the conviction that certain times and certain phenomena are charged with cosmic potency.]

Likewise it is reprehensible for the sexual union to take place in a state of nudity, or following noctural emission, before its impurity is removed by washing and ritual ablutions. There is no harm, however, in having sexual relations several times in succession on the same occasion, and postponing the ablutions until the end. It is also reprehensible for anyone to watch the sexual act being performed, and for the man to look upon the sexual organs of his wife both during the union and at other times. The partners should not face Mecca while performing the sex act, nor should they turn their backs to Mecca. Sexual relations should not take place in a boat. During the union there should be no talking, except the mention of the name of God. [Other important questions discussed in *The Book of Marriage* are the contract, the dowry, and the reasons for invalidating a marriage.] . . .

MORALS

Al-Amr bi-l-Ma'rūf wa-l-Nahy 'an al-Munkar (Commanding the Good and Forbidding the Evil) by Ibn Taymiyyah

The communal duty in Islam of commanding the good and forbidding the evil is the principal provision made for maintaining a healthy moral environment. Muslims say that if it is faithfully observed, order and peace will prevail in the community. The duty is based upon an injunction in the *Qur'ān* which says, "May you form a nation of those who summon to blessing, who command what is good and forbid what is evil" (Surah 3:104, translator's version). All Muslims are expected to exercise this ethical judgment, for their society is intended to be one of complete equality. In it social justice and individual probity are the concern of every citizen. Several public functions have served, in the course of history, to emphasize this duty, such as those of caliph, police force and inspector of commercial activities (*muḥtasib*). These offices and functions were intended to be representative of the communal responsibility to promote the "rights of God" and the "rights of man." The final paragraphs of this selection, dealing with justice, give a succinct and forceful expression of the supreme concern in Islam for social ethics.

Taqī Al-Dīn Ibn Taymiyyah (d. 1328 AD), the author of this short treatise, was a theologian and jurisconsult of the Ḥanbalī school of law and one of the towering personalities of his age.[3] He lived most of his life in Damascus.

Commanding the good and forbidding the evil: by this principle God revealed His Scriptures and sent forth His Apostles. It is a part of religion.

The message of God is both a revelation and a teaching. He reveals things concerning himself, such as the truth of his unity (*tawḥīd*), and things concerning his creatures, for example, the promises and threats which are incorporated into the Quranic narratives. His teaching is found in what is commanded, what is forbidden and what is permitted to do.

This is as the *ḥadīth* says, "Say, He is God [Surah 112:1], and you have rendered a third of the Qur'ān." That is, this affirmation includes the third which is the truth of God's unity, because the content of the Qur'ān can be classified in three categories: narratives, the truth of God's unity and commands.

God (may He be praised) said, in describing his Prophet, "He commands them to do good and forbids them to do evil. He makes good things lawful for them and bad things unlawful" [Surah 7:157, translator's version]. This is a statement of the full scope of his mission. The Prophet (may God bless him and grant him salvation) is the one by whose mouth God commands all good and forbids all evil, makes good things lawful and bad things unlawful.

For this reason it is told of him (may God bless him and grant him salvation) that he said, "In truth I was sent to perfect morality."

So then, commanding good and forbidding evil are among the most important of duties or recommendations. These necessarily exist to promote general welfare, and to eliminate evil. It is for this purpose that Apostles were commissioned [referring to Prophets sent with divine revelations to other peoples, before the time of Muḥammad, as well as to the Prophet of Islam] and that scriptures were revealed. God does not love evil. Rather, all that He commands is for righteousness. He commends righteousness and the doers of righteousness, as well as those who believe and practice good works. In many places He rebukes evil and the doers of it.

Wherever the command and the forbidding result in more evil than good, then they do not issue from God's command. Rather, this shows that some duty has been left undone and that some forbidden deed has been performed, for it is incumbent upon a believer to fear God in the persons of his fellow men, and not to be responsible for guiding them [an allusion to Surah 2:272. This warning serves as a check to prevent anyone from wilfully taking the direction of his own and others' affairs into his own hands.]

This truth constitutes part of the meaning of the Word of the Most High, "O believers, look after your own souls. He who is astray cannot hurt you, if you are rightly guided" (Surah 5:104). ["Rightly guided" is a Quranic expression signifying the person who lives in submission to God, believing and doing works of righteousness.] In truth, right guidance is achieved by the carrying out of duty. If the Muslim applies himself to observe the good that is commanded and to avoid the evil that is prohibited, even as he applies himself to the performing of other duties, then the error of the one who has gone astray will not harm him.

This observance is sometimes in the heart, at other times with the tongue, and at other times by deed. In fact, in all cases it should be carried out from the heart, for there is no harm in deeds performed from the heart. If they are not performed from the heart, then he who does them is not a believer, even as the Prophet said (may God bless him and grant him salvation), "That (deed) shows the most inferior, or weakest, faith." He also said, "Back of that (deed) there is not even enough faith to resemble a grain of mustard seed." [A deed performed from the heart is one which is grounded in and motivated by faith in God. The Qur'ān links faith and works intimately by such expressions as, "Give thou good tidings to those who believe and do deeds of righteousness" (Surah 2:23).]

It is reported that Ibn Mas'ūd [one of the Companions of the Prophet] said, (may God be pleased with him) "Who is dead among the living?" He answered, "The one who knows not the good nor forbids the evil." This is likewise the state of the one who has been led captive by temptation, who is described as having a heart "like an overturned jug" [that is, unable to contain good, even as an overturned jug is unable to contain liquid]. Then there is the *ḥadīth* of Ḥudhayfah Ibn Al-Yamān (may God be pleased with him), which is reported in the two *Ṣaḥīḥ* collections [those of Al-Bukhārī and Muslim Ibn Al-Ḥajjāj], "Temptations suggest themselves to the heart until they surround it like a spread out mat, etc." [The simile is obscure. Another interpretation is that temptations present themselves to the heart like a beautifully woven and decorated garment spread out to allure.]

Who are those who command the good? Here there are two errors into which people fall. First there are those who neglect their duty of commanding the good by giving their own interpretation to the verse which has been cited. It is as Abū Bakr the Upright [the first caliph of Islam] said in his discourse: "O people, you recite this verse, 'Look after your own souls. He who is astray cannot hurt you, if you are rightly guided' (Surah 5:104) and you apply its meaning out of context. I heard the Prophet (may God bless him and grant him salvation) say, "When people see evil being done and they do nothing to change it, then they run the risk of being included by God among those who are punished for doing the evil." [The assurance from the Qur'ān that they will not be harmed by those who go astray should encourage them to try to restore those in error to the right way.]

In the second place there are those who want to command and to forbid, whether by tongue or by deed, but in an absolute way, without either knowledge, gentleness or patience, without paying attention to what is for the general good and what is not for the general good, to what is possible and what is not possible [i.e. zealous people without tact or discernment.] It is as the *ḥadīth* of Abū Tha'labah Al-Khushanī [a Companion of the Prophet] says, "I asked the Prophet (may God bless him and grant him salvation) about it, that is, the verse, and he said, 'Strive for the good and forbid evil, but when you see inveterate avarice, unbridled passion, preference for the life of the world and self-complacency, and when you give counsel which goes unheeded, then tend to your own business. Do not try to give orders to people. You can wait. Be patient. Patience under such circumstances is like holding live coals of fire [that is, very difficult]. The reward of the one who continues in patience is comparable to the reward of fifty men who have reacted similarly [but with less endurance than his]'".

There are some who command and forbid with the conviction that they are thereby obeying God and His Apostle, but in doing so they go beyond the limits of duty. Blameworthy innovators (*ahl al-bid'ah*) [a technical term of disapproval for Muslims who promulgate notions foreign to the ancient tradition] and sectarians such as the Khawārij [members of one of the earliest movements of dissent in Islam], the Mu'tazilah [see the chapter on Theology], the Rāfiḍah [the name given to the earliest Shī'ah (see the chapter on Theology)], and others are among those who err in the practice of commanding and forbidding, even resorting to armed conflict. The evil that they do is greater than the good.

For this reason, the Prophet (may God bless him and grant him salvation), enjoined that tyrannical leaders should be submitted to with patience. He forbade fighting against them as long as they perform the ritual prayer. He said, "Render to them the rights that are their due, and commit your own rights to God." I have explained this statement in another place.

In considering the scope of what is good and what is evil the criteria of the Divine Law must be applied. As long as a man is able to submit to the texts of the law, he must not deviate from them. If, however, there is no specific text to apply in a particular circumstance, let him carefully compare his opinion with possible analogies and similar cases. It is rare that the texts will be found inadequate, provided the person is well-acquainted with them and with their capacity to guide him to wise judgments.

In addition, if an individual or a group encounter a situation in which good and evil are mingled together, and it is impossible to separate them, they must either do both the evil and the good, or do neither the one nor the other. Under such circumstances it is not possible either to command the good or to forbid the evil in advance. Rather the case must be examined, and if the good predominates, then let it be commanded, even though some evil, albeit less than the good, may be necessitated in carrying out the action. No evil should be forbidden if, by so doing, some good should be missed which is greater than the forbidden evil. Such forbidding would constitute a hindrance to following in God's way, an attempt to avoid obedience to God and to his Apostle (may God bless him and grant him salvation), and an omission of good works.

If, on the other hand, the element of evil predominates, then let it be forbidden, even if it means that some good, albeit less than the evil, is necessarily omitted. If that good is commanded which, to carry it out, necessitates the doing of evil which is greater than the good, then this course amounts to commanding the evil and constitutes an act of disobedience to God and to his Apostle.

If the good and the evil are equal and inseparable the two of them should not be commanded together, nor should the two of them be forbidden together. Sometimes commanding the good will be best, and at other times forbidding the evil will be best. At still other times it will be best neither to command the good nor to forbid the evil. This is because the good and the evil are inseparably associated. These remarks pertain to actual, specific matters.

Sometimes, in zeal, good is commanded absolutely and evil is forbidden absolutely. In such circumstances an individual or a group are in no doubt but that the good is to be commanded and the evil is to be forbidden. Judgment is made both for the individual and for the group, so that their praiseworthy deeds are praised, and their blameworthy deeds are blamed, to such a degree that the good commanded neither takes into account other good greater than it [which might have been attained by a less sweeping judgment], nor the occurrence of evil [resulting from an unqualified judgment] that is greater than the good commanded. Likewise, the evil forbidden in such an absolute way neither takes into account other evil greater than that which is forbidden [resulting from an unqualified judgment] nor the elimination of good, whose loss is greater than the advantage gained by forbidding the evil absolutely. [The author refers in this paragraph to simplistic ethical judgments by overly zealous believers.]

When an issue is complicated, the believer should seek enlightenment until the true interpretation becomes clear. He should not undertake any act of obedience without knowledge and deliberate intention. If he neglects such obedience then he has committed sin. The omission of duty is a sin. To do that which has been forbidden is also a sin. This is a vast subject. There is no might and no power save in God [a stereotyped expression often used by Muslims when they are confronted with some profound aspect of human life].

In truth, the affairs of men are kept in order by means of justice. [The Arabic word for "justice" is *ʿadl* and it refers generally to all right moral behavior and conformity to the revealed law (*sharīʿah*).]

The affairs of men in the world are truly kept in order more adequately by justice, even when some kinds of misdeeds [*ithm,* one of the Arabic words for sin, which, in the use of the author here, has reference to minor infractions of Islamic law, whose social consequences are limited] are associated with it, than by legal injustice [*ẓulm fī-l-ḥuqūq,* or disregard for the rights of others], even if the latter is free of misdeeds. For this reason it is said: "God will sustain a just state, even if it is unbelieving; and He will not sustain an unjust state, even if it be a Muslim one."

It is also said, "With justice, even associated with unbelief, the world will continue; but with injustice, even associated with Islam, it will not continue."

The Prophet (may God bless him and grant him salvation) said, "There are no sins whose punishment is quicker than oppression and breaking the ties of kinship" [that is, renouncing responsibility for taking care of one's relatives]. The oppressor is overthrown in this world, even though he may be forgiven and shown mercy in the hereafter.

That is to say that justice is the principle regulating everything. If the affairs of the world are sustained by justice, then the world is truly sustained, even though its ruler [meaning any particular ruler in the world] may not have a great reward in the hereafter. And when it is not sustained by justice, it is truly not sustained, even though its ruler, because of his faith, deserves reward in the hereafter.

CHAPTER 5

Theology

THE TRADITIONAL WAY

A Creedal Statement Attributed to Aḥmad Ibn Ḥanbal, found in Ṭabaqāt al-Ḥanābilah (The Generations of the Followers of Ibn Ḥanbal)

The first formal expressions of Islamic theology were statements of the articles of belief based directly upon the words of the *Qur'ān* and the *ḥadīth.* Aḥmad Ibn Ḥanbal, who is purported to be the author of the following statement, died in 855 AD in the city of Baghdad.[1] He is considered as the founder of the Ḥanbalī school of jurisprudence, one of the four great schools, or rites, which still prevail in the Sunnī Islamic world. It is difficult to say definitely whether Ibn Ḥanbal actually composed this text, but, on the other hand, there is no reason to consider its content as other than an authentic expression of his ideas.

The importance of the creed is twofold. First, it is a good example of the earliest kind of theologizing that was done in the Muslim community; and second, its articles remain to this day the basic tenets of belief held by the largest number of Muslims in the world, those who call themselves "the people of the right practice (*sunnah*) and the community (*jamā'ah*)," or Sunnī Muslims. The word, *jamā'ah,* has a particular reference to the community of the Companions of the Prophet, whose beliefs and practices are considered to be normative for later generations. So this title can be paraphrased as, "The people who follow the Prophet's example (*sunnah*) and conform to the pattern of faith laid down by the first generation of Muslims."

Ibn Ḥanbal's statement was not intended to be, as are the creeds of Christendom, official or standard expressions of faith. It was rather one among many thoughtful efforts to expound the traditionalist position in view of the serious movements of dissension and heterodoxy which disturbed the Muslim community in the first two centuries of its life. This creed represents prephilosophical Islamic thought; although Ibn Ḥanbal's position is often called the orthodox one, he lived before the fixing of any official orthodoxy in Islam.

Introduction

The words of Abū 'Abd Allāh Aḥmad Ibn Muḥammad Ibn Ḥanbal: These are the doctrines of the people of knowledge, the followers of tradition, and the people of the accepted practice who hold fast to its principles. By doing so they have distinguished themselves and have been emulated by others, from the days of the Companions of the Prophet (may God bless him and grant him salvation) until now. I learned these teachings from scholars of al-Ḥijāz, Syria and elsewhere.

Whoever either contradicts anything in these teachings, or discredits them, or denounces one who advocates them, is an innovator [see the chapter on Law], a dissenter from the community, having departed from the way of the *sunnah* and the path of truth.

Description of Faith

[Faith is described rather than defined. Here the intellectual aspect of faith is minimal.] Their doctrine is that faith consists in verbal assent [to the tenets noted in the chapter on Traditions], deeds, intention [In Islam no deed is praiseworthy unless it is motivated by a good intention. In many cases it is required that this intention be expressed before carrying out the deed. See the chapter on Law] and adherence to the *sunnah*. Faith increases and decreases.

This statement of the possibility for faith to grow or to diminish reflects an important debate in seventh and eighth century Islam. One group asserted that faith cannot be affected, either positively or negatively, by the works believers do. Others took the position of Ibn Ḥanbal that faith and works are intimately associated.

There is the saying, "If God wills," in faith; however, the saying, "If God wills," is not an expression of doubt. Rather, it is an ancient practice of the scholars.

(See Surah 18:23, 24, and in the New Testament, James 4:13–15.) Many Muslims follow this principle to the extent of saying that they cannot even assert positively that they have faith, but that they must condition their own confession of faith upon the will of God. Thus the believer is cast entirely upon the mercy of his Lord. As Ibn Ḥanbal points out, this is not an attitude of doubt, but of trust in a most radical form; see the chapter on Traditions.

[Ibn Ḥanbal] And when a man is asked, are you a believer? he should say, I am a believer, if God wills; or I am, I hope; or he should say, I believe in God, His angels, His Books and His Messengers [see Surah 2:285]. . . .

> Man's destiny is from God, with its good and evil, its paucity and abundance, its outward and inward, its sweet and bitter, its liked and disliked, its good and bad, its first and last [that is, every aspect of human life]. It is a decree that He has ordained, a destiny that He has determined for men. No one ever will go beyond the will of God (may He be glorified), nor overstep his decree. Rather, all will attain the destiny for which He has created them, applying themselves to the deeds which He has determined for them in his justice (may our Lord be glorified). . . .

The idea is not that of a transcendent deity who from eternity imposes His will arbitrarily upon His creatures. God is regarded here rather as an extraordinarily wise sovereign, who, out of the breadth of his knowledge and the strength of his will, arranges the lives and affairs of his subjects so that finally perfect justice is achieved. It should be noted that this whole section views human destiny from God's side alone, with the purpose of justifying his governance of men's lives. The fact of human responsibility is understood but not developed.

> The knowledge of God (may He be glorified) is fulfilled in his creatures by virtue of an act of his own will. The disobedience of Satan and of others who disobeyed him (may He be blessed and exalted) is in his knowledge from the moment of their disobedience until the day of judgment. And He created them for that disobedience. Also the obedience of the obedient is in his knowledge, and He created them for that obedience. Each one will do that for which he was created, and will attain what was decreed for him and known concerning him. No one can go beyond either the destiny that God has fixed for him, or his will. God does whatever He desires; He is the efficient cause of whatever He wills.
>
> Whoever asserts that God willed good and obedience for his people who disobeyed him, but that they willed for themselves evil and disobedience, and so did according to their own will, asserts that the will of man is stronger than the will of God (may He be blessed and exalted). And what greater lie could be forged against God (may He be glorified) than this?

This and the following paragraph define clearly the crux of the argument in this section. The concern of the people of the *sunnah* was to affirm unequivocally the supremacy of God's will and his sole creative power. The fact that this affirmation seemed to contradict the reality of man's will and man's responsibility for his acts did not occupy the community at this stage. However, the polemical tone of this section clearly indicates that some Muslims were calling into question the validity of such statements about God and man, statements that may be said to be unduly unilateral.

> To the one who asserts that adultery is not by decree it is said: Do you see this woman who conceived in adultery and brought forth a child? Did God (may He be glorified) will to create this child? Did this event take place with his prior knowledge? If he says, no, then he asserts that there is another creator with God. This is plainly association of another with God in his deity [*shirk*, the cardinal sin in Islam].

Whoever asserts that theft, wine drinking, and using unlawful gain are not by decree and destiny, but rather that man possesses the power to consume that which belongs to others, this one plainly speaks the doctrine of the Zoroastrians [who held to a radical dualism in the deity]. The truth is rather that one who appropriates the possessions of others really consumes his own goods, and God had judged that he should consume them in the manner in which he did.

The Mu'tazilah, a dissenting school of thought, claimed that if a man takes and uses the belongings of another, he appropriates that which God has given to another, not his own things.

Whoever asserts that murder is not according to the destiny that God (may He be glorified) has fixed and by the act of his will for his creature, pretends that the murdered one has died before his appointed time. What blasphemy is plainer than this? No, rather, this happens by the judgment of God, according to his will in his creatures, his control over them, and his foreknowledge concerning them. He is the Just, the True, who does whatever He desires. Whoever concedes divine knowledge must also concede the divine decree and will, even in the smallest and least significant matters.

Submission to Authority

The caliphate will remain in the Quraish tribe so long as two people exist. No one should dispute with them for the office nor revolt against them. Until the day of judgment we shall never concede the office to other than they.

Questions concerning the caliphate belong in a statement of faith because membership in the political community of Islam was conditioned upon faith rather than upon other factors. The affirmation of the primacy of the Quraish tribe, to which the Prophet belonged, represents an effort to assure a continuity of authority, even a doctrine of succession. It contradicts the equalitarian principles upon which Islam is based, one of which says that the degree of piety is the only distinction that should be made between men (Surah 49:13). In the ninth and tenth centuries AD, authority became effectively decentralized in the Islamic empire and passed out of the hands of the Quraish.

Just War [in defense of Islam or to extend its sway] is the ancient prerogative of the heads of the community, whether they be righteous or corrupt. Its merit will be diminished neither by the tyranny of a tyrant nor by the justice of one who is just.

Friday communal prayer, the two festivals [that of the breaking of the fast of Ramaḍān (*'īd al-fiṭr*) and that of the sacrifice of an animal in memory of Abraham (*'īd al-aḍḥā*)], and the pilgrimage are headed by the authorities, even if they should not be devout, just and pious. [There is no clergy in Islam, so ritual functions are assumed by the leaders of the community.]

The payment of alms, the land tax, tithes, booty, and spoils is to be made to the governors, whether they dispose of them equitably or inequitably.

The reference in the last two paragraphs is not to two types of authority but to two categories of duties, ritual ones and fiscal ones.

Submission is due to whomever God has entrusted with authority over you. You are not to refrain from obedience to him, nor are you to raise your sword against him. Eventually God will grant you relief and a way out [an allusion to Surah 65:2]. Do not revolt against authority. You are to heed and obey. You must not violate an oath of allegiance. Whoever does so is guilty of innovation and is a dissenter and a separatist from the community. But if the one in authority commands you to do something which constitutes an act of disobedience to God, you do not have to obey him. However, you are not to revolt against him, nor refuse him his due.

To remain neutral during a civil war is a well established practice which must be observed. In a time of testing, defend your religion with your life. And do not encourage civil war by your hand or your tongue. Rather, restrain your hand, your tongue and your passion. God will help you. . . .

In Sunnī Islam the unity of the community is a value more to be sought than uniformity of belief and practice. Ibn Ḥanbal insists upon this principle in spite of the bad example set by some authorities and against the claim of the Khawārij sect (see in the chapter on Law, p. 116), which believed that only a pious and just caliph was worthy of obedience and which advocated revolutionary force to purify the community of unworthy leaders.

Eschatology

The one-eyed one, the Antichrist (*dajjāl*) [a legendary eschatological character vaguely suggestive of the Biblical Antichrist], will come forth; there is no doubt or question about it. He is the liar of liars.

The punishment of the grave is a reality [referring to that which takes place between the time of death and the resurrection]. A person will be questioned about his religion, and his Lord, about paradise and hell. Munkar and Nakīr [the two angels who conduct the questioning of the grave. They are not mentioned in the Qur'ān but there may be an allusion to their function in Surah 47:27-29.] are a reality. They are the reporters of the grave. We ask God for endurance [in view of the punishment of the grave].

The Pool of Muḥammad (may God bless him and grant him salvation) is a reality [situated in paradise, as a reward for those who enter therein on the day of resurrection], and his people go to it. And there are vessels which they use to drink from it.

The Bridge is a reality [one of the final testings of mankind before entering paradise]. It is placed directly over hell, and people pass upon it. Paradise is beyond it. We ask safety of God [from the perils of crossing the Bridge].

The Balance is a reality. On it are weighed the good deeds and the evil, as God wills them to be weighed [on the day of resurrection; see Surah 21:47; 23:102, 103].

The Trumpet is a reality [see Surah 23:101; 36:51; 37:19]. Isrāfīl [the archangel of the resurrection, whose name is mentioned in the traditions, but not in the Qur'ān] blows upon it, and men die.

All men must die before there can be a resurrection, contrary to Christian belief, which speaks of some who will remain alive at the end and who will be raised after the dead; see I Thessalonians 4:15-17.

Then he blows upon it again, and they rise to the Lord of the worlds, to reckoning and judgment, to reward and punishment, to paradise and hell, to the Preserved Tablet [the divine record of all men's deeds, recorded before the creation of the world. In other contexts the Preserved Tablet is the eternal prototype of the Word of God, of which all revealed scriptures are partial copies; see Surah 85:22.] according to the text of which the deeds of men are performed, conforming to those things that have been ordained and decreed.

The Divine Pen is a reality. [According to tradition, the Pen was the first thing to be created; see Surah 96:4; 68:1.] God has written with it the destiny of all things, and He has reckoned it among the things to be recalled (may He be blessed and exalted) [perhaps an allusion to Surah 96:1, in which God calls upon the Prophet to declare the truth of his creation].

Intercession on the day of resurrection is a reality. One people will intercede for another people, and the latter will not go to hell. A people will come out of hell because of the intercession of the intercessors. A people will come out of hell after having entered into it and having remained there as long as God wills. Then He will bring them out of it. Others will abide there forever. They are the idolaters, the ones who treat his truth as a lie, the gainsayers and the unbelievers. . . .

On the one hand, the *Qur'ān* seems to teach that intercession is not possible (see Surah 2:48 and 39:44). On the other hand, such texts as Surah 40:7; 42:51; and 21:28 have been interpreted as indication that some privileged ones can intercede before God for the rest of mankind. References abound in the traditions to the intercession of Muḥammad, the other prophets, angels, martyrs, and as here, a whole people. The Mu'tazilah opposed the doctrine of intercession.

The Attributes of God

God created seven heavens, one placed above another, and seven earths, one placed beneath another [an allusion to Surah 65:12 and 67:3, and to the cosmology of the ancients]. Between the highest earth and the lowest heaven is a distance requiring five hundred years to cover. And the distance from sky to sky requires five hundred years to cover. There is water above the highest heaven, the seventh. And the throne of the Merciful is above the water. God is upon the throne. The pedestal [of the throne] is the place on which his feet rest [another way of saying that He is seated on his throne].

The debate in Islam over the nature of the divine attributes is one of the most significant features of the history of Muslim doctrine. An oft-recurring example cited by Sunnī scholars is the Quranic assertion that God is seated upon a throne (Surah 20:5; 57:4; et cetera, see p. 139).

He knows all that is in the seven heavens and the seven earths, what is between them, what is under the ground, what is in the depth of the seas, as well as the source of every hair and every tree. He knows every seed, every plant and the falling of every leaf [see Surah 6:59]. He knows the number of all words, how many pebbles, grains of sand and particles of dirt there are, as well as the weight of the mountains. He knows the deeds of men, their steps, their words and their breaths. He has knowledge of all things. Nothing of all this is concealed from him, while He is on the throne above the seventh heaven. Veils of light, fire, darkness and other things of which He has knowledge hide him from sight.

If an innovator and dissenter argues, using the words of God (may He be glorified): "We are closer to him than his neck vein" (Surah 50:16, translator's version), and further, "And wherever you are, He is with you" (Surah 57:4, translator's version), and again, "Three persons cannot converse together, but He is the fourth . . . He is with them wherever they be" (Surah 58:7, translator's version), and other verses similar to these from the obscure portions of the Qur'ān [attempting to prove that God is present in every place]; then tell him: Verily, by this is meant divine knowledge, for God Most High is upon his throne above the seventh heaven, the highest; and He knows all things. His knowledge is evident from his creation. There is no place that is not included in his knowledge.

To reconcile God's omnipresence with his session on the throne, Ibn Ḥanbal here interprets the texts from the *Qur'ān* in a metaphorical way. God is present everywhere by virtue of his all-embracing knowledge. This passage provides a counterbalance to the creed's heavy emphasis upon the anthropomorphic attributes of God. The way is opened for a limited degree of figurative interpretation of anthropomorphic passages.

God (may He be glorified) has a throne, and the throne has carriers who carry it. God (may He be glorified) is upon his throne, and it has no apparent limits. God knows whether it has limits or not. [By not assigning limits to God's throne, the anthropomorphic nature of the sitting is somewhat mitigated.]

God (may He be glorified) is all-hearing. He does not misunderstand; all-seeing, He does not doubt; all-knowing, there is nothing He does not know; munificent, He does not withhold; all-patient, He is not hasty; mindful, He does not forget; watchful, He is not neglectful; close at hand, He is not unmindful. He moves, speaks and sees. He regards and laughs. He rejoices, loves and detests. He hates and approves. He is angered and condemns. He shows mercy and forgives. He impoverishes, bestows and deprives. [This paragraph is a mosaic of allusions to texts in the Qur'ān.]

God descends each night into the lowest heaven, according to his will [a concept originating in the *ḥadīth,* and expressing the immanence of God, as contrasted with the transcendence of his sitting on the throne]. "Like Him there is naught; He is the All-hearing, the All-seeing" (Surah 42:9).* The hearts of men are between two fingers of the Merciful. He turns them as He wills and directs them as He pleases. He created Adam with His hand according to His image.

This concept originates in the traditions. Its bold anthropomorphism is mitigated by later theologians with the explanation that the "image" refers to the mark of preferential ownership with which God singles out man as the most excellent of all creatures.

---

*All quotations from the *Qur'ān* in this chapter are from *The Koran Interpreted,* translated by Arthur J. Arberry, © Oxford University Press 1964. Reprinted by permission of Oxford University Press.

On the day of resurrection the heavens and the earth will rest in the palm of his hand. He will place his foot in the fire [of hell], and it [the fire] will recede. He will bring a people out of hell by his hand [those who are delivered by the intercession of others; see p. 123]. The people of paradise will look upon his face. They will see him, and He will bestow honor upon them. He will reveal himself to them, and He will reward them [the beatific vision, abundantly documented in the traditions, and hotly contested by the Mu'tazilah and other dissident groups]. Men will be presented to him on the day of resurrection. He himself will attend to their account. He will delegate no one but himself for that.

The Nature of the Qur'ān and Inspiration

The Qur'ān is the speech of God. He has spoken by it. It is not created [that is, it is eternal, even as its speaker is eternal]. Whoever asserts the Qur'ān is created is a Jahmī [a follower of Jahm Ibn Safwān, one of the early forerunners of speculative thought in Islam, an obscure figure belonging to the first half of the eighth century], and an unbeliever. If anyone says only that the Qur'ān is the speech of God, and does not add that it is uncreated, his word is more wicked than that of the previous one. [The affirmation that the Qur'ān is the uncreated speech of God came to be one of the catch phrases of Sunnī orthodoxy.] Whoever asserts that our pronunciation and our recitation of it are created, but that the Qur'ān itself is the speech of God, that one is a Jahmī. [Extreme advocates of the uncreated nature of the Qur'ān went so far as to say, as here, that even man's recitation of its words partakes of its eternal nature.] And whoever does not charge such people with disbelief is just like them.

God has spoken to Moses by his mouth, and handed to him the Tawrāt [the Quranic term for the Jewish Scriptures], from his hand to that of Moses. God did not stop speaking [that is, He continued to grant revelations to his prophets], and may He be blessed, He is the most excellent of creators. . . .

Fundamentals of Law

Religion [that is, *dīn,* man's duty to God] consists in the Book of God (may He be glorified), traditions, customary actions and reliable narratives of valid, authentic and well-known reports from trustworthy authorities, which confirm one another, and which lead back to the Apostle of God (may God bless him and grant his salvation), his Companions (may the favor of God be upon them), those who followed them and their subsequent followers; after them, to the well-known Imams, who are emulated, those who adhere to the *sunnah* and are devoted to the traditions. None of those approve of innovation. No one accuses them of falsehood, or denounces them for dissent. They neither apply analogy nor hold subjective opinions, for analogy in religion is false, and subjective opinion is even worse. Those who hold subjective opinion and apply analogy in religion are guilty of innovation and error; that is, unless there can be found a tradition warranting such practices, upon the authority of a previous trustworthy Imam.

This is an extremely conservative statement of the sources of law in Islam, admitting only the *Qur'ān* and the *sunnah.* Later followers of

Ibn Ḥanbal recognized that a limited use of analogy was valid in legal science.

> Whoever asserts that he does not approve of uncritical faith [*taqlīd,* an important notion, meaning faithful observance of the ancient tradition. To others it signified obscurantism; see pp. 133–134.] and that he will not follow others in matters of faith, that one has made a sinful utterance in the eyes of God and his Apostle (may God bless him and grant him salvation). By such an attitude he aims at the invalidation of tradition, the degrading of knowledge and *sunnah.* He is concerned only with subjective opinion, speculative theology (*kalām*), innovation and dissension.
>
> These beliefs and doctrines that I have described are those of the people of the *sunnah,* the community (*jamā'ah*), and the traditions, those entrusted with the reports [of the ancient practice], and bearers of knowledge. We have access to them, since it is from them that we have received the reports, and have learned the *sunnah.* They were well-known, trustworthy Imams, partisans of truth, who should be emulated and followed, who were not given to innovation, deviation or confusion. They in turn adhered to the teachings of their Imams and of the scholars who were before them.
>
> Adhere to these teachings, and may God be merciful to you. Learn them and teach them to others. God will direct in the right way.

THE TRADITIONAL WAY CHALLENGED

Al-Radd 'alā Al-Mushabbihah (Refutation of the Anthropomorphists) by Al-Qāsim Al-Rassī

The traditionalist view of God's attributes was early stigmatized by other Muslims as being grossly anthropomorphic. This selection, dating from the same era as the preceding one, the first half of the ninth century, contains an attack upon the ideas held by men like Ibn Ḥanbal. The writer, Al-Qāsim Al-Rassī (d. 860 AD), was a dissenter from the traditionalist group not only because of his position on the attributes, but also because of his attachment to the Zaydī branch of the Shī'ah, moderate partisans of the right of the caliph 'Alī's family to the place of leadership in the Muslim community.[2] Theologically he belonged to the tendency which was, during the ninth century, developing the use of philosophical arguments to expound Muslim theology, and which finally came to be known as the Mu'tazilī school of thought [see *The House of Islam,* p. 12]. However, Al-Qāsim's brief treatise here presented shows little tendency toward rational speculation, except for its figurative interpretations of the *Qur'ān*. He employs the same appeal to scriptural authority as does Ibn Ḥanbal.

> The heretical anthropomorphists are a group of professing Muslims who have gone astray. They liken God (exalted be his name) to his creation. They claim that He exists in the image of man, that He is a determinate substance and a visible figure. They use ambiguous scriptural texts to support their position, changing them by their interpretation and going against their literal meaning.

This is what the Jews and the Christians did before them, when they changed the order of passages in the Word of God [an allusion to Surah 4:46]. The anthropomorphists also use, as arguments, traditions that were invented by those who, having plunged into error, revolted against Islam. The ignorant go along with them, falling into heresy and blasphemy against God. Likewise they use traditions of which they do not know the correct interpretation, and they do not take the trouble to find out their correct interpretation. They have gone astray and they have led many into error. They have deviated from the right path. One of the Scriptures which they interpret is the following: "Upon that day faces shall be radiant, gazing upon their Lord" (Surah 75:22). They say that God (may He be glorified) will be seen by the eye in the hereafter, that He will be gazed upon openly. This they affirm contrary to God's Word (may his praise be exalted) which says: "The eyes attain Him not, but He attains the eyes" (Surah 6:103), and in ignorance of the meanings and interpretations of the verse [a denial of the beatific vision which Ibn Ḥanbal and other traditionalists affirmed; see p. 125]. The people of knowledge and of faith [those of whom the author is one] explain this verse differently from the dissembling anthropomorphists. To them, "faces shall be radiant" means "a beautiful resplendence"; "gazing upon their Lord" means "expecting his reward, his generosity, his mercy, and all good and benefits which will come to them from him." This is the meaning of the passage in the language of the Arabs, and that is the tongue in which the Qur'ān was revealed.

It is said that when abundance comes after drought, God (may his praise be exalted) has looked upon his creation, and that He has looked upon his servants. What is meant is that He has brought them relief and prosperity, not that before He did not see them, and then He began to see them.

God (exalted be his remembrance) said as He called attention to the people of hell, ". . . there shall be no share for them in the world to come; God shall not speak to them neither look on them on the Resurrection Day. . . ." (Surah 3:71). The interpretation of this statement is that they can expect no reward from God (may his praise be exalted) nor will He do good for them. By contrast, God will look upon the people of paradise, and they will gaze upon God (exalted be his praise). The meaning of this is that they may expect good from God. It will come to them from him; He will accomplish it for them. It does not mean that they will gaze upon God openly with their eyes (may He be revered, the possessor of majesty and honor). How could they see him with their eyes, when He is neither circumscribed nor limited? So (exalted be his praise), He is not visible. One who is visible is enclosed by limits and requires a locus which contains him. That which contains is greater than that which is contained, and more forceful by virtue of its restricting power [therefore, to affirm that God can be present in a particular place is to make him inferior to the place in which He is found]. . . .

The anthropomorphists have interpreted other words of God (may He be blessed and exalted), such as: ". . . I created with My own hands" (Surah 38:75); "The earth altogether shall be His handful on the Day of Resurrection, and the heavens shall be rolled up in His right hand" (Surah 39:67); ". . . and thy Lord comes, and the angels rank on rank" (Surah 89:23); ". . . and unto Moses God spoke directly—" (Surah 4:162); ". . . God is All-hearing, All-seeing" (Surah 22:60);. . . . "All things perish, except His Face" (Surah 28:88). They have explained these words according to their own imaginings to the effect that God (may He be glorified) is understood by them in all of these verses to be like his creatures in their attributes, in their forms and in their deeds. They have blasphemed Almighty God and have offered worship to another than God the Eminent.

The people of faith and unity have interpreted these verses [figuratively] to mean that nothing can be compared with God (may He be glorified). The words, "I created with My own hands" (Surah 38:75), means my power and my knowledge. He means, I was capable of it and cognizant of it; I took responsibility for it, myself. I have no associate either in my planning or in my workmanship. My power, my knowledge and my essence belong to none other, for I am the One to whom there is nothing similar. The meaning of the verse just cited is clarified by another verse which says, "Truly, the likeness of Jesus, in God's sight, is as Adam's likeness; He created him of dust, then said He unto him, 'Be,' and he was" (Surah 3:52). God said (exalted be his praise), "The only words We say to a thing, when We desire it, is that We say to it, 'Be,' and it is" (Surah 16:42). He means by this, when we bring something into being it exists.

He said (may He be blessed and exalted), "Have they not seen how that We have created for them of that Our hands wrought cattle that they own" (Surah 36:71)? He is saying here that what I have made, I have done myself.

He said (exalted be his praise), "Nay, but His hands are outspread; He expends how He will" (Surah 5:69). The people of knowledge interpret this as meaning that his blessings are extended to his creation: generous provision and limited provision. He dispenses as He wills, that is to say, He does what is best for mankind.

Likewise He said (exalted be his praise), "Blessed be He in whose hand is the kingdom" (Surah 67:1). This means that the kingdom is his. The Arabs say, the kingdom is in the hand of so-and-so, or, so-and-so has taken posession of the kingdom and the land. Also they say, it is in his grasp, or in his right hand, meaning that it is under his control and in his possession. In like manner, the heavens and the earth, with all that is between them and in them, are in the grasp of God and in his right hand, that is to say, they are under his control, sovereignty and power today, on the day of resurrection and at all times. Even as He said (exalted be his praise), ". . . that day the Command shall belong unto God" (Surah 82:19). The command, both then and today, belongs to God.

He said (may He be blessed and exalted) to the one who disobeys him, and whom He hands over to hell fire, "That is for what their hands have forwarded" (Surah 22:10), and, ". . . what your own hands have earned" (Surah 42:29). This means, what you have earned by your words and your deeds. It is not a question of one's hands apart from the body and its limbs.

He said (exalted be his praise) to his Prophet (may the blessings of God be upon him and his family), ". . . except what thy right hand owns" (Surah 33:52), meaning what you yourself own. . . .

The meaning of the verse, ". . . and thy Lord comes, and the angels rank on rank" (Surah 89:23), is that God (exalted be his praise) comes with his mighty signs to manifest the resurrection; He comes with earthquakes and terrors; He comes with the noble angels. Wrongdoing is brought to light and doubters have uncertainty removed. Things are revealed to them from God which they did not anticipate. The expression, "thy Lord comes" does not mean that He set forth from a place, nor that He goes away, nor that He changes. He does not change position from one place to another, nor does He come from one place to another. God is exalted and blessed far above such as that. Instead, He is present in every place, and no place contains him. He is cognizant of every secret conversation and is present at every assembly. . . .

From the verse, ". . . and unto Moses God spoke directly—" (Surah 4:162), the anthropomorphists claim that God (may He be exalted far above what they say) speaks with a tongue and with lips, that words go forth from him even as they do from his creatures. They blaspheme Almighty God when they affirm belief in such an attribute. According to the people of faith and knowledge, God's speech (exalted be his praise) to Moses (the blessings of God be with him) means that He called speech into existence, that He created it as He willed, and that Moses heard it (the blessings of God be with him) and understood it. Every thing heard comes from God, being created, because only He can create it. Indeed, God (exalted be his praise) called him and said, "I am God, the Lord of all Being" (Surah 28:30). This call is not the same as the one who calls. The one who calls thus is God (exalted be his praise), and the call is something else. That which is other than God, and which his creatures are incapable of producing, must be created by him, because it was not, then it was, by the power of God alone, who has no partner. . . .

The traditionalists affirmed that the speech of God was one of his eternal attributes. The Mu'tazilah, with Al-Rassī, claimed that to posit eternal, uncreated attributes in God is equivalent to introducing plurality into the divine nature.

As for the word which says, ". . . God is All-hearing, All-seeing" (Surah 22:60), this means that neither voice, nor uvula nor any other substance can be concealed from him, no matter where it might be, in whatever place: in the dark places of the earth, on land or on sea. It does not mean that God hears and sees by means of organs, or by means of anything other than himself. Otherwise He would be limited, or there would be something else coexistent with him. God is exalted above that.

As for the words which say, "All things perish except His Face" (Surah 28:88), and, ". . . yet still abides the Face of thy Lord. . . ." (Surah 55:27), they only refer to him, to nothing else. They mean that all things perish except him. The word, ". . . yet still abides the Face of thy Lord. . . ." (Surah 55:27) refers neither to a face belonging to a corporal substance, nor a body endowed with a face. God is exalted above these attributes which belong to his creatures. . . .

If anyone describes God (exalted be his praise) with the forms of his creation, making him to resemble anything that He has made, or imagines him in any image, body or spirit, or conceives of his being in one place without being in another, or thinks that He can be contained within limits, that He can be veiled from view, that He is visible, that He did not create his speech and his books, the Qur'ān and others, containing his words and his commands, that He is similar to anything in his creation, or that He is or will be accessible to anything in his creation by means of any part of the body or by the senses, such a person has denied him, comparing him with others and associating others with him. Understand this, and may God enable us to attain verity, to arrive at the truth.

Inqādh Al-Bashar min Al-Jabr wa-l-Qadar (The Deliverance of Mankind from Predestination and Fate) by Al-Sharīf Al-Murtaḍā

The traditionalists' emphasis upon predestination also came under attack by the Mu'tazilah. In the following selection objection is made to making God responsible for the evil deeds of mankind.[3] Muslims who believed like Ibn Ḥanbal felt that they must affirm God's all-embracing responsibility in order to be faithful to the truth of his omnipotence. To them, if any deed or event should not be caused by him, then He would be less than omnipotent. In opposition to this consistent, but difficult, doctrine, the Mu'tazilah affirmed that to make God responsible for the evil deeds of man is to attack or deny his perfect justice.

The author of this extract uses only scriptural argument, like Al-Rassī, in the preceding treatise. Al-Murtaḍā was a Baghdad Shī'ī of the Twelver branch, a renowned theologian and poet. He died in 1044 AD.

The following answer may be given to one who asks, "Do you say that good and evil both come from God Most High?"

If you mean that God is the source of well-being and affliction, of poverty and riches, of health and sickness, of fertility and barrenness, of hardship and ease, then it is granted that all of this comes from God. The misfortunes of life are called evil, whereas in reality they are wise, reasonable, true and just.

But if you mean that God is the source of immorality, depravity, lying, deceit, oppression, unbelief, crime and shameful deeds, then God forbid that we should say that. Rather, oppression comes from oppressors, and lying from liars, immorality from immoral people, and polytheism from polytheists. Justice and equitable dealings issue from the Lord of the Worlds.

God Most High confirms what we have said, by his word: "Many of the People of the Book wish that they might restore you as unbelievers, after you have believed, in the jealousy of their souls" (Surah 2:103). He did not say that the jealousy came from their Creator. We know that disobedience comes from his servants and that it is not from him. He said (may He be glorified), "And there is a sect of them twist their tongues with the Book, that you may suppose it part of the Book, yet it is not part of the Book; and they say, 'It is from God,' yet it is not from God, and they speak falsehood against God, and that wittingly" (Surah 3:72). We know that lying and unbelief are not from God. If they are not from God then they are neither of his doing nor of his making. He said (may He be glorified), "Evil are the deeds which they have presented themselves" (Surah 5:83, translator's version). What was presented was by themselves, not by their Lord to them. He also said, "Then his soul prompted him to slay his brother" (Surah 5:33) [referring to Cain, the son of Adam and murderer of Abel]. It is not said that his Lord caused him to murder, nor did his Creator force him to do it. Again, God said, "And they say, 'The All-merciful has taken unto Himself a son.' You have indeed advanced something hideous! The heavens are wellnigh rent of it and the earth split asunder, and the mountains wellnigh fall down crashing for that they have attributed to the All-merciful a son" (Surah 19:91–93) [referring to the Christians' belief in the divine sonship of Jesus Christ]. He informed them that they had perpetrated a terrible thing, not that "I have perpetrated it and put it into your hearts." He said, "And they say, 'The All-merciful has taken unto Himself a son.'" (Surah 19:91), thus informing them that they had attributed it to him, not that He had attributed it to himself.

Then God (may He be exalted) has informed us regarding the Prophets (may the blessings of God be upon them), that when they were censured for neglecting a task or such like, they acknowledged their errors in a most meritorious way. Adam and Eve (may peace be upon them) said, "Lord, we have wronged ourselves, and if Thou dost not forgive us, and have mercy upon us, we shall surely be among the lost" (Surah 7:22).

Jacob (upon him be peace) said to his sons, "No; but your spirits tempted you to do somewhat" (Surah 12:18). He did not say, "Your Lord tempted you." Then the sons of Jacob said, "Our Father, ask forgiveness of our crimes for us; for certainly we have been sinful" (Surah 12:98). They did not say, "Our sins come from our Lord. . . ."

Moses' servant said, "I forgot the fish—and it was Satan himself that made me forget it" (Surah 18:62). He did not say, "It was the Merciful himself who made me forget. . . ." God said: "Conspiring secretly together is of Satan" (Surah 58:11). He does not say that it is from the Merciful. Again, He said, "Let not Satan tempt you as he brought your parents out of the Garden" (Surah 7:26), that is, by means of his temptation and his deceit. God (may He be exalted) said: "Made I not a covenant with you, Children of Adam, that you should not serve Satan—surely he is a manifest foe to you—and that you should serve Me? This is a straight path. He led astray many a throng of you; did you not understand? (Surah 36:60–62) He told them that Satan had led them astray from the truth. He said, "For surely Satan provokes strife between them, and Satan is ever a manifest foe to man" (Surah 17:55). . . .

If we had wanted to continue to recount how God attributed disobedience of his servants to Satan, we should have had much more to write.

Al-Mukhtaṣar fī Uṣūl al-Dīn (A Synopsis of the Principles of Religion) attributed to the Qāḍī ʿAbd Al-Jabbār

The anonymous treatise from which this selection is taken presents in succinct form the basic tenets of the Muʿtazilī theologians. There is little reason to contest its attribution to the eminent theologian of Baghdad and Rayy (in Persia), ʿAbd Al-Jabbār Al-Hamadhānī (d. 1025 AD).[4] The introductory chapter, here translated, not only outlines the content of the whole treatise, but it also deals in an interesting way with the intellectual and spiritual approach of the Muʿtazilah to theology.

O God, I seek your help. I rely upon you and pray that you will guide me in the way of righteousness; and I beg you to bless our Prophet Muḥammad and his family, the excellent ones. [Mention of the Prophet's family in the blessing usually shows Shīʿī sympathies.]

This is a synopsis of the principles of religion. It includes a summary of information and of differences of opinion. We can afford neither to be ignorant of nor to neglect the things which are contained in it. . . . I have arranged the work in the form of questions and answers so that it might be easier and more accessible. God is the best of helpers!

QUESTION: What should a responsible person know about the principles of religion?

ANSWER: Four things: 1) the truth of God's unity (*tawḥīd*); 2) justice; 3) prophethood; 4) divine law. The whole of religion depends upon these principles.

QUESTION: What is meant by the truth of God's unity?

ANSWER: It means the knowledge of the qualities which God (may He be glorified) alone possesses, or the principles for understanding those attributes by which He is distinguished and set apart from all others, as, for example, the fact that He is eternal, whereas everything other than He is created; the fact that He is one, with no second, and with nothing like him in his dissimilarity; the fact that He knows, that no ignorance can be possible in him, and that He has no equal in his knowing. These are things which we shall set forth in detail later.

QUESTION: What is meant by the principle of justice?

ANSWER: It means the knowledge that the Most High is declared to be exalted far above three things: all wickedness, all failure to do whatever is required, such as giving rewards for good deeds, and any possibility of being served by doers of evil or by any action that is not beneficial. Justice also involves the demonstration that all of God's works are wise, just and proper.

QUESTION: Do you not speak normally [in Mu'tazilī circles] of five principles, including the Promise and the Threat [a distinctive emphasis of the Mu'tazilah, having to do with their insistence upon divine retribution for the commission of grave sins], the Intermediary Position [another important Mu'tazilī distinctive, according to which a Muslim who commits grave sin is relegated to a position between that of a believer and that of an unbeliever], and the Commanding of Good and the Forbidding of Evil? [This principle, while not peculiar to the Mu'tazilah (see in the chapter on Law, pp. 113–117), was nevertheless one of the hallmarks of their system. It provided the basis for putting their principles of justice and human freedom into practice in the community.]

ANSWER: All of that is included in justice. When we eliminate from the nature of God all variance, all deceit and all vagueness, we effectively refute the sect of the Murji'ah [who were known for the laxness which they attributed to God's attitude toward those who commit sins. They emphasized God's promises and minimized his threats]. When we make clear the kind of service which God requires then we confirm what has been said about the Intermediary Position, as well as about the Commanding of Good and the Forbidding of Evil.

QUESTION: What is meant by the principle of prophethood?

ANSWER: It means the knowledge of God Most High's ability to send prophets, together with the fact that He has sent them. It includes the duty of believing in the divine law which they transmitted, and the duty of obeying it.

QUESTION: What is meant by divine law?

ANSWER: It means knowing the divine precepts and duties which the Prophet (may God bless him) promulgated, including the indication of licit practices and illicit ones. The science of jurisprudence (*fiqh*) belongs in this connection, and its importance is seen by the fact that through it the divine law becomes known. There are two kinds of *fiqh,* first, that which everyone must know, such as the rules of ritual acts (*'ibādāt*), for example, the number of ritual prayers, the fast of Ramaḍān, etc. The second kind of *fiqh* consists of the systematic elaboration of the subject matter. Here recourse to convention (*taqlīd*) is allowed in the case of those who do not know the science of *fiqh*.

In the realm of belief *taqlīd* means accepting truth on the authority of others, and in the realm of practice it means uncritical imitation of others. See p. 126 for Ibn Ḥanbal's approval of *taqlīd.*

QUESTION: For this last principle, is it not necessary that the responsible believer be well versed in Arabic, grammar and elocution?

ANSWER: Scholars need such knowledge in order to understand the messages which God Most High and his Apostle have spoken. So, this one principle, divine law, requires linguistic competence, but not the other principles which have been mentioned. Those can be known by sound reason alone. Ignorance of language will not affect the validity of one's knowledge of those principles.

QUESTION: What is the first thing that a person is required to do?

ANSWER: To contemplate and to reflect on the way to knowledge of God Most High.

QUESTION: What is the origin of this requirement to contemplate and to reflect? Some people, such as the advocates of tradition (*ḥadīth*) [as Ibn Ḥanbal, see p. 126] and others, disagree and say that the first requirement is to act in uncritical imitation of others. Also, some intelligent people disagree and say, "We know what is incumbent upon us as duty, so we have no need for reflection and contemplation."

ANSWER: The intelligent person knows that among people there are those who make mistakes and there are those who do what is right. However, all of them claim to have done the right thing. Why should the practice of one group be preferred over the practice of the other group? What should the practice of one who professes the unity of God be preferred over that of a heretic? Why should the practice of one who says that God will be seen by mankind be preferred over that of one who denies that vision? [a point of contention between the Mu'tazilah and the traditionalists; see p. 125, for the position of Ibn Ḥanbal.] Thus the weakness of uncritical imitation (*taqlīd*) is made clear, and evidence is furnished that truth is not learned by following the example of men. It is for this reason that the Commander of the Faithful ['Alī Ibn Abī Ṭālib (d. 660 AD), the fourth Caliph of Islam] said to Al-Ḥārith: "O Al-Ḥārith, you have failed to discern that truth is not known by following the example of men. Know the truth first, and then you will recognize the people of truth."

QUESTION: Is it not preferable to imitate the behavior of a person who practices his religion in quiet seclusion?

ANSWER: Is not a zealously religious person capable of doing wrong, whether he acts in seclusion or in the open, even as the Christian monks [who practice their faith in seclusion] have done wrong? [In spite of at least one approving remark in the Qur'ān (Surah 5:82), Islam has generally disapproved of Christian monasticism (see Surah 9:34; 57:27).] So, how can what you have said be true?

QUESTION: Is not the practice of the majority to be preferred?

ANSWER: Is not the majority capable of doing wrong and the minority of doing right? What you have said is not warranted.

QUESTION: The Prophet (may God bless him and his family and grant them salvation) said, "Address yourselves to the masses!" Did he not indicate thereby that he wanted people to follow the majority?

ANSWER: Anyone who advocates acting by uncritical imitation does not recognize that the Apostle was a prophet. To follow him by imitation would be no better than to follow Musaylimah the false prophet [an enemy of the Muslim community in Arabia immediately after the death of the Prophet].

A prophet necessarily brings to his people, according to Mu'tazilī thought, a message which confirms and makes accessible that which thoughtful, reasoning men are capable of discovering by reflection. So, the right way to follow the Prophet Muḥammad is by the full exercise of reason, not by the same blind allegiance that unthinking people give to any forceful demagogue.

> How can this tradition be advanced as an argument? What it means is that one should follow the whole nation [united as a Muslim community, the *ummah*], because its testimony is authoritative. The nation represents the greater portion of the people. Any part of the population less than that aggregate which is described by the term, "nation," cannot be identified with the expression, "the masses," in the Prophet's saying.

Although this interpretation suggests the principle of consensus (*ijmā'*) in jurisprudence (see chapter 4, Law), the authority of the community here is based on reason rather than on scripture (*Qur'ān* and *ḥadīth*).

> If the knowledge of God and his Apostle were primary, admitting no variance, then all intelligent people would be agreed. The fact that they disagree is evidence that such knowledge is acquired by reflection, even as we have said. This fact also furnishes evidence for what we shall say about information which is received by revelation, for the Most High has required and encouraged contemplation upon such information. He praises those who engage in it and He rebukes those who shun it. He said (may He be glorified), "Consider what is in the heavens and the earth" (Surah 10:101, translator's version), and, "What, do they not consider how the camel was created" (Surah 88:17)? The Most High also said, "In the earth are signs for those having sure faith; and in yourselves; what, do you not see" (Surah 51:20, 21)? And, "How many a sign there is in the heavens and in the earth that they pass by, turning away from it" (Surah 12:105). The arguments which God (may He be exalted) has used in his Book to inform point out the necessity for contemplation and the weakness of accepting truth on the authority of others.
>
> QUESTION: What is the basis for the assertion that the intelligent person must reason to attain knowledge of God Most High?
>
> ANSWER: This assertion comes from the experience of hearing the differing opinions of various schools of thought, how they accuse each other of unbelief and how one intimidates another for his divergent opinion. It is based on the knowledge that all of these schools of thought cannot be right. They hold contradictory opinions, as for example, those who say that knowledge is eternal and those who say that it is created, or as those who say that God will be seen by believers and those who deny that vision. If these divergent schools of thought cannot all be right, they cannot all be wrong either. Truth will not totally abandon them. It is impossible to believe that the world is neither eternal nor created. In these opinions there must be some elements of truth and some elements of falsity.
>
> When a person is frightened and is told, "If you do not reflect in order to attain knowledge of the truth, we fear that you will be among those who are thwarted, and that this will lead you to eternal fire, to terrible consequences," then he must fear and be aware that he should be on guard against that which he fears. He must contemplate and reflect, even as he would, for example, if, while he was obliged to follow a certain path, someone told him that he was going to meet a savage beast. Even if no beast

were actually there, he would be frightened at the warning; he would inquire about and investigate the matter. This is why we recommend the necessity for reasoning. Even though a person reflects and ponders upon the signs of God's blessings, such as health and strength, tools and implements, appetite and enjoyment, taking knowledge of the difference between himself and someone who is weak and sickly, he should be told, "Unless you meditate and come to know the Creator and the Giver of all your blessings, we cannot be sure that you will not have the audacity to deny him. Obedience to him depends upon your attaining correct knowledge of him."

QUESTION: State to me in summary form that which it is necessary to know about the truth of God's unity.

ANSWER: This subject may be treated under five fundamentals: 1) proof of the creation of the world; 2) evidence for a Creator; 3) explanation of the attributes which the Creator must have; 4) knowledge of which attributes possessed by his creatures cannot possibly belong to him; 5) proof of his uniqueness. If you know these, then you will have learned what is necessary concerning the truth of God's unity.

THE TRADITIONAL WAY ESTABLISHED

Al-Jawāhir al-Kalāmiyyah fī Īḍāḥ al-'Aqīdah al-Islāmiyyah (Theological Pearls, Setting Forth the Islamic Doctrine) by Ṭāhir Afandī Al-Jazā' irī

For a glimpse at the theological position that prevailed in Sunnī Islam after the intensive debates of the first three centuries of its history, we turn to a twentieth century author, Al-Jazā'irī (d. 1920), who lived most of his life in Damascus.[5] This choice is not as incongruous as it might at first seem, for Al-Jazā'irī presents, in *Theological Pearls,* a faithful picture of classical theology (*'ilm al-kalām*). Insofar as there can be said to be an official doctrinal system in a religious community that from its early days until now, has avoided the centralization of authority, this is it, at least for the Sunnī branch of Islam. Much of the formulation of these doctrines goes back to Al-Ash'arī (d. 935 AD; see *The House of Islam,* p. 12), who, while remaining firmly grounded in the traditionalist framework (see the selection by Ibn Ḥanbal, pp. 118–126), adopted some of the rational methods of the Mu'tazilah to express and to expound the faith of the community. This text reflects much of the theologizing of the Ash'arī school up to the twelfth century. *Theological Pearls* was prepared with a pedagogical concern. It was intended to be studied by average Muslims without training in philosophy, and has enjoyed widespread favor all over the Islamic world.

Introduction

QUESTION: What is the meaning of the expression, "The Islamic Doctrine?"

ANSWER: The Islamic Doctrine is the ensemble of things in which the people of Islam believe, that is, the things which they hold to be true.

QUESTION: What is the meaning of the expression, "Islam?"

ANSWER: "Islam" means the confession of the tongue and the belief of the heart that all which our Prophet Muḥammad (may God bless him and grant him salvation) has brought is true and trustworthy.

QUESTION: What are the Pillars of Islamic Doctrine, that is, its bases?

ANSWER: The Pillars of Islamic Doctrine consist of six things: belief in God Most High, belief in his Angels, belief in his Books, belief in his Apostles, belief in the Last Day and belief in Predestination.

Faith in God

QUESTION: What does it mean, generally speaking, to believe in God (may He be praised and exalted)?

ANSWER: It means to believe that God (may He be praised and exalted) is endowed with all of the attributes of perfection and is free from all attributes of imperfection.

QUESTION: What does it mean, in detail, to believe in God (may He be praised and exalted)?

ANSWER: It means to believe that God (may He be praised and exalted) possesses the attributes of existence, of infinite anteriority, of infinite continuance, of dissimilarity to contingent beings, of self-subsistence, of unity [attributes which emphasize the transcendence of God. These are sometimes explained as qualities which reside in the subject (God), but without causes.], of life, of knowledge, of power, of will, of hearing, of sight, of speech [attributes which emphasize relationship, or the immanence of God. These are sometimes explained as the qualities which issue from causes residing in the subject (God).], and that He is living, knowing, powerful, willing, hearing, seeing and speaking.

The last seven qualities can also be understood as names for God, the living, the knowing, et cetera. This repetition, in the form of divine names, of seven attributes previously listed reflects some of the intricacies of the debate between the Mu'tazilah and the followers of Al-Ash'arī, on the subject of the attributes. To Al-Jazā'irī, the facts of God's living, knowing, et cetera, attested by the *Qur'ān,* are based on the corresponding attributes of life, knowledge, et cetera. And in his thought, both sets of qualities are eternally distinct from God's essence, even while remaining inseparable from that essence. A much used formula to express this thought is, "God lives by virtue of his eternal life; He knows by virtue of his eternal knowledge, et cetera." Evidently, such a subtle formulation would not have been necessary, if the Mu'tazilah had not denied the existence of eternal attributes. They accepted the Quranic witness that God lives, knows, et cetera, but they affirmed that He manifests these qualities, not by virtue of corresponding eternal attributes, life, knowledge, et cetera but simply by virtue of his essence. In other words, the attributes are identical with the essence. Some of this school of thought went further to say that as expressed in the *Qur'ān,* the attributes are only rational formulations of that which is essentially unknowable, that is, the nature of God, so the qualities practically lack real existence. Other Mu'tazilah asserted that God possesses knowledge, power, et cetera by being cognizant, by exercising power, et cetera that is the attribution of a quality to God is contingent upon the manifestation of that quality in time.

On the contrary, for the Ash'ariyyah, the exericse of power, knowledge, et cetera derives from eternal attributes of power, knowledge, et cetera. And in addition, the divine names, expressing God's possession of the attributes, are themselves eternally true. For example, God is the eternally knowing one by virtue of his eternal attribute of knowledge, both eternal realities being identified as distinct from God's essence and yet not existing apart from him.

QUESTION: What does it mean to believe in the existence of God Most High?

ANSWER: It means to believe that God Most High exists and that He exists by virtue of his essence, not by virtue of any intermediary, and that his existence is necessary [that is, contingent on nothing], not affected by non-existence [nothingness].

QUESTION: What does it mean to believe in the infinite anteriority of God?

ANSWER: It means to believe that God is pre-existent. We mean by this that He existed before everything, that at no time was He non-existent, and that His existence had no beginning.

QUESTION: What does it mean to believe in the infinite continuance of God (may He be praised and exalted)?

ANSWER: It means to believe that God (may He be praised and exalted) is permanently existent, that his permanence has no end, that He will never cease to exist, and that nonexistence can never come to him.

QUESTION: What does it mean to believe that God Most High is dissimilar to contingent beings, that is, to creatures?

ANSWER: It means to believe that nothing is like God Most High, neither in his essence, nor in his attributes, nor in his acts.

QUESTION: What does it mean to believe that God (may He be praised and exalted) is dissimilar in his essence to creatures?

ANSWER: It means to believe that the essence of God (may He be praised and exalted) does not resemble creatures in any way. Whatever you might conceive in your mind, God is not like that, "Like Him there is naught" (Surah 42:9).

QUESTION: What does it mean to believe that the attributes of the Most High are dissimilar to the attributes of contingent beings?

ANSWER: It means to believe that the knowledge of God Most High does not resemble our knowledge, that His power does not resemble our power, that His will does not resemble our will, that His hearing does not resemble our hearing, that His sight does not resemble our sight and that His speech does not resemble our speech.

QUESTION: What does it mean to believe that the acts of the Most High are dissimilar to the acts of contingent beings?

ANSWER: It means to believe that the acts of the Lord Most High do not resemble the acts of any being, because the Lord does things without either intermediary or instrument ("His command, when He desires a thing, is to say to it, 'Be,' and it is." Surah 36:82), to believe that He does nothing out of need, and that He does nothing in vain, that is, uselessly; for the Most High is wise.

QUESTION: What does it mean to believe in the self subsistence of the Most High?

ANSWER: It means to believe that God Most High needs nothing. He needs neither locus nor place of inherence, nor any creature whatever. He can dispense with everything, but everything needs him.

QUESTION: What does it mean to believe in the life of God Most High?

ANSWER: It means to believe that God Most High is living and that his life is not like our life. Our life is produced by intermediaries, such as the circulation of blood and breathing, whereas the life of the Most High is not produced by any intermediary. It is of infinite anteriority and of infinite continuance. It is absolutely unaffected by nonexistence or by change.

QUESTION: What does it mean to believe in the unity of God Most High?

ANSWER: It means to believe that God Most High is unique; He has neither associate nor anyone comparable to him nor anyone analogous to him, nor anyone contrary to him, nor anyone opposed to him.

QUESTION: What does it mean to believe in the knowledge of God Most High?

ANSWER: It means to believe that God possesses the attribute of knowledge, and that He knows everything. He knows all things, both outward and inward. He knows the number of the grains of sand, the number both of the drops of rain and the leaves of the trees. He knows that which is secret and hidden. No secret is hidden from him [see Surah 69:18]. His knowledge is not acquired, rather He knows things from eternity before their existence.

QUESTION: What does it mean to believe in the power of God Most High?

ANSWER: It means to believe that God Most High possesses the attribute of power, and that He is omnipotent.

QUESTION: What does it mean to believe in the will of God Most High?

ANSWER: It means to believe that God Most High possesses the attribute of will, and that He wills. Nothing happens except by his will. All that He wills, is; whatever He does not will cannot be.

QUESTION: What does it mean to believe in the hearing of God Most High?

ANSWER: It means to believe that God (may He be praised and exalted) possesses the attribute of hearing and that He hears everything, be it secret or public. But the hearing of the Most High is not like our hearing, for our hearing takes place by the intermediary of the ear, whereas the hearing of the Most High takes place without any intermediary.

QUESTION: What does it mean to believe in the sight of God Most High?

ANSWER: It means to believe that God Most High possesses the attribute of sight, and that He sees everything. He sees even the black ant in the dark night, and whatever is even smaller than that. Nothing is hidden from his view, either on the earth and within it, either above the sky or below. But his sight is not like our sight, for our sight takes place by the intermediary of the eye, whereas the sight of the Most High takes place without any intermediary.

QUESTION: What does it mean to believe in the speech of God Most High?

ANSWER: It means to believe that the Most High possesses the attribute of speech, and that his speech does not resemble our speech. Our speech is created in us and is produced by the intermediary of instruments, such as the mouth, the tongue, the lips, whereas the speech of the Most High is not like that.

QUESTION: Tell us which attributes it is impossible to attribute to the Lord Most High?

ANSWER: The attributes which are impossible with reference to God Most High, that is, those which we cannot attribute to Him are non-existence, contingence, annihilation, resemblance to contingent things, need for other than himself, existence of an associate, weakness, "antipathy," that is, the possibility of something happening without his having willed it, ignorance, and other similar things. It is impossible to attribute these things to him only because they are attributes of deficiency and the Lord Most High possesses only the attributes of perfection. . . .

This paragraph echos the philosophical doctrine of atomism coming from the ancient Greeks and elaborated by Al-Baqillānī (d. 1013 AD) to serve the theology of Al-Ash'arī. According to atomism, creation consists of a large number of basic particles, called atoms, each one endowed with an accident. In combination the atoms form substances. Their existence is for an instant only, and God is continually recreating them. This philosophy safeguards the absolute freedom of God and renders unnecessary a system of cause and effect. Whatever recurring patterns are observed in creation cannot be called natural laws. They are simply oft-repeated sequences of continuous creation by God, which can be interrupted at anytime. Another element in atomism is the antithesis of opposing accidents. It is this milieu of thought that is reflected in the statement of the attributes that it is impossible to attribute to God. The meaning of course is not that divine attributes are accidents but that atomism causes the theologian to think in antithetical terms.

QUESTION: What is meant by the "sitting" in the words of the Most High: "The All-compassionate sat Himself upon the Throne" (Surah 20:4).

ANSWER: The sitting indicated here is that which suits the majesty of the All-compassionate. The fact of sitting is known, but its "how" is unknown. The way in which God sits on his throne is not the same as the way a man sits in a boat, on the back of an animal or on a royal throne, for example. If anyone has such ideas then he is a victim of his imagination, having made the Creator similar to the creatures, whereas reason and tradition have confirmed that nothing is like him. Thus in the same way that his essence resembles that of no creature, so nothing that is attributed to God can resemble that which is attributed to creatures. [See Ibn Ḥanbal's treatment of the "sitting," pp. 123–124. By denying that God resembles anything and yet at the same time holding to the anthropomorphic expressions of the Qur'ān, the Ash'ariyyah remain in the line of the people of the *sunnah* and yet cannot be accused of gross anthropomorphism.]

QUESTION: Can we attribute to God (may He be praised and exalted) two hands, eyes or other such things?

ANSWER: It is mentioned in the Noble Book that God Most High has a hand, according to the words, "God's hand is over their hands" (Surah 48:10), that He has two hands, according to the words, "Said He, 'Iblis, what prevented thee to bow thyself before that I created with My own hands?'" (Surah 38:75), and that He has eyes, according to these words, "And be thou patient under the judgment of thy Lord; surely thou art before Our eyes" (Surah 52:48). However it is permitted to attribute to God only that which He has attributed to himself in his revealed Book, or which his Prophet has attributed to him.

QUESTION: What is meant by "hand?"

ANSWER: The meaning of "hand" as well as that of "eyes" is that which suits his majesty; for that which is attributed to him does not resemble that which is attributed to a creature. Whoever believes that He has a hand like that of a creature, or an eye, is a victim of his imagination, having made God resemble his creatures, whereas nothing is similar to him.

QUESTION: Who holds the opinion that you have given concerning the meaning of the "sitting," the two hands and the eyes?

ANSWER: Most of the Ancients [the people of the *sunnah* and the first generation of Ash'ariyyah] held that opinion. As for the Moderns [later thinkers of the Ash'ariyyah], most of them interpret the "sitting" as meaning "supreme mastery," the "hand" as "blessing" or "power" and the "eyes" as "protection" or "providence." They give this interpretation because many of them think that if these expressions are not interpreted metaphorically and changed from their literal sense, they will lead to the ascription of human characteristics to God. . . .

Faith in Angels

QUESTION: What are angels?

ANSWER: They are subtle bodies created from light. They neither eat nor drink. "They are honoured servants" (Surah 21:26). They "disobey not God in what He commands them and do what they are commanded" (Surah 66:6).

QUESTION: Can men see the angels?

ANSWER: Except for the Prophets, no man can see the angels in their original forms, for they are subtle bodies, even as the air cannot be seen, although it is a body filling space, because it is a subtle body. However, when angels take the form of a dense body, such as that of a man, then they can be seen. . . .

QUESTION: What are the functions of angels?

ANSWER: Some angels are messengers between the Lord Most High and his Prophets and his Apostles, like Gabriel (may peace be with him). Others protect human beings, others register the good and bad deeds of men. Some are put in charge of paradise and its blessings, others in charge of hell and its torment. Still others are carriers of God's Throne. Some angels take care of the interests and benefits of men as well as other matters concerning which they receive orders.

Faith in the Books of God (may He be praised and exalted)

QUESTION: What does it mean to believe in the Books of the Most High?

ANSWER: I believe that God Most High possesses Books which He has made to descend upon his Prophets. He has revealed in them that which He commands, that which He prohibits, that which He promises and that which He threatens. These are the veritable speech of God Most High. They come forth from him, without our knowing how, in the form of words. He made them to come down as a revelation. Some of these Books are the Torah, the Gospel, the Psalms and the Qur'ān.

QUESTION: What do you believe about the Qur'ān?

ANSWER: I believe that the Qur'ān is a very noble Book which God revealed to the most noble of his Prophets, Muḥammad (may God bless him and grant him salvation). It is the last of the divine Books to be revealed. It abrogates all of the Books that came before it, and its authority will last until the day of resurrection. It cannot be affected by either change or alteration. It is the most important sign of the prophetic office of Muḥammad (may God bless him and grant him salvation), by virtue of the fact it is the greatest of miracles.

QUESTION: Why is the Qur'ān the greatest of miracles?

ANSWER: In truth, the Qur'ān is the greatest of miracles because it is a permanent rational sign, visible at all times to the eye of the mind. Other miracles terminate when their time comes to an end, and no trace remains of them except what is reported concerning them. One aspect of its wondrous nature is that it attains a degree of purity of language and of eloquence that goes beyond human capacity. . . .

A second point is the fact that no matter how much the recitation of the Qur'ān is listened to, one never grows tired of it.

A third point is the fact that the Qur'ān contains a collection of knowledge unknown either to Arabs or to non-Arabs.

Fourthly, it gives accounts of past events and of conditions among the nations, whereas the one to whom these things were revealed (may God bless him and grant him salvation) was illiterate, knowing neither how to write nor to read. The revelation made such knowledge unnecessary for him. The fact of illiteracy also makes it more appropriate to accept the book's inimitability.

Faith in Apostles (may blessing and salvation be theirs)

QUESTION: What do you believe about the Apostles of God Most High?

ANSWER: I believe that God Most High has Apostles whom He has sent in his mercy and by his grace, to announce rewards for those who do good, to warn of punishment those who do evil, to explain to mankind religious and worldly matters which they need to know and which are useful to them in enabling them to reach the highest level of development. God has confirmed his Apostles by manifest signs and striking miracles. The first Apostle was Adam and the last was our Prophet, Muḥammad (may blessing and salvation be his).

QUESTION: What is the meaning of the word, "prophet?"

ANSWER: The Prophet is a man to whom God has revealed a Divine Law, even if he did not receive the command to transmit it. If he received the order to transmit it, he is also called an Apostle. So, every Apostle is a Prophet, but not every Prophet is an Apostle.

QUESTION: How many Prophets are there?

ANSWER: Their number is not known with certainty. In the Noble Book there are twenty-five whose names are listed. These are Adam, Idrīs, Noah, Hūd, Ṣāliḥ, Abraham, Lot, Ishmael, Isaac, Jacob, Joseph, Job, Shu'ayb, Moses, Aaron, Dhū Al-Kifl, David, Solomon, Elijah, Elisha, Jonah, Zacharias, John the Baptist, Jesus and Muḥammad (may blessing and salvation be theirs). These are also Apostles.

QUESTION: What is required of Prophets (may blessing and salvation be theirs)?

ANSWER: Four qualities are required of Prophets (may blessing and salvation be theirs): veracity, faithfulness, communication and intelligence. With reference to Prophets, veracity means that their message conforms to reality, to things as they actually are. Absolutely no untruth can emanate from them. The meaning of faithfulness, in their case, is that their outer acts and their inner thoughts are preserved from falling into that which would displease God the Real, the One who has chosen them from among all creatures. Communication means that they explain to mankind as clearly as possible all that God has commanded them to explain, without hiding anything. Intelligence means that they are the most perfect of creatures in discernment and understanding.

QUESTION: In summary, what is necessary for us to believe on the subject of Prophets (may blessing and salvation be theirs)?

ANSWER: We believe that the Prophets (may blessing and salvation be theirs) are characterized by every quality which adorns and free of everything which dishonors, both inwardly and outwardly, both in deed and in word. We believe that it is permissible for human accidents [such as sickness and suffering] to happen to them, for these do not detract from their high position. We believe that God chose them from among mankind and sent them in order that men might know his commands and his ordinances. We believe that they have not diverged from each other in matters of religion, for religion is basic, by virtue of its relationship with faith, which itself admits of neither multiplicity nor variation. Where the Prophets differ, it is in certain precepts of the law, which are by nature derivative, having to do with practice, and in which wisdom dictates variation, depending on the different eras, locations and situations in which peoples live, and their different characteristics.

QUESTION: In how many qualities did our Prophet (may blessing and salvation be his) differ from the rest of the Prophets?

ANSWER: Our Prophet (may blessing and salvation be his) differs from the rest of the Prophets in three ways: first, he is superior to them, second, he was sent to all mankind, and third, he was the Seal of the Prophets, so that after him no other Prophet will come.

QUESTION: Why was our Prophet (may blessing and salvation be his) the Seal of the Prophets?

ANSWER: Our Prophet (may blessing and salvation be his) was the Seal of the Prophets because the underlying reason for sending Prophets is to call mankind to worship God the Real, and to guide them in the way of right behavior with reference both to the present life and the life to come. . . . The noble Divine Law which he [Muḥammad] brought undertakes to reveal all of these things in a way that could not be imagined more perfectly clear, since it suits all peoples in all times, places and circumstances. After him mankind needs no more Prophet because in him perfection reached its summit. . . .

QUESTION: Mention to me the miracles of our Prophet (may blessing and salvation be his).

ANSWER: The miracles of our Prophet Muḥammad (may blessing and salvation be his) are many. Among them there is the noble Qur'ān, and it is the most important of his signs, the greatest, the most brilliant and most magnificent. Its inimitability has already been mentioned, as well as the fact that it is an abidingly permanent sign, having been transmitted by the Seal of the Prophets. Another of his miracles was the gushing forth of water from between his fingers during a journey when his distinguished companions suffered from thirst because of a shortage of water. He placed his noble palm into the water and it became so abundant that all of those present were able to satisfy their thirst, and there was even some left over. This was repeated on several occasions. Another miracle was the multiplication of a small amount of food so that it might satisfy the needs of a large number of people. This also happened on several occasions. In addition there are other miracles which are mentioned in the books on the proofs of prophethood.

QUESTION: What was the life of our Prophet (may blessing and salvation be his) like?

ANSWER: It is unanimously agreed that the life of our Prophet (may blessing and salvation be his) was absolutely the best of lives. Even the unbelievers have recognized his excellence. And how could they not do so, for his life shines like the sun in broad daylight. The biographers report that he (may blessing and salvation be his) was of the most noble lineage and that he had the highest of personal qualities. He was faithful to blood ties; he helped the needy. He was of great endurance; he knew how to be indulgent and to persevere. He never tired of showing favor, of forgiving and of being kind and gentle. He never sought vengeance unless the rights of God or of men were at stake. He was often silent in meditation upon the secrets of the kingdom of God. When he did speak it was with succinctness, in few words, but what he said was full of meaning and of remarkable judgment. No one could explain with such clarity as he. Upon occasion he joked, but he always told the truth in his joking. He lived in the certainty of God's protection under all circumstances. When other great heroes would retreat, he would go forward, remaining firm in the presence of any danger. He was very humble, but in spite of his great humility and his affable manner, he inspired awe in his fellow men, to such a degree that none of his Companions would fix his eyes upon his noble visage. When he met with them they observed the strictest politeness. One would have thought that a bird was sitting on their heads [because they stood or sat so quietly]. No one would interrupt another; no one would say anything indiscreet. In his childhood the pagans named him, "Faithful." Then, after he had made his claims to prophethood his enemies never found any grounds for slandering him or for discrediting him, in spite of their fierce hostility and their eagerness for calumny. He taught people wisdom and the precepts of the law. He called them to the House of Peace [Islam and paradise]. Those who followed him attained the highest level of intellectual and moral virtue. Even those who did not follow him were influenced by him incidentally and subsequently. God revealed his religion as superior to all other religions and perpetuated the beautiful memory of him upon the lips of his partisans and his opponents. Whoever has read his biographies, full of his great and admirable character, knows that he is the noblest of creatures, in both his inner and his outer qualities.

Faith in Predestination

QUESTION: What does it mean to believe in Predestination?

ANSWER: It means that we believe that all human acts, be they by choice, such as rising, sitting, eating and drinking, or be they coercive, such as falling, all of them take place by the will of God Most High, by His eternal decree, according to the knowledge that He had of them before they were performed.

QUESTION: If God Most High is the Creator of all man's works, then is not man compelled to do them, and does not one who is compelled deserve neither reward nor punishment?

ANSWER: Not at all. Man is not compelled, because he has a particular will which he can direct toward good and toward evil. He also has a mind with which he distinguishes between the two. When he directs his will toward good, the good which he wills manifests itself, and he is rewarded for it, because by his effort it appears. His particular will is related to the good action. If he directs his will toward evil, the evil manifests itself, and he is punished for it, because by his effort it appears. His particular will is related to the evil action.

QUESTION: Cite an example, easy to understand, which will make clear to me the fact that man is not compelled in his deeds.

ANSWER: Every man can know that he is not compelled to do all of his acts by virtue of the fact that he is able to distinguish, for example, the movement of his hand in writing from the movement of his hand caused by trembling. When his hand moves to write, he attributes this act to himself, saying, "I wrote by my own choice and will." But when his hand moves because of trembling, he does not attribute this act to himself. He does not say, "I moved my hand." He says rather, "It happened without my choosing."

QUESTION: What benefit can be had from this example?

ANSWER: By this example every man can perceive immediately that his deeds are of two kinds: those which he performs by his own choice and will, such as eating, drinking, fighting, etc. and those which occur without his choosing, such as falling.

QUESTION: Does anything follow from the fact that man's deeds are performed according to his choice?

ANSWER: It follows that when man does good deeds by his choice, he is rewarded, and when he does evil ones he is punished. On the other hand the things that he does of necessity do not involve reward or punishment.

QUESTION: If a person strikes another unjustly, as a hostile act, or performs some similar evil, sinful act, and then he excuses himself by saying that his deed was predetermined for him, is such an excuse acceptable?

ANSWER: Neither God Most High nor man will accept the excuse of Predestination, because man has a particular will, a capacity for action, and the ability to choose, and to reason.

QUESTION: Summarize the subject.

ANSWER: Every responsible person must believe with certainty that all of his acts, all of his words and all of his movements, be they good or bad, are produced by the will, the decree and the knowledge of God Most High. Good deeds take place with his good pleasure, but bad deeds without his good pleasure. One must believe also that man has a particular will by which he performs acts by choice, that he is rewarded for those acts which are good and punished for those which are evil. Finally one must believe that man has no excuse for doing evil, and that God Most High is never unjust toward his servants. . . .

ESOTERIC DOCTRINE

Ta'wīl al-Da'ā'im (Interpretation of the Pillars) by Al-Nu'mān Ibn Muḥammad

The choice of a selection to represent Shī'ī doctrine taken from a book of law illustrates the fact that law and theology cannot be neatly separated in Islam. Treatises on law normally begin with a section on doctrine. The book, *Interpretation of the Pillars,* is a commentary on one of the basic law treatises of the Ismā'īlī branch of the Shī'ah. Both text and commentary were written by a Tunisian judge, Al-Nu'mān Ibn Muḥammad, who died in 962 AD.[6] He was the chief theoretician of the Fatimid dynasty, the most important political expression of Shī'ī Islam that the world has known.

The passages chosen for translation bring out the following points regarding Shī'ī theology: 1) its affinity with Mu'tazilī thought; 2) its liking for allegorical interpretations; 3) its division of truth into exoteric and esoteric categories; and 4) its dependence upon a strict hierarchical structuring of society, based upon a divinely ordained continuity of leadership through the progeny of the caliph 'Alī.

This selection does not cover the range of theological subjects, but it introduces the reader to the often recondite thought world of the Shī'ah.

The First Discourse of the First Section

In the name of God, the Merciful, the Compassionate.

Praise be to God, who makes the rain to fall, who foreordains blessing, who creates men in the wombs of their mothers, creation after creation [an allusion to Surah 39:6]. May the blessings of God be upon the best of his creatures, Muḥammad his Prophet, and upon the Imams [the divinely guided, infallible leaders of the Muslim community, according to the doctrine of the Shī'ah] of his noble, preeminent and pure progeny.

The Creative Process

You have heard, O believers, in what has gone before [perhaps an allusion to the author's previous writings], how you have progressed from one state to another in the stages of religion, just as you progressed in outward creation. In truth, the creative process in religion is inwardly similar to the outward creation, for God (may He be glorified) has said, "Thereafter We produced him as another creature" (Surah 23:14) [This verse concludes a passage which speaks of the gradual stages in the creation of man in the womb of his mother.], and also, "He creates you in your mothers' wombs creation after creation" (Surah 39:8).

The basic esoteric interpretation of the foregoing is as follows. "Mothers," in their inner meaning, represent those who seek access to one who is above them in the spiritual hierarchy, and who impart knowledge to others below them in rank. These seekers' "wombs" are interpreted as the esoteric knowledge which they have, in which the seekers move from degree to degree. This progression constitutes what is meant by the "birth of religion." The word of God Most High in the same verse, ". . . in threefold shadows" (Surah 39:8), refers literally to that which encloses the embryo, the "shadows" of the abdominal wall, the wall of the uterus and the placenta. This last actually contains the embryo and immediately encloses it. Then the uterus encloses the placenta and the abdomen encloses the uterus.

These "shadows" in their esoteric meaning are like a veiling from view, or a concealment, even as the darkness of the night may be compared with the esoteric truth, and with the one who practices it. This truth [figuratively designated by the womb] is enclosed by three ranks [corresponding to the three "shadows"] : 1) that of the Imam, who owes his origin to the one who inaugurated him [or, the *asās* (first principle), the rank immediately below the highest level of the Ismā'īlī hierarchy] : 2) that of the Ḥujjah (Guarantor) who issues from the Imam and proceeds to him, the one who endorses the Imam, 3) and finally the rank of the one designated to be the means through whom the Imam becomes accessible to those below.

In summary the image of the three "shadows" provides a setting for the description of three stages in the Ismā'īlī spiritual hierarchy. According to this system human history unfolds in seven cyclical eras, each one giving mankind access to esoteric knowledge through the intermediary of a series of leaders. First there is the Prophet, who reveals an exoteric message. Then for each Prophet a messenger is sent called the first principle (*asās*) who has immediate access to the esoteric meaning of the Prophet's message. In the era of Muḥammad, 'Alī Ibn Abī Ṭālib (d. 660 AD) was the *asās.* Seven Imams are provided for each era, and in the threefold listing above, the Imam is the closest to the source of esoteric truth. The Ismā'īliyyah believe that the seventh Imam, Muḥammad Ibn Ismā'īl, disappeared in the eighth century AD and that he will return to be the seventh and final speaking Prophet. Until his advent at the climax of human history, he will be represented by twelve leaders called Ḥujjah, or Guarantor. Finally, in the third degree of remoteness from the source of esoteric meaning are the persons charged with the role of missionary, or *dā'ī,* who spread the summons (*da'wah*) of Shī'ī Islam among the masses.

The Pillars of Islam

In the *Book of Pillars* Muḥammad Al-Bāqir [the fifth Shī'ī Imam in the era of the Prophet Muḥammad, d. 731 AD] (may God bless him and grant him salvation) is reported as saying that Islam is based on seven pillars: 1) Divine Custodianship (*walāyah*) [the name of the office of the members of the spiritual hierarchy. This office, elevated to be a pillar of Islam, is peculiar to the Shī'ī branch of Islam.], which is the most excellent of the Pillars. By means of this Custodianship and by the intermediary of those charged with it, the Men of God, one finally comes to full knowledge; 2) Ceremonial Purity; 3) Ritual Prayer; 4) Almsgiving; 5) Fasting; 6) Pilgrimage; 7) Just War.

As the Prophet said (may God bless him and grant him salvation), these are the Pillars of Islam, its bases and its principles, which God has prescribed for his people. They have their similitudes in the esoteric interpretation. Divine Custodianship has its similitude in Adam (may God bless him) [the first of the seven speaking Prophets of the Ismā'īliyyah], for he was the first to be charged by God (may He be glorified) with Divine Custodianship. The angels were commanded to prostrate themselves before him [see Surah 2:34], and prostration implies submission. This is the exercise of Divine Custodianship. This is all that they were charged to do, and all of them prostrated themselves except Satan, according to the information that God Most High has given. Adam (may God bless him) was tested by being charged with Divine Custodianship. He was an example of it, in which all mankind must believe. If anyone refuses to accept Adam as Man of God, then the Custodianship of subsequent Men of God will be of no benefit to him, since he has neither yielded to Adam's authority nor admitted the authenticity of his position as the first one in the line of those Apostles, Prophets and Imams of divine religion to whom God has delegated his authority. Adam is their progenitor, their father.

Ceremonial Purity has its similitude in Noah (may God bless him) [the second of the speaking Prophets]. He was the first one commissioned and sent from God to purify mankind from the sins and iniquities which they had committed and which had taken place among them since the time of Adam (may God bless him). He was the first speaking Prophet (*nāṭiq*) after Adam, the first of the Men of Action (*'azm*), one of the Apostles charged with promulgating the Divine Law. God granted him his sign which was sent forth by water, intended for purification, and called, "purifying" [an immediate allusion to Surah 25:48, and in a more general sense a linking of the flood which destroyed Noah's enemies with the idea of purification].

The similitude of Ritual Prayer is Abraham (may God bless him). He it was who built the Ka'bah and set up the Maqām [the area of the sacred enclosure in Mecca where prayers are offered during the pilgrimage ceremonies]. God made the Ka'bah to be the focal point toward which prayer is directed (*qiblah*) and the Maqām to be a place of prayer [an allusion to Surah 2:125]. His words are recorded in the Word of God Most High, "I have turned my face to Him who originated the heavens and the earth, a man of pure faith; I am not of the idolators" (Surah 6:79). This speech inaugurated the practice of Ritual Prayer for those who pray.

Almsgiving has its similitude in Moses. He was the first one to call for it and to be instructed regarding it. God Most High said, "Hast thou received the story of Moses? When his Lord called to him in the holy valley, Towa: 'Go to Pharaoh: He has waxed insolent. And say, "Hast thou the will to purify [the word for almsgiving, *zakāt,* comes from a verb which means "to purify oneself"] thyself?" ' " (Surah 79:15-18). Moses was the first one whom God commanded to call men to purify themselves.

Fasting has its similitude in Jesus (upon him be peace). He was the first one to speak about it to his mother, saying that she should speak to whatever person she saw. His speech to her is told in the Word of God Most High, "And if thou shouldst see any mortal, say, 'I have vowed to the All-Merciful a fast, and today I will not speak to any man' " (Surah 19:26, 27). Thus during his lifetime he fasted. He abstained from sexual relations, even as it is incumbent upon those who fast to do during the time of their fasting.

The Pilgrimage has its similitude in Muḥammad (may God bless him and grant him salvation). He was the first to determine the ritual practices of the Pilgrimage, and to establish it as a customary procedure. Before him the Arabs of the Time of Ignorance and other peoples had gone on pilgrimage to the House [A pilgrimage to the Ka'bah in Mecca was one of the practices of preislamic polytheistic religion.], but they had performed none of its ceremonies, even as God Most High communicated regarding them through his Word, "And their prayer at the House is nothing but a whistling and a clapping of hands" (Surah 8:34). They used to circumambulate the House in the nude, and this was the first thing which was forbidden. The Prophet said during the pilgrimage [the *'umrah,* or minor pilgrimage, which can be performed at any time during the year, as distinguished from the *ḥajj*] which he made before the conquest of Mecca, after he had taken leave of his unbelieving relatives, "Hereafter, do not circumambulate the House in the nude." They set up idols around the House and worshipped them. Then when God granted the conquest of Mecca the Prophet broke up the idols, bringing them to an end. He established the customary procedures of the Pilgrimage, with its ceremonies.

He determined its sites according to the command of God, and set forth its prescriptions. The Pilgrimage was the seal of all prescribed works, even as Muḥammad (may God bless him and grant him salvation) was the Seal of the Prophets.

After the Pilgrimage the only one of the Pillars of Islam which remains is the Just War. Its likeness is seen in the seventh Imam [referring to a distinctive tenet of Ismā'īlī doctrine, the legitimacy of seven Imams belonging to the family of 'Ali; see p. 146, who will be the last of the Seven, the Master of the Resurrection. Even as you have heard before, he was prepared as the seventh speaking Prophet (*nāṭiq*), since God will gather all mankind according to his command, and not one person will be left alive who opposes the religion of Islam and the divine ordinances of faith. This person is one of the Imams of Muḥammad (may God bless him and grant him salvation), the last Imam of his descendants, the last representative of his summons [see p. 146], and the summons of all the Imams to the Law of Muḥammad (may God bless him and grant him salvation). . . .

The Just War is not one of the basic religious works, since it consists of a summons to compliance with the Divine Law and the elimination of any who stand in the way of such compliance. Thus, in the time of the one who is the likeness of the Just War, that is, the Seal of the Imams, there will be no place for deeds of piety, even as God Most High has informed us, saying, "On the day that one of thy Lord's signs comes it shall not profit a soul to believe that never believed before, or earned some good in his belief" (Surah 6:159). [The coming of the seventh Imam, who becomes himself the final speaking Prophet, will mark the time of the end; religious law will be abrogated and mankind will be judged.] . . .

THE SECOND DISCOURSE OF THE FIRST SECTION

Faith and Islām. This section refers to the important question of the relationship between *islām,* or the outward performance of religious duties, and faith (*imān*), the inner adherence of the believer to God. The Mu'tazilah considered the two to be identical, whereas the Ash'ariyyah made a distinction between them. The external nature of *islām* as contrasted with the inwardness of faith makes the two concepts fit well into the Shī'ī dichotomy of the exoteric and the esoteric.

On the subject of faith and *islām* [not to be confused with Islam, the name of the religion of the Muslims], the *Book of Pillars* maintains their distinction, one from the other. However, whereas faith has something in common with *islām, islām* has nothing in common with faith. The exoteric meaning of this is explained in the *Book of Pillars.* Its esoteric meaning is that *islām* corresponds to exoteric interpretation, whereas faith corresponds to the esoteric interpretation. Both faith and *islām* must be held to, believed in, and practiced. It is not possible to hold to one without the other, nor to believe in one and to disbelieve in the other. It is not possible to hold to the esoteric interpretation without holding first to the exoteric interpretation, even as a man cannot be a believer without being a Muslim. Accordingly, the Imam Muḥammad Ibn 'Alī (may God bless him and grant him salvation) [the same as Muḥammad Al-Bāqir, see above, p. 146] likened the exoteric and the esoteric interpretations to two circles, one within the other. *Islām,* being the exoteric meaning, is like the outer circle, whereas faith, being the esoteric meaning, is like the inner circle. This imagery and this form of perception are explained in the *Book of Pillars,* making clear that *islām* corresponds to the exoteric meaning and faith to the esoteric. The exoteric cannot exist without the esoteric, nor can the esoteric exist without the exoteric.

Definitions of Faith. It should be noted that *islām,* the exoteric element, is no longer the subject under consideration but that faith, the esoteric element, is now viewed as having itself both exoteric and esoteric aspects.

The Imams (may God bless them) say also on this subject that faith consists of verbal assent, deeds and intention. Verbal assent corresponds to the exoteric meaning, and deeds correspond to the esoteric meaning, for verbal assent to the twofold testimony [that is, to the sole deity of God and to the apostleship of Muḥammad] is the requirement for entry into the religious community. Whoever makes this testimony becomes subject to the jurisdiction of his religious confession. The deeds which are prescribed by the authority of Divine Law correspond to the esoteric meaning. They are hidden from other people for they concern only the believer and his Lord. So the believer says, "I have purified myself ritually; I have prayed; I have fasted; I have given alms; I have learned that which God has required of me." It is not necessary that this should be announced, or that there should be witnesses to it, except when other people are involved and they make some claim regarding his actions. But as for those acts of worship which are between him and God, if he is faithful in them, God knows and will reward him. Those who, like the Murji'ah [a movement of dissent in Islam, dating from the eighth century; see p. 132], say that faith consists of verbal assent, apart from deeds, are in the position of those who say that religion has its exoteric side, but has no esoteric side.

Verbal confession, which the Murji'ah and others insisted as the essential element in faith, should not be understood simply as the expression of a judgment concerning an objective truth. Verbal confession meant, to these Muslims, the total involvement of the believer in the reality to which he renders an efficacious testimony. The Murji'ah did not deny the necessity of good works for a full expression of faith, and in addition, some of them insisted on the element of knowledge as a part of the basic definition of faith.

The *Book of Pillars* exposes the wrongness of their assertion. It also explains the likeness of intention [an important safeguard against perfunctory religious practice in Islam], without which no statement or work is valid, to Divine Custodianship. Intention is the firm belief of the heart, and it is in the heart that the divine precept abides. According to allegorical interpretation, the heart corresponds to the Imam, as has previously been pointed out. If anyone does not believe in the Divine Custodianship through an Imam of the epoch, then neither his verbal assent nor his deeds will profit him, neither exoteric nor esoteric religion will be authentic with him. In addition, no faith in the Divine Custodianship of the Imams is authentic without previous faith in the Apostles who originated and established the Divine Law. The Imams followed them in observing this law, taking from them that which had been entrusted to them. Every Prophet among the Apostles was served during the period of his prophethood by cycles of Imams, even as we have mentioned previously. All Apostles and Imams must be believed in and their law for each epoch must be practiced. The authority of each Imam must be recognized and submission must be accorded to him. Anyone who separates himself from the Apostles and the Imams must be disavowed, as well as anyone who arrogates to himself the position of one of them.

In the *Book of Pillars* are set forth the exoteric meanings of religious duties involving the members of the body. In addition there is an allegorical interpretation of these, giving their esoteric meaning, even as there are similitudes for each of the members of the body.

Some say that faith consists entirely of deeds, and that verbal assent is one of these deeds [another well-known definition of faith, common among the Mu'tazilah]. The allegorical interpretation of this statement is that faith, as consisting entirely of deeds, represents the esoteric meaning, because everything included in faith, so understood, consists of acts of the bodily members and belief in the heart [which concern primarily the believer and his Lord; see p. 149]. All of these, according to this definition, are deeds, as has been explained in the *Book of Pillars*.

There is another aspect of this matter, namely, since faith is a similitude of the esoteric meaning, as we have previously mentioned [p. 148], and since likewise deeds are a similitude of the esoteric meaning, as we have explained [p. 149], then these two are the same thing. It is as though one said, the esoteric meaning consists entirely of the esoteric; there is no need of any outward manifestation, for once there is outward expression, then the matter becomes exoteric.

By this and the following argument all that is involved in faith is gradually drawn into the esoteric realm.

Then follows the statement that verbal assent is one of the deeds. As we have already mentioned, verbal assent is a similitude of exoteric meaning [p. 149], so the statement that verbal assent is one of the deeds [as in the definition above] means that the exoteric meaning was, before it was outwardly manifested, actually a part of the esoteric meaning. Then, when it was manifested outwardly it became exoteric, while still remaining a part of the esoteric. This is seen in the fact that the total message which any Apostle of God (blessed be his name) has brought to the people of God, with which previous Apostles had not been charged, has its origin in God (may He be glorified), who disclosed it to whichever of his Apostles He willed, even though they may not have been charged to divulge the revelation. [Not all Prophets are commissioned to deliver a divine revelation to the people; see p. 141, although strictly speaking, according to the Sunnī formulation, the name "Apostle" is given only to those Prophets who receive such a commission.] Before God commissioned Apostles with an esoteric message for the people, Apostles who would put into devout practice the message given them, and whose people would put it into devout practice, his message already existed, since He informed them of the names of those Apostles who would come after them, and of the esoteric knowledge which they would bring, his knowledge which

> He would entrust to them. This is part of the secret of their knowledge, its esoteric meaning, which has been entrusted to those sincere ones [the Imams of the Shīʿah] who follow the Apostles, who were appointed by them as Guarantors for their peoples. . . .

The import of this passage is first of all to illustrate the passage of truth from esoteric meaning to exoteric, without losing its esoteric nature, even as is stated to be the case of verbal assent as a component part of faith. Secondly the information about God's esoteric message, which at the time willed by him is divulged through his chosen Apostles, but without losing its esoteric nature, is meant to show the continuity of the Shīʿī doctrine, which has always existed in the hearts of God's Apostles, even if they were not authorized to divulge it, and which is guaranteed to the people through the intermediary of those who follow the Apostles, that is, the Imams.

CHAPTER 6

Art and Architecture

ART

"Magnify Him greatly," says the concluding verse of Surah 17, using the familiar device of Arabic grammar by which the verb supplies its own object, giving a meaning of intensity. "Make Him greatly great," it might be translated, or more freely, "Give to God a praiseful praise."

One of the surest forms of Islamic response to this command is in the patterns of its art. The first of these in time and honor is calligraphy—the inscribing on page or tile or stone, on innumerable artifacts, and items in pottery, wood and brass the letters and sequences of the sacred text of Scripture. The skill that cherishes the *Qur'ān* itself has been the source and tutor, as well as the stimulus, of other expressions of Muslim craftsmanship and joy in design. Hence, it is imperative to begin any presentation of Islamic art with that of the pen—the instrument so much celebrated in the *Qur'ān* itself.

The earliest and severest style in calligraphy was the Kufic, so named from Kūfā, a vital center of original Islam in southern Iraq. With its angular forms, Kufic writing is the closest Arabic comes to the shapes of its neighbor Syriac—a language which, it is said, Muḥammad directed his secretary, Zaid, to learn. Kufic uses short or light vertical strokes with exaggerated horizontals.

The solid heavy features of Kufic were later developed into the more rounded, flowing character of the Naskhī script, which reached its highest quality under the Fāṭimids in Cairo in the twelfth century. In western Islam the Maghribī script achieved a kind of fusion between the straightness of the Kufic and the curves of the Naskhī.

(Addressed to Muḥammad at a time of near despair about opposition.)

> In the name of the merciful Lord of Mercy.
> By the shining noon and the brooding night!

وَمَا قَلَىٰ ۝ وَلَلْآخِرَةُ خَيْرٌ لَّكَ مِنَ الْأُولَىٰ ۝ وَلَسَوْفَ يُعْطِيكَ رَبُّكَ فَتَرْضَىٰ ۝ أَلَمْ يَجِدْكَ يَتِيمًا فَآوَىٰ ۝ وَوَجَدَكَ ضَآلًّا فَهَدَىٰ ۝ وَوَجَدَكَ عَآئِلًا فَأَغْنَىٰ ۝ فَأَمَّا الْيَتِيمَ فَلَا تَقْهَرْ ۝ وَأَمَّا السَّآئِلَ فَلَا تَنْهَرْ ۝ وَأَمَّا بِنِعْمَةِ رَبِّكَ فَحَدِّثْ ۝

(٩٣) سُورَةُ الضُّحَىٰ مَكِّيَّةٌ وَآيَاتُهَا إِحْدَىٰ عَشْرَةَ

بِسْمِ اللَّهِ الرَّحْمَٰنِ الرَّحِيمِ

وَالضُّحَىٰ ۝ وَاللَّيْلِ إِذَا سَجَىٰ ۝ مَا وَدَّعَكَ رَبُّكَ

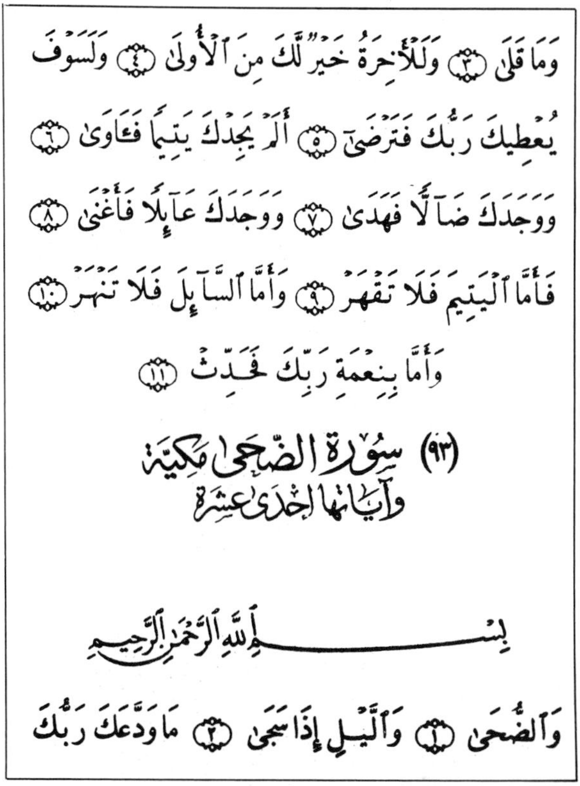

FIGURE 3. Surah 93 in Naskhī style: Egypt: Fourteenth century.

Your Lord has not abandoned you, nor turned against you.
The last will be better for you than the first.
Truly the gift your Lord will yet give will altogether satisfy.
Did He not find you an orphan and sheltered you?
Find you wandering and led you?
Find you needy and sufficed you?
Then do not oppress the orphan, nor repel the suppliant.
The grace of your Lord—let that be your theme.

The thirteenth century saw the rise of the Nasta'liq script with its hanging or sloping line, which abandoned the horizontal sequence of the earlier types and so created a perpendicular dependence. This style disposed of space more freely and gave a new dimension to the lateral links. It distinguished the upward and downward strokes of the pen and filled its spaces with floral flourishes. Writing thus became as much an article of decor as a vehicle of thought. The elaborated loops of Nasta'liq provide elbows of protection where words could be convoluted in parallels or curves and folds and so wrought into almost indecipherable subtleties. Ottoman signatures, or *tughras*, count among the most ingenious and vexing examples of this intriguing penmanship.

Documents and imperial directives apart, calligraphers devised endless motifs for Quranic verses. Texts could be crystallized into emblematic forms, artistic license turning the shapes into patterns and pictures. Animals, turrets, minarets, and flowers all suggested shapes for this ingenuity, until the fabric of the alphabet became a kind of arabesque of letters. Even staid Kufic could turn its structure to representational ends. But it was the Nasta'liq above all which afforded these indulgences, disporting as it did in circles, rectangles, triangles, or squares. It could make its lines the framework of a margin or even wind itself rope-wise around a center piece.

The art of calligraphy had many to instruct and celebrate its skills. Among them the poet, Abū-l-Ḥasan al-Kātib al-Baghdādī who is quoted by Ibn Khaldūn, the historiographer, in his *Al-Muqaddimah*. His poem runs as follows:

> O you who want to write a calligraphic hand
> And desire to write and draw [the letters] well,
> If you are truly desirous to master the art of writing,
> Pray that your master make it easy (for you)!
> Prepare a calamos that is straight and strong,
> Capable of fashioning elegant writing with craft.
> If you propose to nib the calamos, aim
> At applying to it the greatest symmetry.
> Look at both ends of it, and then nib it
> At the end where it is thin and narrow.
> Give the part of the calamus that is nibbed a moderate size,
> Neither too short, nor too long,
> And make the split precisely in the middle . . .
> So that the space nibbed
> On both sides of it will be exactly equal.
> Eventually, when you have done all this as carefully
> As the careful craftsman who knows what is wanted,
> Then, turn all your attention to cutting the point
> For cutting the point is the crux of the procedure.
> Do not beg me to reveal its secret.
> I am chary of its secret, a thing concealed.
> But the sum total of what I want to say is that
> The [point] should be something between oblique and round,
> Stir the [ink in the] inkstand with soot that is treated
> With vinegar or verjuice.
> Add to it red pigment that has been diluted
> With orpiment and camphor.
> Eventually, when [the ink] has fermented,
> Go to the clean, pleasant, tested paper.
> After cutting it, press it with a press, so as
> To remove all trace of crumpling and soiling.
> Then make patient imitation your habit.
> Only a patient person achieves what he desires.
> Begin by writing on a wooden slate, wearing it out
> With a resolution kept free from haste.
> Do not be ashamed of your bad writing
> When you begin to imitate [the letters] and draw lines.
> The matter is difficult (at the beginning) and then becomes easy . . .
> Eventually, when you achieve what you have hoped for,
> You will be filled with joy and gladness.
> Then thank your God and do His pleasure!

God loves all those who are grateful.
Furthermore, pray that the fingers of your hand will write
Only what is good for you to leave behind in the house of deception.
Everything a man does, he will be confronted with
on the morrow,
When he is confronted with the written decree [on the day of Resurrection].[1]

Among the earliest to achieve a personal celebrity as a calligrapher was the great Ibn al-Bawwāb (c. 1022). The famous pioneer of the Nasta'liq style was Yāqūt al-Musta'ṣimī (d. 1299). The Herat Academy in Afghanistan attained a wide celebrity in the sixteenth century, producing notable exponents of the art of the pen, among them Mir'Alī of Tabrīz and 'Alī Mashhadī, who gained the title of 'sultan of the scribes.'

But, for the most part, the visitor to the Islamic museum must be ready for calligraphic anonymity, or, if their handiwork is identified, it is more often by their academies than their personal names. There is something deeply impressive about this anonymity. As with the icon painters of the Greek and Russian Orthodox Christian tradition, every *Qur'ān* copy was a work of piety, requiring a quality of symmetry and beauty commensurate with the instinct of devotion. The steady flow of meticulous script, under the discipline of the trained hand, the rhythmic conformity of line and turn and angle, the letters linking and breaking by the unfailing rules of scribal law, and the sustained constancy of the will behind the pen—all expressed a consecration of spirit. Writers set themselves to match the oral cares of the reciter. Their fulfillment was in the immaculate copying of the Scripture, the illuminating of chapter headings, the gilding of marginal medallions, marking the thirty sections, the sixty subsections into which recitation divided it.

It would be fair to say that Islamic aesthetics as a whole belongs with the esteem of the written page. Calligraphy reaches into every area of Islamic art. It was the source from which color and design flowered into their Islamic place. It is proper to detect a predisposition for the curving line even in the living figures of painting and the miniature. The brush behaves like a pen. Often inclining human and animal forms, in Islamic art, conform in leaning head and neck, or in the line of limbs, to the rounded patterns of the script. The horse-shoe arch, so characteristic of Islam in Spain, departs from the vertical as its line descends and rounds itself after the manner of the alphabet. The very uniformity of a page of writing, where receding and succeeding lines have equal value, can be related to the practice by which, until the sixteenth century, Muslim art was unconcerned about perspective of the distant and the near. Quranic script merits the perpetual pride of hand and eye because it holds in trust the ultimate text. "By the pen and what they write. . . ." is the opening invocation of Surah 68, while the inaugural vision of Surah 96 celebrates man's education "by the pen." Traceable back to Adam himself, the pen is seen as giving gladness to all his posterity.

It was on this account that calligraphers called in gilders, engravers and illuminators to assist their product. In the margins of written texts the arts of color came into their own. Texts other than the *Qur'ān* could be adorned with miniatures relating to the subject matter. The *Qur'ān* itself could be decorated only by marginal decor and geometrical design. But the several skills proceeded together. On the high dignity of writing all else depends.

Figure 4, is the *Shahadah,* or confession of faith: "There is no god but God: Muḥammad is the apostle of God," in the intriguing form of minarets and towers. The letters read from the right to the middle and then, contrary to Arabic usage, from the left to the middle (marked by an arrow). But the artist has not quite produced a reflection as in a mirror, because he has inserted the third tall minaret from the right on a letter which would not normally have length as the others do. The name 'Muḥammad' is the squared shape immediately below this third minaret. (See p. 171.)

In figure 5, a calligrapher's imagination penned a verse in Surah 17:80 in the form of a ship, to catch the implication of the sense, which reads: "Say: 'O Lord, make my entering to be into truth and my exit a departing in truth and appoint me from before Thee a captain for my aid.'" "The truth of God the great" attests it as Quranic.

There are two outstanding features of Islamic art that afford significant clues to the nature of the religion itself. They are the flowing patterns of arabesque and the love of geometrical design. To appreciate the former it is well to trace the approach to artistic representation in early Islam. Painting begins in book illumination, gilding the letters and

FIGURE 4. The Islamic Shahādah *with an artist's ingenuity. (From* Islamic Studies, *Institute of Islamic Research, Islamabad, Pakistan. Reproduced by permission.)*

the margins of the *Qur'ān*, and illustrating in the margins of non-Quranic works the themes discussed and handled. The common assumption that early Islam was antagonistic to all representation because of its veto on idolatry needs to be modified. The Quranic passages are much less explicitly prohibitive than is often thought. Islam needed to emulate, as well as censor, the skills it found in the civilizations it overran. These were rich in arts. There were still treasured in Persia, for example, the holy books of the Manicheans. Mānī himself had been an admirable painter and had relied strongly on artistic means to inculcate his faith. An oft-told story relates how, as late as the third Muslim century (923 AD), during an outbreak of persecution against some surviving Manicheans, fourteen sacks of their precious books were burned in Baghdad. Trickles of gold and silver were seen running from the fire, so lavish was their decoration.

The story may be taken as a parable of what persists through what is repudiated. The skills, and often the practitioners themselves, survived into Islam's service. Also—as evidenced in the building of the *Ḥaram* at Jerusalem—it was necessary for Islam to assert its authority and competence within cultures, which, though conquered, were still artistically far superior. In its sudden and unfamiliar acquisition of a wealth of art, early Islam seems to have been caught between fascination with the level of cultural expression around it and a sense of threat to the purity of a final faith.

The visual symbol of calligraphy was, of course, utterly safe from being confused with the usages of any alien world. For the rest, as Islam gathered confidence, based on its physical triumphs, so its artists, recruiting from the conquered, became more venturesome. There are remarkable wall paintings and mosaics from the Umayyad period within

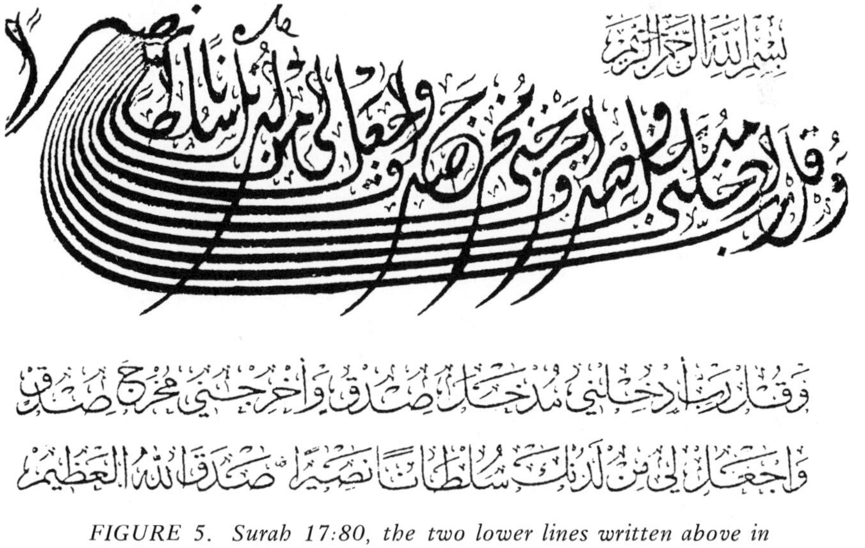

FIGURE 5. Surah 17:80, the two lower lines written above in the form of a ship. (From Education and Community Relations, *May/June 1976, vol. 6, no. 3. Reproduced by permission of the Commission for Racial Equality, London.)*

the first century, such as those at Qaṣr al-Ḥayr and Quṣayr Amrah. But it was, more than all, the art of the miniature that developed, especially after the rise of the Seljūks in the eleventh century, into the treasures of book illumination that are the great pride of Islam. It was an art that decorated a long sequence of science writings, of fables, and of poetry. The fact that the same works were illustrated through many generations gave the painters a unity of theme and allowed a steady development of style. They were not so much painting to inform about the unknown but to interpret anew the familiar. Medical works, astronomies, mirrors for princes (as works of politics and government tended to be called), fables, treatises, and poems (of Firdausī, Sa'dī, Nizāmī, Ḥāfiẓ and the rest) all figured in a long and rich sequence. There were also familiar incidents from the *Sīrah*, or biography, of Muḥammad, astride his horse Burāq, or preaching his last sermon to attentive rows of disciples. Often in these paintings the face of Muḥammad is left blank, or a white nimbus surrounds the head, both suggesting authority and divorcing the figure from the background.

In all this painting, which was only two-dimensional for many centuries, the artists made no effort to create spatial illusion. They were free to idealize a landscape and dot their flowers, or trees, or people, as they would, without concern for perspective. They were free to tilt a horizontal plane into a vertical, to view objects from front or side or overhead, at will, and without consistency. They were not drawing what they saw, but rather what they visualized. Lines of landscape do not recede: figures incline rather like the curving calligraphy: there is often an evident unconcern to differentiate the sexes. Yet a charming quality of expression is achieved. The lioness in the fable, who has been won over to vegetarianism by the wily jackal, has a telling look of a well-disposed and pious purpose. On the faces of the mourners grouped around the bier of Alexander, in a fourteenth century leaf from the *Shāh Nāmā* of Firdausī, one reads the enigmatic reservations, as well as the prudent grief or sheer bewilderment, of the onlookers. Illuminating Al-Bīrūnī's *Chronology of Ancient Peoples*, the artist presents the Eden temptation registering both the dubious indecisiveness of Adam and the queryful fascination of Eve, negotiating with a blandly persuasive tempter.

Here is a Persian historian, Khwandamīr in tribute to the most famous of all miniaturists, Kamāl al-Dīn Bihzād:

> Since the album of the sky has been fashioned with the light-scattering form of sun and moon, the rays of the intelligence of no expert draughtsman have ever fallen on the like of the forms which decorate these pages.
>
> His brush, like Mānī's, wins eternal fame:
> Beyond all praise his virtuous qualities:
> Bihzād, acknowledged as supreme in art,
> The master of the painters of the world,
> Unique among the artists of his age,
> Has turned the name of Mānī to a myth.
> Hairs of his brush, held in the master hand,
> Give life unto the forms of living things.

His talent is so fine that 'tis no boast
If we maintain his brush can split a hair.
If you still doubt that in the painter's art
His mastery has reached perfection's height,
You need but look with an impartial gaze
And contemplate the marvel of these forms,
Wherewith he has adorned these beauteous leaves
And perfected the marvels set therein.[2]

It was such skill and the instincts that guided it which underlay the arabesque style so characteristic of Islamic art. Arabesque delights in endless lines of foliage, or branching trees and interlacing leaves, of curving forms and geometric roses growing perpetually out of each other. It is an artistic form that repudiates individuation. The line runs through every part: the center is in all, in such sense that none can claim it. Scenic elements, of air, water, light, and space itself, are harmonized into unity. Some commentators derive the style from theology itself, believing it to register a distinctive relationship to divine creation. Nature is thought to exist, not in its own right, but only by a series of arbitrary acts constantly shaping it in the divine will. There is a flux about all things. Nature is not particular phenomena subsisting of themselves, but only a flowing in the divine will. "Everything," says the *Qur'ān*, "is perishing except His countenance." (Surah 28:88). There are no enduring forms or relations outside the perpetual causing activity of God. Art, therefore, is not capturing, or tracing, a thing in itself: it is reflecting the momentary action of the divine Sustainer. So the artist does not merely avoid representation because it might conduce to idolatry. He excludes impressions of nature which might imply, as pictorial art does, that it has any self-sufficiency.

Lines of arabesque present the sort of abstractions that divert eye and mind from concrete reality, from particulars, into universals. Nothing in the sequence is left to chance, nothing is bizarre, perverse, or tragic. We are free of "the coarse and unkempt facts of man." The orthodox Muslim is secured in his assurance of the nonautonomy of natural things. For his part, the Sufi mystic (chapter 7) discerns the unitive experience of reality, the *tauḥīd* of tranquil absorption into God.

Arabesque is in deliberate contrast with pictorial art. "It does not seek to capture the eye to lead it into an imagined world but, on the contrary, liberates it from the preoccupations of the mind, rather like the view of flowing water, fields waving in the wind, falling snow or rising flames. It does not transmit any specific ideas, but a state of being which is at once repose and inner rhythm."[3]

Akin to this quality of arabesque is the still more abstract nature of geometrical design, so frequent in Muslim decoration. Whether tooled in leather on the covers of books, or carved in wood on the surfaces of pulpits, doors and balustrades, or wrought in brass and iron, or inlaid in tile and ivory, Muslim patterns are dedicated to mathematical symmetry. For geometrical design corresponds to something essential to Islam.

Interpreters differ as to what that something is. Do the convolutions suggest that the reality of God is not 'centered' in any manifestation?

FIGURE 6. A simple form of geometric sequence.

Are we to read the infinity and invisibility of God in those endlessly recurring sequences of line and angle? As the complexity increases, so layers or degrees of knowledge are implied and this suggests, further, the element of conformity as against choice and desire. All these explanations have been offered. Or should we understand that the regularity and order of these designs deliberately excludes the disorder, the tragedy, the chaos of a perverse humanity? Do they insist instead on the ultimate irresistible sovereignty of God? There is no drama and no tension. All is crystalline clarity, growing in conformity to its inner principle.

Analysis of the rich variety of Islamic patterning reveals the triangle, the square, the hexagon, the heptagon, the octagon, even the dodecagon, as the several 'grids' on which the sequences are based. But the average observer will admire the over-all impression of fascination and delight rather than the intricacy of the geometry, which determines them. That Islam has to be sought and known from within these most characteristic forms of its artistic genius is undeniable. The perceptive student will decide the lesson for himself.

FIGURE 7. Geometric design: the art of symmetry.

FIGURE 8. Patterns in wood, metal, leather, and print.

It should be known that God singled out some places of the earth for special honor. He made them the homes of His worship. [People who worship in them] receive a much greater reward and recompense [than people who worship elsewhere]. God informed us about this situation through the tongue of His messengers and prophets, as an act of kindness to His servants and for the purpose of facilitating their ways to happiness.

We know from the two traditions that the most excellent places on earth are the three mosques of Mecca, Medina and Jerusalem. Mecca is the house of Abraham. God commanded Abraham to build it and to exhort the people to make the pilgrimage thither. He and his son, Ishmael, built it, as is stated in the Qur'ān. He fulfilled God's commandment in this respect. Ishmael dwelt there with Hagar and the Jurhum [tribe] who lived with them, until they both died and were buried in the *ḥijr* of the Ka'bah.

Jerusalem is the house of David and Solomon. God commanded them to build the mosque there and to erect its temples. Many of the prophets, descendants of Isaac, were buried around it.

Medina is the place to which our Prophet emigrated when God commanded him to emigrate and to establish the religion of Islam there. He built his sacred mosque in Medina, and his noble burial place is on [Medina's] soil.

These three mosques are the consolation of the Muslims, the desire of their hearts, and the sacred asylum of their religion. Many are the well-known traditions about their excellence and the great reward awaiting those who live near them and pray in them.[4]

So wrote Ibn Khaldūn early in the fifteenth century. While the three mosques he praises in their historical uniqueness are without peer, most would agree that for architectural glory the Ḥaram al-Sharīf at Jerusalem has the crown. It is the supreme achievement of the Umayyad period and the first great monument of the Islamic spirit. It demonstrates in superb degree the splendor of the dome as the builder's glory. The earliest mosques in Arabia had been constructed with tree trunks as pillars and these developed, as in Cordoban Spain, into halls of columns supporting single, sometimes double, arches, and providing an almost forest-like setting for the acts of prayer. Magnificent as these might be and fascinating in their symmetry, they disallowed that conscious incorporation into a whole which marks a single congregation. For the twin needs of congregational unity and prayer in unison in visible array before the prayer niche, the dome alone was perfect. It both created and unified the space in which to pray and the Dome of the Rock at Jerusalem was its first splendid Islamic exemplar. The interior decoration was thoroughly worthy of the setting. Entirely covered with mosaic, the octagon, the circle and the drum beneath the dome conspire in a singular beauty that in the opinion of many, makes the first flower of Muslim architecture still the finest. Its calligraphy, and the baskets, jewels, scrolls, flowers, and crowns, which abound in its decoration (the last meant to impress upon the Holy City that Islam was in possession) are unsurpassed elsewhere.

The ground plan of the Muslim house of prayer, unlike the Jerusalem

FIGURE 9. Minaret in Marrakesh, Morocco. Pattern in wall design.

Mosque, has, for a variety of reasons, been traditionally square, or rectangular. But to crown a square with a dome demands the art of turning the angle into the circle. Here the building genius of Muslim architecture displays its quality in the device of the squinch and pendentives and the *muqarnas*, or stalactite form, by which the right angle of the wall ascends in a series of niche-like quarter circle supports into the base of the dome's full circle. The cunning structural function provides a surface where the ingenuity of art and color, and the play of light and shade, find perpetual occasion. It was in Persian and Ottoman designs that these came to their perfection, creating honeycombs of shadow and bright surface, blending with color. At the place where walls, rising from the solid earth, turn and taper into the celestial round, imagination could almost read a meeting of the finite with the infinite. (See figure 12).

Of all the shrines of Islamic architecture, the Tāj Mahal, at Agra, India, (see figure 10) expresses grace and tragedy more tellingly than any other structure. Sixteen years in building, it has been justly described as the most noble monument of the love of man for woman. It is certainly the finest flowering of the culture it celebrates. There is

FIGURE 10. The Tāj Mahal. (Courtesy of Government of India Tourist Office, New York.)

no precise knowledge about the master architect to whose genius it is owed. European admiration has been loathe to abandon the groundless idea that some Venetian had the honor. Shāh Jahān, fifth of the great Mughals, was its presiding inspiration. From his palace round the curve of the Jumna River, he daily followed its construction, cherishing his grief at the death in childbirth of his wife, Mumtāz Mahal, whose remains it was to house.

He was a prisoner of his own son, Aurangzīb, who held him captive for eight years in tragic humiliation, his family decimated, and his spirit broken. He was deprived of all society save that of mullahs and of the *Qur'ān,* over which he brooded for long hours, gazing at the masterpiece his craftsmen were shaping. With them his vengeful son did not interfere, though he tried later to emulate them, unsuccessfully, with a mausoleum of his own. When, at length, Shāh Jahān was released by death and laid within the Tāj Mahal, a chapter ended in the interplay of art and tragedy which represents a deep moment in the story of religion. Perhaps some imaginative poet, or playwright, east or west, will yet give authentic voice to the thoughts of Shāh Jahān sustaining his sorrows with his holy Book and his master builder.

The setting of the mosque is a rectangular garden, the lines of whose water courses carry the eye to the square dais where the central edifice stands. At each corner, as if in perpetual, reverential meditation, are four slender, circular minarets, each terminating in columns and a dome. The great dome itself rises above arched alcoves that lift the converging horizontals of the garden into the perpendicular. Each is flanked by lesser, double alcoves repeated in the beveled corners of the structure. Four attendant domes, atop arched columns, curtsey to the climax of the whole, swelling into full dimension midway between base and apex, and wreathed below the pointed summit in a draping mantle of fluted stone.

The glistening white marble with its rich inlay of gold, the tracery in the angles of the alcoves, the girdle of arabesque around the circle of the dome, the delicate platforms dividing the line of the minarets, and the firm horizontal carrying all, combine into an entrancing unity of line and curve, of light and shade, of purity and strength.

It was predominantly Persian workmanship, coming into India via Afghanistan, by which the triumphs of Mughal architecture were achieved. These were the skills that on their native ground, accomplished the splendors of the Safavids in the same sixteenth and seventeenth centuries. Isfahan, *Nuṣf-i-Jahān* or 'half of the world,' as its citizens entitled it, was their crowning city.

Isfahan under the Safavids was a city resplendent with mosques, tombs, *madrasahs* and palaces, with the *Masjid-i-Shāh*, or royal mosque, as their splendid focus at the southern end of the great *Maidān*, or rectangle, which formed the city's heart. For all the arresting quality of the minarets at *Masjid-i-Shāh*, it is finally the superb dome which holds the imagination. It was in domes that the Persian architects were supreme.

> They rise majestic and serene. Gold or azure, they are unencumbered by shadows or by counter weights. With high drums, slightly bulging sides and an exquisitely delicate curve, they convey a feeling of grace, of utter self-sufficiency and of a volume so perfectly defined and intensely realized that a new quality of space seems to have been called into being.[5]

The great court of the *Masjid-i-Shāh* is worthy of its climax. With its surrounding galleries and recesses and its wide ablution pool, it presents an inviting spaciousness in which the individual is at once insignificant and relevant, in that everything is open, on a single floor level, where space renews itself in a single comprehensiveness where each has an unimpeded share. Not here are the receding perspectives of Gothic, leading into solemn distance and remoter mystery.

Since the north-south axis of the great *Maidān* did not tally with the *Qiblah* towards Mecca, the architects skillfully devised a sort of circular pivot in the form of a hall leading in from the great *īwān* (porch) on the *Maidān*, and opening into the great court. The arched portals, and their deep recesses, are decorated with white calligraphy and rich faience mosaic in dominant blue and gold. A prayer mat design on the perpendicular face of the front *īwān* reminds all comers of the purpose of the whole. The high horizontal lintels overhead contrast with the intricate quarter-circle niches and *muqarnas* structures supporting them below.

The great dome possesses a resonant echo. Within and without it is decorated by a flowing wealth of arabesque descending to the margin of the ringed calligraphy at the base, broken only by a series of patterned surface arches that lead into the drum windows below. These afford a diffused light inside which imparts an almost floating quality to the mass of the structure. The foliate cartouches, like some draping textile, stream in perfect symmetry from the central medallion (as in figure 11 of Luṭfallah).

There are, it is reckoned, eighteen million bricks in the *Masjid-i-Shāh* and half a million tiles. That quantitative measure may suggest to the imagination the focus of skills, of engineering and mathematics, of masonry and tiling, with all the attendant *dramatis personae* of scaffolders, carpenters, stucco-carvers, glass workers, carpet weavers, ceramicists and dyers.

Art and architecture, then, are among the student's best allies in his search for Islam from within. It is fascinating to reflect on the career of just one among the numerous eminent builders and designers who belong with the Islamic story, namely Sinān 'Abd al-Mannām. Choosing him takes us to the Ottomans and to a more ponderous style of mosque grandeur than that of Persia and the Mughals. The great mosques of Istanbul have domes of more exacting stresses and square their circles with a heavier load-taking technique. The incredibly spacious dome of

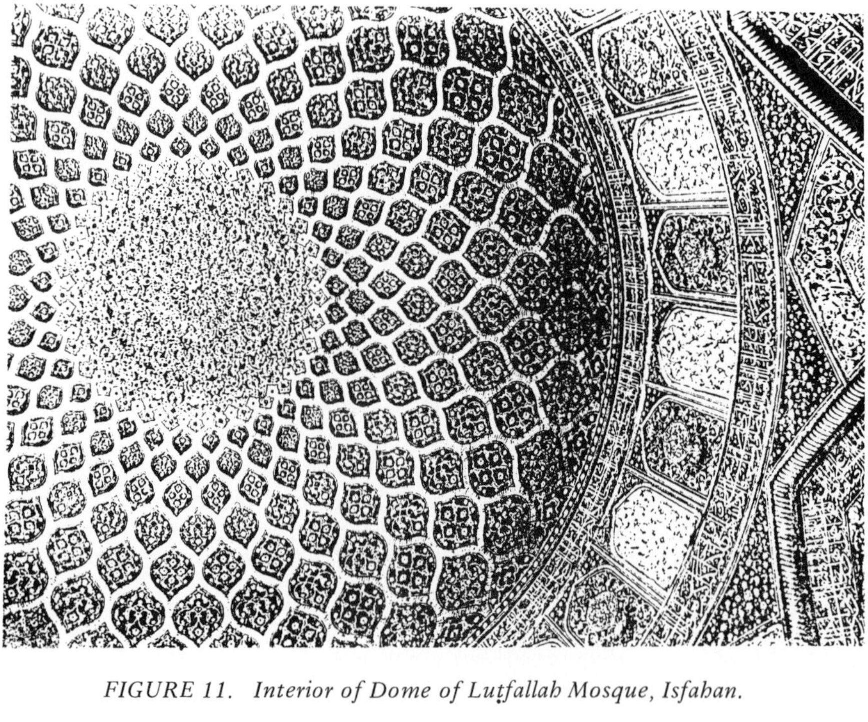

FIGURE 11. Interior of Dome of Luṭfallah Mosque, Isfahan.

Haghia Sophia, successively cathedral, mosque, and museum in Istanbul, is enormously buttressed by masses of masonry—a far cry from the lithe perfection of Isfahan. Yet the nobility of that vast shrine, the work in the sixth century of the Emperor Justinian and his architect, Anthemius, seems to have cast a double spell of challenge and of imitation upon the builders for the Islamic Justinian, Sulaymān the Magnificent, in the sixteenth century. The greatest of these builders, who served four successive Ottoman Caliphs, was Sinān.

Born a Greek (or perhaps an Albanian) he was first a captive slave and then, after Islamizing, he became an apprentice engineer to the Janissaries and finally Chief Imperial Architect to the Caliph. He reputedly erected more buildings than any other known architect in history. He has the unique distinction of being the restorer of three most sacred shrines in monotheism—the Great Mosque and *Ka'bah* in Mecca, the *Ḥaram al-Sharīf* in Jerusalem with the Wailing Wall, and the Haghia Sophia in Istanbul where he added the four minarets as well as the buttresses that have perpetuated the dome of his Byzantine predecessors. His first mosque was built in Aleppo while he was a military engineer. At the age of seventy he climbed to the summit of his masterpiece, the Sulaymāniyyah in Istanbul, to set the finial in place atop the dome. He made the pilgrimage to Mecca again when in his nineties and died, in 1588, with almost a century of Islamic years to his account.

FIGURE 12. From square to circle: a corner of the Iwan Masjid-i-Shāh, Isfahan.

Sulaymāniyyah Mosque is at once his response to, and his independence of, the Haghia Sophia. He adopted the same ground-plan—a central domed square with two semidomes on the long axis of the *Qiblah* and flanking areas with upper curtain walls above the arches that sprang from the central masonry. There were semicircular lights around the dome's base and attendant lower semidomes beside the two axial ones. But in his own edifice, Sinān introduced corbel mouldings between wall and arch, laying greater emphasis on the contrast between the cubic and the circular. He also used stalactite forms for his corners, instead of the rounded pendentives of the Haghia Sophia. With a splendidly arcaded court and with its tall fluted minarets like limestone candles with laden snuffers in permanent application, the Sulaymāniyyah marks a supreme moment in Islamic architecture. The genius it embodies was renewed—some would say excelled—in the Selīmiyyah Mosque in Edirnë, built to an hexagonal plan and buttressing its dome superbly.

"Houses God has given leave for. . . ." says Surah 24:35—words that Sinān's illuminator, Kara Hiṣārī, inscribed around the base of the Sulaymāniyyah dome by express order of the caliph. It is by that sense of the divine sanction, however corroborated and invoked by the skill of human craft, that we must understand the achievements of Sinān and his peers. Anthologies can only draw on written printed texts. But a religion cannot be fully read without its artists and its architects.

INTERPRETATIONS

Dr. Ishtiaq Husain Qureishi, formerly Minister of Education in Pakistan and a noted Muslim teacher and Vice-Chancellor of the University of Karachi, relates the forms of Islamic art to the essential temper of Islamic faith, in the following analysis:

> The guiding tendency in Muslim art is its passion for abstraction. . . . The Muslims chose calligraphy as their primary medium of aesthetic expression because no other art embodies so complete and so absolute an abstraction. Calligraphy is based on beauty of form but the form is detached from an imitation of any object. Calligraphy brought the Muslims to an appreciation of the rhythmic curve and the place that is occupied by the rhythmic curve in all forms of Muslim art is so significant that I look upon it as fundamental and all-embracing. . . .
>
> The other expression of this love for abstraction is the Muslim artist's obsession with geometrical patterns. The geometrical pattern is pure and simple abstraction. It embodies the beauty of form without tying it down to the form of any natural object. It is the involvement with the abstract geometrical pattern that has created in the Muslim artists a passion for symmetry. . . .
>
> Another form of abstraction takes us to the conventional floral motif. Once again, the artist's mind is not attracted by any particular flower, leaf or tree. It tries to find the essence of the shapes of flowers, leaves and trees and reduce this abstraction into symmetrical geometrical proportions through a

combination of curves and straight lines. . . . The artist repeats them in geometrical regularity in surface decoration, whatever may be the medium, stone, plaster, mosaic, tesselation or pietra dura. This, or course, has no alignment with naturalism, because naturalism is tied to the forms as they exist.

Naturalism emphasizes the particular, not the type or the essence. . . . This passion for abstraction could be the result of a strong feeling against idolatry. To a point the theory of inhibition can hold ground, but as for being the root cause it has to be dismissed. . . .

It is generally conceded that Islam is a rational faith. There is no religion that does not have to contend with the mysterious, the unknown, the inconceivable. Hence no religion can divorce itself from a mystic apprehension of the truth, of God Himself and of His relation to man and the universe. Islam has these elements. But outside them it relies upon the openness of reason and does not encourage imaginative speculation. It possesses an openness which tries to lay bare its very soul to the believer. Its rituals are simple and do not incorporate mystery. The truth and teaching of Islam are sought to be explained and inculcated in a rational manner. The mysteries of creation and the logical order of the universe are brought in as arguments but the deductions from these arguments are rational and logical. In this process the mind remains free from mystification and acquires an openness of approach that becomes its very nature. This openness is a part of the Muslim spirit. It is only another name for clarity and unhindered, unhampered vision. Hence there is an attachment to light and not to darkness: the appeal is to comprehension and not to a sense of mystery. This spirit pervades all Muslim rituals. There is no attempt at mystifying the worshippers in a place or worship through the agencies of semi-darkness and subdued and controlled lights. Muslim architecture, therefore, never attempts to shut out the light. All places of worship are built to admit the maximum amount of light in consonance with comfort and tectonic propriety. . . .

One finds this same love of light in the miniature paintings where objects do not fade into one another. In each picture, its components stand clearly defined. They are surrounded, as it were, by an invisible light: more often than not, shadows are cut out. . . .

Abstraction, as well as an uninhibited joy in light, has produced the quality of restraint. The rhythmic curve demands that the sillhouette should be uncluttered: clarity demands that objects should not hide one another. . . .

The last point I would like to make is that logic and reason inculcate a sense of proportion. Logic does not permit the imagination to run wild and holds it under restraint. The psychology created by logic emphasizes not only restraint but also proportion. It is strengthened by the general attitude of Islam towards life, where a believer is expected to earn his salvation, not by running away from the world but by living in it and discharging his social responsibilities in the light of the inspiration that he derives from a living faith in God. . . . The psychology created by the teachings of Islam is all pervading and has manifested itself in every sphere of art.[6]

The link between the faith of Islam and the forms of Islamic art has been interpreted in the following terms by Dr. Sayyid Ḥossein Naṣr, an eminent educator and writer in Persian Islam today.

The relation between art and spirituality is extremely profound and in all traditional societies [and here the Islamic offers particularly striking examples] the guilds of craftsmen, and the spiritual organizations, such as Sufism

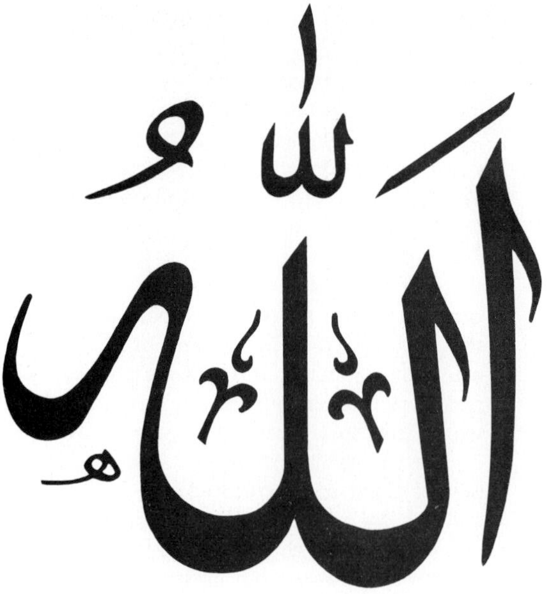

FIGURE 13. The Arabic (ALLĀH), as written in round medallions, on the walls of innumerable mosques.

FIGURE 14. The Arabic (MUḤAMMAD) as it appears in round medallions counterparting the Divine Name.

in Islam, have been closely linked. To make matter beautiful, to remove its opacity and make it the symbol of a higher level of reality . . . there must be a living intellectual and spiritual tradition which makes the vision of the intelligible world possible and provides the means to penetrate into the inner meaning of the symbol. The relation of true art and spirituality is like that of the body and the soul. . . .

Because sacred art is the bridge between the material and the spiritual worlds, it is inseparable from the particular religion with which it is connected. There is no sacred or liturgical art possible in a vacuum, any more than it is possible to 'write' a sacred scripture without a revelation from heaven. . . . Sacred art makes use of a symbolism which is related to the form of the religion in question. . . .

FIGURE 15. The name (MUḤAMMAD) in squared designed script.

Dr. Naṣr explains the association of crafts with religious cults.

The masters of the guilds [in Islam] became initiated into the mysteries of Sufism and learned the metaphysical and cosmological doctrines which underlay the symbolism of Islamic art. The rest of the members of the guild emulated the methods, techniques and symbols involved without necessarily understanding all of the profound levels of their meaning, although on their own level of understanding the work had meaning for them. They can use all their creative energy in making it and are far from mere imitators of something they do not understand. . . . It is because of this depth of expression innate to symbols and images, transmitted from the master to the craftsmen who study and work with him, that often a work produced by a so-called uneducated craftsman has more profundity and intelligence than a so-called educated onlooker has the capability to understand.

This same intimate relationship exists between Islam in general and Sufism in particular and the other forms of art. It is not accidental that the vast majority of the great musicians of Persia were connected in one way or another with Sufism or that the most universal poetry of the Persian language is Sufi poetry. Even in calligraphy the number of men associated in one way or another with the esoteric dimension of Islam who were masters of the art is great indeed.

The sacred art of Islam is related in both form and spirit to the divine Word as revealed in the Holy Qur'ān. The word having been revealed as a book, rather than as a human being, as is the case with Christianity, the sacred art concerns the manifestation of the letters and sounds of the Holy Book, rather than the iconography of a man who is himself the Logos. The sacred art of Islam in the domain of the plastic arts is more than anything else mosque architecture and calligraphy. One creates a space in which the divine Word is echoed and the other lines and letters which can be said to be the external form of the Word in the alphabet in which it was revealed, the alphabet of the Arabic and Persian languages. . . .

The space created inside a mosque, far from being arbitrary and accidental, is planned deliberately to remove those coagulations and tensions which would prevent the Word from spreading in an illimitable and harmonious space, a space filled with peace and equilibrium in which the Spirit is everywhere, rather than being localized in a particular icon or statue. The iconoclasm of Islam, about which so much has been said, does not mean that Islam is opposed to sacred art, without which no religion can create an appropriate ambience for its earthly manifestations. Rather it means that Islam refuses to imprison the Spirit or the Word in any form which would endanger the freedom innate to the Spirit and kill its reflections through imprisonment in matter. It is also related . . . to the insistence of Islam upon Divine Unity [*Tauḥīd*] which cannot be represented in images and the spiritual style of Islam which is 'nomadic' rather than 'sedentary'. . . .

In the decorated mosque architecture so typical of the tiled mosques of Persia, the two basic forms of sacred art, architecture and calligraphy, join hands to create a crystal in which is reflected a ray of the light of heaven amidst the darkness of material existence. . . .

The so-called minor arts . . . surround man in his daily life and hence influence him deeply. In this realm the 'seal of the sacred' is to be seen even in the most common everyday objects. The rugs are a recapitulation of paradise, bound by a frame and looking inward toward the center like the courtyard and the Persian garden. . . . The miniature, which is intimately bound with book illustrations, is an extension of calligraphy. . . .

Revelation can be compared to the dropping of a stone in a pool of water that causes ripples to move out as concentric circles from the center. The descent of the Holy Qur'ān, with its poetic structure based on sharply defined rhythms and a very subtle rhyming pattern, caused ripples which reflected this genius for rhyme and rhythm in the other forms of Islamic literature, of which, after Arabic, the most important is certainly Persian, itself the mother of several other Islamic languages. Persian poetry in its rhyme and rhythm reflects the echo of the Holy Qur'ān in the minds of the men who created this poetry. In its turn this poetry causes a reminiscence of this echo in the minds and souls of the men who read it. . . .

To appreciate Ḥāfiẓ [celebrated Persian poet] fully is to be already in the proximity of the divine.

There is an exuberance over the esoteric and the mystical characterizing Sayyid Ḥossein Naṣr's writing, which some exponents would wish to examine more critically. But none will quarrel with the sentiment of his conclusion:

The creative power of the artist . . . can become like the song of the bird, above the sound and clamor that fatigue and sicken the soul of man, to remind him of the peace, tranquility and joy for which he was created and which he seeks at all times knowingly or unknowingly, but which he can only find when he gains an awareness of the sacred and surrenders himself to the will of Heaven.[7]

CHAPTER 7

Mystics and Saints

SUFISM

Ibn Khaldūn discusses the 'science' of Sufism in his famous *Al-Muqaddimah.*

> The (Sufi) approach is based upon constant application to divine worship, complete devotion to God, aversion from the false splendor of the world, abstinence from pleasure, property, and position, to which the great mass aspires, and retirement from the world into solitude for divine worship. These things were general among the men around Muḥammad and the early Muslims. . . .
>
> The Sufis came to represent asceticism, retirement from the world, and devotion to divine worship. Then, they developed a particular kind of perception which comes about through ecstatic experience. This comes about as follows. Man, as man, is distinguished from all other animals by his ability to perceive. His perception is of two kinds. He can perceive sciences and matters of knowledge, and these may be certain, hypothetical, doubtful or imaginary. Also, he can perceive 'states' persisting in himself, such as joy and grief, anxiety and relaxation, satisfaction, anger, patience, gratefulness and similar things. . . . Thus knowledge originates from evidence, grief and joy from the perception of what is painful or pleasurable, energy from rest, and inertia from being tired. In the same way, the exertion and worship of the Sufi novice must lead to a 'state' that is the result of his exertion. That state may be a kind of divine worship. Then it will be firmly rooted in the Sufi novice and become a 'station' for him. . . The 'stations' form an ascending order. The Sufi novice continues to progress from station to station until he reaches the [recognition] of the Oneness of God [*tauḥīd*] and the gnosis [*ma'rifah*] which is the desired goal of happiness. . . The basis of them all is obedience and sincerity. Faith precedes and accompanies them all. Their result and fruit are states and attributes. . . . The novice must scrutinize [*muḥāsabah*] himself in all his actions and study their concealed import, because the results of

necessity originate from actions, and shortcomings in the results, thus originate from defects in the actions. The Sufi novice finds out about that through his mystical experience, and he scrutinizes himself as to its reasons.

Very few people share the [self-scrutiny] of the Sufis, for negligence in this respect is almost universal. Pious people, who do not get that far, perform, at best, acts of obedience freed from the juridical study of how to be satisfactory and conforming. They [Sufis], however, investigate the results [of acts of obedience] with the help of mystical and ecstatic experience, in order to learn whether they are free from deficiency or not. Thus, it is evident that the Sufis' path in its entirety depends upon self-scrutiny with regard to what they do or do not do, and upon discussion of the various kinds of mystical and ecstatic experience that result from their exertions. . .

Furthermore, the Sufis have their peculiar form of behavior and a linguistic terminology which they use in instruction. . . . Where there occur ideas not commonly accepted, technical terms facilitating the understanding of those ideas are coined to express them. . . . Sufis wrote on the laws governing asceticism and self-scrutiny, how to act and not to act in imitation of model (saints). . . . Thus the science of Sufism became a systematically treated discipline in Islam.

Mystical exertion, retirement, and *dhikr* exercises are as a rule followed by the removal of the veil of sensual perception. The Sufi beholds divine worlds which a person subject to the senses cannot see at all. The spirit belongs to those worlds. The reason for the removal of the [veil] is as follows. When the spirit turns from external sense perception to inner [perception], the senses weaken and the spirit grows strong. It gains predominance and a new growth. The *dhikr* exercise helps to bring that about. It is like food to make the spirit grow. The spirit continues to grow and increase. It had been knowledge, now it becomes vision. The veil of sensual perception is removed and the soul realizes its essential existence. This is identical with perception. [The spirit] is now ready for the holy gifts, for the sciences of the divine presence and for the outpouring of the Deity. Its essence realizes its own true character and draws close to the highest sphere, the sphere of the angels. The removal of the veil often happens to people who exert themselves [in mystical experience]. They perceive the realities of existence as no one else [does]. . . .

The men around Muḥammad practiced that kind of [mystical] exertion. . . . The recent Sufis who have occupied themselves with this kind of removal [of the veil] talk about the real character of the higher and lower *existentia* and about the real character of the [divine] kingdom, the spirit, the [divine] throne, the [divine] seat, and similar things. Those who did not share their approach were not able to understand their mystical and ecstatic experiences in this respect. The *muftis* partly disapprove of these Sufis and partly accept them. Arguments and proofs are of no use in deciding whether the Sufi approach should be accepted or rejected, since it belongs to intuitive experience.[1]

Khāliq Aḥmad Nizāmī, a contemporary Indian Muslim scholar, examines the origins of Sufism as follows:

Mysticism, it is said, has no genealogy. It is the eternal yearning of the human soul to have direct experience of the Ultimate Reality. . . . The birth and growth of the mystic ideal in Islam were due to several factors. First, the mystic sentiment grew out of human aspiration for a personal, direct approach to, and a more intensive experience of, the Supreme Being and the religious truth. When strong religious emotions could not be satisfied by orthodox or formal approach to the Ultimate Reality, the mystic ideals came to be cherished and cultivated. The orthodox theologians looked upon religion as a set of lifeless rituals and ceremonies. Intensely religious spirits, hungering after a deeper communion, naturally turned to mystic speculation and experience as the real source of religious progress and development. A consciousness of contradiction in the metaphysical and ethical aspects of popular theology further encouraged the mystic attitude which, in its ultimate analysis, is an attempt to transcend discord and reduce all contradictions into an absolute unity.

Secondly, Islamic mysticism was a reaction against over intellectualism, formalism and hair splitting theology. It was under the influence of Greek thought that Muslim scholars had adopted a sophisticated approach toward religion. Their attitude was characterized by artificialism and they tried to represent the simple facts of faith in terms derived from Greek logic and metaphysics. . . . People who yearned for a direct and natural approach to religion turned towards the spiritual aspects. They developed cosmic emotions as an antidote to over intellectualism. . . .

Thirdly the rigidity and formalism of the various schools of Muslim jurisprudence found its reaction in the development of mystic thought. It became the exponent of the higher religious values and attracted to its fold all those who were not satisfied with formal and static aspects of religion. Mysticism is, at its highest level, a form of free thinking. The following couplet neatly expresses the mystic challenge to the jurists:

You cannot see God in *Kanz* and *Hidāyah* [Two celebrated law books]
Look into the mirror of your heart:
There is no better book.

Lastly, the mystic call in Islam was the result of an inner rebellion of conscience against the social injustices of the age. . . . The impious ways of the Muslim governing classes provoked disgust in sensitive minds. . . .

After citing several Quranic verses loved by Sufis, Khāliq Aḥmad Nizāmī continues:

The Prophet has always occupied a central and pivotal place in the ideology of Islamic mysticism. His vigils, his meditation at Ḥirā' and his direct relationship with the Lord has inspired travellers on the mystic path. Some seventy persons, known as *Ahl al-Ṣuffah,* lived in his mosque and prayed day and night during his life time. They had no earthly attachments and no worldly engagements. Some of the Quranic verses, according to many exegetes, refer to their piety. This small group of intensely devoted religious men constitutes the earliest batch of mystics in Islam . . .

The ascension of the Prophet [*Mi'rāj*] has greatly fascinated the Sufis and they have sometimes enjoyed narrating their adventures in the realm of the spirit more or less on the lines of the Prophet's experience. Shaikh Bayāzīd Bistāmī [d. 875 AD] was probably the first distinguished saint who took the *Mi'rāj* as a theme for expressing his own mystical experience.[2]

Al-Ghazālī's (1058–1111) (see *House of Islam*) decisive experience of intuitive conviction of truth as told in his autobiographical treatise, *The Deliverer from Wandering,* is a classic document in Sufi history.

It had already become clear to me that I had no hope of the bliss of the world to come save through a God-fearing life and the withdrawal of myself from vain desire. It was clear to me too that the key to all this was to sever the attachment of the heart to worldly things by leaving the mansion of deception and returning to that of eternity, and to advance towards God most High with all earnestness. It was also clear that this was only to be achieved by turning away from wealth and position and fleeing from all time-consuming entanglements. . . .

I reflected on this continuously for a time, while the choice still remained open to me. One day I would form the resolution to quit Baghdad . . . the next day I would abandon my resolution. I put one foot forward and drew the other back. If in the morning I had a genuine longing to seek eternal life, by the evening the attack of a whole host of desires had reduced it to impotence. Worldly desires were striving to keep me by their chains just where I was, while the voice of faith was calling: "To the road! to the road! What is left of life is but little and the journey before you is long. All that keeps you busy, both intellectually and practically, is but hypocrisy and delusion. . . ." On hearing that, the impulse would be stirred and the resolution made to take flight.

Soon, however, Satan would return. "This is a passing mood," he would say. "Do not yield to it for it will quickly disappear: if you comply with it and leave this comfortable and influential position, these dignified circumstances . . . then you will probably come to yourself again and you will not find it easy to return to all this."

For nearly six months . . . I was continuously tossed about between the attractions of worldly desires and the impulses towards eternal life. In the month of Rajab 486 AH the matter ceased to be one of choice and became one of compulsion. God caused my tongue to dry up so that I was prevented from lecturing. . . . This impediment in my speech produced grief in my heart, and at the same time my power to digest and assimilate food and drink was impaired: I could hardly swallow or digest a single mouthful of food. My powers became so weakened that doctors gave up all hope of successful treatment. "This trouble arises from the heart," they said, "and from there it has spread through the constitution. The only method of treatment is that the anxiety which has come over the heart should be allayed."

Thereupon, perceiving my impotence, and having altogether lost my power of choice, I sought refuge with God most High as one who is driven to Him because he is without further resources of his own. He answered me, for He "answers him who is driven [to Him] when he calls Him." [Surah 27:63] He made it easy for my heart to turn away from position and wealth, from children and friends. I openly professed that I had resolved to set out for Mecca, while privately I made arrangements to travel to Syria. I took this precaution in case the Caliph and all my friends should oppose my resolve to make my residence in Syria. This stratagem for my departure from Baghdad I gracefully executed, intending in my mind never to return there. There was much talk about me among all the religious leaders of Iraq, since none of them would allow that withdrawal from such a state of life as mine could have a religious motive. For they looked upon that as the culmination of a religious career. Such was the sum of their knowledge. . . .

I left Baghdad then. I distributed what wealth I had, retaining only as much as would suffice myself and provide sustenance for my children. . . . In due course I entered Damascus, and there I remained for nearly two years with no other occupation than the cultivation of retirement and solitude, together with religious and ascetic exercises. I busied myself purifying my soul, improving my character and cleansing my heart for the constant recollection of God most High, as I had learned from my study of mysticism. I used to go into retreat for a period in the mosque of Damascus, going up the minaret of the mosque for the whole day and shutting myself in so as to be alone.

At length I made my way from Damascus to the Holy House [Jerusalem]. There I used to enter into the precinct of the Rock every day and shut myself in.

Next there arose in me a prompting to fulfill the duty of the Pilgrimage, gain the blessings of Mecca and Medina and perform the visitation of the Messenger of God most High.

Thereafter he returned to Baghdad, drawn by the entreaties of his children and other anxieties, yet still in meditative search.

I continued at this stage for the space of ten years and during these periods of solitude there were revealed to me things innumerable and unfathomable. This much I will say in order that others may be helped. I learnt with certainty that it is the mystics above all who walk on the road of God: their life is the best life, their method the soundest method, their character the purest character. Indeed, were the intellect of the intellectuals, the learning of the learned and the scholarship of the scholars, who are versed in the profundities of revealed truth, brought together in an attempt to improve the life and character of the mystics, they would find no way of doing so. For to the Sufis all movement and all rest, whether external or internal, brings illumination from the light of the lamp of prophetic revelation, and behind the light of prophetic revelation there is no other light on the face of the earth from which illumination may be received.[3]

THE WAY: STATES AND STAGES

One of the most influential manuals of Sufi story and vocabulary was that of Abū Bakr al-Kalābādhī (d. 990 AD). Written in Bukhārā it owed its great reputation and its circulation in part to its brevity and sweetness, and in part to the careful effort it made to affirm the essential orthodoxy of Sufism. Its account of Sufi patterns and terms was prefaced by a careful, succinct exposé of the basic theology of Islam. Its title, *Kitāb al-Ta'arruf li Madhhab Ahl al-Taṣawwuf,* "The Book to Make Knowledgeable about the School of the Sufi People," is well chosen. Among its attractions are the snatches of quotation in prose and poetry from the saints of earlier centuries.

Al-Junayd was asked: "What is intimacy?" He replied: "Intimacy is the removal of nervousness, together with the persistence of awe."

Dhū al-Nūn, being asked the same question, said: "Intimacy is the lover's boldness with the Beloved."

A certain Sufi said: "Intimacy means that a man should be so familiar with the recollection of God, that he is absent from the vision of [all] others." Ruwaym is quoted in this connection:

Thy beauty is my heart's delight,
And holds my mind unceasingly:
Thy love hath set me in Thy sight,
Estranged from all humanity.
Thy recollection comes to me
With friendly tidings from the Friend:
"Behold as He hath promised thee
Thou shalt attain and gain thine end."
Wherever Thou mayest chance to light,
O Thou Who art my soul's intent,
Thou comest clearly to my sight,
And in my heart art immanent.

One of our shaikhs explained 'presence' [with God] as follows: "Presence means that whatever one may witness one is oblivious of it, and it is as if non-existent, because of the overwhelming presence of God."

Presence signifies that a man regards his passions as belonging to God, not to himself: whatever he may indulge in, he indulges in it in the spirit of servanthood and the submission of his human nature, not for the sake of pleasure and lust. There is yet a second absence beyond this, in which a man is unconscious of his passing away. . . . Presence is a consciousness of being overwhelmed, not a visual consciousness.

One of the Sufis composed the following:

When truth its light doth show,
I lose myself in reverence,
And am as one who never travelled thence
To life below.
When I am absented
From self in Him, and Him attain,
Attainment's self thereafter proveth vain,
And self is dead.
In union divine
With Him Him only do I see:
I dwell alone, and that felicity
No more is mine.
This mystic union
From self hath separated me:
Now witness concentration's mystery
Of two made one.

Passing away [*al-fanā'*] is a state in which all passions pass away, so that the mystic experiences no feelings towards anything whatsoever, and loses all sense of discrimination: he has passed away from all things and is wholly absorbed with that through which he has passed away. . . . Abidingness [*al-baqā'*] which follows passing away means that the mystic persists through what is God's. One of the Sufis said: "Persistence [abidingness] is the station of the prophets." They were clad in the peace of God [*sakīnah*] and whatever comes to them cannot prevent them from doing their duty to God and receiving His bounty. . . .

Certain of the Sufis count these states as a single state, in spite of the various terms that are applied to them. Thus they equate passing-away and continuance, concentration and separation, and similarly absence and presence, intoxication and sobriety. For the mystic passes away from what belongs to himself and persists through what belongs to God: while conversely he persists through what belongs to God, and so passes away from what belongs to himself. . . .

They are at variance as to whether the mystic who has once passed away ever returns to remain in his own attributes. Some say that the mystic does so return, and that the condition of passing away is not permanent. For, if it were so, then the mystic . . . would be incapable of doing a single thing connected with his life in this world and his members would necessarily be useless for performing religious duties. . . . The great Sufis, however, and those who have had true experience, among them Al-Junayd, Al-Kharrāz and Al-Nūrī, do not hold that the mystic returns to his own attributes after passing away. They argue that passing away is a divine bounty and gift to the mystic. . . . If He were to return the mystic to his own attribute, He would be taking away what He had given, and recalling what He had accorded, and this would not be at all in keeping with God's nature.

The Doctrine of the Seeker and the Sought

The seeker is in reality the sought, and the Sought is the Seeker. For the man who seeks God only seeks Him because God first sought him. So God says: "He loves them and they love Him": [Surah 5:59] and again, "God was well-pleased with them and they were well-pleased with God": [Surah 5:119] and again, "Then He turned to them that they might turn." [Surah 9:119] His seeking of them was the cause of their seeking of Him. For the cause of everything is God's act and God's act has no cause. If God seeks a man it is not possible for that man not to seek God: so God has made the seeker the sought, and the Sought the Seeker. Nevertheless the seeker is the man whose toiling preceded his revelation, while the Sought is He whose revelation preceded his toiling. The seeker is described in God's words: "But those who fight strenuously for Us We will surely guide them into our way." [Surah 29:69] Such a man is sought by God Who turns his heart and implants in it a grace, to stir him to toil for Him, and to turn to Him and to seek Him. Then He accords him the revelation of the spiritual states. So it was with Ḥārithah, who said: "I turned myself from this world and thirsted in the daytime and watched at night." Then he said: "And it was as though I beheld the Throne of my Lord coming forth." With these words he indicated that the revelation of the unseen came to him after he had turned from this world. The 'sought' man, on the other hand, is drawn forcibly out by God, and accorded the revelation of the states that through the power of the vision he may be stirred to toil for God, and turn to Him, and bear the burdens laid on him by God.

Further, Al-Kalabādhī observes: A man said to Abū Bakr al-Wāsiṭī: "With what motive must the mystic engage in his motions?" He replied: "With the motive of having passed away from his motions, which exist through another than he."

The words of God: "Surely the mention of God is greater," [Surah 29:44], are interpreted as meaning that they are greater than your understanding can attain, or your intellects contain, or your tongues express. True recollection consists in forgetting what is other than God.

Al-Junayd said: "Let not thy purpose in thy prayer be to perform it, without taking pleasure and joy in the union with Him to Whom there is no means of approach save through Himself."

Another wrote:

Grant that I cherish and remember Thee, in hope of gain—
So yearn the children of inconstancy for pleasures vain.
How, Lord, shall I Thy glorious revelation aspire to bear
And leave this world of veiling and temptation, in transport rare?

One of the companions of Al-Jurayrī was heard to say: "I remained for twenty years, my tongue only listening to my heart: then my state changed, and I remained for twenty years, my heart only listening to my tongue." The meaning of his saying: "My tongue only listening to my heart" is: "I only spake because of a reality which I possessed": and of "my heart only listening to my tongue" "God preserved my tongue," according as the tradition says: "By Me he hears and by Me he sees and by Me he speaks." One relates that he heard a great Sufi say: "One day I was sitting opposite the *Ka'bah* and I heard a wailing noise proceeding from the building and the words: "O wall, move out of the way of my saints and my friends. For whoso visits thee, processes about thee, but whoso visits Me processes in My presence."

Ruwaym said: "The people heard their first *dhikr* when God addressed them saying: 'Am I not your Lord?' This *dhikr* [a reference to the call to man the creature in the creation] was secreted in their hearts, even as the fact, thus communicated, was secreted in their intellects. Thus, when they heard the [Sufi] *dhikr*, the secret things of their heart appeared, and they were ravished."[4]

The purity of hearts is the key of the unseen. Purify your heart, for it is the house of the Lord. The heart is the mirror of the manifestations: therefore seek the adorning worth of the heart that is emptied. The heart is the throne of your Lord, the divine consciousness. . . . Read the tablet of the heart, your "preserved tablet" [Surah 85:22], you the beloved, the observed one, and it shall reveal your secrets to you. What He discloses to the heart shall never become deficient, while that which 'self' acquires will not be free from drudgery and monotony. Knowledge of your self in its hallowing is the door to the presence of sovereignty.

Meanings are gifts and stations are ranks. Feelings pass away, all that is, except the real, shall vanish. . . .

The saints of God are the mine of the guarded secret. These are in touch with His revealed mystery. The saints of God are the brides of the presence: on them is drawn the veil of zeal. They are treasures hidden from the mass of humanity. The saints of God have parted from the people of this world in spirit, although in physical bodies they dwell among them. The saints have hearts whose light is brighter than the sun of which we are conscious. . . . Thus they are the stars of earth in the view of the people of heaven.

Manifestation comes to men by acceptance and perfection [that is, the expression in outwardness of their status in sainthood]. Remembrance [*dhikr*] is worship by the tongue with the consent of the heart. . . . It marks the coming nearer to God of the knowing, the intelligent. If the worshipper is absorbed in worship, remembrance will add nothing to him. . . . Those who are annihilated through contemplation reach the end and purpose of remembrance. There is a vast difference between the one who remembers in order to receive enlightenment and one who has already received enlightenment before remembrance. Whoever imagines that he really remembers the Remembered One is surely forgetful of the presence. . . .

Music is stimulating to the people of the beginning, whereas to the people of the goal it is without influence. For you might consider the mountains stationary on which you look, whereas they travel with the speed of clouds. Verily, music comes not through the ears, but through the hearts in the realm of the unseen. The man of the beginning seeks the music of the camel-driver's song in order to quieten his longings, while the man of the goal is at peace in the presence of meeting.

Long did your singer excite my longings for you
Till we met where longing and singer flew.

In principle, the Sufi is one who would refresh you with his purity when you are in dismay. He is one who is purified and free from harshness. The Sufi prefers secrecy. He dons the garment of the chosen. The Sufi travels on the Path and his travel prospers. The Sufi is not one who wears wool and makes pretenses. . . . He is a man who knows and does, one who is purified and journeys in the path of enlightenment. Sufism became a subject for men's controversial discussions. They disagreed and made inacceptable descriptions of their own. As for me, I would give the epithet only to the man who is at peace with others and with whom others are at peace: therefore he is called a Sufi.

Know . . . that your wish to draw nearer means rebellion against your nature. Follow the consensus of opinion, for in so doing there is benefit for you: loss follows upon innovation. Let piety be the foundation stone. Observe the coming of divine thoughts and utterances. In asking be of infinite gentleness, sweet in word and good in action. Pursue devotion and avoid greed. Beware of errors and commit no wrong. Be humble with the great and friendly with the small. Accompany the poor and forsake the princely. Among the Sufis be of utter contentment. Depart from men and confide in the Provider. Let the knowledge of God be sufficient unto you, whereby you do not need to ask from the creatures of God. Occupy yourself with the divine revelations and forget material assistance. Stand at the thresholds and knock at the door. . . . Abide by your silence and adoration intermingled with loneliness and surging thoughts. Make your reply consistent with the discourse. Eat what is lawful and cleanse your character. Deny yourself and avoid [lavish] clothes. Be not deceived by praise. Make not your worship a matter of habit . . . Look upon the world with the eye of annihilation and you will rest from care. . . . Hold yourself in submission before the Sufi dignitaries: offer service to men on the carpet of veneration. Take care not to be self-confident, for in that lies abasement. Should they [the Sufis] draw you near unto them and disclose to you themselves, do not divulge the secrets lest you be expelled from the company of the good. For to be exiled after being brought nigh is the greater cause for misery and suffering. Therefore, seek God's help against the loss of your gift, for truly that is a catastrophe. If you find that your self has been conquered by desire and that your heart has been filled with harshness, advise them that hope is gone and make ready for immediate death. Chastise yourself and remember the Day of Resurrection at the end, the standing for judgment, the terror of punishment, the examination of sins through the use of the balance, the fear of the stumbling foot upon the way, repentance and the asking for some station of privilege.[5]

A revealing expression of the Sufi experience of *Fanā'* as the passing away of the self, through the tutelage of a loved guide, is put into the mouth of the great Al-Ḥallāj by a modern playwright in Cairo, Ṣalāḥ

'Abd al-Ṣabūr, in a verse play modelled on T.S. Eliot's *Murder in the Cathedral,* with the title: *The Tragedy of Al-Ḥallāj.*

Just as the longing thirsty desert meets abundant rain,
So did I meet my teacher. . . .
And love united us. I loved to ask and he loved to reply,
And to give. My soul became tender, and he gave,
And my veins swelled and faith shone through them.
He gave and my being became younger:
He gave and my speech and knowledge bloomed.
He took off my clothing and dressed me
In the garments of the learned.
He used to say that love is the secret of salvation.
'Love and you will be saved.
You will be rich in your beloved.
You will become the praying and the prayer.
You will become the faith, the Lord and the mosque.'
So I loved until I fell in love.
I imagined until I saw: I saw my Beloved.
And He favoured me with the perfection of beauty
And the beauty of perfection.
And I favoured Him with the perfection of love,
And I lost myself in Him.[6]

In his *Gulshān-i-Rāẓ* or *Mystic Rose Garden,* Maḥmūd Shabastārī (1250–1325) notes how the divine spoke to Moses in the midst of a burning bush and continues:

The saying: 'I am the Truth' was lawful for the bush.
Why is it not lawful in the mouth of a good man?
Every man whose heart is pure from doubt
Knows for a surety that there is no being but One.
Saying: 'I am' belongs only to the Truth . . .
The glory of the Truth admits no duality.
In that glory is no 'I' or 'We' or 'Thou.'
'I,' 'we,' 'Thou,' 'He' are all one thing.
For in unity there is no distinction of persons.
Every man who as a void is empty of self
Re-echoes within him the cry: 'I am the Truth.'
Travelling, travel and traveller, all become one.
Incarnation and communion spring from 'other,'
But every unity springs from the mystic journey.[7]

The Persian poet Jāmī uses his love lyric to convey the same mystical oneness of lover and beloved: Yūsuf and Zulaikha.

Whatever heart doth yield to love, He charms it.
In His love the heart hath life.
Longing for Him, the soul hath victory. . . .
Beware! Say not: 'He is All Beautiful

And we His lovers.' Thou art but the glass
And He the face confronting it, which casts
Its image in the mirror. He alone is manifest
And thou in truth art hid.
Pure love, like beauty, coming but from Him,
Reveals itself in thee. If steadfastly thou canst regard,
Thou wilt at length perceive He is the mirror also,
He alike the treasure and the casket. 'I' and 'Thou'
Have here no place, and are but phantasies
Vain and unreal. . . .

Then, addressing absolute Being, the poet continues:

In Thy universe all things are one.
Thy world captivating beauty, to display its perfections,
Appears in thousands of mirrors, yet is One.
Thy beauty accompanies all the beautiful,
Yet, in truth, the unique, the incomparable
Heart-enslaver is One. All this turmoil and strife
In the world is from love of Him.[8]

Muḥammad al-Ḥarrāq (died 1845) wrote:

The sum of quests is in Thy loveliness.
All else we count not worth a glance
Nay! when we look we see that nought is there
Beside Thy wondrous Countenance.

According to Ibn al-'Arabī, as cited by Shaikh al-Darqāwī, this is the experience of *fanā'*:

It is that the Infinite Majesty of God should appear unto the slave and make him forget this world and the next with all their states and degrees and stations and all memories of them, extinguishing him both from all outward things and also from his own intelligence and soul, and from his extinction therefrom, and from his extinction from extinction therefrom, inasmuch as he hath been utterly overwhelmed in the waters of Infinite Realization.

My existence has come to naught in my vision and
I have parted from the 'I' of my vision, effacing it, not affirming it.

Whoso is Its (truth's) seeker, maketh his quest
Sole object of his eyes. Then strippeth he his soul
Of all faults he can detect, and when stripped, robeth it
In their opposites. God's slave at each time and place,
His bounden debt of worship fulfilling,
He addeth thereto of his own free will,
Until the Truth is his Hearing, Sight,
Tongue and Utterance, and Hands and Feet.
He dieth before his death to live in the Lord,
Since after this death is the supreme migration.
He calleth himself to account 'ere he be called,
He herein most fitted to act for the Truth.
The Truth's Being he seeth before his own,

And after it, and wheresoever he turn.
Alone God was, and with Him naught else.
He is now as He was, lastly as firstly,
Essentially One, with naught beside Himself,
Inwardly hidden, outwardly manifest,
Without beginning, without end. Whate'er thou seest,
Seest thou His Being. Absolute Oneness
No 'but' hath and no 'except.' How should God's Essence
Be confined with a veil? No veil there but His Light.

Whoso is ignorant of My Essence beneath My veil,
He asketh where I am. Say 'am' without 'where'
For in my Being is no gap, as from one 'where' to another. . . .
Nay, He alone was is and shall be.
I then am absolute in Essence, Infinite.
My only 'where' is 'through Myself I am.' . . .
I am essentially One, Single, Unencroachable
By the least object. Leave I any crevice,
Any space vacant that to another might go? . . .
Doth other than Me exist, empty of My attribute?
My Essence is the essence of Being, now,
Always. . . . To behold creation is to behold the Truth,
If creation be interpreted as it truly is.
Interpret then all in the light of *He is near*.
And thou thyself of that nearness shall partake.
Deem not this localization. That were impossible,
For He cometh not to dwell in any place.
Extol the Essence of God above the touch
Of other than It. It is borne by none,
Beareth no burden. It is hidden in Its own
Outward Manifestation, wherein it doth appear
As Veil after Veil made to cover its Glory.

By Heaven here are no doubts, no vague imaginings:
I know God, with a knowledge part secret, part proclaimed.
I drank the cup of love and then possessed it,
And it has become my possession for all time. . . .
Then when the Giver vouchsafed that I proclaim it,
He fitted me—how I know not—to purify souls,
And girded me with the sword of steadfastness,
And truth and piety, and a Wine He gave me,
Which all who drink must needs be always drinking,
Even as a drunk man seeketh to be more drunk. . . .
Marvel not that I speak thus for the Lord.
Himself hath said that He singleth out for grace
Whomso He will and giveth unsparingly.
This is God's grace: He giveth it whom He will,
Surpassing praise and glory and thanks be His!

In another poem, Shaikh al-'Alawī wrote:

Accept none other for thy love but God.
All things apart from Him are pure illusion.

Here is my counsel if thou canst counsel take.
The rememberers are ever absent in their Beloved,
For none have life save those that are near to Him.
Between such and the Truth there is no veil.
What are the blessings of Paradise to them?
Passion God's slaves have melted: they have drunk,
And still drink, His eternal-treasured Wine,
The draught whereof has robbed them of themselves.
Would thou could take one sip out of their cup!
'Twould help to bridge the gap twixt thee and me.
A good slave he who saith: "I am at thy service,"
Hearing God's call which I address to him.
If God thou seekest then companion me:
For thee, be very sure, there is no way else.[9]

Here are characteristic Sufi verses and sayings:

Reason is like an officer when the king appears.
The officer then loses his power and hides himself.

Other people have their affairs and our affair is God.[10]

God is not veiled from you by some reality existing apart from Him, since there is no reality outside Him. What veils Him from you is but the illusion that there can be any reality apart from Him.[11]

See now, I hold a mirror to mine eyes,
And nought but thy reflection therein lies:
The glass speaks truth to them that understand.[12]

Life is the vessel: union the clear draught in them.

His Name will flee when it sees an attempt at speech.
In the world of divine unity, there is no room for number.
Every form you see has its archetype in the placeless world.
If the form perished, no matter, since its original is everlasting. . . .

Conceive the Soul as a fountain and these created things as rivers:
While the fountain flows, the rivers run from it.
O indestructible Love, O divine Minstrel,
We are pieces of steel and Thy love is the magnet.
He is at once all reason and brings all reason to nought.[13]

What is worship? To realise reality.
What is the sacred law? To do no evil.
What is reality? Selflessness.

He who desires heaven is a laborer working for wages,
But he who desires God is on the path to glory.[14]

Though in this world a hundred tasks thou triest,
'Tis love alone which from thyself will save thee.
Even from earthly love thy face avert not,
Since to the Real it may serve to raise thee.
Ere A, B, C, are rightly apprehended,
How canst thou con the pages of the Qur'ān?
A sage [so I heard] unto whom a scholar

Came craving counsel on the course before him,
Said: "If thy steps be stranger to love's pathways,
Depart, learn love, and then return before me!
For, should'st thou fear to drink wine from Form's flagon,
Thou canst not drain the draughts of the Ideal.
But yet beware! Be not by Form belated:
Strive rather with all speed the bridge to traverse.
If to the bourn thou fain would'st bear thy baggage
Upon the bridge let not thy footsteps linger."

Thou art absolute Being:
All else is naught but a phantasm.
For in Thy universe all things are one.
Thy world-captivating beauty, to display its perfections,
Appears in thousands of mirrors, but is one.
Although Thy Beauty accompanies all the beautiful,
In truth the unique and incomparable Heart-enslaver
Is One.

O God, Thou knowest that in mine eyes the eight Paradises weight no more than the wing of a gnat compared with that honor which Thou hast given me by the commemoration of Thy Name, or that freedom from all else which Thou hast vouchsafed to me when I meditate on the greatness of Thy glory.[15]

There is no wonder at him who is slain at the door of the Beloved's tent:
The wonder is at the survivor, in what way he saved his soul alive.[16]

Sufi prayer abounds in rich metaphors having to do with veiling and unveiling, with sobriety and inebriation, with shadows and lights, with journeys and taverns. Another is that of "the beggar at the door," or the petitioner at the gate.

The Worship of Petition: The Beggar at the Door

Without the link, there would be nothing linked. For the shaikh is the door to God and there is no access to God save through His door. Therefore Sidi Muṣṭafa al-Bakrī said: "Haunt the door of the Master and thou shalt be through this a chosen friend."

He haunted the thresholds and stood at the door like a doorkeeper. For all who travel arrive and he who haunts the threshold enters. And Rābi'ah al-'Adawiyyah said: "Cleave to the door if thou desire access."

Muḥammad is sometimes referred to as God's door.

He who is Thy very door itself. Bless the door of love. Servants of His door, cleaving close to Him, spending themselves in his path.

At the door of the best of creation my purpose has stationed me, from my knowledge that the chosen one is generous in succor. I come, bringing no knowledge and no piety, rather all is defilement, my lord, with me.

But, more usually, it is at the door of God Himself, rather than the Prophet that the suppliant stands.

Open to me the door of Thy generosity which Thou dost never close to those who are dear to Thee.

Endow me with patience, for patience is the greatest of Thy doors. For Thou hast said, and Thy word is truth: "They that endure . . to them is the reward of the abode . . . and the angels will enter to them by every door. . . . Peace be to you through what you have endured, how excellent then is the reward of the abode." [Surah 13:22]

As to the patient camel when made to kneel on stones tries to kneel, so the believer stands at his Lord's door patient with Him over his misfortunes.

For Thou art the generous One at whose door stand the beggars, Thou wider in generosity than all to whom the hands of poor clients are outstretched.

I take up my station at Thy door, the poor, expectant one.

Night and morning find me at one of the doors of Thy bestowal, a beggar beseeching.

Thy little slave is at Thy door, Thy poor one is in Thy courtyard. Thy destitute one is in Thy courtyard.

We, Thy destitute and poor and weak servants, are standing at the threshold of the courtyards of Thy mercy.

The Muslim worshipper is trained in such an aweful sense of the infinite, distant majesty of God, ever present yet ever distant in the incomparability of His majesty that he will not, when thinking theologically, urge upon his Lord any standards of human behavior. It is all the more touching to note that so deep-rooted is his sense of the duty of host to guest that he is unable to think of a God who is not bound by the great standards of eastern hospitality. In prayers which picture travelers, short of provisions, arriving at the great house, the worshipper speaks to God in the assurance that He would be ashamed that any failure in divine hospitality should be attributed to Him.

O best of those besought, O most glorious of those sought, Thy servants the Arabs, when a fugitive seeks shelter at the ropes of their tents, will shelter him. And Thou, Creator of the Arabs and the non-Arabs, at Thy door I seek shelter, in Thy courtyard I alight.

O be generous in Thy kindness, my God, to one whose travel provision is small: penniless he stands at Thy door, O Thou Friend. His sin is a great sin, do Thou forgive that great sin. Lo, he is a stranger, a sinner, a miserable slave.

Thou who givest to a slave when he asks of Thee, and when he hopes for what is in Thy house sendest it to him, and when he approaches Thee dost draw him nearer, my God, whoever came seeking Thy hospitality without Thou giving it to him? Whoever halted his camel at Thy door hoping for Thy liberality, without Thou bringing him in? Is it seemly that I should return from Thy door driven away with contumely when I know no other Lord than Thee whose quality is beneficence?

Far be it from Thee to send off with reproaches the beggar from Thy door, when Thou art the generous King.

Thy generosity is wider, Thy glory greater, than when a poor man could stretch out his hands asking Thee to pour down pardon and be turned away ashamed.

My Lord, I stand a beggar at one of the doors of Thy bestowal, turning away from the exposure of my case to others. It is not consonant with the lovely bestowals of grace to turn away a broken-hearted beggar, a needy one hoping for Thy generosity.

He said to me: "O succor of the Almighty, if a thirsty one came to Thee in a day of burning heat and thou didst own cold water for which thou hadst no use, wert thou to refuse it him thou wouldest be of all misers the most miserly. Then how can I refuse them My mercy when I have set my seal to My Name of 'the most merciful of them that show mercy?'"

Lo, I am Thy servant at Thy door:
Thine abject one at Thy door;
Thy captive at Thy door: Thy client at Thy door:
Thy destitute one at Thy door, O Lord of the worlds.
A weary one is at Thy door,
O Thou Helper of them that seek for help.
Thine anxious one is at Thy door
O Thou Who dost lift away the care of all the careworn.
And I, Thy rebel, O Thou Who seekest for penitents,
Thy rebel who acknowledges his faults is at Thy door.
O Thou Who forgivest sinners,
One who confesses his sin is at Thy door.
O most merciful, he who has erred is at Thy door.
O Lord of the worlds, he who has wronged is at Thy door.
Have mercy upon me, my Lord.

I have nought but my destitution to plead with Thee for me. And in my poverty I put forward that destitution as my plea. I have no power save to knock at Thy door,
And if I be turned away, at what door shall I knock?
Or on whom shall I call, crying his name,
If Thy generosity is refused to Thy destitute one?
Far be it from Thy generosity
To drive the disobedient one to despair.
Generosity is more freehanded, graces are wider than that.
In lowly wretchedness I have come to Thy door,
Knowing that there degradation finds help.
In full abandon I put my trust in Thee,
Stretching out my hands to Thee, a pleading beggar.

My God, in my very riches I am poor. How great then my destitution when I am poor! My God, I am ignorant in my very knowledge, how shall I not be crassly ignorant in my ignorance? My God, from me comes what accords with blame, but from Thee comes what accords with generosity. My God, Thou didst show Thyself kindly and compassionate to me before my evil deeds were done. Wilt Thou then deprive me of Thy kindness and compassion after those deeds?

Thy door is open to the beggar . . . all means have failed Thy servant and all doors are locked against him.

Thou who dost open when the busy doors of kings are locked.

His door never closes and the beggar is never turned away.

(A night prayer) My God and my Lord, eyes are at rest, stars are setting, hushed are the movements of birds in their nests, of monsters in the deep. And Thou art the Just who knowest no change, the Equity that swerveth not, the Everlasting that passes not away. The doors of kings are locked, watched by their bodyguards: but Thy door is open to him who calls on Thee. My Lord, each lover is now alone with his beloved, and Thou art for me the Beloved.

The foregoing prayers of the suppliant at the door are drawn from familiar prayer books, of wide popular circulation, from masters such as Al-Mirghānī, Al-Jilānī, Al-Tījānī, Muṣṭafā al-Bakrī, and that paragon of piety the Imām 'Alī Zain al-'Ābidīn.[17]

In the prayer manuals of the Naqshabandi Order of Sufism come the following prayer phrases.

I praise God with praises that are for evermore His due.

Let hands be lifted up to Him in supplication and petition, alike in hardship and in ease. For He is the hearer of all voices in all the diversity of tongues and languages.

Do not lay upon us burdens beyond our power to take: pardon us, forgive and do us mercy.

O Thou Lord of majesty and honor, cleanse our hearts from every trait that would distance us from the vision of Thy love.

Graceful are the secrets of Thy Being and in every thing that is do they appear. The light of Thy holy purity shines on high and is manifest in every thing seen.

O Thou with Whom is a goodness no gratitude can suffice, whose patience knows no term, Whom place cannot contain, nor time exhaust, to Thee is my desire. 'Tis Thou I fear.

O Thou than Whom there is no 'He' save 'He', inspire us with truth and wisdom.

O God, we ask Thee by the light of Thy face filling the pillars of Thy throne, sow the knowledge of Thee in our hearts—the knowledge that we ought to have of Thee.

Make our wildness to be rightly ordered: bring our distresses into light: accomplish our hopes and cleanse our tongues and have mercy upon our state of exile.

Take from me my own wilfulness and make me patient. Companion me and meet my need, O Thou of caring kindness. Make real to me Thy proximity wherein there is no disquiet.

O my God, transgressions are mine, between me and Thee, between me and Thy creation, transgressions from which neither Thou nor Thy creation leave me an escape, being wholly mine. Forgive me and remove them from me. Enrich me of Thy goodness, O Thou of wide forgivingness.

Occupy my body in Thy obedience, busy my mind with reverence and cleanse me inwardly from all sedition of the heart.

O God, send down blessing upon Thy Apostle, our Master and Lord, Muḥammad, so that we may inherit the earth and whoso is therein. For Thou art the best of those who make to inherit.

Bind us in the ties of security from falling into transgression against Thee.

The musings of the mind are far from the inner mystery of the nature of Thy essence and come short of conceiving it. O Thou succor of those who call for aid, come to our help.

Cause us at this hour to be among those who called upon Thee and were heard, who made requests and were answered, who besought Thee and found mercy and were brought near to the knowledge of Thee through Thy goodness. Do well with us O Lord, according to Thy fame and do not deal with us according to ours. We ask Thee to satisfy our needs. Let only Thy pardon encompass us.

O God, we call upon Thee by the might of the strength-imparting power of Thy mightiness [a threefold play on words], by the measure of the competence of Thy authority, and by the height of the soaring of Thy sovereignty and by the forbearance of the forgivingness of Thy pardon, by Thy mercy come and aid us.

We ask of Thee a taking hold of Thee in Thy pardon both of what is outward to us and what is inward and humility in word and deed.

O Thou Who art the holder of the balance, enlarge for me my bosom and ease me in my business. [A prayer quoting two Quranic verses: 3:18 and 20:25.] [18]

The adamant will for detachment from human entanglements, disallowing all roots of local dwelling and attachment, makes the true dervish a perpetual wanderer. The *Mathnawī* of Jalāl al-Dīn Rūmī thus describes the saint, Al-Daqūqī.

> He rarely tarried in one place and seldom stayed two days in one village. For he said: "If I tarry in one house two days, attachment to that house becomes a passion for me. I guard myself from being deceived into loving a home. Up! soul, and travel in search of eternal wealth. My heart's inclination is not satisfied by houses, lest they should be places of temptation for me." Thus by day he travelled and by night he prayed. His eyes were always gazing on the King's like a falcon's, cut off from mankind, though not for any fault, severed from men though not for baseness, having compassion on mankind and wholesome as water, a kind intercessor and one whose prayers were heard. . . . Thus Al-Daqūqī, in devotions, prayers and praises, was forever seeking the particular favorites of God. Through all his long journeyings, his object was this: to interchange a word with the favorites of God. He cried continually as he went his way: "O Lord, let me draw near Thy chosen ones."[19]

The unresting travel of the Sufi is in pursuit of kindred souls, not of the sights of this world. For, as Ibn Abū-l-Khair had it in the twelfth century, "the more a man knows of the world, the less he knows of God." The true Sufi is the son of time present, a passive instrument moved by the divine impulse of the moment.

> O heart, why art thou captive in the earth that is passing away? Fly forth from this enclosure, since thou art a bird of the spiritual world. . . . Regard thine own state, go forth and journey from the prison of this formal world to the realm of ideas. Illumine thy bodily senses by the light of the soul.[20]

An illuminating account both of the role of the *murshid*, or guide in Sufism, and of the nature of mystical experience is found in the fragment of autobiography left among the papers of Shaikh Abū-l-'Abbās al-'Alawī (1869–1934), a paragon of Islamic spirituality, born at Mostaghenam, Algeria. He was a famous master of Sufi discipline whose legacy is well-known from Fez to Damascus. Recalling his early experiences of snake-charming, he describes how he met Shaikh Muḥammad al-Būzīdī, who warned him of the need to learn to 'charm' the 'snake' that lay "between the two sides of his body," namely, the self and soul of man. Shaikh al-'Alawī continues:

> I went out wondering about the soul and how its poison could be more deadly than a snake's. . . .
>
> After the Shaikh had transmitted to me the litanies for morning and evening recitation, he told me not to speak about them to anyone, "until I tell you" he said. Then in less than a week he called me to him and began to talk to me about the Supreme Name (Allāh) and the method of invoking it. He told me to devote myself to *dhikr Allāh* in the way generally practised in our order at that time; and since he had no special cell of retreat for *dhikr*, I was unable to find a place where I could be alone undisturbed. When I complained of this to him, he said: "There is no better place for being alone than the cemetery." So I went there alone at nights, but it was not easy for me. I was so overcome with fear that I could not concentrate on the *dhikr*, although for many nights I tried to do so.
>
> I complained again to the Shaikh and he said: "I did not give you a binding order. I merely said there was no place better for being alone than the cemetery." Then he told me to limit my *dhikr* to the last third of the night, and so I invoked at night and made contact with him during the day. Either he would come to me, or else I would go to him, although his house was not always a good place for meeting on account of the children and for other reasons. In addition to this, at midday, I went on attending the lessons in theology which I had attended previously. One day he asked me: "What lessons are those I see you attending?" I said: "They are on the doctrine of the Unity [*Al-Tauḥīd*] and I am now at "the realization of proofs." He said: "Sidi So-and-so used to call it 'the muddy mire doctrine (*tawḥīl*).'" Then he added: "You had better busy yourself now with purifying your innermost soul until the Lights of your Lord dawn in it and you come to know the real meaning of Unity. But as for scholastic theology it will only serve to increase your doubts and pile up illusion upon illusion." Finally he said: "You had better leave the rest of those lessons until you are through with your present task, for it is an obligation to put what is more important before what is of lesser importance."
>
> No order that he ever gave me was so hard to obey as this. I had grown very fond of those lessons and had come to rely on them so much for my understanding of the doctrine that I was on the point of disobeying him. But God put into my heart his question: How do you know that what you are receiving from the Shaikh Al-Būzīdī is not the kind of knowledge that you are really seeking, or something even higher than it? Secondly, I comforted myself with the thought that the prohibition was not a permanent one: thirdly I remembered that I had taken an oath of allegiance to obey him: and fourthly I told myself that perhaps he wanted to put me to trial, as is the way of Shaikhs. But all these arguments did not stop the ache of heart that I felt within me. What sent that away was my spending in solitary invocation the hours which I had previously devoted to reading, especially after I had begun to feel the effects of this invocation.
>
> As to his way of guiding his disciples, stage by stage, it varied. He would talk to some about the form in which Adam was created, and to others about the cardinal virtues and to others about the divine Actions, each instruction being specially suited to the disciple in question. But the course which he most often followed, and which I also followed after him, was to enjoin upon

the disciple the invocation of the single Name with distinct visualization of the letters until they were written on his imagination. Then he would tell him to spread them out and enlarge them until they filled all the horizon. The *dhikr* would continue in this form until the letters became like light. Then the Shaikh would show the way out of this standpoint—it is impossible to express in words how he did so—and by means of this indication the spirit of the disciple would quickly reach beyond the created universe provided that he had sufficient preparation and aptitude—otherwise there would be need for purification and other spiritual training. At the above mentioned indication the disciple would find himself able to distinguish between the Absolute and the relative, and he would see the universe as a ball or a lamp suspended in a beginningless, endless void. Then it would grow dimmer in his sight as he persevered in the invocation to the accompaniment of meditation, until it seemed no longer a definite object but a mere trace. Then it would become not even a trace, until at length the disciple was submerged in the World of the Absolute and his certainty was strengthened by its Pure Light. In all this the Shaikh would watch over him and ask him about his states and strengthen him in the *dhikr* degree by degree until he finally reached a point of being conscious of that he perceived through his own power. The Shaikh would not be satisfied until this point was reached, and he used to quote the words of God which refer to one who "His Lord has made certain and whose certainty He then followed up with direct evidence." [Surah 11:17 in Sufi translation.]

When the disciple had reached this degree of independent perception, which was strong or weak according to his capability, the Shaikh would bring him back again to the world of outward forms after he had left it, and it would seem to him the inverse of what it had been before, simply because the light of his inward eye had dawned. He would see it as Light upon Light [Surah 24:36], and so it had been before in reality.

In this degree the disciple may mistake the bowstring for the arrow as has happened to many of those who are journeying to God, and he may say, as more than one has said: "I am He that I love, and He whom I love is I," and the like—enough to make anyone who has no knowledge of the attainments of the mystics and is unfamiliar with their ejaculations throw at him the first thing that he can lay hands on. But the master of this degree comes before long to distinguish between the spiritual points of view, and to give to each of the different degrees of existence its due and to each of the spiritual stations what rightly belongs to it. This station took hold of me and it has been my home for many years.

When I had reaped the fruit of the *dhikr*—and its fruit is no less than knowledge of God by way of contemplation—I saw clearly the meagreness of all that I had learned about the doctrine of the divine Unity, and I sensed the meaning of what my Master had said about it. Then he told me to attend once more those lessons which I had attended previously, and when I did so I found myself quite different from what I had been before as regards understanding. I now understood things in advance before the Shaikh who was teaching us had finished expounding them. Another result of the invocation was that I understood more than the literal sense of the text. In a word, there was no comparison between the understanding I now had and that which I had before, and its scope went on increasing, until when anyone recited a passage from the Book of God my wits would jump to solve the riddle of its meaning with amazing speed at the very moment of recitation.

> When after many long days I was freed from the obligation of devoting myself exclusively to the Divine Name, my Master said to me: "Now you must speak and guide men to this path inasmuch as you are now certain where you stand." I said: "Do you think they will listen to me?" And he said: "You will be like a lion: whatever you put your hand on you will take hold of it." It was as he had said. Whenever I spoke with anyone in the intention of leading him to the path, he was guided by my words and went the way I pointed out to him, and, so, praise God, this brotherhood increased.[21]

Sufi personality at its finest can perhaps be more readily measured in the words of a modern account than in the intimations that come from remoter, medieval sources. An eye-witness, for example, in Algeria thus described the fascination exercised by the charisma of Shaikh al-'Alawī:

> You would find sitting in front of him [in the mosque] hundreds, nay thousands, with heads bowed as if birds were hovering round them and hearts full of awe and eyes wet with tears, in silent understanding of what they heard him say.

Another writer, shortly after the Shaikh's death in 1935:

> In his brown *jallābah* and white turban, with his silver grey beard and his long hands which seemed when he moved them to be weighted down with the flow of his *barakah* [blessing], he exuded something of the pure archaic ambience of Sayyidnā Ibrāhīm (Abraham), the Friend of God. He spoke in a subdued gentle voice. . . . His eyes, which were like two sepulchral lamps, seemed to pierce through all objects, seeing in their outer shell merely one and the same nothingness, beyond which they saw always one and the same reality—the Infinite. Their look was very direct, almost hard in its enigmatic unwaveringness, and yet full of charity. Often their long ovals would grow suddenly round as if in amazement or as if enthralled by some marvellous spectacle. The cadence of the singing, the dances and ritual incantations seemed to go on vibrating in him perpetually: his head would sometimes rock rhythmically to and fro while his soul was plunged in the unfathomable mysteries of the Divine Name hidden in the *dhikr*, the Remembrance. . . . He gave out an impression of unreality, so remote was he, so inaccessible, so difficult to take in on account of his altogether abstract simplicity. . . . He was surrounded, at one and the same time, with all the veneration due to saints, to leaders, to the old and to the dying.
>
> Yet, as another observes: He belonged to that class of men, often to be met with in North Africa, who can pass without transition, from deep thought to action, from the mysteries of the next world to the life of this, from the vast sweep of ideas to the smallest details of native politics.[22]

THE SUFI ORDERS

Describing the Suhrawardiyyah Order of Sufism (see *House of Islam*, pp. 71–72). Khāliq Aḥmad Nizāmī attributes to its founder the following fundamental principles governing organized *khānqāhs,* or 'monasteries.'

i. The people of the *khānqāhs* should establish cordial relations with all men.
ii. They should concern themselves with God through prayers and meditation, et cetera.
iii. They should abandon all efforts at earning a livelihood and should resign themselves to the will of God.
iv. They should strive for the purification of their inner life.
v. They should abstain from things that produce evil effects.
vi. They should learn the value of time.
vii. They should completely shake off indolence and lethargy.

The *ahl-al-khānqāh* were divided into two categories: permanent residents [*muqīmūn*] and travellers [*musāfirūn*]. A traveller desiring to stay in a *khānqāh* was expected to arrive before the *'aṣr* prayer. If he arrived late, he was advised to pass the night in some mosque and join the *khānqāh* the next day. As soon as a guest arrived he was expected to offer two genuflections of prayer and then greet the residents of the *khānqāh.* If the visitor decided to stay on after the third day, he had to undertake duties in the *khānqāh,* and help the inmates in their day to day work. The servants of the *khānqāh* were instructed to show extreme hospitality to all guests and were strictly warned against ridiculing those who were ignorant of the mystic customs and conventions.

The permanent residents were divided into three grades: *Ahl al-Khidmah, Ahl al-Suḥbah* and *Ahl al-Khalwah* [servers, companions, intimates] according to their standing and the nature of the duties assigned to them.

Strict discipline was maintained in the *khānqāhs* and elaborate rules were laid down for the guidance of the inmates—how to talk to the Shaikh, how to deal with visitors, how to sit in the *khānqāh,* how to walk, how and when to sleep, what dress to wear. On these and similar topics minute instructions were given. The Shaikh dealt sternly with those inmates who were found guilty of the slightest irregularity.

If a *khānqāh* had no endowment for its maintenance, the Shaikh could either instruct his disciples to earn their livelihood or permit them to beg or ask them to sit in the *khānqāh* resigned to God's will. If a *khānqāh* had no shaikh but was run by a group of men of equal spiritual status [*ikhwān*] the same three courses were open to them.[23]

In a manual of the *Tījāniyyah* Order in the nineteenth century, the following directions are given for the admission of postulants to the *Ṭarīqah.*

You must be an adult Muslim in order that it may be correct for you to take the *aurād* [prayer liturgies] for they are the work of the Lord of men. You should ask permission from your parents of your own free will before you take the *Ṭarīqah,* for this is one of the means of *wuṣūl* or entering into God. You must ask for one who has a genuine permission to initiate you into the *aurād,* so that you will be well-connected with God.

You should abstain absolutely from any other *aurād* than those of your shaikh, since God did not create two hearts within you [a reference to Surah

33:4]. Do not visit any *walī*, living or dead, for no man can serve two masters. You must be strict about performing the five prayers in the congregation and in observing the legal obligations, for they are prescribed by the best of creation [the Prophet]. You must love the shaikh and his *khalīfah* throughout your life, since for the generality of created beings such love is the main means of Union: and think not that you can safeguard yourself from the workings of the Lord of the universe, for this is one of the characteristics of those who fail. You must not malign nor bear enmity against your shaikh, otherwise you will bring destruction upon yourself. You must not desist from reciting the *aurād* as long as you live, because they contain the mysteries of the Creator. You must believe and trust in all that the shaikh says to you about the virtues, because they are amongst the sayings of the Lord of the first and the last. You must not criticize any good thing that seems strange to you in this *Ṭarīqah*, or you will be deprived of the virtue of the Just Ruler. . . .

Gather together for the office and the Friday *dhikr* with the brethren because this is a safeguard against the wiles of the devil. . . . Do not interrupt [the recitation of] anyone, especially one of the brethren, for such interruption is one of the methods of the devil.[24]

That most celebrated of Muslim travelers, Ibn Baṭṭūṭa of Tangier [1304–1369], tells an intriguing story that illustrates the vast dispersion of Sufi communities and also the aura of mystery and occult wisdom that is attached to the leading shaikhs and *murshidīn* of the several Orders. He was *en route* from Sylhet in eastern Bengal to the mountains of Assam.

My purpose in travelling to these mountains was to meet a notable saint who lives there, namely Shaikh Jalāl al-Dīn of Tabriz [not Rūmī]. At a distance of two days journey from his abode I was met by four of his disciples, who told me that the Shaikh had said to his dervishes who were with him: "The traveller from the west has come to you: go out to welcome him." He had no knowledge whatever about me but this had been revealed to him. I went with them to the shaikh and arrived at his hermitage, situated outside the cave. There is no cultivated land there, but the inhabitants of the country, both Muslim and infidel, come to visit him, bringing gifts and presents, and the dervishes and travellers live on these offerings. The Shaikh, however, limits himself to a single cow, with whose milk he breaks his fast every ten days. It was by his labors that the people of these mountains became converted to Islam, and that was the reason for his settling among them. When I came into his presence he rose to greet me and I embraced him. He asked me about my native land and my travels, and when I had given him an account of them he said to me: "You are the traveller of the Arabs." Those of his disciples who were there said: "And the non-Arabs, too, our Master." "And of the non-Arabs too," he repeated, "so show him honor." Then they took me to the hermitage and gave me hospitality for three days.

On the day when I visited the Shaikh I saw that he was wearing a wide mantle of goatshair. It took my fancy and I said to myself: "I wish the Shaikh could have given it to me." When I visited him to bid him farewell, he went to the side of the cave, took off the mantle and placed it upon me, together with a skull-cap from his head, himself putting on a patched garment. The dervishes told me that the Shaikh was not in the habit of wearing this mantle and had put it on only when I arrived, saying to them: "This mantle will be asked for by the Moroccan, and it will be taken from him by an infidel sultan, who will give it to our brother Burhān al-Dīn of Sagharj, whose it is and for whom it was made." When they told me this I said to them: "I have obtained the blessing of the Shaikh through his clothing me with his garments and I, for my part, shall not enter the presence of any sultan, infidel or Muslim, wearing this mantle." With this, I withdrew from the Shaikh's presence.

Now it came about a long time afterwards that I visited China and eventually reached the city of Khansa. My party were separated from me by the pressure of the crowd and I was wearing this mantle. I happened to be in a certain street when the *wazīr* came by with a large suite. His eye fell upon me, and summoning me he clasped my hand, asked me about my arrival, and continued talking to me until I came to the sultan's palace with him. At this point I wished to take leave of him, but he would not hear of it and introduced me into the sultan's presence. The latter questioned me about the Muslim sultans and when I replied to his questions, he looked at the mantle and took a liking to it. The *wazīr* said to me: "Take it off," and I could not resist his order. So the sultan took it and ordered me to be given ten robes, a horse and harness, and a sum of money.

This incident roused my anger, but afterwards I recalled the Shaikh's saying that an infidel sultan would seize it and I was deeply amazed at the fulfilment of the prediction.

The following year I entered the palace of the King of China at Khan-Beliq [Peking] and sought out the convent of the Shaikh Burhān al-Dīn of Sagharj. I found him reading and wearing that identical mantle. I was astonished and took it in my hand to examine it. He said to me: "Why examine it when you know it already?" "True," I replied, "it is the one that was taken from me by the sultan of Khansa." "This mantle," he went on, "was specially made for me by my brother Jalāl al-Dīn, who wrote to me saying: 'This mantle will reach you by the hand of so and so.'" Then he brought out the letter and I read it and marvelled at the Shaikh's perfect knowledge. I told Burhān al-Dīn the beginning of my story and he said to me: "My brother Jalāl al-Dīn can do more than all this, he has the powers of creation at his disposal but he has now passed to the mercy of God. I have been told," he added, "that he prayed the dawn prayer every day at Mecca, and that he made the pilgrimage every year, for he used to disappear from sight on the days of 'Arafāt and the festival, and no one knew where he went."

While in South India, Ibn Baṭṭūṭa encountered another shikh of local renown but, apparently, of rather less esteem with the traveler.

In this city there is a fine mosque, built of stone, and it has also large quantities of grapes and excellent pomegranates. I met here the pious shaikh Muḥammad of Nishapur, one of the crazy dervishes who let their hair hang loose over their shoulders. He had with him a lion which he had tamed and which used to sit and eat along with the dervishes. Accompanying him were about thirty dervishes, one of whom had a gazelle. Though the gazelle and the lion used to be together in the same place, the lion did not molest it.

Ibn Baṭṭūṭa had the liveliest of tributes in very florid vein when he recorded his sojourn in Cairo:

. . . mother of cities and seat of Pharaoh the tyrant, mistress of broad regions and fruitful lands, boundless in multitude of buildings, peerless in beauty and splendor, the halting place of feeble and mighty, whose throngs surge as the waves of the sea. . . .

There are [he went on] a large number of religious establishments, which they call *khānqāhs* and the nobles vie with one another in building them. Each of these is set apart for a special school of dervishes, mostly Persians, who are men of good education and adepts in the mystical doctrines. Each has a superior and a doorkeeper and their affairs are admirably organized. They have many special customs, one of which has to do with their food. The steward of the house comes in the morning to the dervishes, each of whom indicates what food he desires, and when they assemble for meals, each person is given his bread and soup in a separate dish, none sharing with another. They eat twice a day. They are each given winter clothes and summer clothes, and a monthly allowance of from twenty to thirty *dirhams*. Every Thursday night they receive sugar cakes, soap to wash their clothes, the price of a bath, and oil for their lamps. These men are celibate: the married men have separate convents. Their duties include attendance at the five ritual prayers, passing the night in the *khānqāh* and attendance at their *dhikr* gatherings held in the hall. It is also customary for each one to occupy his own special prayer-mat.

When a new arrival makes his appearance he has to take up his stand at the gateway, girded around the middle, with the prayer-mat slung over his back, his staff in his right hand and his ablution-jug in his left. The gatekeeper informs the steward who goes out and ascertains from what country he has come, what *khānqāhs* he has resided in during his journey [or training] and who was his initiator. If he is satisfied as to the truth of his replies, he brings him into the *khānqāh,* arranges a suitable place for him to spread his prayer-mat and shows him the wash-room. He then restores himself to a state of ritual cleanliness, goes to his mat, ungirds himself and prays two prostrations. After this he clasps the hand of the shaikh and of those who are present and takes his seat among them.[25]

Stories of the Sufis, illustrating the vigilance of their spirituality, are many.

Abū-l-'Abbās al-Muhtadī said: "I was once in the desert and I saw a man walking before me with feet bare and head uncovered, and he was carrying no wallet. I said to myself: 'How can this man pray? He has neither purity nor prayer.' Thereupon he turned to me and said: 'God knows what is in your heart, therefore fear Him.' [Surah 2:236] Immediately I fainted: and when I recovered, I asked God's pardon for the regard which I had cast upon him. Then, as I was walking along the road, he came again before me. And as I looked at him, I feared him and stopped.

But he turned to me and recited: 'It is He that accepts the repentance of His servants and pardons their evil-doings.' [Surah 42:24] Then he disappeared and I never saw him again."

One reported that he heard Abū-l-Ḥasan al-Muzayyin say: "I went into the desert alone, to be apart from men. When I was at Al-'Umaq [on the road to Mecca], I sat down on the margin of the pool there, and my soul began to speak to me about how it had gone apart from men, and journeyed through the desert, and a sense of pride entered into it. Then, behold, Al-Kattānī appeared to me—or it may have been another, the doubt is mine—on the other side of the pool and called me, saying: 'O cupper! how long wilt thou speak to thyself of vain things?'"

Dhū-l-Nūn said: "I once saw a youth wearing old rags, and my soul revolted against him: yet my heart attested that he was a saint. So I remained divided between my soul and my heart, reflecting. The youth perceived what was in my mind. For, looking toward me, he said: 'O Dhū-l-Nūn, do not look at me in order to see what is my character. The pearl is only to be found within the shell.' That spiritual insight is a genuine phenomenon is attested by the following tradition: 'Fear the insight of the believer, for verily he sees with the light of God.'"

Al-Darrāj said: "I examined the sleeve of my master, looking for a kohl-box, and I found in it a piece of silver. I was astonished thereat, and when I came to him I said: 'Lo, I found a piece (of silver) in thy sleeve!' He replied: 'I have seen it. Give it back.' Then he said: 'Take it and buy something with it.' I asked: 'What was the purpose of this piece, in view of the rights of Him thou worshippest?' He answered: 'God provided me with nothing yellow or white [that is, gold or silver] in this world, save this: and I intended to make a deposition that it should be wrapped in my winding sheet, so that I could give it back to God.'"

Abū-l-Qāṣim al-Baghdādī told the following anecdote which he heard from Al-Dawrī: "On the night of the festival [ending Ramaḍān], we were in the company of Abū-l-Ḥusain al-Nūrī in the Shūnīzī mosque. A man came up to us and said to Al-Nūrī: 'Master, tomorrow is the festival. What wilt thou wear?' Al-Nūrī began to recite these verses:

'Tomorrow is the festival! they cried,
What robe wilt thou put on? And I replied:
The robe He gave me, Who hath poured for me
Full many a bitter potion. Poverty
And patience are my garments, and they cover
A heart that sees at every feast its Lover.
Can there be a finer garb to greet the Friend
Or visit Him, than that which He doth lend?
When Thou, my Expectation, art not near
Each moment is an age of grief and fear:
But while I may behold and hear Thee, all
My days are glad, and life's a festival.'

"I saw a certain poor man who bore the marks of hunger and I said to him: 'Why dost thou not ask of men that they may give thee to eat?' He replied: 'I fear to ask them lest they refuse me, and not prosper. I have heard that the Prophet said that if the beggar were sincere, he who refused him would not prosper.'"[26]

The deep reaches of mystical intention and the high ideals of spirituality, as evident in Sufi prayers, poems and experience, should not obscure the wealth of odd idiosyncrasies, the vagaries, and sometimes the sheer human compromises, even charlatanry, that belong equally with the Sufi story. Wherever there are saints in the pursuit of sanctity there are liable to be hypocrites in the indulgence of vanity or worse; there are practitioners of piety who, in the temptations of authority or of repute, succumb to lesser levels. The autobiography of Ṭāhā Ḥusain, cited in chapter 8, yields one obscure glimpse of these, in the recollections of his rural childhood in Upper Egypt.

> Shaikhs of the Sufis—what might they be? They were many in number and scattered throughout the regions of the land. . . . Their sects were different and they split up the people between them into schisms and divided their affections to a very great degree. There was acute rivalry in the province between two families of the Sufis.

Ṭāhā Ḥusain goes on to indicate how his own father and mother stood within this strife of leaders and, speaking of himself throughout in the third person as 'the lad,' he describes the annual visit of the Sufi 'chief.'

> When he came, he did not come alone or with a few people but with a mighty army, the number of which, if it did not reach a hundred, fell not far short of it. He did not take the train or any Nile boats, but instead he proceeded on his way, surrounded by his companions mounted on horses, mules and asses. As they passed through villages and small towns, they alighted and mounted in strength and magnificence, victorious in a place where they alone held sway, and united in a place where their opponents were all-powerful.
>
> Thus they came when they visited the lad's family and when they arrived the street was filled with them and their horses, mules and asses. . . . 'Ere long a lamb was killed and tables laid out in the street, and soon they fell upon their food with a gluttony that was almost unbelievable.
>
> Meanwhile the shaikh was sitting in the guest room surrounded by his chosen friends and devotees, and the owner of the house and his household were in front of him carrying out his behests. When they had finished their lunch they went away and left him to sleep where he was. Later he got up and wished to perform the ceremonial ablutions. Then see how the people vie with one another and quarrel as to who shall pour the water upon him. And when that is done, see how they race and quarrel to get a drink of the water of his ablutions! But the shaikh was too pre-occupied to heed them. He prayed and made supplications at great length.
>
> When at last he had finished all this he gave an audience to the people and they flocked to him, some kissing his hand and going meekly away, some holding conversation with him for a moment or so, and others asking him about some affair, and the shaikh would answer them with strange, vague expressions that they could interpret pretty much as they liked.
>
> The lad was brought to him and he touched his head, quoting a verse from the Qur'ān: "And He taught you what you knew not and the grace of God was mighty upon you." From that day the lad's father was convinced that his son was destined to become great.
>
> After the sunset prayer the tables were laid again and they ate. Then followed the evening prayer and then the assembly was held. The holding of the assembly is an expression for people assembled at a dervish circle for *dhikr.* This they perform sitting in silence. Then they began to move their heads and raise their voices a little. Then a shudder runs through their bodies and lo! they are all standing, having leapt up into the air, like jacks-in-boxes. The shaikhs move about the circle reciting the poems of Ibn al-Fāriḍ and similar poems.
>
> Now this shaikh was particularly fond of a well-known ode in which there is mention of the Prophet's Night Journey and Ascent. It begins as follows:
>
> "From Mecca and the most glorious House,

To Jerusalem travelled by night Aḥmad."

The shaikhs used to chant this continually and the performers of the *dhikr* used to move their bodies in tune with this chant, bending and straightening themselves as though these shaikhs were making them dance.

Whatever the lad forgets he will never forget that night on which one of the reciters made a mistake and interpolated a phrase in the ode. Forthwith the shaikh got excited and boiled and foamed and frothed, crying at the top of his voice: "You sons of bitches. May God curse your fathers and your fathers' fathers, and your fathers' fathers' fathers as far as Adam. Do you want to bring down destruction on this man's house?"

And whatever the lad forgets, he will never forget the effect of this outburst of wrath upon the hearts of the performers of the *dhikr* and the other people present. It was just as if the people were convinced that the mistake in the ode was a source of bad omen without parallel.

The lad's father at first showed agitation and consternation, but later appeared more confident and tranquil. When, on the morrow, after the shaikh had taken his departure, the family talked about him and what had taken place between him and the performers and reciters of the *dhikr*, the owner of the house laughed in a way that left no doubt in the lad's mind afterwards that the faith of his father in this shaikh was not free from doubt and contempt. . . .

When he took his departure he took with him anything that took his fancy and pleased him. At one time he would take a carpet, at another a Kashmiri shawl, and so on. The family . . . hated the visit for what it cost them in the way of money and trouble. In fact it was an ineluctable evil, established by custom and meeting the desire of the people. . . . The country people, including their old men, have a particular mentality in which is simplicity, mysticism and ignorance. And those who have had the greatest share in producing this mentality are the Sufis.[27]

SUFISM AND POETRY

There is no reckoning with Islamic mysticism that does not surrender to the fascination of the poets. For Sufism plays a major role in the genesis and the genius of many poets in the long and splendid tradition of Arabic, Persian, Urdu, and Turkish poetry. An Afghani writer in Peshawar in the seventeenth century characterized the poet as "a lover drawing the veil of allegory across the brow of his mistress, truth, placing jewels upon her fingers and adorning her with the sandalwood and saffron of metaphor."

Translation, of course, is a necessary condition, and a hobbling one, in the appreciation of Sufi verse. But it is clear that in several cases inspired poetry has generated inspired translation, a fact that may be itself a measure of the contagion of the spirit. Four representative poets will be included in this chapter of anthology.

The first is Ibn al-Fāriḍ (1182–1235) who was certainly the greatest among those who were Arab born. He lived and died in Cairo where his tomb in the Muqaṭṭam Hills is still a place of loving veneration. His father lectured in the Azhar and was a Sufi *faqīr*, or devotee, resigning his law office to become so. The son acquired his father's love of discipline and spiritual search, partly in the hills where his tomb now lies and partly, for a long period in a defile close to Mecca. His *Dīwān*, or house of verse, celebrated the tests and joys of mystic *fanā'*, or absorption into God. He also developed a familiar Sufi metaphor, that of intoxication, in a "Wine song," the *Khamriyyah,* about "the inebriate of God," dwelling in the "taverns" of the heart. He achieved a range and wealth of imagery quite unsurpassed in Arab writing. His composition, *The Great 'T'*, sang of mystical love, each stanza devised around the recurrence of the letter 't.'

There was also *The Poem of the Way* in which he imagined the spirit of Muḥammad speaking and conveying the meaning of the Quranic inspiration.

> From his [Gabriel's] light
> The lantern of my essence shone on me:
> My eve in me was radiant as my morn . . .
> And I was he: and I beheld
> That he was I, that light my radiance,
> In me the holy vale was sanctified . . .
> I founded firm my Sinai-s, and there
> Prayed to myself, and all my wants fulfilled:
> My essence was my interlocutor.
> By me are guided all the guiding stars
> Upon their courses: all the planets swim
> About my heavens as my will controls:
> All things I own: my angels prostrate fall
> Before my sovereignty.

Orthodoxy would find such absorption of the Prophet into the very soul of the divine universe quite alien and heretical. But it was instinctive to the Sufi loyalty to Muḥammad's significance as they received it. Ibn al-Fāriḍ wrote of divine wisdom in the feminine:

> In poverty I sought her yet was rich
> In having poverty my attribute.
> Wherefore I cast away impoverishment
> Alike and riches. When to jettison
> My poverty and wealth assured to me
> The merit of my quest, I thrust aside
> My merit also: and therein appeared
> Evident my good fortune: she who would
> Reward me [and naught else] became my prize . . .
> Through her I issued from myself to her
> Nor to myself came back . . .
> . . . my being was effaced
> In my beholding, and I was detached
> From my beholding's being. . . .
> I count every day my festival
> Whereon I contemplate with jocund eye
> The loveliness of her sweet countenance . . .
> I through her became oblivious of myself . . .

So occupied was I that I forgot
My first pre-occupation to forget myself . . .
Such is the soul. If it throw off desire
Its faculties are multiplied.[28]

But elsewhere, with masculine pronouns, he elaborates on the warning of Surah 7:143 to Moses: "Thou shalt not see Me," and finds, nevertheless, the mystic vision given.

. . . the vision blest
Was granted to my prayers . . .
The while amazed between
His beauty and His majesty
I stood in silent ecstacy
Revealing that which o'er my spirit came and went.
Lo! in His face commingled
Is every charm and grace:
The whole of beauty singled
Into a perfect face
Beholding Him would cry:
"There is no god but He and He is the most High."[29]

That sense of the divine splendor and its all-compelling wonder in the soul makes the poet aware of the whole crowded canvas of history and nature around him as unreal and transient. Yet, as a poet, he is loathe to forego all the rich visual scene and he describes it with eager enthusiasm as if his poetic eye was reluctant to concede to unreality the panorama of the world. This tension between visual beauty and mystical absorption has nowhere been so vividly conveyed. His lines celebrate the bird on wing and song, camels matching their color with the sands, ships on high seas, armies embattled, cavalry and infantry in the thrust and sway of conflict, fishermen and fowlers, leviathans of the deep and all the breeding, preying, world, and the mysteries of the jinns and spirits. Yet all is wrapped in what Ibn al-Fāriḍ calls "the veil of concealment" and when the curtain is lifted, there is confusion no longer. The soul beholds only God, whose deed is all.

The name of Jalāl al-Dīn Rūmī (1207–1273) is, for many, the supreme point of Islamic mystical story. His poetry, so long sustained, seems to have been the direct sequel to his Sufi experience, since he had written none before; but, thereafter, his muse never seemed to fail of fertility. The son of a Sufi, born at Balkh, he passed a checkered youth in a world of political turmoil and exile in search of security. His family migrated westwards, via Baghdad and Damascus, and finally settled at Konya in Turkey when he was twenty. His conversion to Sufism released his poetic genius around the age of forty. It sprang from his contact with an itinerant dervish named Shams al-Dīn Tabrīzī. An ardent love grew up between the two and when in 1247 Shams al-Dīn died by violent hands, Jalāl seems to have found him again in his own mystical vocation. He devoted fourteen years to the composition of his masterpiece the *Mathnawī*, a poem in six books from which a great many of the anecdotes about saints and Sufis are drawn in popular anthologies. It yields also, with his *Dīwān*, a great medley of aphorisms, parables, songs, and imagery where Muslim faith and culture are set, as it were, to one master's music. Here in the *Dīwān* is Rūmī's counsel to the seeker:

Grasp the skirt of his favor, for on a sudden he will flee:
But draw him not as an arrow
For he will flee from the bow.
What delusive forms does he take, what tricks invent!
If he is present in the form, he will flee by way of the spirit:
Seek him in the sky,
He shines in water like the moon.
When you come into the water, he will flee to the sky.
Seek him in the placeless, he will sign you to place:
When you seek him in place, he will flee to the placeless.
As the arrow speeds from the bow,
Like the bird of your imagination,
Know that the Absolute will certainly
Flee from the imaginary.

David said: "O Lord, since Thou hast no need of us,
Say, then, what wisdom was there in creating the two worlds?"
God said to him: "O temporal man, I was a hidden treasure,
I sought that that treasure of loving-kindness
And bounty should be revealed, I displayed a mirror—
Its face the heart, its back the world—
Its back is better than its face—if the face is unknown to thee.
. . . O spirit, make thy head in search and seeking
Like the water of a stream,
And, O reason, to gain eternal life
Tread everlastingly the way of death.
Keep God in remembrance till self is forgotten,
That you may be lost in the Called,
Without distraction of caller and call.

. . . Make my last better than my first.
When Thou art hidden I am of the infidels:
When Thou art manifest I am of the faithful.
I have nothing except Thou hast bestowed it:
What dost Thou seek from my bosom and sleeve?[30]

The lovers who dwell within the sanctuary are moths burnt with the torch of the Beloved's face.
How long wilt thou dwell with words and superficial things?
A burning heart is what God seeks.
Consort with burning.
Kindle in thy heart the flame of love . . .
This fault is better than a thousand correct forms:
No need to turn to the *Ka'bah* when one is in it.
Divers have no need of shoes.[31]

Few celebrations of death excel Rūmī's lines in the *Dīwān* of Shams al-Dīn:

When my bier moveth on the day of death,
Think not my heart is in this world.
Do not weep for me and cry: Woe! Woe!
Thou wilt fall in the devil's snare: that is woe.
When thou seest my hearse, cry not: Parted! Parted!
Union and meeting are mine in that hour.
If you commit me to the grave, say not: Farewell! Farewell!
For the grave is a curtain hiding the communion of Paradise.
After beholding descent, consider resurrection.
Why should setting be injurious to the sun and moon?
To thee it seems a setting, but 'tis a rising:
Though the vault seems a prison, 'tis the release of the soul.
What seed went down in the earth but it grew?
Why this doubt of thine as regards the seed of men?
What bucket was lowered but it came out brimful?
Why should the Joseph of the spirit complain of the well?
Shut thy mouth on this side and open it beyond,
For in placeless air will be thy triumph song.[32]

A similar sense of immortality breathes in the verse of Ḥāfiẓ, named Shams al-Dīn Muḥammad, of Shiraz, our third representative Sufi poet. We might call him, the Keats of Islam who cherished external nature, human grace, the wine of love, yet was alive to life's transient urgency and was impelled to capture all experience in song.

Ḥāfiẓ (13?–1390) was so named for his recitation of the *Qur'ān*, but he was also given the title of "tongue of the secrets and master of mysteries." Shiraz, in southern Persia, was beset throughout the time of his life by war, pillage, and political strife—it was the time of Tamarlane. In consequence, and through personal tribulations, Ḥāfiẓ's poetry is full of wistfulness and the sense of tragedy. Even his love lyrics have a pathos wrought into their texture, like the tears with which, according to legend, God had first kneaded the dust of the human clay. He lamented his dying son, like a player who can make no further move:

What shall I play? Upon the chequered floor
Of night and day, death won the game—forlorn
And careless now, Ḥāfiẓ can lose no more.

It is customary for a poet to weave his own name into the final stanza of each poem. In one, he wearied at the parting of friends, the blight of nature, the puzzles of time, and the dearth of love, and concluded:

Ḥāfiẓ, the secret of God's dread task
No man knoweth, in youth or prime
Or in wisest age: of whom would'st thou ask
What has befallen the wheels of time?

Ḥāfiẓ's fame, which attracted great throngs of students to his sessions on the *Qur'ān* in Shiraz, rests for posterity on the sheer beauty of his imagery and the charm of his refrains. He set to music the pains and joys of life's now smiling, now clouded, face. He infused the literal, or apparent, sense of his lines with mystical import, delicate enough to be fragile even to himself; yet the lines were fraught with deep suggestion for those prepared to read it there. The taverns, wines, and roses of his verses and the love feasts within the veils seem all too vivid, even carnal. Yet interpreters of Sufi ecstacy claim for them a subtlety that transmutes their sensuous feeling into religious wonder. Physical joy becomes a parable of spiritual delight. The poet himself remains a figure of ambiguity. Some at his death saw him as a dubious atheist, unworthy of Muslim burial; but for others he was the pure singer of the mystic quest, a *ḥāfiẓ*, not simply of the Quranic text but of the Quranic hiddenness. So there is a continuing question about what he meant by his innkeepers, and garments laid aside in penitence. Does the *saqī*, or cupbearer, unloose ribald tongues, or silence the contemplative? Are the breezes in the gardens of delight the ardors of caressing lovers, or whispers of the unitive mystery? The questions allow no categorical answer and so preserve their fascination.

> Brave tales of singers and wine relate
> The key to the hidden 'twere vain to seek:
> No wisdom of ours has unlocked that gate.
> And locked to our wisdom it still shall be.
> But of Yūsuf's beauty the lute shall speak
> And the minstrel knows that Zulaikha came forth,
> Love parting the curtains of modesty.

These were the famed lovers of Egypt.

So the poet rests in his Shirazi garden, his tomb adorned in tiles and script with verses from his own pen. It would seem that he anticipated his own enigmatic fame, as the best of poets and the most elusive of mystics.

> But to you, O Ḥāfiẓ, to you O tongue
> That speak through the mouth of the tender reed,
> What thanks to you when your verses speed
> From lip to lip the song you have sung?
> Wind of the dawn that passes by
> Swift to the strut of my fairie hie,
> Whisper the tale of Ḥāfiẓ, true,
> Fresh and fresh and new and new.[33]

The Sufi spirit has often showed a wistful openness to the diversity of religious faiths, dissociated as it is in large measure, from the definitions and interests of dogma and the dogmatists. Ḥāfiẓ's words are justly celebrated:

> Love is where the glory falls
> Of Thy face on convent walls,
> Or on tavern floors, the same
> Inextinguishable flame.

Ibn al-Fāriḍ warns the orthodox Muslim:

If the mosque's *miḥrāb* (prayer niche) be lighted
By the Qur'ān, no church's massive pile
Is wasted with the Gospel open there,
Nor synagogue, wherein the Torah's scrolls
Moses delivered to the chosen folk
Are nightly read by rabbis at their prayers.
But if, in idol house, the devotee
Bows down to stones, rush not in zealous rage
Beyond the disavowal faith requires.
Many a one, unspotted by the shame
Of polytheist idol mongering,
In spirit worships Mammon.

The true mosque in a pure and holy heart
Is builded. There let all men worship God.
For there He dwells, not in a mosque of stone.[34]

Jalāl al-Dīn Rūmī also castigates the implicit 'sectarianism' of all religion, when seen from the angle of mystical knowledge.

When the prophets raise their cry to the outward ear,
The souls of each sect bow in adoration within.
But never, in this world, has the soul's ear
Heard from any man the like of that cry
Where the poor man in the strange, sweet voice,
Recognizes the voice of God: "Verily I am nigh."

Here is the contrast between the formalist and the devotee:

He observes obedience and fasting and prayer
And devotions and almsgiving and so on,
Yet never feels the least expansion of soul.
He performs the devotions and acts enjoined by the law,
Yet derives not an atom of relish from them.

But the mystic?

At times my state resembles a dream:
My dreaming seems to them infidelity.
Though my eyes sleep, my heart is awake:
My body, though torpid, is instinct with energy.
The Prophet said: "Mine eyes sleep
But my heart is awake with the Lord of mankind.
Your eyes are awake and your heart fast asleep;
My eyes are asleep and my heart at the open door.
My heart has other five senses of its own . . .
What seems night to you is broad day to me,
What seems a prison to you is a garden to me,
Busiest occupation is rest to me . . .
'Tis not I who companion with you, 'tis my shadow:

My exaltation transcends your thoughts
Because I have transcended thought."

Thou hast run after 'form' O ill-informed one:
Wherefore thou lackest the fruit of the tree of substance . . .
'Tis one, though it has a thousand manifestations.
He has thousands of names, yet He is One.
Answering to all description, yet He is indescribable.
Everyone who seeks names, if he is a man of credulity
Like thee, remains hopeless and frustrated of his aim . . .
Pass beyond names and look to qualities,
So that qualities may lead thee to essence.
Differences of sects arise from His Names:
When they pierce to His essence, they find His peace.[35]

CHAPTER 8

Contemporary Issues

An anthology of contemporary issues requires library shelves rather than book pages. Here we concern ourselves with selective matters, taking the end of the Islamic Caliphate in 1924 (see *House of Islam,* p. 110) as a symbolic point of departure. Nationalism and Islamic unity, secularism and the problem of religious authority, and factors of economic and social change are the salient features of the middle decades of this century. One vigorous area of debate has to do with the liberation of women.

NATIONALISM WITHIN ISLAM

The deep significance of the demise of the Caliphate may be measured in the enthusiasm with which the Turkish writer, Ziya Gökalp (1875–1924), greeted the designation of 'Abd al-Majīd as Caliph late in 1922, a bare eighteen months prior to the liquidation of the whole caliphal office by the new Atatürk policy of secular statehood. (See *House of Islam,* p. 120.) Ironically the very nationalism that Gökalp favored brought to a decisive end the symbol of Islamic 'internationality' that he preached. What he refers to here as 'election' was in fact the first mention of the name of the new Caliph in the mosque Friday prayers.

> The Islamic *Ummah* has taken the one-ness of this highest *imām* or Caliph as the expression of its existence, unity and solidarity. How could it be permissible to defame such an office, the symbol of the unity of the Islamic *Ummah?* . . .
>
> The ceremony of the election of the Caliph in all mosques of Islam last Friday was a day of great rejoicing which spiritually united all Muslims of the world. That day all Muslims, who had gained a supreme *imām* as the head of

> the *Ummah* exclusively, realized their solidarity in a sense more intense than in the past. . . . Now that the Caliph will no longer be subject to the politics of any nation, he will enjoy free communication with the *muftis* of all lands: he will issue decrees to all *imāms* and *khaṭībs*: in short, he will exercise his right of religious authority over all religious institutions. No Muslim or non-Muslim state will prevent the fulfillment of this religious function.[1]

In point of fact, this merely 'international' Caliphate, shorn of a base of political power, had no future. "The fulfillment of this religious function" was, in fact, prevented by a 'Muslim' ruler.

Comparable evidence of the centrality of the Caliphate to Muslim emotions and Islamic order up to 1924 comes forcibly from the Indian subcontinent, where the Muslims clearly saw in this over-all Islamic symbol a cherished safeguard of their own communal position vis-à-vis the Hindu majority.

Ziya Gökalp was a notable thinker whose threefold formula, Turkism, Islam, and Modernism, lay behind many of the changes by which Turkey, under the famous Muṣṭafā Kamāl Atatürk (1881–1938), achieved its vigorous program of secularism in the second quarter of this century. Gökalp argued that the absolute, abiding authority of a religious *Sharī'ah* could be sustained without precluding free and radical change in response to the flux of times. He did this by insisting on a careful distinction between revelatory law and the *'urf*, or traditional customary patterns of society which came so largely into Islam during and after its wide expansion. He claimed that this double source of Islamic jurisprudence justified the fullest expression of his central principle of Turkism, or nationalism of the Turks, without colliding sharply, as Atatürk's reforms were to do, with the sacrosanct areas of Islam. These could be at once honored and where necessary, relegated.

After explaining that Islamic jurisprudence has two sources, he continues:

> The first is the *nass* and the second is *'urf*. The *nass* is expressed in the Book and in the *Sunnah*, while the *'urf* is the conscience of the society expressed in the actual conduct and living of the community. Actions with respect to goodness or badness are judged obligatory [*wājib*] or forbidden [*ḥaram*] in terms of the *nass*, and as customary, equitable [*ma'rūf*] or rejected [*munkar*] in terms of the *'urf*. The actions that are neither obligatory nor forbidden, and neither customary nor rejected, are accepted as permissible [*mubāḥ*].
>
> Yet, the function of *'urf* does not consist only in distinguishing between actions that are socially acceptable and those that are socially rejected. The tradition ["What the faithful regard as good is good with God"] and the maxim of the *Fiqh* ["Action according to *'urf* is like acting on the *nass*"] imply that, under necessity, *'urf* may take the place of *nass*.
>
> Muslims have to obey the commands and prohibitions expressed in the *nass* as they have to command that which is customary [*ma'rūf*] and forbid that which is rejected [*munkar*]. But the latter is nothing more than those actions which are cherished or rejected by the social consciousness.
>
> Therefore, on the one hand, *fiqh* is based on revelation, and on the other, on society. In other words, Islamic *Sharī'ah* is both divine and social. The

transmitted principles of *fiqh* are absolute and unchangeable. The Holy *Qur'ān* is preserved and the *Sunnah* is recorded as far as possible. The divine part of the *Sharī'ah,* being a divine act, is in a state of absolute perfection: hence it is exempt from any evolution or progress. The fundamentals of the faith cannot be subject to the law of evolution like social institutions. Religion is religious when it is believed in as free from any defect. A religion ceases to be religion when its ultimate principles are believed not to be absolute and unchangeable.

The social principles of *fiqh,* on the other hand, are subject to the transformations taking place in the forms and structures of society, and hence are subject to changes along with society. Every *'urf* is invariably the *'urf* of a certain social type. A norm which is customary in a certain social type may be a norm rejected in another social type. . . .

The social *sharī'ah* is in a continuous process of 'becoming' like all social phenomena. It follows, then, that that part of *fiqh* is not only liable to evolution in accordance with social evolution, but also *has* to change. The fundamentals of *fiqh* related to *nass* are eternally constant and unchangeable, whereas the social applications of these fundamentals which are based on the *'urf* of the public and on the *ijmā'* [consensus] of the scholars of *fiqh* have to adapt themselves in accordance with the necessities of life.[2]

In developing his view of religion and society, Gökalp distinguished carefully between "culture" and "civilization." The former was where religion belonged, in close harmony with the concept of the nation; whereas the latter meant, for contemporary man, the western techniques and sciences that Islam was free, indeed impelled, to imitate and acquire.

As an old Turkish saying runs: "Know your work, your food, and your mate," so modern sociology would tell us: "Know your nation, your religion, and your civilization."

The conversion of the Turks to Islam and their entrance into the area of eastern civilization took place simultaneously. For this reason many would call the eastern civilization Islamic civilization. [However] , peoples belonging to different religions may belong to the same civilization. In other words, civilization and religion are two different things. Otherwise, there could not be any institution common to the groups who belonged to different religions. Since religion consists only of sacred institutions, beliefs, and rituals, non-sacred institutions such as scientific ideas, technological tools, aesthetic standards, constitute a separate system outside of religion. Positive sciences such as mathematics, physics, biology, psychology and sociology, industrial methods, and fine arts, are not concerned with religions. Thus, no civilization can ever be called after a religion. There is neither a Christian civilization nor an Islamic civilization. Just as it is incorrect to call western civilization a Christian civilization, so it is equally incorrect to call eastern civilization an Islamic civilization. . . .

There is only one road to salvation: to advance in order to reach—that is, in order to be equal to—Europeans in the sciences and industry as well as in military and judicial institutions. And there is only one means to achieve this—to adapt ourselves to western civilization completely.

This effective distinction between a religio-culture and a civilization open to diverse religions is paralleled in Gökalp's view of Turkism as nationality and Islam as 'internationality.' He writes:

> When the Turks, as an ethnic people, joined Islamic civilization, the Turkish language assumed an Islamic character with the introduction of the Arabic script and terms.
>
> Thus, the factor that creates the spirit of internationality, and hence civilization, is the book. Consequently, there is no incompatibility between Turkish nationalism and Islam, since one is nationality and the other is internationality.

If there is an inconsistency here in his own description of a 'civilization' as 'Islamic,' it seems clear that his general point is that Turkish Muslims are within a larger collective of 'international' religion, which is in no way inconsistent with their participation, as nation, in a technological order of things, which, he claims, is independent of any religion and properly open to any nation.

> Those peoples are 'contemporary' who make and use all those machines made and used by the peoples most advanced in the techniques of the age. For us today being contemporary with modern civilization means to make and use the battleships, cars and aeroplanes that the Europeans are making and using. But this does not mean being like them only, in form and living.
>
> As there is no contradiction between the ideals of Turkism and Islam, there is none between these and the ideal of modernism. The idea of modernity necessitates only the acceptance of the theoretical and practical sciences and techniques from Europe. There are certain moral needs which will be sought in religion and nationality, as there were in Europe, but these cannot be imported from the west as if they were machines and techniques.
>
> The Turkish nation today belongs to the Ural-Altai group of peoples, to the Islamic *Ummah,* and to western nationality. We should accept the three ideals at the same time by determining the respective fields of operation of each. To put it in a better way, we have to create 'an up-to-date Turkism,' realizing that each of the three ideals is an aspect of the same need taken from a different angle.[3]

The vital factor in the advocacy of Pakistan (see *House of Islam,* p. 111ff.) prior to partition was the rejection of the *community* concept as an account of Muslims in India (where they were a numerical minority), and the intransigent insistence on the *nation* concept. Two nations in one territory cannot subsist, though two communities can. Ishtiāq Ḥusain Qurashī, scholar, educator, and one-time Minister of Education in the new Pakistan, set out the Islamic necessity of the nationhood-statehood concept in very clear terms. After a historical review in which he celebrated the Mughal (Muslim) efforts to create an Indian unity within Islamic auspices, he attributed the necessity of Islamic separatism to a Hindi revivalism that repudiated the Islamic form of unity and thereby threatened Islamic existence. He conjectured (1953) that: "In a hundred years, perhaps in a shorter time, the Muslim people may cease to exist in that country" (that is, in India—a prediction representing a view that has done much to complicate and vex the problems of the

Muslim community in partitioned India and which, meanwhile, shows no sign of being vindicated). His account of the case for separate Islamic statehood highlights the instinctive conviction that Islam cannot be itself as a religion unless it is also politically expressed. The State is indispensable to a viable, not to say a true, Islam.

> The Hindu looked upon the pre-Muslim past as his golden age. The Muslim replied by idealizing the achievements of his ancestors in India. The tale of Muslim conquest, looked upon by Hindus as a story of national humiliation, was to the Muslim the record of the glory of his forefathers. All this brought about an estrangement in the relations of the Muslims with the Hindus which made the Muslims conscious of being a separate entity. . . . As Muslim opinion became more articulate it tended to emphasize this truth. Westernization did not check this process, because it did not affect the springs of group consciousness either of the Hindus or of the Muslims. It only accentuated the feeling by its emphasis on grouping humanity into nationalities. The Hindus found in their doctrine of Indian nationalism an opportunity to consolidate their position, because they hoped to hold all the resources of the State with the help of their numbers, economic strength and superior education. The Muslims discovered they were a nation by themselves. Hindu revivalism left them in possession of all the distinctive characteristics of a separate nation.
>
> To the student of sociology, this is a significant phenomenon because it was inevitable. . . . The Muslims in India started with demands for separate representation and safeguards, but they soon discovered the futility of such methods and ultimately developed the conviction that nothing short of independence could guarantee their existence as a distinct entity. Fortunately there were well-defined geographical areas where they formed the majority. They demanded that these areas should form a separate country and their determination has won them this cherished goal which today stands fulfilled in Pakistan. . . .
>
> The majority of the Indian Muslims were not in a mood to accept absorption. They wanted to live.[4]

That will to live, it was held, was inexpressible except in terms of separate statehood, as distinguished from the will to all-India unity. Yet such a will was present in many sincere Hindus and was shared by numerous Muslims, millions of whom (on the wrong side of the geographical divide when partition happened) were being required to live and survive under just those circumstances of Hindu majority presence which the Pakistan advocates said were lethal to a true Islam. It is thus that there is no clearer, sharper focus of contrasted self-definition within Islam than the two sides of Muslim population in the subcontinent—those with and those without, the supposed *sine qua non* of the Islamic state.

Muḥammad Iqbāl's case for Islamic nationalism (see *House of Islam* p. 112) was formulated in 1930 in a presidential address to the All-India Muslim League at Allahabad.

> I lead no party: I follow no leader. I have given the best part of my life to a careful study of Islam as it unfolds itself in time, its law and polity, its culture, its history and its literature. This constant contact with the spirit of Islam has,

I think, given me a kind of insight into its significance as a world-fact. It is in the light of this insight, whatever its value, that, while assuming that the Muslims of India are determined to remain true to the spirit of Islam, I propose, not to guide you in your decisions, but to attempt the humbler task of bringing clearly to your consciousness the main principle which, in my opinion, should determine the general character of these decisions. . . .

I do not know what will be the final fate of the national idea in the world of Islam. Whether Islam will assimilate and transform it, as it has assimilated and transformed many ideas before that were expressive of a different spirit, or allow a radical transformation of its own structure by the force of this idea is hard to predict. . . . At the present moment the national idea is racializing the outlook of Muslims and thus materially counteracting the humanizing work of Islam. And the growth of racial consciousness may mean the growth of standards different and even opposed to the standards of Islam.

Iqbāl is clearly aware that nationalism is alien to the ideal of Islamic unity. Since it cannot be other than territorially expressed—and Iqbāl himself in the same speech was to make precisely that territorial demand for separate statehood—nationalism cannot escape "racializing" except by retreating into optimistic verbiage about an imaginary exemption from all the pressures of human politics. Iqbāl continued, in his presidential address:

Is religion a private affair? Is it possible to retain Islam as an ethical ideal and to reject it as a polity? . . . The nature of the Prophet's religious experience, as disclosed in the Qur'ān . . . is creative of a social order. Its immediate outcome is the fundamentals of a polity with implicit legal concepts whose civic significance cannot be belittled because their origin is revelational. The religious ideal of Islam, therefore, is organically related to the social order which it has created. The rejection of the one will inevitably involve the rejection of the other. Therefore, the construction of a polity on national (that is, all-India lines), if it means a displacement of the Islamic principle of solidarity, is simply unthinkable to a Muslim. . . . The Muslim demand for the creation of a Muslim India within India is, therefore, perfectly justified. . . . Personally I would go further . . . I would like to see the Punjab, North-West Frontier Province, Sind, and Baluchistan, amalgamated into a single state. . . . The formation of a consolidated North-West Indian Muslim State appears to me to be the final destiny of the Muslims at least of North-West India. . . .

The truth is that Islam is not a church. It is a state conceived as a contractual organism . . . and animated by an ethical ideal which regards man not as an earth-rooted creature, defined by this or that portion of the earth, but as a spiritual being understood in terms of a social mechanism, and possessing rights and duties as a living factor in that mechanism. . . .

The Muslims of India are the only Indian people who can fitly be described as a nation in the modern sense of the word. . . . Seventy millions [that is, Muslims] in a single country constitute a far more valuable asset to Islam than all the countries of Muslim Asia put together. . . . One lesson I have learned from the history of Muslims. At critical moments in their history it is Islam that has saved Muslims and not vice versa. . . . I do not wish to mystify anybody when I say that things in India are not what they appear to be. The meaning of this, however, will dawn upon you only when you have achieved a real collective ego to look at them. In the words of the Qur'ān: "Hold fast to yourself: No one who erreth can hurt you, provided you are well guided." [Surah 5:105] [5]

By that advocacy, Iqbāl had set in motion a trend of thought that, sixteen years later, concluded in the creation of Pakistan with the East Bengal segment joined to his contemplated State of North-West India. His thinking had not only sketched an ultimate decision; it had also implicitly set out the ambivalence in a politico-religious identity requiring, and at the same time claiming to disavow, anything territorial. There was the same problem in Iqbāl's famous Lectures, in the same year, on *The Reconstruction of Religious Thought in Islam.* The national principle here emerged as a necessary condition for the ousting of imperialism, which could be transcended once that goal had been achieved.

> An international ideal . . . forming the very essence of Islam has been hitherto overshadowed or rather displaced by Arabian Imperialism of the earlier centuries of Islam. . . . [However] For the present every Muslim nation must sink into her own deeper self, temporarily focus her vision on herself alone, until all are strong and powerful enough to form a living family of republics . . . It seems to me that God is slowly bringing home to us the truth that Islam is neither Nationalism nor Imperialism but a League of Nations which recognize artificial boundaries and racial distinctions for facility of reference only and not for restricting the social horizon of its members. . . . The race idea which appears to be working in modern Islam with greater force than ever may ultimately wipe off the broad human outlook which Muslim people have imbibed from their religion.
>
> . . . The modern Muslim in Turkey, Egypt and Persia is led to seek fresh sources of energy in the creation of new loyalties, such as patriotism and nationalism. . . . The modern Muslim fondly hopes to unlock fresh sources of energy by narrowing down his thought and emotion. . . . Both nationalism and atheistic socialism, at least in the present state of human adjustments, must draw upon the psychological forces of hate, suspicion and resentment which tend to impoverish the soul of man and close up his hidden sources of spiritual energy.[6]

Abū-l-Kalām Āzād (1888–1958) sharply rejected the claim of the pro-partition elements in Indian Islam that the Muslim population (at least in its majority areas) was a *nation,* rather than simply a community capable of authentic existence and fulfillment *within* an all-India unity. His thinking was deeply grounded in Quranic study and represented a notable Muslim effort to participate in a single India. He is, therefore, the most significant witness against the absolute necessity of Islamic statehood to a true Islam which was the adamant conviction of Muḥammad 'Ali Jinnah and the Muslim League in the years before the end of the British Raj.

Maulānā Āzād distinguished between *Dīn* and *Sharī'ah,* between Islam as a vision and Islam as a code. Alam Khundmiri offers this interpretation of Āzād's "religious philosophy."

> According to Āzād it is the basic teaching of the Qur'ān that Islam or the Faith, *Dīn al-Islām,* is the name of that fundamental spirit of every historical

religion. . . . In his Commentary on the Qur'ān he develops the idea that the real intention of religion is to assert the oneness of God and the unity of mankind. In his own words: "This unity of man is the primary end of religion. The message which every prophet delivered was that mankind were in reality one people and one community, and that there was but one God for all of them, and on that account they should serve Him together and live as members of one family. Such was the message which every religion delivered. But curiously the followers of each religion disregarded the message, so much so that every country, every community and every race resolved itself into a separate entity and raised groupism to the position of religion. *Dīn* or real religion is devotion to God and righteous living." . . . Just as the followers of other religions have lost their way, so have the Muslims lost the vision or Faith or the spirit of Islam. (There is a) distinction between Islam as the underlying spirit of all historical religions and Islam as a historical religion itself.

There are, according to Khundmiri's presentation of Āzād, sociological factors operating to bring about the distinction between essential truth and communal expression. Muḥammad's prophethood, truly seen, is an essential and final reaffirmation of the primary vision. But in line with other possessive and appropriating communities, the Islamic community through the centuries has formalized and institutionalized that vision by failing to keep in view the distinction between *Dīn* and *Sharī'ah.*

The followers of the different religions tend to forget the real message of the revealed religion and the law of the practical way is over-emphasized. The emphasis is shifted from the end to the means. . . . Is Islam basically a law or a vision? Āzād's answer is clear. Islam is a vision and its laws are the manifestations of this vision. . . . This . . . should not mislead one to believe that Āzād considered that the laws of Islam, as they are revealed in the Book, are obsolete or need any revision by the modern world. He is simply maintaining the priority of vision over law, and nothing more. This vision is not an exclusive property of any religious group. . . . The real aim of religion is the spiritual transformation of man and law is a guide or a means for such a spiritual transformation. The greatness of Islam does not consist in the special legal structure but in its acceptance of the fundamental truth that God is one and mankind is one community.

There are times when the neutral observer has to wonder whether, in these terms, Āzād is not seeking to have both sides of the case.

Law can never become an end in itself and love, to become authentic, must have a form. *Sharī'ah* provides such a form to love. It is to make devotion to God meaningful that adherence to law is necessary, but the true ends of religion are not to be sought in law alone. Āzād presents the true ends of religion without undermining the importance of the outward aspects. The modernists disregard the legal aspect of Islam or *Sharī'ah.* Āzād in this sense is not a modernist, he is a true orthodox. No verse of the Qur'ān supersedes the other, according to him and no verse of the Qur'ān is obsolete. What is needed most is to change the religious perspective and shift one's gaze to the essential and make religion a unifying force rather than make it an instrument of dividing humanity.[7]

This still leaves us with a query about the proper relation of the vision to the code and how an unmodified allegiance to the latter tallies with a true response to the priority of the former. But the questions thus left unsatisfied were at least in the cause of a steady venture after harmony with Hinduism; all Āzād's thinking must be seen in the light of that intent. Pakistan advocates saw it as an intent they thought incompatible with the loyalties Islam required of Muslims.

After outlining what he calls the rationalist reformist movement (Muḥammad 'Abduh), the romantic apologist (Aḥmad Khān and others) and the nationalist secularist (as in Turkey), Dr. S. Abid Husain offers this current Indian view:

> In every country there are people who are not fully satisfied with any of these three modernist philosophies and want to strike a new line. Leaving aside some amateur scholars who pursue the subject of religious reform as a hobby, or at best an intellectual exercise, and whose study of Islam is confined to the perusal of the writings of western Islamicists, there are in this category many serious minded and knowledgeable practising Muslims to whom a reinterpretation of the teachings of Islam from a liberal point of view is of vital importance. They have carefully studied the three movements of modernist reforms which we have briefly discussed and found that each of them had a useful role to play in helping Muslims in a particular region to grapple with the most serious problems which they faced at a particular time. The rationalist reformist movement of Muḥammad 'Abduh in the second half of the 19th century enabled Muslims in Egypt and the countries of the fertile crescent to bring about a working understanding between the highly conservative *'Ulamā'* and the ultra modernist westernized group of people, to meet the threat of their cultural and political domination by western powers. The romantic apologist movement led by Sayyid Aḥmad Khan in its first phase helped Indian Muslims to recover from the state of utter dejection and frustration into which they had fallen after the holocaust of 1857 and, in its second phase, made them, under the inspiration of the poet Iqbāl, conscious, perhaps over conscious, of their cultural identity and their great destiny. The nationalist secularist movement sponsored by Muṣṭafā Kemāl cured Turkey of the malignant growth of its Empire, relieved it of the encumbrance of its nominal religious leadership and turned it into a healthy, united, strong nation. But they feel that none of these three movements is calculated to meet even the total need of the region within its own sphere of influence, much less the general need of the whole world of Islam, to understand the true spirit of Islamic teachings and to apply them to the problems facing them in the latter half of the twentieth century.
>
> Their views have not yet found a clear and precise expression but there are vague indications of what they think and feel. Their idea of a modernist reform in Islam seems to be that first of all an objective study, without any preconceived notions, should be made of the fundamental spiritual and moral principles of Islam and their application to the social and cultural life of its followers through the ages, in accordance with the changing needs of time and place. They would like the study to be carried on, not by the apologetic method, but through the scientific historical method, first outlined by the medieval Muslim historian Ibn Khaldūn and later developed by modern western thinkers. The next step they would like to be taken is a critical but unprejudiced examination of the theoretical basis and the practical institu-

tions of modern western civilization, in order to distinguish what is of positive, permanent and universal value, from what is negative or destructive or of merely local and ephemeral significance. Only after this comparative study has been completed could it be possible, they feel, to reinterpret the legal, social and cultural doctrines of Islam so as to relate them to the problems of the present age.

After reviewing something of the thinking of Maulānā Āzād, whom he regards as a pioneer of this pattern of response to modernity, Dr. S. Abid Husain concludes:

This trend [neo-reformist] has not yet acquired the character of an organised movement. Still it is a fairly widespread trend which can be perceived, in slightly different forms, in many Muslim countries and is likely to grow into a powerful movement as soon as it finds the individual or collective leadership to give it definite shape and direction.[8]

SECULARITY, AUTHORITY, AND CHANGE

The geographical source of the influences that has brought soul-searching and intellectual challenge to modern Islam is, of course, western. This means that the general spiritual and mental issues are emotionally complicated by political factors. If not a love-hate relationship, certainly an imitate-repudiate relationship characterizes Muslim reactions to western presence, western power, and western intellectual impact. The confrontation was further accentuated by the fact that Muslims who knew their own past felt that they were now made to feel inferior by a culture and an ethos, in Europe, which really owed its achievements to Islamic sciences and legacies in earlier centuries. The pupil, as it were, had outdone the tutor. This meant yet another psychological concern, namely to diagnose and understand why this worsting had happened and what Islam needed to recover its lost leadership—if recover it could, given the long start the west enjoyed in techniques and resources.

Shaikh Muḥammad 'Abduh gave his perceptive mind to these problems in the concluding pages of his *Risālat al-Tauḥīd* and gave currency to a parable that has since been often in mind in Muslim writing. He was trying to find a way beyond imitation-repudiation mentalities into a right self-assurance.

Islam's full light is in the east. Yet precisely there its own people lie in the deepest gloom and cannot see. Does this seem intelligible? Is there any parallel in the annals of men? Does it not appear that the very Muslims who have known something of science are precisely those who, for the most part, instinctively regard Islam's doctrines as superstitious and its principles and precepts as a farce? They find pleasure in aping the free-thinking people who scoff and jeer and think themselves forward-looking. Do you not see Muslims whose only business with the Scriptures is to finger their pages, while they preen themselves on being expert in their laws? How far they are from the rational study of the Qur'ān which they despise and regard as worthless to religion and the world! Many of them simply pride themselves on ignorance, as if thereby they had evaded prohibited things and achieved some distinction. Those Muslims who stand on the threshold of science see their faith as a kind of old garment in which it is embarrassing to appear among men, while those who deceive themselves that they have some pretension to be religious and orthodox believers in its doctrines regard reason as a devil and science as supposition. Can we not, in the light of all this, call God, His angels and all men to witness that science and reason have no accord with this religion?

It may well be that the foregoing has not exaggerated the plight of Muslims today, indeed these several generations past. But is the objection the whole story? Parallels could be found in the descriptions of Islam in their day, given by Al-Ghazālī, Ibn al-Ḥajj and other writers on religion, filling whole volumes, both about the general population and the intelligentsia.

But the reading of the Qur'ān suffices of itself to vindicate what I have said about the essential nature of Islamic religion, provided it is read with care to understand its real import, interpreted according to the understanding of those among whom it was sent down and to the way they put it into practice. To admit the validity of what I have said about its fine effects, it suffices to read the pages of history as indited by those who truly know Islam and the objective writers in other nations. Such Islam was—and is. We have earlier said that religion is guidance and reason. Whoever uses it well and takes its directions will gain the blessedness God has promised to those who follow it.

As a medicine for human society its success when truly tried is so manifest that not even the blind and the deaf can deny or gainsay it. All that the objection just elaborated leads to is this: a physician treated a sick man with medicine and he recovered. Then the doctor himself succumbed to the disease he had been treating. In dire straits from pain and with the medicine beside him, he has yet no will to use it. Many of those who come to visit him or seek his ministrations or even gloat over his illness, could take up the medicine and be cured, while he himself despairs of life and waits either for death or for some miraculous healing.

We have now set forth the religion of Islam and its true character. As for those Muslims who by their conduct have been an argument against it, these must be dealt with not here but in another book, if God wills.

The several items, as he saw them, in such an indictment of Muslim unworthiness, Shaikh Muḥammad 'Abduh had already listed in a series of questions to which his parable of the physician not healing himself was no more than a summary answer. Here are the 'If's' as he saw them on the threshold of the twentieth century.

It is said by some that if Islam truly came to call diverse peoples into one common unity and if the Qur'ān says: "You have nothing to do with those who divide over religion and make parties," [Surah 6:159] how does it come about that the Islamic people has been sundered into sectarian movements and broken up into groups and schools?

If Islam is a faith that unifies, why this numerous diversity among Muslims? If Islam turns the believer in trust towards Him who created the heavens and the earth, why do multitudes of Muslims turn their faces to powerless things that can neither avail nor harm, and apart from God are helpless either way, even to the point of thinking such practice part of *Tauḥīd* itself?

If it was the first religion to address the rational mind, summoning it to look into the whole material universe, giving it free rein to range at will through all its secrets, saving only therein the maintenance of the faith, how is it that Muslims are content with so little and many indeed have closed and barred the door of knowledge altogether, supposing thereby that God is pleased with ignorance and a neglect of study of His marvellous handiwork?

How does it happen that the very apostles of love have become in these days a people who nose around for it in vain? They who were once exemplary in energy and action are now the very picture of sloth and idleness.

What are all these accretions to their religion, when all the time Muslims have the very Book of God as a balance in which to weigh and discriminate all their conjectures and yet its very injunctions they abandon and forsake?

If Islam really is so solicitous for the minds and hearts of men, why today in the opinion of so many is it somehow beyond the reach of those who would grasp it?

If Islam welcomes and invites enquiry into its contents, why is the Qur'ān not read except by chanting and even the majority of the educated men of religion only know it very approximately?

If Islam granted to reason and will the honor of independence, how is it that it has bound them with such chains? If it has established the principles of justice, why are the greater part of its rulers such models of tyranny? If religion eagerly anticipates the freeing of slaves, why have Muslims spent centuries enslaving the free?

If Islam regards loyalty to covenants, honesty and fulfillment of pledges as being its very pillars, how does it come about that deception, falsehood, perfidy and calumny are so current among Muslims?

If Islam forbids fraud and treachery and warns imposters that they have neither part nor lot in it, how is it that Muslims practice deception against God, the sacred law, and the true and loyal believers? If it prohibits all abomination, whether evident or hidden, what is it we see among them both secret and open, both physical and spiritual?

If Islam teaches that religion consists in sincerity before God, His Apostle and fellow believers in both immediate and general relationships, if "man is the loser save those who believe, do good works, and enjoin upon each other justice and patience," [Surah 103:1-3] and yet, not enjoining kindliness or forbidding evil, they go altogether to the bad and their honest folk call and get no response, and if this which they quite fail to fulfill is in fact their most bounden duty, why is it that they thus so totally fail to counsel each other and lay upon each other squarely what the divine will requires? Why do they not hold to it with fortitude and speak truth about right and wrong?

Why do they in fact take each their own way, letting things go as they will in rabid individualism, ignoring each others' affairs as if they were totally unrelated the one to the other, having nothing in common? Where are the bowels of mercy, of compassion for a neighbor? Where is the just dealing the rich owe to the poor with their possessions?[9]

In the second volume of his autobiography, *A Student at the Azhar,* Ṭāhā Ḥusain, the celebrated Cairo scholar, makes painful reference to the antagonism Shaikh Muḥammad 'Abduh suffered and to the way fickle approbation lapsed after his death.

While I was studying with more or less profit as a probationer, the Imām retired from the Azhar as the result of a celebrated incident, after the Khedive had delivered his famous speech before some of the learned shaikhs.

I imagined that the Imām's pupils, of whom a large number crowded every evening into the Porch of Al-'Abbās, would start a movement which would make it clear to the Khedive that the youth of the Azhar were affronted and intended to devote not only their time but also their hearts to the defense of their Rector.

Nothing of the kind. The Imām left the Azhar and took a house for his work as Mufti. His students secretely sympathised with him but kept their thoughts to themselves. A few of them visited him at his house in 'Ain al-Shams, but the majority deserted him: and that was the conclusion of the whole affair. As for me, my heart was full of shame and anger for shaikhs and students alike, though I had never known the Imām or been introduced to him.

A little later the Imām died and his death caused a great stir throughout Egypt. But Azharite circles were less affected than any by this tragic event. The Imām's pupils were sorry and perhaps some of them shed a few tears but after the summer vacation they returned to their studies as if the Imām had not died, or indeed had never lived, except that now and again his own special pupils spoke of him regretfully. . . .

But I noticed something else which increased my aversion for the Azhar and my contempt for both the shaikhs and students. I found that the men who mourned sincerely for the Imām did not wear turbans, but tarboushes. I conceived a secret inclination towards them and a desire to make some acquaintance with their society. But how was such a thing possible for a blind boy condemned without escape to the Azhar and its circle? I memorized one of the lines of Shaikh Bakhīt . . .

"The turban on his head was like a net
Stretched on a camel's load of straw."[10]

Turban or tarboush? a ready way of focusing the question whether the interpretation of Islam and its application to changing situations in society and history, can rightly, or safely, be left to religious authorities, shaikhs, mullahs, and Azhar-style scholars. For these alone command the skills of exegesis and the minutiae of traditional studies. But are such skills an essential factor or, perhaps, actually an impediment? What of the right, and the capacity, of the devout Muslim who is out in the daily world as the surgeon, the banker, the diplomat, the engineer? Are not they, given sincerity of commitment, proper partners in the renewal and self-definition of Islam? But will the pundits admit their partnership? Do sincerity and experience in the actual world suffice without the lore of traditional scholarship? How might these cooperate or may they, can they?

These are the questions encircling the role of *Ijtihād,* that institution which Iqbāl called "the principle of development in Islam," the appeal to the mind of the community as the right source of decision about what is, or is not, Islamic, within the control of the *Qur'ān* and the *Sunnah.* The diehards hold that the "door of *Ijtihād*" is closed, or closed to all but scholars. Others insist that it is, and must be, forever open—open to problems that never cease to demand answer and open to the *whole* community of Muslims of integrity.

Here a brief passage first dismisses the claim that a role for the "laity" in Islam means a secular state. Then follows one writer's opinion from India (where this issue is crucial).

(The controversy over *Ijtihād* is usefully illustrated in later discussion about marriage in Pakistan. See pp. 235–237).

In his *Letters on Islam*, Dr. Muḥammad Fāḍil Jamālī writes on laicism and the idea of the secular state. He sees the separation of religion and the state as justified only on grounds of European history that now no longer apply. Those conditions:

> . . . led some political thinkers, who were champions of freedom, peace and stability, to seek refuge then in the separation of religion from the state. As for today, when public education is spreading among peoples, and when civil governments are not subject to men of religion, and when tolerance and brotherhood among all sects are accepted facts by all wise men everywhere, and when a scientist or a research worker is completely free in his researches and in making his theories public without anyone deterring him, no justification remains for the separation of religion from the state, that is, for laicism. We may even say that laicism today may be considered as a reactionary movement, reactionary from a historical point of view, for the historical circumstances which demanded it have gone: and reactionary because it required the state to neglect one of its most important duties and shrink from performing it, namely the care for the souls of its citizens in addition to their bodies and minds.
>
> We believe it is necessary that the state should be civil and religious in Arab and Muslim lands. The state should pay attention to the life of man, materially and spiritually. Its attention should be undivided and unseparated, for the unity of the life of man, spiritual and physical together, should be the concern of the state. If the state cares for the hygienic, mental and social aspects of man, what sense and what logic justifies the neglect of the spiritual aspect? The state, then, should be religious. It should adopt the religion of the majority of the inhabitants, but at the same time it should care for the feelings and religious interests of the adherents of other religions on the basis of equality. It should provide opportunities for religious education for all, irrespective of their religious differences. It should also care for the religious affairs of individuals like marriage and inheritance, and allow charitable institutions and institutions of worship for all. . . .
>
> The readiness of the Muslims to promote the spirit of tolerance and respect for religious freedom of all and their avoidance of blind fanaticism and narrow-mindedness makes thinking of laicism a matter of blind imitation of others and nothing more. . . .
>
> As for Turkey, Muṣṭafā Kamāl established laicism after World War I, as a reaction to the Ottoman Caliphate with all that it implied in terms of reactionary forces. But the Muslim people of Turkey have not accepted this laicism and have not assimilated it. That is why the Democratic Party were acting in accordance with the sentiments of the Turkish people when the late Adnan Menderes undertook to build nearly two thousand mosques in the Turkish villages and undertook the renovation of the beautiful great mosques of Istanbul. Some people considered Adnan Menderes reactionary for this policy. The truth is that he was responding to one of the urgent wishes of the Turkish people. . .
>
> The laicity of the state in Muslim lands would mean that the state had divorced itself from the Islamic *Sharī'ah*, that is, from the most important

factor directing the daily life of the people, plus divorcing itself from spiritual life as such. That is what laicity demands. . .

The separation between religion and the state would mean that Arab states had abandoned the most important force of their nationalism. For the Arab nation, separated from Islam and its mission, becomes like a body separated from its life and its soul. Such a separation would turn the body into an empty shell with no kernel, in which case it would be quite easy for invading ideologies to enter the shell and fill the vacuum.[11]

Dr. Asaf A.A. Fyzee (born 1899), a notable jurist and philosopher of India, has set out his approach to Islamic interpretation and loyalty in his book, *A Modern Approach to Islam.* His emphasis is strongly historical. This still leaves open the criteria by which what is read in the context of its past is to be reliably fulfilled in the different present. Here many in Islam would strongly resist Asaf Fyzee's position and some would also reject his historicism altogether, preferring (if possible) to find their security in an absolute revelation not, on this view, time-conditioned at all.

The message of Islam was sent to the world fourteen centuries ago. Does it need reinterpretation? Is it not meant for the whole world and for all time? The answer to both questions is in the affirmative. Even if a message is true and, in a sense, eternal, it is, by those very premises, essential to understand it in accordance with the science, philosophy, psychology, metaphysics and theology of the modern world; nay, the sum total of the world's thinking and its blazing light should be brought to bear upon it.

In the history of man it is only some ten thousand years ago that he conceived the idea of certain divinities as ruling his destiny. . . . Some five thousand years later, in Mesopotamia or thereabout and also in India, man for the first time in recorded history came to believe that it was not a thousand deities but one Supreme Being, the One, the Brahman, the Absolute, the Creator, Ram, or Rahim, by whatever name you call Him, which was the *one* object of worship. After a prolonged tribulation of the spirit came this great discovery, probably the greatest single discovery in the history of man. It is greater than the discovery of zero, greater than the discovery of fire, of iron, of relativity, of any known thing. The concept itself is unique: it has a mysterious compelling power: it revivifies broken spirits, it gives meaning to life, it makes man see that which he cannot see, makes man hear that which he cannot hear, makes man know that which he cannot know. It does not depend upon human science and its changing moods: it is an eternal concept, not liable to change, decay or imperfection.

This message has often come to man through the vibrant spirit of a sensitive soul and one among the elect was the Prophet Muḥammad. The history of his quest, his mental agony and final illumination is to be found in the Qur'ān, and the Book is full of that inward perception of truth which shows the history of man's gradual cognition of God. [Here Fyzee quotes Surah 81:1–20]

The belief in the existence of God is based upon *experience*, it can neither be proved nor can it be disproved. Therefore it has stood the test of time. Not so the works of human reason or knowledge or science. The postulates, the hypotheses, theories and 'facts' of science, are in their very essence capable of change, but the belief in God is one and unchangeable, immediate and intuitive. . .

But such truth can only be communicated through an imperfect instrument, language. Language is human, variable, subject to change. No language can be read or understood for more than five or ten thousand years. We have many writings of man on earth the meanings whereof are forgotten. The classical language of the Arabs has undergone considerable change in the last two thousand years and philological studies make it perfectly clear that the meanings of words, their nuances and shades, are subject to evolutionary change. . . . Whence it is clear that the very meanings of the words, phrases, idioms, metaphors and imagery of the language used by the Arabs in the days of the Prophet have changed, are changing and will go on changing, until in the course of time they may be as difficult to comprehend as the language of Mohenjo Daro.

But we Muslims believe that the central message will last longer than its language, and that is the belief in God. Therefore, to me it is clear that we cannot go 'back' to the Qur'ān: we have to go 'forward' with it. I wish to understand the Qur'ān as it was understood by the Arabs of the time of the Prophet Muḥammad only to *reinterpret* it and apply it to my conditions of life and to believe in it, so far as it appeals to me as a twentieth century man. I cannot be called to live in the desert, to traverse it on camel back, to eat locusts, to indulge in vendetta, to wear a beard and a cloak, and to cultivate a pseudo-Arab mentality. I must distinguish between poetic truth and factual truth. I must distinguish between the husk and the kernel of religion, between law and legend. I am bound to accept and understand the message of Islam as a modern man, and not as one who lived centuries ago. I respect authority, but cannot accept it *bilā kaif* the traditional formula: 'Without asking how?' in the matter of conscience.

Islam is based upon the Qur'ān, and the Qur'ān is to be interpreted in its historical setting and on chronological principles. . . .

We in India are in a peculiarly favorable position with regard to the interpretation of religion. . . . Thus situated, the Indian Muslim has to test and compare his faith and actions with those of his compatriots, each day of his life. Common saints—Hindu, respected by Muslims and Muslim respected by Hindus—are a unique feature of this land. An Indian interpretation of Islam, as this professes to be, enjoys the advantage of a common religious life and a shared mystical experience which militates against bigotry and fanaticism and makes for catholicity and eclecticism. These are great advantages for a world religion such as Islam.

After noting past "hybridization of religious ideals" and expressing what many Muslims would regard as a very sanguine view of its desirability, Fyzee goes on to relate his concept of Islamic loyalty to issues of law, leadership, and toleration.

The first task is to separate the dogmas and doctrines of religion from the principles and rules of law. The essential faith of man is something different from the outward observance of rules: moral rules apply to the conscience but legal rules can be enforced only by the state. Ethical norms are subjective, legal rules are objective. The inner life of the spirit, 'the idea of the holy,' must be separated to some extent from the outward forms of social behavior. The separation is not simple: it will even be considered un-Islamic. But the attempt at a rethinking of the *Sharī'ah* can only begin with the acceptance of this principle. . . .

Religion should place emphasis on devotion to God, cleanliness of spirit, orderliness of life, and not be enmeshed in the minutiae of particular do's and don't's. Apart from everything else, the Islamic virtues of generosity, humility, brotherliness, courage and manliness, should be taught by examples drawn from early Muslim history. Additionally, the ethics and morality of Islam should be fortified by the teaching of the ethical and philosophical teachers of the modern world. . . . We cannot make the Qur'ān a book "which imprisons the living word of God in a book and makes tradition an infallible source." The Rabbis, it has been said, "don't listen to their conscience: they consult their law books." So do the religious mentors of Islam. . . .

The spiritual beauty and strength of fasting can be inculcated without insisting on its hidebound prescriptions. . . .

When a rule is laid down in the Qur'ān or the *Sharīʻah*, it is necessary to determine whether it is a rule of law or a rule of ethics. If it is a rule of law, the state should enforce it. If it is a rule of ethics the state cannot enforce it. Once it is determined in accordance with this principle that there is a clear rule of law laid down in the Qur'ān, the question assumes importance. The law of God, it is said, cannot be disobeyed. This statement, it is respectfully submitted, requires careful re-examination. The Qur'ān may lay down a fundamental rule governing the actions of man: or it may speak of a particular by-law, restricted by time and circumstance, not laying down an eternal verity, or it may speak in the language of poetry, metaphor, myth or legend. . . . In such a case we may come to the conclusion that it is a question of interpretation and that the law can be changed, but religion is more permanent and need not be altered.

Rejecting what he calls 'fossilization' and the pundits' claim to a closing of "the door of *Ijtihād*" or enterprise, Fyzee continues:

True Islam cannot thrive without freedom of thought, in every single matter, in every single dogma. . . . It must be asserted firmly, no matter what the *'ulamā'* say, that he who sincerely affirms that he is a Muslim, is a Muslim: no one has the right to question his beliefs and no one has the right to excommunicate him. That dread weapon, the *fatwā* of *takfīr* [branding an unbeliever] is a ridiculous anachronism. It recoils on the author, without admonishing or reforming the errant soul. Belief is a matter of conscience and this is the age which recognizes freedom of conscience in matters of faith. What may be said after proper analysis is that a certain person's opinions are wrong, but not that "he is a *kāfir*." . . .

My faith is my own, fashioned by my own outlook on life, by my own philosophy, my own experience, my own intuition. I give to every Muslim, indeed to every man, the right to fashion his own faith. "To you your religion, to me mine," [Surah 109:6]. I do not believe that the gate of interpretation is bolted and barred.

I believe that the Qur'ān is a message from God. It is the voice of God heard by Muḥammad, in the Speech of Muḥammad, the Arabic language. I believe that in every age these words must be interpreted afresh and understood anew. I believe it is the duty of every Muslim to understand this message for himself. I do revere the great interpreters of Islam, but I crave their indulgence if I cannot fully share their beliefs. For belief is at bottom a matter of individual conscience. I cannot agree that they are the keepers of my conscience. It is the duty of the scholars of each age to interpret the faith of Islam in their own times. . . .

I believe that law must be separated from religion. I believe that science and religion are distinct spheres. . . . I believe in the Islamic form of prayer, but not in prescribing and enforcing a soulless ritual which has no meaning in modern life. Prayer must be taught to the young, not as a ritual, but as an outpouring of the human spirit to the All-knowing, All-loving and All-powerful God. . . .

After serving the cause of civilization for some seven centuries, Islam came under a shadow. Its spirit was throttled by fanaticism, its theology was gagged by bigotry, its vitality was sapped by totalitarianism. For the last two centuries efforts are being made to free it from its shackles. . . . Let us release this bright spirit of joy, compassion, fraternity, tolerance and reasonableness, and modern man will be happier for its presence.[12]

THE ROLE OF POWER

A significant document in recent Islamic thinking about central problems in life and religion was the late Egyptian President's, Jamāl 'Abd al-Nāṣir, *Falsafat al-Thaurah (The Philosophy of the Revolution),* published in Cairo in 1954. It dealt, among other things, with the issue of violence and what might be called the search for purity of heart.

Describing his revolutionary will to kill in the interest of an ideology, he went on:

Deep in my heart, however, I had not been at all satisfied that violence could serve as the positive action we must take to save the future of our country. I fell prey to perplexity, to a mixture of overlapping factors that ran the gamut of patriotism and religion, leniency and ruthlessness, knowledge and the lack of it.

Gradually I came to realize that the idea of political assassinations that glowed once in my imagination was beginning to dim and lose its value as a means of bringing about this positive action.

I remember particularly a night which marked a turning point in the course of my thoughts and dreams in this respect. We had planned a course of action and decided that a certain man should cease to exist. We studied his movements and habits before carrying out our plan, which was perfected in all respects. The plan was to shoot him by night on his way home. An execution squad was appointed to do the shooting, covered by a second squad for protection, and a third squad for the get-away. The appointed night came and I went out with the attack group. Everything went according to plan. As we had expected, the field was clear. The squads concealed themselves in their assigned positions, waiting for our man. As soon as he was sighted, he was met with a volley of bullets. The execution squad then withdrew, covered by the protective force, and we hurried to safety. . .

But suddenly there rang in my ears the sounds of screaming and wailing. I heard a woman crying, a child terrified and a continuous, frightened call for help.

While speeding away in my car, I was overwhelmed and excited by a multitude of emotions. A strange thing was happening to me. The sounds were still loud in my ears: the screaming and wailing and the crying and the frightened calls for help. I was now too far away from the scene to hear the actual sounds, but nevertheless they seemed chasing me and pursuing me.

I arrived at my house and threw myself on my bed, my mind in agitation, my heart and conscience in unceasing turmoil. . . . I did not sleep all night. I remained laying on my bed in darkness, smoking continuously, trying to direct my agitated thoughts, which were no sooner collected than again distracted by the sounds that chased me.

Had I done right? I answered myself with conviction that it was for the sake of my country that I had taken this action.

Was there another way? Again I answered myself, but this time in doubt. What else *could* we have done? But is it really possible to change the future of our country by eliminating this or that person? Is the problem deeper than this?

Perplexed by this question, I answered myself: the problem appears to be deeper. We dream of the glory of our nation. But which is the better way to bring it about: to eliminate those who should be eliminated, or to bring forward those who should be brought forward?

There on my bed I thought it through with flashes of understanding illuminating my reflections. . . . Still tossing on my bed in a room now full of smoke and permeated with emotions, I said to myself: And so, therefore? I heard an inner voice asking: Therefore what? This time I answered myself with certain conviction: I mean that our method must be changed. What we have been doing is not the positive action to which we are dedicated. The problem has roots that are deep, and is too profound to be solved in this negative way.

I felt a serene inner relief. . . . Suddenly I hoped that the man would not die. It was strange to find myself at dawn wishing life for the man whom I had wished death for only the previous evening! I waited anxiously for the morning paper. The man whose assassination I had planned was out of danger. I was relieved.

But the main problem remained. We must find out what the positive action should be.

From that time on, our thinking was directed to doing something more deeply rooted, more important and further reaching. Thus we began to draw the outline of the picture which materialized on the night of July 23rd: a revolution springing from the heart of the people, expressing their hopes, following the same path they had already envisioned as the great highway to freedom. . . .

Did the events of July 23rd realize all we wanted? The answer is definitely No! Those events were but the first step. In fact, I was not diverted by the joy at our success. That joy was not enough to convince me that our hopes could now become real and that the spring of a new life had come to Egypt. I felt almost the contrary. . . . Before July 23rd I had imagined that all the nation was on the alert and ready. I thought that the nation was only waiting for a vanguard to tear down the barrier that stood in its way and would then consolidate behind that vanguard in an ordered, organized move.

[On the contrary] dissension, chaos, vindictiveness and selfishness were unleashed at the very first moments. Every man wanted selfishly to benefit by the Revolution and attain certain individual aims. . . .

At an earlier point in his reflections, this is how ʿAbd al-Nāṣir described that egotism in society:

How different is the reality from the dream. . . . At this moment I felt, with bitterness and sorrow, that the task of the vanguard, far from being completed, had only begun. . . . Every man we questioned had nothing to recommend except to kill someone else. Every idea we listened to was nothing but an attack upon some other idea. If we had gone along with everything we heard, we would have killed off all the people and torn down every idea, and there would have been nothing left for us but to sit down among the corpses and ruins. . . . Most of the cases referred to us were no more or less than demands for revenge, as though the revolution had taken place in order to become a weapon in the hand of hatred and vindictiveness.

If anyone had asked me in those days what I wanted most, I would have answered promptly: to hear an Egyptian speak fairly about another Egyptian: to sense that an Egyptian had opened his heart to pardon, forgiveness and love for his Egyptian brethren. To find an Egyptian who did not devote his time to tearing down the views of another Egyptian.

In addition to all this, there was a confirmed individual egotism. The word 'I' was on every tongue. It was the solution to every difficulty, the cure for every ill.[13]

Algeria and the Algerian Revolution of the 1960s have an important place in the twentieth century life of Islam, by virtue of the bitterness of the campaign to terminate the French presence and of the economic power the state wields. One of the actors and interpreters of that revolution is Aḥmad Ṭāleb whose *Lettres de Prison* comment on the approach of Islam, as he sees it, to issues of violence and human rights. The writer later became Minister of Education in the new republic.

La Santé, August 25th, 1958. To a French friend.
My dear R,
For the first time you raise the problem of the attacks and take occasion to ask my opinion about violence. Believe me, I am not a systematic partisan, but I will never concede that one can respond to blows with benediction [to use Camus' phrasing]. Blows call for blows: I am not a disciple of Christ. For me retaliation is a law.

To be sure, I am among those for whom moral principle has a role to play in politics or, more precisely, I am one for whom the role of politics is to make the technique express the ethical. I am a person of scruple, a *scrupulard*, as one of the honorable ministers of the IVth has it. In the struggle in which we are engaged, we have always acted conformably to certain principles. But it is an exceptional conflict, a life and death struggle, and, what is more, it is against an adversary who does not hesitate to use torture, who scrapes you to the bone.

Our acts of violence, then, are in reply to a violent situation. You will understand me better when you have read again this passage from Mounier [again I quote him]: "One thinks too much about acts of violence, so that one fails to recognize what are more often situations of violence, in which today millions of people languish, die and are dehumanized, without defense, in the name of order. It is the tyrant who is the real source of sedition. Violence, in the reprehensible sense of the word, is the continuing régime."

To a militant Algerian. Fresnes, February 10th, 1960.
My dear A,
Islam, you write to me, is at the heart of politics and you complain that many militants who feel so do not find anywhere any response to the questions

which they ask and which are posed to them, when they want to link reflection and action firmly together. Here, then, are some hasty observations on the "inability of Islam to accommodate to the modern world."

Let me say that your brother prisoners ask the same questions—which has led some among them to ask me to draft some notes on the problem of involvement from within Islam. It is these reflections I am going to pass on to you. I am not proposing anything exhaustive but only a few guide marks which, I hope, may stimulate your own thinking.

It is all a very complex problem and has to do with more than involvement. I will not lose myself in philosophical intricacies but will stay with the practical aspects, namely, action. One could pose the issue as follows: Are the hands of man really on the wheel of history? But you will say to me that this problem has clearly been resolved a century since. . . .

However, it is our obligation as Muslims to go back to our own origins and make good, as it were, "a pilgrimage to our sources," to see if Islam (that is, essentially, the Qur'ān as it was revealed and then applied) has attained a solution to the problem and, in the event of a positive response, to make clear the originality of that solution.

The first question may be formulated thus: does Islam counsel commitment or apathy? If we run through the sacred text, we discover that action is explicitly affirmed. Two verses in particular seem to me to be specially relevant and, of themselves, to eliminate completely all the theories of western sociologists about the supposed fatalism of Islam. "For God does not change what belongs to a people, until they transform their own selves." [Surah 13:11] and: "That is because God would never change the favor He had granted a people until they changed their own selves." [Surah 3:53] These two verses, in laying the accent on human effort, demonstrate that the duty of the Muslim is to be always manning the breach, whether it be to bring a detested régime to an end or to maintain and preserve a satisfactory situation.

The Prophet himself did not opt to live far away from the camp of men. He did not say to youth: "Sell what you have and follow me." On the contrary, he worked and toiled among things as they are. He did not achieve the glory of the just, except by way of the risk of his life. He only made triumphal entry into Mecca after confronting every danger and being subjected to every taunt of sarcasm. At Medina, he was not content merely to be the preacher of the new faith: he became also the leader of the new city, where he organized the religious, social and economic life. We see him sharing personally in the construction of the Mosque and the dwellings of the emigrants. Later, carrying arms, he put himself at the head of his troops. Charged to deliver a message he opted for action, because he was convinced that a message can only pass from the realm of idea to the realm of life by taking the hard road of involvement.

Thus, Islam commends action—we plainly see—just as, no less explicitly, it condemns craven aloofness from it. We can set this out under two aspects.

(a) First the fainthearted, those of whom the Qur'ān says, "When a surah is sent down bidding them believe in God and struggle on behalf of the messenger, the superior among them pray to be excused, saying: 'Let us stay with the non-combattants.'" [Surah 9:86]. And there is another verse: "The ones who ask to be excused are those who have no belief in God nor in the last day, those of dubious heart who vacillate in their doubtful minds." [Surah 9:45]

Islam in no way encourages us to keep to the household hearth while the city burns or when the fatherland is in danger. It stirs us to engage when our brothers have need of us or when misery spreads its fearful leprosy or cries of the innocent tear at our hearts or when injustice reigns with its toll of bitterness and suffering. There are numerous verses condemning deserters who abandon the duty of solidarity in the common cause. These verses offer an admirable lesson in courage and unflinching self abnegation. The true Muslim will always shoulder his responsibilities and never screen himself behind pretexts which for the most part are idle pretence.

(b) Here we encounter the second class of defaulters, namely the idealists, those who would be 'pure,' isolating themselves in their ivory tower in flight from the world and its problems. They forget that the Prophet often repeated the dictum: "There is no monasticism in Islam," insisting that purity is no abstraction in some empyrean of bliss, but that it is to be gained only in daily, strenuous encounter with the multiple patterns of the real world. They forget, too, that without incarnation the most beautiful ideal will remain ideal alone.

Furthermore, the Qur'ān gives us to know that there is no middle, or third, way between *Ḥizballāh* and *ḥizb al-shaiṭān* (taking God's part, and taking Satan's). The Muslim must make his choice, cost what sacrifice it may. He cannot stay out of the conflict: to see events from some lofty perch is to forfeit contact with reality.

Among this second category of defaulters, there is often concealed under the plea of purity an individualism that relishes ease and repose. In this connection, let me cite a tradition with a truly foresighted quality, since it illustrates a condition of things in Islamic society right up to the present: "There will come a time," said the Prophet, "in which the nations of the earth will rush upon you like dogs that pounce upon their quarry." When the Prophet was asked whether that would be because they were feeble in numbers, he replied: "No! for then you will be a great throng. It will be because God will fill your hearts with *wahan.*" Finally one of them asked him precisely what this word *wahan* meant and he said: "It is the love of this world's goods and the fear of danger."

Having responded to the first question to the effect that Islam is a philosophy of engagement and roundly condemns all forms of desertion from duty, it remains to show how this philosophy is distinguished from those doctrines of action which abound in our day. It seems to me that the answer to that can be found in this verse: "Say: 'Act, and God and the Prophet and the believers will see your doing.'" [Surah 9:105]. In other words, the Muslim must be a man of action ["Act"] but his doings must be ruled by a moral factor ["God sees what you do."] and should conform to the perfection of a model ["and his Prophet"] and also have the good of the community as their goal ["and the believers"].

Here, then, are the three characteristics of the Muslim as a man of action.

(a) All his actions obey a moral criterion—the term so decried and sullied in our time must be reconstituted among us. This moral quality centers on probity, justice, courage, modesty and love of the truth. To reach these goals a Muslim must never take any and every means as good, and he will never abandon himself to mere opportunism. For him Quranic precepts are no dead letter but the constant inspiration of his acts. He knows that God loves those who fear Him and who operate within the framework of a morality of honesty, respect for others and duty done. God says to us: "Did you imagine that you would enter the garden and God not know which of you had striven and who the patient be?" This verse turns on two words—"strive" and the fact that such endeavor is "in the way of God." [Surah 3:141]. The Muslim finds himself moving between these two poles—engagement and the way of God.

(b) This Quranic morality has been embodied in the Prophet who thus represents for us a model in which this synthesis between combat and duty to God, between the revolutionary and the man of God, has been achieved. And after him there have been numerous Muslims who have known how to hold in harmony the most entire engagement with things temporal and a spiritual life of great richness. We find them in the history of our Maghrib here—and not least so! Let me cite only Ibn Tumart and 'Abd al-Qādir. The first, a mystic and an ethical reformer, founded the greatest empire our country has known—the Almohads, which sealed the unity of the Maghrib in the 12th century. As for the Amīr, 'Abd al-Qādir, he was—to quote Kierkegaard's phrase, taken up by our friend M.C. Sahli—"a knight of the faith," in whom national and religious feeling were marvellously blended.

(c) The Muslim, finally, in all his activity, does not lose sight of the fact that he is part of a community. "He who does not love the wellbeing of our community," said the Prophet, "is not one of us." We are committed, then, always to the spirit of the common interest, the good of the nation to which we belong. That is why it is forbidden to us to enter into any pact with the evil doers.

For the rest, the Muslim man of action is not an anarchist. "The earth shall be the inheritance of my righteous servants," [Surah 21:105, quoting from the Psalms.] If he is involved in destruction, in scorching the earth, it is in order the better to rebuild. When the Prophet shattered the idols of the Quraish in the *Ka'bah,* I see there a symbol from which one can evidently derive all the extrapolations we need.[14]

In the light of these sentiments, it is perhaps natural to find, in another letter, a very critical attitude to the mysticism that occupied the extracts in chapter 7.

Fresnes, March 8th, 1960. To a French friend.
My dear C,
I was more than agreeably surprised to have your letter after a long silence. But I do not go along with you when you make apology for Massignon [Louis Massignon, 1883-1962, was an eminent French Islamicist who translated many Sufi texts, notably the *Tawāsīn* of Al-Ḥallāj.]

Numbers of Europeans dream of a Muslim society of *Khouans* [hermits] confined to their paternosters and their monastic sermonizings, while they abandon any care to shoulder the demands of the temporal world.

The history of Islam shows us that mysticism flourishes in two extreme situations, namely in societies that are very developed, where cities and countryside alike are flourishing, where misery and servitude are banished, as was the case in the early 'Abbāsid period. Or it occurs in oppressed societies which are condemned to ignorance and poverty [our job is to find another answer than mysticism] as was the situation in the Muslim world in the eighteenth and nineteenth centuries.

In our time mysticism in its first form is a luxury we cannot allow ourselves. In its second form it is a thing we must combat. When the city needs the arms and the brains of its children to liberate and rebuild it, it becomes a crime to take refuge in an ivory tower or in a convent. I have repeatedly insisted that to us the notion of a private individual salvation is quite foreign.

Aḥmad Ṭāleb has some interesting comments on the theology of activism in God's Name in a letter to a Lebanese intellectual.

> Fresnes, March 15th, 1960. To René Habachi
> Dear Friend,
> I have not replied sooner to your note of February 7th, my excuse being that I have less leisure back here in the infirmary than I had in the hospital.
>
> In this month of Ramaḍān, when one feels so close to God, I want to tell you what response you have kindled in me by your pages on the theme of atheism. . . .
>
> What is really tragic about it is that our atheism, in line with so many other things that are occurring, is an imported atheism. It is by imitation that one proclaims one is an atheist. Or it is by snobbery and because this stance constitutes a screen behind which one can allow oneself anything? [Listlessness of this order has nothing in common with the "everything goes" of Ivan Karamazov.] That is why one rarely finds among our atheists those grand spirits, rich in human qualities, of whom the West affords us many examples [I think at this moment of R. Martin du Gard].
>
> Our atheism has still about it a characteristic refusal to reckon with our past in its comprehensiveness. It is tied to the notion that religion was the cause of the centuries of humiliation [some of Renan's theories have been greatly prized among us]. Having this attitude to the past, it assumes that abandoning the faith is the essential condition of all revival.
>
> If you are aware of how much scorn there is in the mouth of our atheists for the descriptive 'medieval', you will see how totally they fail to understand the splendid Middle Age which you invoke and which certainly deserves a resounding rehabilitation. Our atheists loudly hail the slogan: "Faith is each one's private business, civics is the affair of all." Thus they want to eliminate God just at the very time when "God alone can save us." Mounier has it rightly: "Because those who stand for the eternal have lost the sense of the temporal, let us not lose in the refound temporal the sense of the eternal."
>
> It remains for the young believers, Christians and Muslims, holding as they do a measure of responsibility for our much troubled Arab world, to take deeper your attractive formula: "Revolution in the temporal *via* the spiritual." For the important thing for us, as you yourself have said so well, "is not on no account to change the past, but above all on no account to forfeit God."[15]

QUESTIONS IN SOCIETY

Dr. 'Ali Mazrui, a Kenyan political scientist and author, has some lively observations on Islam and Islamic issues in his *On Heroes and Uhuru Worship,* which bear on several of the themes of this chapter. His African perspective makes his analysis of Muslim patterns of mind and their likely bearing on affairs all the more useful for the student. Observing that, contrary to the notion of some political scientists, belief systems are significant determinatives of human behavior, he continues:

> What this paper is attempting to do is to formulate broad hypotheses about Islam in Africa and its relation to the impact of the West and to ideas of eco-

nomic radicalism. . . . Islam can become an ally of revolutionary commitment in Africa.

Of all the charges against Islam which westerners made in the nineteenth century, perhaps the one which hurt Muslim intellectuals most deeply was the accusation that Islam was incompatible with modernity. In politics modernity at the time was associated with liberal individualism. In economics it was linked with entrepreneurial skills and spirit of private achievement characteristic of the new ethos of industrial capitalism. By both criteria of modernity Islam in the Middle East was found wanting. Islamic reformism gained momentum in Turkey and in the Arab world. And the direction of change which most intellectual reformers tended to advocate was towards greater similarity with western norms. In Turkey the movement finally found a revolutionary climax in the loss of Turkey's Islamic Empire and in the triumph of Kemāl Atatürk. With the secular transformation launched by Kemāl, Turkey became less Muslim in her determination to be more modern. Changes toward secularism in the rest of the Middle East were less spectacular, but Islam was never the same again after the Western impact.

This brings us to the second crucial hypothesis. It is to the effect that Islam, under certain conditions, has a propensity to produce both rebellious leaders and submissive followers. The rebelliousness of the leader and the submissiveness of the followers go back to Muḥammad himself and his original following. Of all the major religions of the world perhaps none was born with a greater outburst of militancy than Islam. . . . Muḥammad was a rebel against the ways of his ancestors. The militant tradition of rebellious leadership and submissive following has recurrently broken out in Islamic history ever since. . . . This is a tradition which can lie dormant for generations. . . . The mating of egalitarianism and authoritarianism in the modern world provides possibilities for a new form of rebellious leadership and submissive following.

Commenting on the frequent question about Islam and its actual or potential attitude to communism, 'Ali Mazrui reflects on the remarkable commercial (and, therefore, presumably capitalist) instincts of Islam. But he sees these balanced and differentiated, for example, from western, Protestant procapitalist factors, by the effective countercapital workings of Islamic laws of inheritance.

Commercial activity is . . . part of the origins of Islam. . . . Muḥammad might well be the only founder of a major religion who was once a man of commerce. He attended to some of the trading interests of his wealthy wife. Mecca itself was at that time, and before Muḥammad's time, almost as much a center of commerce as a religious focus for Arabs from distant parts of the peninsula. A verse from the Qur'ān assures Muslims that it is not wrong to seek a livelihood in trade and exchange in the course of the pilgrimage [Surah 2:198]. Moreover, the Prophet himself is credited with the saying: "Nine portions of God's bounty are in commercial activity." In Africa, too, the spread of Islam came to be associated with trade. . . . Yet the encouragement of commerce in Islam is not quite the same thing as the Protestant ethic defined by Weber. . . . Islam stands in an intermediate position between the asceticism and self-denial of some aspects of Buddhist and Hindu thought . . . and the accumulative spirit of Calvinistic and Lutheran doctrines on the other. . . . The Islamic equivalent fell short of developing into capitalism because of other factors in Islam which inhibited it. One factor was the collectivistic nature of Islamic loyalties. It is true that commerce was encouraged in Islam.

But so were a host of responsibilities toward relatives and co-religionaries. These responsibilities hampered accumulation. As for the Islamic laws of inheritance, they were almost calculated to thwart intergenerational capital formation. There is a built-in distributive device in the Islamic code of inheritance. The wealth of a man is inherited by too many relatives. . . . In East Africa early in the century the Islamic law of inheritance was a major obstacle to the introduction of some of the legal aspects of western economic individualism. In short, the encouragement of commerce in Islam did not go with the kind of economic individualism which made the Protestant Ethic in the west so accumulative. . . . The old Islamic encouragement of commercial activity served to keep alive the achievement incentive, while the collective and egalitarian aspects of Islam restrained that incentive from becoming too accumulative. The resulting cultural climate is one that can be easily hospitable to a centralized economy with certain rewards for individual achievement, certain limited incentives for individual exertion. . . .

If we go back to the very origins of Islam in Arabia, we find the Muslim state under the early Caliphate was almost excessively distributive in its attitude to its own resources. Tradition has it that the Caliph 'Umar clothed himself in coarse linen and wore sandals of fibre in which he walked the streets refusing to ride. In a sense, he saw himself as the state and wanted to ensure a kind of military socialism as a principle of sharing the spoils of conquest. . . .

The distributive aspect of Islam is, of course, intimately related to the egalitarian. The Prophet Muḥammad himself was, in a sense, the paradox of a "proletarian aristocrat." He was born of the noble tribe of the Quraish but he came from a poor family and had worked in humble jobs. At first, his modest upbringing, in spite of noble blood, was an impediment to his religious mission. . . . But his marginal status as a poor, camel-driving aristocrat later became his strength. The poor were captivated and the noblemen eventually capitulated. A relative egalitarianism based in common faith in Islam, emerged quite early as a basic precept of the religion.

Modern socialists in the Middle East sometimes exaggerate the egalitarian aspect of early Islam. Islam was more egalitarian in intention than in achievement. But there were enough levelling tendencies within it to make the capitalistic spirit of creative individual accumulation difficult to sustain.

Another aspect of Islam is basically anti-accumulative, [namely] the Islamic attitude toward certain forms of risk-taking. . . . Islam's disapproval . . . of interest on loans and savings is also anti-accumulative in its implications. Islam in East Africa continues to frown on the whole idea of receiving interest on one's savings account in a bank. . . . This is an inhibition which is withering away. But that it has ever existed is a matter of some pertinence in the economic history of Muslim communities in such areas.[16]

'Ali Mazrui's reflections stay naturally within the sphere of the economic and the political-ideological. When the susceptibility of Islam to Marxist ideas and theories is assessed from the religious angle it is usual to suppose that its rigorous theism is entirely antithetical to atheistic communism. But it would be simplistic to press that conclusion too readily. Much depends on the degree to which, in the active if not in the abstract, the other areas of Marxist thinking can be detached from its strictly religious denials. For insofar as they can, there are many elements of Islamic ideology, tradition, and instinct that lend themselves to socialist and communist enlistment and fulfillment.

Among the liveliest and most controversial of authors within Arab Islam at mid-twentieth century has been Khālid Muḥammad Khālid (born 1920) whose spirited *Min Hunā Nabda'* "Here We Start," published in Cairo in 1950, provoked an intriguing debate on social and intellectual issues within current Arab Islam. Here, under the heading "Stay This Torrent," is his plea, and case, for birth control.

> The final means to a truly socialist plan of action—and an absolute necessity it is—lies in limiting and controlling the birth rate.
>
> It may be asked: What connection has socialism with birth control? Our reply is that it has the most intimate connections, especially when an attempt is made to apply socialism to a society like ours which is in veritable flood of human progeny, spawning from the womb, with neither thought nor accounting.
>
> Socialism here must do two things:
>
> (a) Control material production
>
> (b) Control human fertility.
>
> It is certain that disparity between the two, production and fertility, brings upon the nation debilitating troubles. It has truly become imperative for our society, if it is to be happy, to recognize its duty in respect to this problem and to discharge it in the best ways, and completely.
>
> We address ourselves here to our own people upon whose shoulders alone falls the burden of battling against this evil. There is one fact which needs to be clearly understood. It is that there is absolutely no hope of an improvement in the standard of living among us as long as the rate of births is so excessive. 400,000 come to swell our population every year—(the figure has doubled in the seventies)—a population totally unprepared to welcome them and unable to care for them. But for the high rate of infant mortality life would have become a chaos of folly and futility.
>
> The most urgent aspect of this problem is that people know nothing of it. They are entirely unaware that they are faced with a catastrophe threatening their happiness and their prosperity. Marriage is the done thing among us all. Then husband and wife become a busy generating station, going for the record in producing boys and girls. The parents do not pause to consider whether or not there is a place for their offspring in the community and whether or not they will have the opportunity and the capacity to ensure the victims a chance of real life.

After citing various statistics and comparative ecological problems, Khālid Muḥammad Khālid comes to the gist of his message and handles religious tradition and prejudice in a most illuminating way.

> We know that the basic cause of this torrential birth rate is a misunderstanding of religion, fate, and faith—all of which summons us to consider the religious aspect of this fearful issue. Our conviction is that Islam enjoins birth control in the interests of the community and of the individual and considers prodigality in this area, under conditions of poverty and destitution, an intolerable calamity.
>
> According to a fine tradition, the Prophet [upon whom be peace] repeatedly prayed: "O Lord, I seek refuge with Thee from the struggle with affliction." "And what, O Prophet, is that?" he was asked. "Scarcity of means," he replied, "and a large family." He was asked about abstaining from intercourse

and he replied that it was certainly what they should do. At that time abstaining from intercourse was the sole means by which it was possible to control and limit fertility. The apostle declared it to be permissible without condition, as we have seen in the preceding tradition and as can be seen from the following story, recorded on strong authority by the reliable traditionalists.

It is recorded that ʻUmar was visited by ʻAli, Zubayr and Saʻīd, and others of the companions [upon whom be peace]. Abstaining from intercourse was the subject raised and he said: "There is no objection to it." A man got up and said: "People say that, in a small way, to do so is equivalent to burying alive." However, ʻAli said: "Not so, until the seed has been through seven stages. It is first a particle of clay, then a drop of water, then a blood clot, an embryo, then bone and flesh, and finally it becomes another creature." ʻUmar's comment was: "You have rightly spoken: God lengthen your days." Now, if Islam approves abstention, which is simply a way of preventing the living sperm from reaching the ovum where it lodges to grow into a personality and goes on to become a man, then it approves by analogy every other modern means to the same end.

It oftentimes occurs to simple people that birth control does not square with trust in God or faith in Him, and that no soul whose existence God has willed can fail to come into existence. whether *we* will it or whether *we* would disallow it. We deny, however, the first part of the argument and agree with them on the other. But we must point out to them that faith in the coming to be of anything that God has willed shall be, does not conflict with our appeal for birth control and restraint.

We believe that when pestilence rages among the population, there is no one, whose death by it God has decreed, who will not in fact die, and none whose survival God has willed, who will not survive. This conviction of ours, though, does not prevent us from straining every effort to wipe out the pestilence and destroy it. We take up the same position in regard to the plague of human reproduction, which is on the point of engulfing the community, or leaving it destitute on the shore of the flood, if that flood has not already engulfed it. . . .

Children are certainly a delight and make a paradise. They are a supreme joy to parents and a wealth of unsurpassed value to the nation, if they are proportionate in their time and are not more numerous than the level of the ability of their families and their community to sustain, so that, if they fall sick, they are cared for; that they find what they seek and can enjoy what they want in life and more than they want. But when they multiply like a pouring torrent, then they are a curse to themselves and a misery to their parents and their country. Then society echoes the complaint of Abū-l-ʻAlā al-Maʻarī [the epitaph he directed for his tombstone]:

"This is my father's crime against me.
I have not so wronged anyone."

and the cry of our own Egyptian poet, Abū-al-Wafā':

"In the fire is the dwelling of every mother
And every father who together have begotten to adversity the likes of me."
[See *House of Islam,* p. 124].[17]

Two Pakistani sociologists, Muḥammad Iqbāl Choudhury and Mushtāq Aḥmad Khān, have analyzed the problem of population growth but deal far more tentatively than Khālid Muḥammad Khālid with the religious elements in the situation. After some statistical facts they proceed to list the causes that apply, and in most of them the Islamic attitudes, at least in popular terms, are paramount.

> 1. Control of Infant Mortality
> 2. Introduction of Modern Medicine
> 3. High Fertility among Muslims . . . reasons as under: a. Polygamy. For the Muslims four wives are allowed (under new family law there are some restrictions), if a person can treat them equally. The factor has been enhancing the chances of more children in comparison to other, monogamous, religious groups. b. The remarriage of a widow is in vogue among Muslims (as contrasted with Hindu custom) . . . c. It is one of the sacred duties of the parents of Muslim children to get their children married as early as possible (though under new family law there is an age limit). Thus the children get married in their most fertile age so there was higher birth among Muslims. Celibacy is also disallowed among Muslims. d. Antagonistic attitude of the Muslims against family planning, while on the other hand more children are considered the blessing of God. . . . e. Misinterpretation of religious values pertaining to reproduction and attitude towards the new population, have stimulated the birth rate among Muslims.
> 4. No aspiration after higher living standards and the general contentment of the masses also affects adversely the idea of planned parenthood. The masses are fatalistic and have firm belief that whatever has been written in fate cannot be changed by the efforts of human beings. They hate and discourage the idea to achieve higher living standards at the cost of fewer children.
> 5. Illiteracy of the masses and especially among the women folk further aggravates the situation. . . .
> 6. In most of the rural areas due to factions and feuds large families are regarded as a matter of prestige. A family with a large number of males is feared and respected in rural areas.
> 7. The climate is hot and pleasant, favorable to high fertility rate.
> 8. Desire for a male child . . . as a felt need. So the parents of female children go on having a large number of issues in hope of getting a male child. . . .
> 9. Better sanitation. . . .
> 10. Control over natural and other calamities. . . .
> 11. Lack of Family Planning Publicity. . . .
> 12. Philosophical support. . . . Man is above all other creations and thus he should not be used as means towards other ends and he should not be denied the enjoyment through contraceptives and late marriage etc.
> 13. Some people believe that the greater the number of people the greater the political power in the country.

After this discussion of the factors, the authors go on to suggest remedies, including various educational and social steps, later marriage, and literacy education. Under "Monogamy" they say:

> We do not want to interfere in religious matters, but it is obvious, if there is one wife, the number of children will definitely be less in comparison to a person having more wives. In the former case during pregnancy a husband is

not in a position to engage his wife in sexual intercourse while in the latter case he has got other wives. . . .

Religious sanction should be sought from the '*Ulamā*' to get favorable public opinion for late marriage and planned parenthood. . . .[18]

In his notable exposition of Muslim Personalism, Dr. Muḥammad Laḥbābī, of Morocco (see pp. 47–50) reaches what he agrees, at first sight, might seem a disqualification of his thesis about the Islamic version of the human dignity, namely, the role assigned to women. His response to his own raising of this issue leads into one of the best statements of the hopeful and positive side of a vexed question.

We have already said that woman is the equal of man. Nevertheless, her juridical position leaves us aware rather of flagrant inequality. For example:

a. While polygamy is licit, polyandry, in any form or under any circumstances, is considered as adultery and fornication, subject to the severest penalties in this world and the next.
b. While it is allowable for a believer to marry a non-Muslim, without demanding her conversion, no woman has the liberty to marry a non-Muslim.
c. The man disposes unilaterally of the right to pronounce divorce.
d. To this list must be added the fact that the share accorded to women in inheritance is always inferior to that of the males.
e. A woman's witness does not have the same juridical value as that of the man in the courts.

In face of these, can one talk of Muslim personalism? Surely. All we need do is go back to the sources of Islam.

Polygamy

The Qur'ān strongly conduces to monogamy. It suffices to reflect on Surah 4:3–4, 127–130, to be convinced of this. Before commenting on these verses, a few preliminary remarks are in order. In the first place, polygamy has never been either required or commended. On the contrary, the woman has the right to include in the marriage contract forms a pledge from the husband to observe monogamy, and, in the case of divorce, to pay indemnity. The wife has also the right to ask and obtain from the *Qāḍī*, given adequate grounds, the dissolution of the conjugal tie (if for example the husband is guilty of cruelty, grave injury, or if the life of the marriage is endangered by impotence, madness or contagious disease). Also the wife has the right to have the marriage dissolved if the husband refuses, of his own free will, to fulfill his conjugal duty, if he sets up any erotic tyranny over her, or if he does not provide decently for her maintenance.

Now for Surah 4 of the Qur'ān, where there are several verses, some relating to polygamy, others, in more general terms, to marriage. The Surah begins: "O man, fear your Lord who created you from a single soul whence He created its mate, and from the two He has caused to proliferate great numbers, men and women. Fear God in whose Name you demand one of another, and the wombs. God is watchful over you."

There is, then, from the beginning, complete equality between the two sexes, specifically grounded in mutual affection and gentleness [see Surah 30:21].

After this preamble, the Surah proceeds to the matrimonial bonds between the sexes. Man is permitted to be polygamous, but on condition that he is equitable in respect of each spouse. However, "If you fear not treating them equally, then marry only one, or a female slave: so you will be more sure of not being partial. Give to the women their dowries duly. If they are minded to make a gift to you or part thereof, profit by it peaceably and quietly."

The same chapter has other provisions [v. 127–130] respecting marriage and polygamy: "O Prophet-messenger, believers will consult you about women. Say to them: 'God . . . instructs you about them and the orphans [who are under your care] to whom you have not given what is prescribed for them and whom you desire to marry. God instructs you about minors who have no protection and directs that you do justly by the orphans. Whatever good you do, God knows of it.'"

The Qur'ān reverts to marriage with the orphans many times because, were these not protected by the law, they could well be at the mercy of guardians marrying them for the sake of carting off their fortune. Furthermore the law aims at protecting woman in general from every whim of tyranny or injustice from the husband. "If a woman fears any harshness or indifference from her husband, there is no wrong in their dealing with it between them, for such conciliation is better than divorce. Egoism is always besetting human souls [in such circumstances, "but] if you show yourselves beneficent and if you fear God [God knows it]. For He is well aware of what you do." Piety, then, consists in conforming to the orders given by God. Nothing escapes God of our intentions and our deeds. The primordial virtue is equity, most of all towards the wife. "You will not be able to be equitable between your [plural] wives, however you try! Still, do not incline [towards one at the expense of another to the point where you leave the latter] in suspense [neither a loved wife nor a wife divorced]. If you prefer concord and if you are God-fearing, God Who is all forgiving and all pitying [will take account of it]. If two spouses separate, God will provide each of them another destiny. God is omnipotent and wise." [v. 128–130]

These verses make clear the intention of Islam in regard to polygamy. It allows it to come in at the window in order to throw it out at the door. By dint of restrictive rules, and the appeal to impartiality between wives [which is moreover virtually impossible] one arrives at a virtual prohibition of polygamy. He who wishes to be in the grace of God and who fears lest he be unjust *must* opt for monogamy. "In truth, there is herein a reminder for him who has a heart, or who knows how to listen attentively." [Surah 50:36–37]

The Equality of Man and Woman

The 'I' of the woman, is her name, She is not Madam X, née Y: she is, and all her life will remain, bearer of the name she received at birth. She is at liberty to take up any other name she will, but there is no law requiring her to 'depersonalize' in favor of her husband.

Personal law relating to women contains many rights: the right to marriage, to family, to inheritance, to private property [inviolate and her own, legally ensured against all trespass even that of the husband himself]. True, a woman receives in inheritance only half what her brother takes, but that is explained by the fact that in marriage it is the man alone who gives the dowry [which becomes the inalienable personal property of the wife] and it is the man who assumes all the costs of the domestic hearth and its upkeep. Is not that just and equitable?

The woman, then, has to take up her responsibilities devolving from these rights and from her liberty to handle her own property. She has a role in the family and in the *Ummah*. Her selfawareness as an 'I' and her social role are based on this cluster of rights. Woman is a person. In liberating her from the yoke of the tribe and from most of the taboos and customs of the *Jāhiliyyah*. Islam gave to woman her essential liberties and a legal framework allowing her to secure other liberties [political rights, right to work, et cetera.]

It is up to woman to strive, to set herself in the van of human evolution. The Qur'ān always associates the female with the male in every situation: she does not exist as the entity relative to man but as his equal [see for example Surah 4:35; 17:75]. This equality must be made real within a pure and sacred love. This is illustrated in a tradition which might be considered a poetic evocation of conjugal love and a most beautiful celebration of it. "When a man looks upon his wife and she upon him, God Himself looks upon them in mercy. When they take one another's hands, their sins disperse through the interstices of their fingers. When he cohabits with her, angels surround them from earth to the zenith. The ardor and desire between them is as splendid as the mountains. When the wife is pregnant her recompense equals the merit of fasting, of *Ṣalāt* and of *Jihād*.

With Islam, woman reaches to a higher level of evolution, not merely in degree, but decisively. Instead of thralldom we have religious individualism and a juridical personality. The individual is detached from group existence and becomes subject and object of jurisprudence *per se*. Religion speaks to all the members of the *Ummah* and a new wind of democracy blows. The Qur'ān, the *Sunnah* and *fiqh*, or jurisprudence, are concerned with woman as much as with man. Woman comes before God with the same rites as man and with no intermediary [Surah 2:184] . . . .

Between female and male, in Islam, there are no inequalities, only differences. The *Shahādah*, the first fundamental of Islam, is the same for each. And it is likewise with the other four pillars of religion. The differences relate only to matters of law and do not belong at all with ontological status.

"O men, fear your Lord Who has created you from a single soul . . ." [Surah 4:1, earlier quoted]. Every time God addresses the human world, woman finds herself always associated with man. Take for example, one passage among dozens: Surah 33:35, where all the terms descriptive of men are given also the feminine plural form, making clear unmistakably the inclusion of women—believers, *muslims*, praying ones, sincere ones, those who fast, the chaste, "for all these God has prepared pardon and a rich reward."

The *Sunnah* includes many marks of solicitude for women. Note particularly the Farewell Sermon of the Prophet where there are many important passages on the subject, such as: "As for your wives, you and they have just the same rights on each other. Those that are yours should not foul your bed (a footnote indicates that 'bed' here means also honor and reputation) with any other person than yourselves, and they should not admit to your homes, without your permission any whom you do not love, and they should not commit adultery. Should they do so, God in truth has permitted you to put them away, to establish separate beds and to strike them—but not immoderately. If they desist and obey you, you must maintain them properly in food and dress. Be sure to treat your wives well. In truth they are yours by trust from God and it is by a word of God that you are permitted to consort with them. Be God-fearing then in all that has to do with your wives and be sure to treat them well. O people, verily believers are brothers."[19]

Muḥammad Laḥbābī's statement of this theme is broadly representative, even apart from his particular philosophy of personalism. There is much modern exegesis of Surah 4, which finds in it a *virtual* prohibition of plural marriage, and the rest of his apologia, too, could be found in other recent sources. One writer, however, a woman, also from Morocco, calls for a much more radical, less theoretical, treatment of the issues in terms of social realism and sexual mores. Her analysis, though unusual, deserves serious attention as being the shape of likely preoccupations to come. It will be followed by a representative statement of a rearguard conservatism.

Beyond the Veil: Male-Female Dynamics in a Modern Muslim Society is a recent (1965) study by Fāṭimah Mernissi, which takes a very different line from that of Muḥammad Laḥbābī. She brings his idealism down to earth by challenging in a fundamental way what she believes to be the built-in dominance of the male in Islamic society. This dominance finally stands, as she believes, not in ideology as such (where Laḥbābī and others have rightly denied it) but in the entrenched patterns of family mores and assumptions. These are seen by her as the ultimate bastion, which tends to be the more sharply defended by conservatism in proportion as modernizing changes take place inexorably in other spheres (economic and technological) and so inspire the fearful to resist totally on the family front. According to Fāṭimah Mernissi, the ultimate problem lies in the fact that the Muslim understanding of heterosexual love is that, within it, the female is liable to endanger the order God has willed and must, therefore, be restrained by male dominance.

> In this book I want to demonstrate that there is a fundamental contradiction between Islam as interpreted in official policy, and equality of the sexes . . . Muslim marriage is based on male dominance. The desegregation of the sexes violates Islam's ideology of the woman's position in the social order: the woman should be under the authority of fathers, brothers or husbands. Since she is considered by God to be a destructive element, she is to be spatially confined and excluded from matters other than those of the family. The woman's access to non-domestic space is put under the control of males.
>
> Paradoxically, and contrary to what is commonly assumed, Islam does not advance the thesis of women's inherent inferiority. Quite the contrary, it affirms the potential equality between the sexes. The existing inequality does not rest on an ideological or biological theory of women's inferiority, but is the outcome of specific social institutions designed to restrain her power, namely segregation and legal insubordination of the woman to the man in the family structure. . . . In Islam there is no belief in female inferiority. On the contrary, the whole system is based on the assumption that the woman is a powerful and dangerous being. All sexual institutions (polygamy, repudiation, sexual segregation) can be perceived as a strategy for containing her power. . . .
>
> At stake in Muslim society is not the emancipation of women [if that only means equality with men] but the fate of the heterosexual unit.

Stressing that this unit is understood in Islam as the due curb on what, outside it, would be socially disruptive and ruinous, Fāṭimah Mernissi quotes Al-Ghazālī:

> If the desire of the flesh dominates the individual and is not controlled by the fear of God, it leads men to commit destructive acts. . . . Sexual desire was created solely as a means to entice men to deliver the seed and to put the woman in a situation where she can cultivate it, bringing the two together softly in order to obtain progeny, as the hunter obtains his game, and this through copulation." Al-Ghazālī . . . sees civilization as struggling to contain the woman's destructive, all-absorbing power. Women must be controlled to prevent men being distracted from their social and religious duties. Society can only survive by creating the institutions which foster male dominance through sexual segregation.
>
> The explicit theory is epitomized by 'Abbās Maḥmūd al-'Aqqād, in *Woman in the Qur'ān*. He attempts to describe the male-female dynamic as it appears through the divine Book. He opens his book with the quotation: "Men are superior to them by a degree," and deduces hastily that "the message of the Qur'ān which makes men superior to women is the manifest message of human history. . . ." What 'Aqqād finds in the Qur'ān . . . is a complementarity between the sexes based on their antagonistic natures. The characteristic of the female is a negative will to power. All her energies are vested in wanting to be conquered, in wanting to be overpowered and subjugated. . . . "Males in all kinds of animals are given the power, embodied in their biological structure, to compel females to yield to the demands of the instinct [that is, sex] . . . . There is no situation where the power to compel is given to the women over the men."

But, whether in terms of an implicit theory of women as a source of male temptation and disorder (so that veiling for example arises from men's fear to lose control over their wills in the proximity of women) or the explicit theory that sees the female as inviting subjugation, the result is the same. This result is a view of sexuality that sees it as potentially destructive, disruptive, and dangerous, rather than relaxed, complementary, mutual, and productive of friendship, fulfilment, and joy, not temptation and loss of control. Mernissi's plea, therefore, is for an attack upon the whole concept of polarity between the sexes and upon the social forms, which perpetuate it. For lack of such heterosexual mutual at-ease-ness, which Fāṭimah Mernissi insists must be found,

> . . . the Muslim woman is endowed with a fatal attraction which erodes the male's will to resist her and reduces him to a passive, acquiescent role. Then he has no choice: he can only give in to her attraction, whence her identification with *fitnah*, that is, chaos, disorder. . . .
>
> "The Prophet saw a woman. He hurried to his house and had intercourse with his wife, Zaynab, then left the house and said: 'When a woman comes towards you, it is Satan who is approaching you. When one of you sees a woman and is attracted to her, he should hurry to his wife. With her, it would be the same as with the other one.'"
>
> Commenting on this quotation, Imām Muslim, an established voice of Muslim tradition, said the Prophet was referring to ". . . fascination, to the irresistible attraction to women God instilled into man's soul, and he was

referring to the pleasure man experiences when he looks at the woman, and the pleasure he experiences with anything related to her. She resembles Satan in his irresistible power over the individual."

This attraction is a natural link between the sexes. Whenever a man is faced with a woman, *fitnah* might occur. Al-Tirmidhī said: "Whenever a man and a woman are isolated in the presence of each other, Satan is bound to be their third companion." . . . The married woman whose husband is absent is a particular threat to men. . . .

Moroccan folk culture is permeated with a negative attitude towards femininity. . . . The best example is the sixteenth century poet, Sidi 'Abd al-Raḥmān al-Majdūb. His rhymes are so popular they have become proverbs:

"Women are fleeting wooden vessels
Whose passengers are doomed to destruction."

Woman is *fitnah*, the polarization of the uncontrollable, a living representative of the dangers of sexuality and its rampant disruptive potential . . . Sexuality *per se* is not the danger. On the contrary, it has three positive, vital functions: it allows the believers to perpetuate themselves on earth . . . it serves as a foretaste of the delights secured for men in Paradise, thus encouraging men to strive for Paradise and obey God's rule on earth, and sexual satisfaction is necessary to intellectual effort. [But] . . . woman is a dangerous distraction which must be used for the specific purpose of providing the Muslim nation with offspring and quenching the tensions of the sexual instinct. But the woman should not in any way be an object of emotional investment or the focus of attention. . . . The Muslim wariness of heterosexual involvement is embodied in sexual segregation and its corollaries: arranged marriage, the important role of the mother in the son's life, and the fragility of the marriage bond [as revealed by the institutions of polygamy and repudiation]. The whole Muslim social structure can be seen as an attack on, and a defense against, the disruptive power of female sexuality.

After a documented sociological survey of Moroccan marital patterns and experiences, Fāṭimah Mernissi concludes that there are:

. . . legal, ideological and physical barriers which subordinate the wife to the husband and condemn heterosexual relation to mistrust, violence and deceit. Young people demanding love marriages not only create tremendous conflicts with their parents, they also almost guarantee conflict in their own marriages. Given the way they have been brought up, the traditional patterns of sexual relatedness in their society and the government's lack of support, they are almost sure to fail in their effort to create a fulfilling heterosexual relationship based on love rather than conflict.

The traditional pattern for heterosexual relations is being destroyed before meaningful alternative patterns of relatedness can develop. Traditionally sexuality was controlled by separating the sexes spatially, but modern sexual desegregation is swiftly eroding those spatial boundaries.

By "spatial boundaries," Fāṭimah Mernissi means primarily the domestic confines of women and the mores of noninteraction outside the admissible limits of family, marriage, procreation, and conformity, all within the "public universe of the *Ummah*", which dominates the self-understanding of Islamic existence, as the community of the rule of God.

Aside from economic and political factors necessary to social change in this sphere, Fāṭimah Mernissi, writing in her very emphatic terms, declares:

> Muslim sexuality sets ranks, tasks and authority patterns. Spatially confined, the woman was taken care of materially by the man who possessed her, in exchange for her total obedience and her sexual and reproductive services. The whole system was organized so that the Muslim *Ummah* was actually a society of male citizens who possessed among other things the female half of the population. . . . This territoriality [the confining of women] is in process of being dismantled, modernization having triggered mechanisms of socio-economic change no group is able to control. . . . Modern Muslim societies have to face the fact that the traditional family mutilates the woman by depriving her of her humanity. What modern Muslim societies ought to strive toward is a family based on the unfragmented wholeness of the woman. Sex with an unfragmented human female is a glorious act, not a soiling, degrading one. It implies and generates tenderness and love. Allegiance and involvement with an unfragmented woman do not take men away from their social duties because the woman is not a marginal, tabooed individual: rather, she is the center, source and generator of order and life. . . .
>
> To the dismay of rigid conservatives desperately preoccupied with a static tradition, change is shaking the foundations of the Muslim world. Change is multidimensional and hard to control, especially for those who deny it. Accepted or rejected, change gnaws continuously at the intricate mechanisms of social life and the more it is thwarted, the deeper and more surprising are its implications. The heterosexual unit is not yet officially admitted by Muslim rulers to be a crucial area in the process of national development. . . . Development plans devote hundreds of pages to the mechanization of agriculture, mining, and banking, and only a few pages to the family and woman's condition. I want to emphasize on the one hand the deep and far-reaching processes of change working in the Muslim family, and on the other the decisive role of women and the family in any serious development plan in a Third World economy.[20]

A measure of the temper, the arguments too, characteristic of the traditional understanding of the rule of the *Sharī'ah* in marital affairs, can be gauged from the resistance of that school to a commission's proposals for the establishment of compulsory registration of marriages and of a minimum age of marriage in Pakistan. Ihtishām al-Ḥāqq dissented sharply from the main objectives and plans of the Commission. He rejected its appeal for a progressive interpretation of Islam, and in a sharply polemical vein insisted on the continuity of polygamy and the traditional patterns of marriage, despite the case made about their unhappy and deleterious effect in society. The whole issue, of course, involved the legitimacy and prerequisites of *Ijtihād* (discussed elsewhere, see pp. 111–113). The vigor of the debate is indicative of the sense of both parties that the creation of Pakistan had made the battle for the interpretation of Islam crucial.

> It is a matter of surprise that persons utterly ignorant of the elementary propositions concerning God, His glory, the Prophethood and the comprehensiveness and universality of religion should have the temerity to write

on such subjects. Perhaps our Introduction-writer [that is, in the majority report] does not know that the Qur'ān is the sacred Word of God and embodies His divine guidance, Who has the fullest knowledge and prescience of every minor event of every period and every epoch from the beginning of time to its end. He knows all the infinite varieties of human relationship which can happen in any period or epoch in all futurity. Hence His revealed Book and His appointed Prophet with prophetic wisdom, are all based on the truth that until Doomsday the teachings and injunctions of the Holy Qur'ān and the *Sunnah* shall be the authoritative guidance and final word for all the infinity of events that may take place in the universe. This is the basic and fundamental article of faith in Islam owing to which Islam is a religion for all times. If the scope of the Qur'ān and the *Sunnah* were limited to the circumstances and events that arose during the Prophet's lifetime or while the Qur'ān was being revealed, then it would be meaningless to call the Holy Qur'ān and the *Sunnah* the revealed word of God and Islam as His revealed Religion. It would then be more correct to dub the Qur'ān and the *Sunnah* as the work and compilation of an individual who could not see beyond the limited horizon of his own time. . . . If want of knowledge about future events is conceded then what meaning can this divine declaration have: "This day I have perfected your religion. . . ." [Surah 5:3]? Will the introduction-writer translate it thus: "O ye Muslims, of the period of revelation: Your religion has been perfected in regard to the circumstances of your period but as regards future events it is imperfect and you can have it completed with the help of Commissions." . . .

As a matter of principle, reference to public opinion on purely *Sharī'ah* matters amounts to trifling with Islamic *Sharī'ah* and ridiculing the religion, which cannot be tolerated. . . .

Turning to some of the specific reforms Ihtishām al-Ḥāqq held out adamantly for the preservation of the old traditions, either contesting the validity of the change or arguing that the "old is better."

Sharī'ah has neither fixed any age limit nor prescribed any condition of puberty for the parties entering a marriage contract. . . . The fixation of age limit is not reasonable even from the point of view of common sense. . . . If a person is on his death bed and his only child is a small young daughter he should marry her off at once and not leave her to the mercy of his relatives or neighbors. . . . If we accept this prohibition [that is, of early marriage] we would be encroaching upon the rights of the parents which they enjoy as the guardians of their children. It is obvious that we are not entitled to do so. . . .

In the light of their judgement [that is, the majority for reform] *nikāḥ* [marriage] should be prohibited before the marrying parties are mentally mature, just as entrusting property to the orphans has been prohibited before they have developed sufficient maturity of intelligence. . . . The difference between the two cases has been overlooked, where one relates to the entrusting of property to an orphan who has lost his loving father and his property lies in the trust of others. As for the question of the marriage of young boys and girls, it should be noted that their guardians are their parents more than whom neither the Court nor any government authority can claim to cherish love and sympathy for them. . . . I hold that any restrictions on early or pre-puberty marriages amount to *mudākhalat fī-l-Dīn* [interference with Faith]. The custom has, no doubt, its own defects which should be removed by other means than legislation. . . .

The recommendation that women should have an equal right to pronounce divorce is not only incompatible with human nature but tends to make the future of women themselves uncertain. . . . This right is not an absolute right but [may be] delegated to the wife by the husband [that is, if it has been required as a condition of the *nikāḥ* contract].

Polygamy is not a matter for any human society to be ashamed of. . . . We do not have the slightest excuse for imitating the ways of a people with a social set-up and a legal system which tolerate sexual satisfaction by means other than marriage. . . . If the question of polygamy is considered purely from the point of view of whether . . . nature allows it or not to man, it will be found that the verdict of nature is in favor of allowing polygamy.

The responsibilities of men and women linked in matrimony are quite different from each other in respect of procreation. One is the active agent, the other the passive agent. One is the giver, the other is the receiver. So a piece of land, the function of which is to take the seed into its bosom for its nourishment may bring into play its power of nourishment only for the benefit of one cultivator at a time. It is not possible for more cultivators than one to make full use of their abilities at one plot. Intermixture and partnership may, on the one hand, result in the wasting of the seed and on the other hand there may be danger of intermingling of produce. Contrary to this, one cultivator can do justice to the sowing of seeds in several plots of land without any such dangers.

The Holy Qur'ān compares woman to a field when she is one of the parties brought together in wedlock. It is laid down: "Approach your tilth when and how you will." [Surah 2:223] . . . The conclusion, therefore, is that in the system involving procreation the plurality of the active agent is unnatural and that of the passive agent is in perfect conformity with nature. . . . Polygamy is such an essential part of family life that no matrimonial system can be adequately comprehensive or perfect without it. . . .

The conclusion is this that the Quranic injunction is general and there is no restriction or restraint on marriages up to the limit of four. [Contrast Muḥammad Laḥbābī's exegesis of Surah 4:3.] This being the position, it would be an interference in the revealed religion if the plurality of marriages is declared to be unlawful or any restriction is imposed on it. The Quranic injunction must remain general and unrestricted in its application.

Ihtishām al-Ḥāqq makes his final point one of disqualifying all difference of view and making nugatory all procedures he rejects. His position, trenchantly expressed and oblivious of its sharp implications, indicates in some measure the struggle in which writers like Fāṭimah Mernissi are engaged, as well as the tasks a sanguine temper like that of Laḥbābī is liable to overlook.

All our matrimonial and family problems are governed by *Sharī'ah*. Whatever law is made should be subject to *Sharī'ah*. If any change is attempted to adapt *Sharī'ah* to these laws, it would be giving laws superiority over *Sharī'ah*. In that case, matrimonial relations may be outwardly legalized but, so long as they are not regulated strictly according to *Sharī'ah*, they will remain *ḥaram* [unlawful] from the point of view of *Sharī'ah*.

The most outstanding feature of Islamic matrimonial laws is that, because of their divine origin, they meet all the requirements of men, women and children. Even the slightest change made in them would create disruption and any step to improve one thing would result in the deterioration of the other.

> . . . Hence the salvation of the individual as well as the *Millah* [community] rests on strictly abiding by the provisions of the divine law, avoiding all interventions therein.
>
> The Islamic social system is a complete system. It shall have to be accepted or rejected in its entirety. It is not possible to accept or reject it in part and act against the warning of the Holy Qur'ān: "Do you believe in some parts and reject others?" [Surah 2:85]
>
> This report is an undesirable attempt of this sort and from every point of view, religious or intellectual, deserves complete rejection. This is my recommendation.[21]

Let the last word in this anthology go to Dr. Muḥammad Ṭalbī, writing in Tunis, on the fascinating theme of contemporary relations between religions—an issue for which we have here no scope. His words are apposite to our entire retrospect within Islam.

> Neither Islam, nor any other theistic faith, has any other choice today than to accept adventure. For science is every day setting further and further forward the frontiers of mystery and of the universe, and, so doing, poses questions from which neither philosophers nor theologians can excuse themselves without a radical and fundamental denial of humanity. It requires on the part of all an increase in reflective thought, and on the part of believers a rereading of the meaning of Revelation in line with the new problematic. . . . There is need for an opening up of issues without reservations, and we have need of multiple antennae.
>
> A new exegesis is necessary, one that will not arbitrarily deny the riches and positive elements of the past, and this needs a climate of adventure, of exchange and of tension, in order to be timely and responsive to all susceptibilities. . . . If, as every Muslim believes, the Word of God is eternal, it follows necessarily that, whatever may be disclosed in time and space, it still tran-

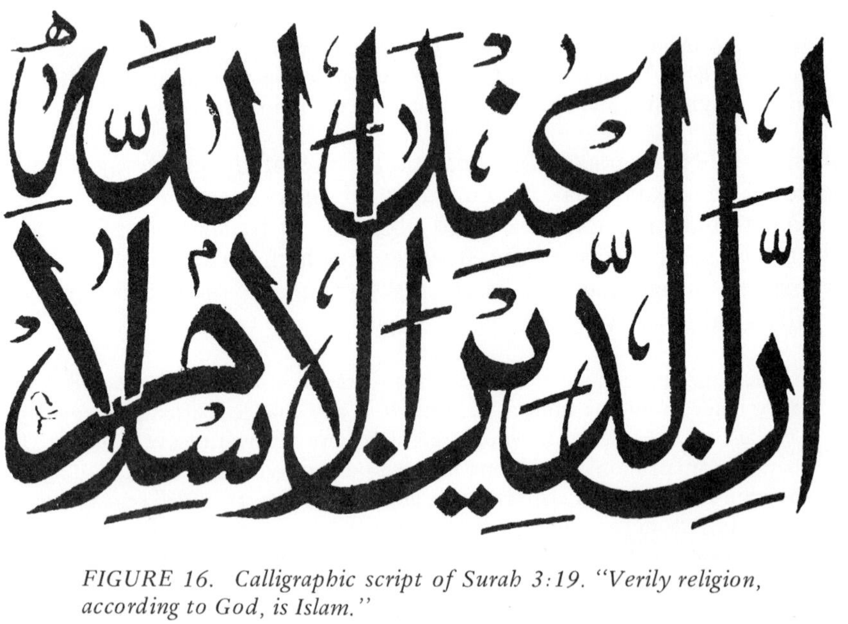

FIGURE 16. Calligraphic script of Surah 3:19. "Verily religion, according to God, is Islam."

scends these and is always and everywhere, audible, present, and forever new. It must, then, be perceived and received, in no static way. . . . We have this need of urgently hearkening to God today, with contemporary ears, in the insistent present. The indispensable condition, if God is not to be expropriated from the world, but present anew in the human scene, is the arousal of a modern exegesis, holding together at one and the same time, both prudence and audacity, and grappling directly with the questions, the restlessness, the anguish, of our time. . . . Is it not the natural vocation of a religion to be perpetually in crisis, that is to say, in tension, going beyond itself?[22]

Notes

CHAPTER 1

1. *Qur'ān,* trans. by Kenneth Cragg.

2. Driss Chraïbi, *Le Passé Simple* [Heirs to the Past], trans. by Len Ortzen (London: Heinemann Educational Books, 1971), pp. 43–44.

3. Alan Villiers, *Sons of Sinbad* (New York: Charles Scribner's Sons, 1940), p. 35.

4. Lawrence Durrell, *Mountolive* (London: Faber and Faber; New York: E.P. Dutton, 1958), p. 265.

5. Henri Mercier, *The Koran,* trans. by L. Tremlett (London: Luzac & Co., 1956).

6. Muḥammad al-Nāṣir al-Ṣaddām, *Ibtihālāt,* trans. by Kenneth Cragg (Tunis: Maison Tunisienne de l'Edition, 1968), pp. 27–28.

7. Muḥammad 'Alī, *My Life, A Fragment,* ed. by Afzal Iqbal (Lahore, Pakistan: Shaikh Muḥammad Ashraf, 1942) pp. 107–28.

8. Al-Sūyūṭī, *Al-Itqān,* trans by Kenneth Cragg (Cairo edition, n.d.), bk. ii, pt. 64, pp. 197–212.

9. Muḥammad 'Abduh, *The Theology of Unity,* trans. by Kenneth Cragg (London: George Allen & Unwin, 1965), pp. 118–22, 140–41.

10. K.W. Morgan, ed., *Islam: the Straight Path* (New York: Ronald Press Co., 1958), pp. 21, 23, 26-27, and 34–36.

11. Al-Baidāwī *Commentary,* Surah 3 [Chrestomathia Baidawiana], trans. by D.S. Margoliouth (London: Luzac and Co., 1894), pp. 3–10.

12. Ibn Khaldūn, *The Muqaddimah: An Introduction to History,* ed. and trans. by Franz Rosenthal, Bollingen Series 43 (Princeton, N.J.: Princeton University Press, 1958), vol. 1, pp. 438–39, 439, and 443–446.

13. Sayyid Quṭb, "Commentary," *Fi-Ẓull al-Qur'ān,* no. 1.

14. Hashim Amir Ali, *The Student's Qur'ān* (Hyderabad, India: Shalimar Publishers, 1959), pp. 121–22.

15. Martin Lings, *A Muslim Saint of the 20th Century* (London: George Allen & Unwin; Berkeley, Ca.: University of California Press, 1961), pp. 89–90.

16. Muḥammad Iqbāl, *The Reconstruction of Religious Thought in Islam* (Lahore, Pakistan: Shaikh Muḥammad Ashraf, 1944), pp. 10, 11, 17, 18, 56, 57, 127, 128, 138–40, 147, 167–68, 179.
17. Muḥammad 'Alī, *My Life*, pp. 274–79.
18. Khalifa Abdul-Hakim, *Islamic Ideology*, rev. ed. (Lahore, Pakistan: Institute of Islamic Culture, 1961), pp. ix–x, xi, xvi, 20, 21–26, 27, 29–31, 37, 63, 74, 83, 104, 149–50, 154, 159–64, 169, 180.
19. E.H. Whinfield, trans., *Masnavi* (London: Trübner's Oriental Series, 1898), p. 169.
20. Sayyid Ḥossein Naṣr, *Ideals and Realities of Islam* (London: George Allen & Unwin; Boston: Beacon Press, 1966), pp. 47–48, 50–51.
21. A.J. Arberry, *Discourses of Rumi* (London: John Murray, 1961), pp. 173, 231.
22. Daub Rahbar, *God of Justice: A Study of the Ethical Doctrine of the Qur'ān* (Leiden, Netherlands: E.J. Brill, 1960), pp. 18–19.
23. S.J. Samartha and J.B. Taylor, eds., *Christian Muslim Dialogue: Papers from Broumana* (Geneva, 1972), pp. 68–72.

CHAPTER 2

1. Rudyard Kipling, *Writings in Prose and Verse* (New York: Charles Scribner's Sons, n.d.), vol. 4, pp. 42–43 and vol. 28, p. 274.
2. Muḥammad Laḥbābī, *Le Personnalisme Musulman* (Paris: Presses Universitaires de France, 1964), pp. 4–5, 7–8, 17, and 21–24.
3. Muḥammad 'Abduh, *The Theology of Unity*, trans. by Kenneth Cragg (London: George Allen & Unwin, 1965), pp. 135–36, 145.
4. Alan Villiers, *Sons of Sinbad* (New York: Charles Scribner's Sons, 1940), p. 30.
5. Sirdar Iqbal Ali Shah, *Lights of Asia* (London: Arthur Baker, 1934), pp. 29–34.
6. S.J. Samartha and J.B. Taylor, eds., *Christian Muslim Dialogue: Papers from Broumana*, (Geneva, 1972), pp. 121–25.
7. *Dalā' il al-Khairāt*, trans. by Kenneth Cragg (Cairo, n.d.).
8. Kemal A. Faruki, *Islam, Today and Tomorrow* (Karachi: Pakistan Publishing House, 1974), pp. 264–68.
9. Kenneth Cragg, trans., *The Dome and the Rock* (London: Society for Promoting Christian Knowledge, 1964), pp. 37–39.
10. Najīb Maḥfūẓ, *Midaq Alley*, trans. by Trevor LeGassick (Beirut, Lebanon: Khayat Book and Pub. Co., 1966).
11. Abū-l-'Alā al-Maudūdī, *Towards Understanding Islam* (Lahore, Pakistan: Shaikh Muhammad Ashraf, 1940), pp. 139–42.
12. Faruki, *Islam, Today and Tomorrow*, pp. 316–20.
13. Malcolm X with the assistance of Alex Haley, *The Autobiography of Malcolm X* (New York: Grove Press; London: Hutchinson Publishing Group, 1965), pp. 327–32, 341–42, and 349.
14. Cragg, *The Dome and the Rock*, pp. 68–70.
15. Lewis Pelly, ed., *The Miracle Plays of Hasan and Husain*, revised by A.M. Wollaston, 2 vols. (London, 1879), vol. 1, pp. 17–18, 23, 50, 90, 213, 290; vol. 2, pp. 1, 51, 82, 100.

16. Al-Nabahānī, *Al-Naṭm al-Badī*, trans. by Kenneth Cragg (Damascus, Syria: 1941).

17. Constance E. Padwick, *Muslim Devotions* (London: Society for Promoting Christian Knowledge, 1961), pp. 146–47.

18. Muṣṭafā al-Marāghī, *Dīwān al-Khuṭab al-Ḥadīthah*, trans. by Kenneth Cragg (Cairo: n.d.), pp. 10–13.

19. Muḥammad Fāḍil Jamālī, *Letters on Islam*, trans. from the Arabic by the author (Oxford: Oxford University Press, 1965), pp. 20–22, 39.

20. Aḥmad Amīn, *Ḥayātī*, trans. by Kenneth Cragg (Cairo: Dāral-Ma'ārif, 1950), pp. 200–05, 343–46, 353–59.

CHAPTER 4

1. Al-Marghīnānī, *Al-Hidāyah* [Guidance] (Cairo: Maktabat Muḥammad 'Alī Ṣabīh, 1966).

2. Al-Muḥaqqiq Al-Ḥillī, *Sharā'i' Al-Islām* [The Laws of Islam] (Beirut, Lebanon: Dār Maktabat Al-Ḥayāt, 1965).

3. Taken from a collection of treatises by several authors, called *Shadrāt al-Balātīn Min Ṭayyibāt Kalimāt Salafinā al-Ṣālibīn* [Bits of Platinum from the Good Words of our Venerable Forefathers], Muḥammad Al-Fiqī, ed., (Cairo, 1956), vol. 1. Writers in Arabic of the old style have a predilection for alliterative, rhyming and colorful titles.

CHAPTER 5

1. Ibn Abī Ya'lā, *Ṭabaqāt Al-Ḥanābilah* (Cairo, 1952), vol. 1.

2. Muḥammad 'Amāra, ed., *Rasā' il al-'Adl wa-l-Tawḥīd* [Treatises on Justice and Unity] (Cairo: Dār al-Hilāl, 1971), vol. 1. Translated by permisstion of the editor.

3. Ibid.

4. Ibid.

5. The edition here used was prepared by Father Robert Caspar and translated into French for use in teaching. It exists in mimeographed form and this translation of large extracts from the Arabic text has been made with the kind permission of Father Caspar.

6. Al-Nu'mān Ibn Muḥammad, *Ta'wīl al-Da'ā' im* [Interpretation of the Pillars], 3 vols., ed. by Muḥammad al-A'ẓmā (Cairo: Dār al-Ma'ārif, 1972), vol. 1.

CHAPTER 6

1. Ibn Khaldūn, *The Muqaddimah: An Introduction to History*, ed. and trans. by Franz Rosenthal, Bollingen Series 43 (Princeton, N.J.: Princeton University Press, 1958), vol. 2, pp. 388–89.

2. T.W. Arnold, ed., *Painting in Islam* (New York: Dover Publications, 1928), pp. 36–37.

3. Titus Burckhardt, *Moorish Culture in Spain* (London: George Allen & Unwin, p. 206.

4. Khaldūn, *The Muqaddimah*, pp. 249–50.
5. Arthur U. Pope, *Introduction to Persian Art* (London: Peter Davies, 1930), pp. 28–29.
6. Charles Malik, ed., *God and Man in Contemporary Islamic Thought* (Beirut, Lebanon: American University of Beirut, 1972), pp. 115–21.
7. P.J. Chelkowski, ed., *Studies in the Art and Literature of the Near East* (New York: New York University Press, 1974), pp. 165, 167, 169, 171–72, 173–75, 179.

CHAPTER 7

1. Ibn Khaldūn, *The Muqaddimah: An Introduction to History*, ed. and trans. by Franz Rosenthal, Bollingen Series 43 (Princeton, N.J.: Princeton University Press, 1958), vol. 3, pp. 76–83.
2. 'Abd al-Ḥaqq Anṣārī et al., eds., *Islam* (Patiala, India: Punjabi University, 1969), pp. 50–52, 54–55.
3. W. Montgomery Watt, *Faith and Practice of Al-Ghazālī* (London: George Allen & Unwin, 1953), pp. 56–60.
4. A.J. Arberry, *The Doctrine of the Sufis* (Cambridge: Cambridge University Press, 1935), pp. 98–99, 113, 118, 120, 125–27, 141–46, 152, 165, 166–67.
5. Edward J. Jurji, *Illumination in Islamic Mysticism* (Princeton, N.J.: Princeton University Press, 1938), pp. 121–22.
6. Muḥammad Iqbāl, *The Reconstruction of Religious Thought in Islam* (Lahore, Pakistan: Shaikh Muḥammad Ashraf, 1944), pp. 158–59, 162, 187–88.
7. Maḥmūd Shabastārī, *Gulshan-i-Rāz* [Mystic Rose Garden], trans. by E.H. Whinfield (London: Trübner's Oriental Series, 1880), pp. 45–46.
8. E.J. Browne, trans., *Literary History of Persia* (Cambridge: Cambridge University Press, 1909), vol. 1, pp. 436, 439.
9. Martin Lings, *A Muslim Saint of the Twentieth Century* (London: George Allen & Unwin, 1970), pp. 145, 160, 199–200, 202–03, 204, 207.
10. E.H. Whinfield, trans., *Masnavi* (London: Trübner's Oriental Series, 1898), p. 195.
11. Al-Darqāwī, *Letters of a Sufi Master*, trans. by Titus Burckhardt (London: Perennial Books, 1969), p. 7.
12. Gertrude Bell, ed. and trans., *The Dīwān of Ḥāfiẓ* (London: William Heinemann, 1928), p. 84.
13. R.A. Nicholson, trans., *Dīwān Shams al-Dīn Tabrīzī* (Cambridge: Cambridge University Press, 1898, reprinted 1952), nos. xiii, xx, xxvi, xxxii, and xl.
14. Jogendra Singh, trans., *The Invocations of Ansari of Herat* (London: John Murray, 1939), pp. 40, 42.
15. Browne, *Literary History*, vol. 1, pp. 425, 441, 442.
16. Ibid., vol. 2, p. 537.
17. Constance E. Padwick, *Muslim Devotions* (London: Society for Promotion of Christian Knowledge, 1961), pp. 214–19.
18. *Awrad* of the Naqshabandi Order, trans. by Kenneth Cragg (Cairo, n.d.).
19. Whinfield, *Masnavi*, p. 137–38.
20. Nicholson, *Dīwān Shams*, no. xliv.
21. Lings, *Muslim Saint*, pp. 53–56, 58–59.
22. Ibid., pp. 102, 107, 117.
23. Anṣārī, *Islam*, pp. 65–66.
24. J. Spencer Trimingham, *The Sufi Orders in Islam* (Oxford: Oxford University Press, 1970), p. 191.

25. H.A.R. Gibb, ed. and trans., *Travels of Ibn Baṭṭūṭa in Asia and Africa, 1325–1359* (London: Routledge & Kegan Paul, 1953), pp. 247, 264, 268-70.

26. Arberry, *Doctrine,* pp. 86-87, 88, 155-56.

27. Ṭāhā Ḥusain, *An Egyptian Childhood,* trans. by E.H. Paxton (London: Routledge & Kegan Paul, 1932), pp. 95-102, 105.

28. A.J. Arberry, trans., *Poem of the Way* (London: Emery Walker, 1952), lines 560-68, 682-85, 1140-43, 1608, 1619-21, 1903-04, and 2334-54.

29. R.A. Nicholson, *Literary History of the Arabs* (Cambridge: Cambridge University Press, 1914), p. 397.

30. Nicholson, *Dīwān Shams.*

31. Whinfield, *Masnavi,* pp. 83, 93.

32. Ibid.

33. Bell, *Dīwān of Ḥāfiẓ,* pp. 22, 76, 78, and 83-84.

34. R.A. Nicholson, *Mystics of Islam* (London: Routledge & Kegan Paul, 1975), p. 87.

35. Whinfield, *Masnavi,* pp. 104, 105, 107, and 108.

CHAPTER 8

1. Niyazi Berkes, *Turkish Nationalism and Western Civilization* (London: George Allen & Unwin; New York: Columbia University Press, 1959), p. 226.

2. Ibid., pp. 194-96.

3. Ibid., pp. 75-76, 268, 271-72, and 276.

4. Ishtiāq Ḥusain Qureshī, "Foundations of Pakistani Culture," *The Muslim World Quarterly,* 44 (January 1954):8-9.

5. F.K. Khan Durrani, *The Meaning of Pakistan* (Lahore, Pakistan: Shaikh Muḥammad Ashraf, 1944), pp. 149, 152-54, 156-58, 171-72, and 174-75.

6. Muḥammad Iqbāl, *The Reconstruction of Religious Thought in Islam* (Lahore, Pakistan: Shaikh Muḥammad Ashraf, 1944), pp. 158-59, 162, 187-88.

7. Maulānā Abū-l-Kalām Āzād, *Islam and Nationalism* (New Delhi: Kalamkar Prakashan, 1969), pp. 48-51, 52, 55.

8. 'Abd al-Ḥaqq Ansārī et al., ed., Islam (Patiala, India: Punjabi University, 1969), pp. 96-97, 101. (Dr. S. Abid Husain is secretary of the Islam and the Modern Age Society, and retired professor of philosophy and Urdu literature, Jamia Milla Islamia, Delhi, India.)

9. Muḥammad 'Abduh, *The Theology of Unity,* trans. by Kenneth Cragg (London: George Allen & Unwin, 1965), pp. 151-53, 153-54.

10. Ṭāhā Ḥusain, *A Student at the Azhar,* trans. by Hilary Wayment (London: Longmans, Green and Co., 1958), pp. 105-06, 107.

11. Muḥammad Fāḍil Jamālī, *Letters on Islam,* trans. by the author (Oxford: Oxford University Press, 1965), pp. 96-100.

12. A.A.A. Fyzee, *A Modern Approach to Islam* (Bombay: Asia Publishing House, 1963), pp. 91-95, 99-100, 102, 105-07, and 110-12.

13. Jamāl 'Abd al-Nāṣir, *Egypt's Liberation,* intro. by Dorothy Thompson (Washington, D.C.: Public Affairs Press, 1955), pp. 33-36, 55-59.

14. Aḥmad Ṭāleb, *Lettres de Prison, 1957-1961,* trans. by Kenneth Cragg (Algiers: Editions Nationales Algériennes, S.N.E.D. Alger, 1966), pp. 109-16.

15. Ibid., pp. 121-23.

16. 'Ali Mazrui, *On Heroes and Uhuru Worship* (London: Longman Group, 1967), pp. 159-60, 168, 176, and 178.

17. Khālid Muḥammad Khālid, *Min Hunā Nabda'* [Here We Start], trans. by Kenneth Cragg (Cairo, 1950), pp. 146, 152.

18. Muḥammad Iqbāl Choudhury and Mushtāq Aḥmad Khān, *Pakistani Society: A Sociological Analysis* (Lahore, Pakistan: Noorsons, 1964), pp. 175, 178, 179, and 189.

19. Muḥammad Laḥbābī, *Le Personnalisme Musulman* (Paris: Presses Universitaires de France, 1964), pp. 74-84.

20. Fāṭimah Mernissi, *Beyond the Veil: Male-Female Dynamics in a Modern Muslim Society* (Cambridge, Mass.: Schenkman Publishing Co., 1975), pp. xv–xvi, 2, 4, 11–14, 79, and 102–03.

21. *The Gazette of Pakistan,* No. F 9 (4), August 30, 1956, 56 Leg. pp. 1563, 1565, 1577–79, 1592–93, 1597, and 1604.

22. Muḥammad Ṭalbī, *Islam et Dialogue,* trans. by Kenneth Cragg (Tunis: Maison Tunisienne de l'Edition, 1972), pp. 44–47.